Who's Who in Congress

1991 – 1992

102nd Congress

Who's Who in Congress

1991 - 1992
102nd Congress

Congressional Quarterly Inc.
Washington, D.C.

Congressional Quarterly

Congressional Quarterly, an editorial research service and publishing company, serves clients in the fields of news, education, business and government. It combines Congressional Quarterly's specific coverage of Congress, government and politics with the more general subject range of an affiliated service, Editorial Research Reports.

Congressional Quarterly publishes the *Congressional Quarterly Weekly Report* and a variety of books, including college political science textbooks under the CQ Press imprint and public affairs paperbacks on developing issues and events. CQ also publishes information directories and reference books on the federal government, national elections and politics, including the *Guide to Congress,* the *Guide to U.S. Elections, Open Secrets: The Dollar Power of PACs in Congress, Politics in America* and *Congress A to Z: CQ's Ready Reference Encyclopedia.* The *CQ Almanac,* a compendium of legislation for one session of Congress, is published each year. *Congress and the Nation,* a record of government for a presidential term, is published every four years.

An electronic online information system, Washington Alert, provides immediate access to CQ's databases of legislative action, votes, schedules, profiles and analyses.

ISBN 0-87187-596-9   ISSN 1054-9234

Printed in the United States of America

Second Printing

Managing editor Nancy Lammers
Research director Sharon Perkinson
Contributors Carolyn Goldinger, Ann O'Malley,
     Jenny Philipson
Interior and cover designer Kachergis Book Design
Typesetter Paul Pressau
Photo researchers Michael Jenkins, Jeanne Kislitzin,
     Charlie Mahtesian, Jennifer Silverman

Congressional Quarterly Inc.

Andrew Barnes   *Chairman*
Neil Skene   *Editor and Publisher*
Robert W. Merry   *Executive Editor*
John J. Coyle   *Associate Publisher*
Michael L. Koempel   *Director of Information Services*
Robert E. Cuthriell   *Director of Development*

Book Division

Patrick Bernuth   *General Manager*
David R. Tarr   *Director, Book Department*
Kathryn Suárez   *Director, Book Marketing*
Jacqueline A. Davey   *Manager, Library and Professional
     Marketing*

Computers and Production

Ron Knott   *Computers/Production Director*
I.D. Fuller   *Production Manager*
Michael Emanuel   *Assistant Production Manager*
Jhonnie G. Bailey   *Assistant to the Production Manager*

Table of Contents

Preface

The editors at Congressional Quarterly have designed *Who's Who in Congress* as a pocket guide to the facts behind the faces of our nation's lawmakers. We hope it will be useful when you attend committee hearings, watch congressional floor debate—in the galleries or on C-SPAN—or prepare for a visit to a member's office.

Each profile includes the information CQ's subscribers request most often. The biographical data—including birthdate, education, military service, religion, family, previous occupations and political career—were obtained through CQ surveys and staff reporting. Also included is a pronunciation guide for some of the most-often mispronounced names of members of Congress.

Capitol Hill phone numbers are assigned by district, so they likely will remain constant; however, office addresses may change during the year. CQ researchers gathered information on congressional staffs during December 1990 and January 1991. Listed for each member is his or her chief aide, press secretary and appointments secretary; but not all members employ a person in each of those positions. Included with every profile are standing committee assignments; not all special and select committee assignments were released in time for publication.

Election results are provided for the previous two cycles for incumbent members and for 1990 for freshmen. In cases where a senator's election results are at two-year intervals, the first year was a House election. The symbol "u/o" indicates that a member was unopposed in an election.

The election procedures in three states deserve special note. In Louisiana the primary is open to candidates of all parties. If a candidate wins 50 percent or more of the vote, no general election is held. A candidate with no primary or general election opposition is declared elected and does not appear on the ballot. Alaska and Washington have "jungle" primaries in which candidates of all parties appear on the same ballot; the candidate with the most votes in each party advances to the general election.

Most of the election percentages were calculated from official election returns received from each state; however, official general election returns for 1990 were not received in time from Arkansas, Delaware, Georgia, Hawaii, Michigan, Minnesota, Ohio and Pennsylvania. The results published from those states are based on nearly complete, unofficial returns.

Each member's profile also includes scores from CQ's vote studies for 1989 and 1990. The presidential support score is the percentage of recorded floor votes on which President Bush took a position and on which a member voted "yea" or "nay" in agreement with the president's position. Party-unity scores represent the percentage of recorded votes on which a member voted "yea" or "nay" in agreement with a majority of his or her party. Party-unity roll calls are those on which a majority of voting Democrats opposed a majority of voting Republicans. (Failure to vote on presidential support or party-unity roll calls may lower a member's score.) Voting participation is the percentage of recorded floor votes on which a member voted "yea" or "nay." Participation in quorum calls is not reflected.

For members who served in 1988 and 1989 ratings by four interest groups are given: the Americans for Democratic Action (ADA), the American Conservative Union (ACU), the AFL-CIO and the Chamber of Commerce of the United States (CCUS). Freshmen do not have scores for CQ vote studies or interest group ratings. However, House scores are given for Senate freshmen who were members of the House in 1988, 1989 or 1990.

The appendixes and other ancillary materials include information useful in navigating around Capitol Hill. In the inside front cover is a map of Capitol Hill, and inside the back cover is a list of frequently called legislative phone numbers. The appendix contains state delegations, congressional leadership, committee rosters for the House and Senate, CQ key votes for 1990, Senate terms of office, guides to the televised proceedings of the Senate and House floor action, an explanation of the congressional bell system and a glossary of legislative terms.

All of the facts and statistics included in this guide will be updated and expanded for the next edition of *Politics in America,* available July 1991.

Brock Adams (D-Wash.)
Of Seattle • Elected 1986

Born: January 13, 1927, Atlanta, Ga.
Education: U. of Washington, B.A. 1949;
Harvard U., J.D. 1952.
Military Career: Navy, 1944-46.
Occupation: Lawyer.
Family: Wife, Mary Elizabeth Scott; four
children.
Religion: Episcopalian.
Political Career: U.S. attorney, 1961-64;
U.S. House, 1965-77; U.S. secretary of
transportation, 1977-79.

Capitol Office: 513 Hart Senate Office
Building 20510; 224-2621.
Office Staff: Administrative Assistant,
Ellen Globokar; Press Secretary, Pam
McKinney; Personal Secretary, Sara
Johnson.
Committees: Appropriations; Labor &
Human Resources; Rules &
Administration.

Washington — The statewide vote for
George Bush was 48% in 1988.

CQ Voting Studies

	1989	1990
Presidential	43%	34%
Party	94%	93%
Participation	98%	99%

Interest Groups

	1988	1989
ADA	90%	95%
ACU	0%	4%
AFL-CIO	77%	100%
CCUS	36%	38%

Elections

	1986
General	51%
Primary	46%

Daniel K. Akaka (D-Hawaii)
Of Honolulu • Elected 1990

Born: September 11, 1924, Honolulu, Hawaii.
Education: U. of Hawaii, B.Ed. 1952; U. of Hawaii, M.Ed. 1966.
Military Career: Army Corps of Engineers, 1945-47.
Occupation: Elementary school teacher; principal; state program administrator.
Family: Wife, Mary Mildred Chong; five children.
Religion: Congregationalist.
Political Career: Sought Democratic nomination for lieutenant governor, 1974; U.S. House, 1977-90.

Capitol Office: 109 Hart Senate Office Building 20510; 224-6361.
Office Staff: Administrative Assistant, James Sakai; Press Secretary, Peter McClaran; Office Manager, Patricia Hill.
Committees: Energy & Natural Resources; Governmental Affairs; Veterans' Affairs.

Hawaii — The statewide vote for George Bush was 45% in 1988.

CQ Voting Studies

	1989	1990
Presidential	35%	23%
Party	96%	88%
Participation	97%	99%

Interest Groups

	1988	1989
ADA	85%	85%
ACU	0%	7%
AFL-CIO	93%	100%
CCUS	23%	30%

Elections

	1988	1990
General	89%	54%
Primary	u/o	81%

Max Baucus (D-Mont.)

Of Missoula • Elected 1978

Born: December 11, 1941, Helena, Mont.
Education: Stanford U., B.A. 1964;
Stanford U., LL.B. 1967.
Occupation: Lawyer.
Family: Wife, Wanda Minge; one child.
Religion: United Church of Christ.
Political Career: Mont. House, 1973-75;
U.S. House, 1975-79.

Capitol Office: 706 Hart Senate Office
Building 20510; 224-2651.
Office Staff: Administrative Assistant,
Rodger Schlickeisen; Press Secretary,
Paul Risley; Appointments Secretary,
Tracy Crabtree.
Committees: Agriculture, Nutrition &
Forestry; Environment & Public Works;
Finance; Small Business.

Montana — The statewide vote for
George Bush was 52% in 1988.

CQ Voting Studies

	1989	1990
Presidential	48%	51%
Party	69%	70%
Participation	97%	98%

Interest Groups

	1988	1989
ADA	80%	80%
ACU	8%	19%
AFL-CIO	86%	100%
CCUS	29%	43%

Elections

	1984	1990
General	57%	68%
Primary	79%	83%

CQ Voting Studies

	1989	1990
Presidential	69%	52%
Party	71%	75%
Participation	98%	98%

Interest Groups

	1988	1989
ADA	40%	45%
ACU	42%	36%
AFL-CIO	89%	90%
CCUS	25%	57%

Elections

	1982	1988
General	59%	59%
Primary	78%	85%

Lloyd Bentsen (D-Texas)
Of Starr County • *Elected 1970*

Born: February 11, 1921, Mission, Texas.
Education: U. of Texas, LL.B. 1942.
Military Career: Army Air Corps, 1942-45; Air Force Reserve, 1950-59.
Occupation: Lawyer; financial executive.
Family: Wife, Beryl Ann "B. A." Longino; three children.
Religion: Presbyterian.
Political Career: Hidalgo County judge, 1947-48; U.S. House, 1948-55; sought Democratic nomination for president, 1976; Democratic nominee for vice president, 1988.

Capitol Office: 703 Hart Senate Office Building 20510; 224-5922.
Office Staff: Administrative Assistant, Michael Levy; Press Secretary, Jack DeVore; Executive Assistant, Gay Burton.
Committees: Commerce, Science & Transportation; Finance (Chairman).

Texas — The statewide vote for George Bush was 56% in 1988.

Joseph R. Biden, Jr.   (D-Del.)
Of Wilmington • Elected 1972

Born: November 20, 1942, Scranton, Penn.
Education: U. of Delaware, B.A. 1965; Syracuse U., J.D. 1968.
Occupation: Lawyer.
Family: Wife, Jill Jacobs; three children.
Religion: Roman Catholic.
Political Career: New Castle County Council, 1970-72.

Capitol Office: 221 Russell Senate Office Building 20510; 224-5042.
Office Staff: Chief of Staff, Ted Kaufman; Press Secretary, Evelyn Lieberman; Scheduler, Marianne Baker.
Committees: Foreign Relations; Judiciary (Chairman).

Delaware — The statewide vote for George Bush was 56% in 1988.

CQ Voting Studies

	1989	1990
Presidential	50%	33%
Party	81%	83%
Participation	98%	98%

Interest Groups

	1988	1989
ADA	15%	90%
ACU	0%	14%
AFL-CIO	80%	100%
CCUS	67%	29%

Elections

	1984	1990
General	60%	63%
Primary	u/o	u/o

Jeff Bingaman (D-N.M.)
Of Santa Fe • Elected 1982

Born: October 3, 1943, El Paso, Texas.
Education: Harvard U., B.A. 1965; Stanford U., J.D. 1968.
Military Career: Army Reserve, 1968-74.
Occupation: Lawyer.
Family: Wife, Anne Kovacovich; one child.
Religion: Methodist.
Political Career: N.M. attorney general, 1979-83.

Capitol Office: 524 Hart Senate Office Building 20510; 224-5521.
Office Staff: Administrative Assistant, Patrick Von Bargen; Press Secretary, Janet M. Rivera; Appointments Secretary, Virginia White.
Committees: Armed Services; Energy & Natural Resources; Labor & Human Resources.

New Mexico — The statewide vote for George Bush was 52% in 1988.

CQ Voting Studies

	1989	1990
Presidential	54%	35%
Party	84%	76%
Participation	99%	94%

Interest Groups

	1988	1989
ADA	70%	65%
ACU	20%	15%
AFL-CIO	77%	90%
CCUS	43%	38%

Elections

	1982	1988
General	54%	63%
Primary	54%	u/o

Christopher S. Bond (R-Mo.)
Of Mexico • Elected 1986

Born: March 6, 1939, St. Louis, Mo.
Education: Princeton U., A.B. 1960; U. of Virginia, LL.B. 1963.
Occupation: Lawyer.
Family: Wife, Carolyn Reid; one child.
Religion: Presbyterian.
Political Career: Republican nominee for U.S. House, 1968; assistant attorney general, 1969-70; Mo. state auditor, 1971-73; governor, 1973-77; Republican nominee for governor, 1976; governor, 1981-85.

Capitol Office: 293 Russell Senate Office Building 20510; 224-5721.
Office Staff: Administrative Assistant, Warren Erdman; Communications Director, David Ayres; Scheduler, Anne Ekern.
Committees: Agriculture, Nutrition & Forestry; Banking, Housing & Urban Affairs; Budget; Small Business.

Missouri — The statewide vote for George Bush was 52% in 1988.

CQ Voting Studies

	1989	1990
Presidential	86%	82%
Party	85%	86%
Participation	98%	98%

Interest Groups

	1988	1989
ADA	0%	5%
ACU	88%	85%
AFL-CIO	23%	10%
CCUS	86%	100%

Elections

	1986
General	53%
Primary	89%

David Boren (D-Okla.)
Of Seminole • Elected 1978

Born: April 21, 1941, Washington, D.C.
Education: Yale U., B.A. 1963; Oxford U., M.A. 1965; U. of Oklahoma, J.D. 1968.
Military Career: National Guard, 1968-75.
Occupation: Lawyer.
Family: Wife, Molly Wanda Shi; two children.
Religion: Methodist.
Political Career: Okla. House, 1967-75; Okla. governor, 1975-79.

Capitol Office: 453 Russell Senate Office Building 20510; 224-4721.
Office Staff: Administrative Assistant, David Cox; Communications Director, Matthew Helmerich; Executive Assistant, Beth Byrd.
Committees: Agriculture, Nutrition & Forestry; Finance; Small Business.

Oklahoma — The statewide vote for George Bush was 58% in 1988.

CQ Voting Studies

	1989	1990
Presidential	77%	58%
Party	51%	58%
Participation	97%	92%

Interest Groups

	1988	1989
ADA	25%	30%
ACU	48%	63%
AFL-CIO	62%	50%
CCUS	58%	100%

Elections

	1984	1990
General	76%	83%
Primary	90%	84%

Bill Bradley (D-N.J.)
Of Denville • Elected 1978

Born: July 28, 1943, Crystal City, Mo.
Education: Princeton U., B.A. 1965;
Oxford U., M.A. 1968.
Military Career: Air Force Reserve, 1967-78.
Occupation: Professional basketball
player; author.
Family: Wife, Ernestine Schlant; one
child.
Religion: Protestant.
Political Career: No previous office.

Capitol Office: 731 Hart Senate Office
Building 20510; 224-3224.
Office Staff: Administrative Assistant,
Marcia Aronoff; Communications
Director, Michael Jones; Scheduler, Ellen
Laughlin.
Committees: Energy & Natural
Resources; Finance.

New Jersey — The statewide vote for
George Bush was 56% in 1988.

CQ Voting Studies

	1989	1990
Presidential	46%	32%
Party	82%	80%
Participation	95%	99%

Interest Groups

	1988	1989
ADA	75%	85%
ACU	9%	15%
AFL-CIO	75%	80%
CCUS	25%	25%

Elections

	1984	1990
General	64%	50%
Primary	93%	92%

CQ Voting Studies

	1989	1990
Presidential	71%	57%
Party	62%	68%
Participation	99%	99%

Interest Groups

	1988	1989
ADA	50%	40%
ACU	44%	30%
AFL-CIO	85%	100%
CCUS	43%	50%

Elections

	1984	1986
General	u/o	53%
Primary	86%	37%

John B. Breaux   (D-La.)
Of Crowley • *Elected 1986*
Pronounced BRO

Born: March 1, 1944, Crowley, La.
Education: U. of Southwestern Louisiana, B.A. 1964; Louisiana State U., J.D. 1967.
Occupation: Lawyer.
Family: Wife, Lois Daigle; four children.
Religion: Roman Catholic.
Political Career: U.S. House, 1972-87.

Capitol Office: 516 Hart Senate Office Building 20510; 224-4623.
Office Staff: Chief of Staff, Wallace J. Henderson; Press Secretary, Bob Mann; Executive Assistant, Norma Jane Sabiston.
Committees: Commerce, Science & Transportation; Finance.

Louisiana — The statewide vote for George Bush was 54% in 1988.

Hank Brown (R-Colo.)
Of Greeley • Elected 1990

Born: February 12, 1940, Denver, Colo.
Education: U. of Colorado, B.S. 1961; U. of Colorado, J.D. 1969; George Washington U., LL.M. 1986.
Military Career: Navy, 1962-66.
Occupation: Tax accountant; meatpacking company executive; lawyer.
Family: Wife, Nan Morrison; three children.
Religion: United Church of Christ.
Political Career: Colo. Senate, 1973-77; Rebublican nominee for lieutenant governor, 1978; U.S. House, 1981-91.

Capitol Office: 902 Hart Senate Office Building 20510; 224-5941.
Office Staff: Chief of Staff, Bill Brack; Administrative Assistant, Joel Kassiday; Press Secretary, Denise Wible; Personal Secretary/Scheduler, Susan Riley.
Committees: Foreign Relations, Judiciary.

Colorado — The statewide vote for George Bush was 53% in 1988.

Elections

	1988	1990
General	73%	56%
Primary	u/o	u/o

CQ Voting Studies

	1989	1990
Presidential	59%	44%
Party	75%	81%
Participation	99%	99%

Interest Groups

	1989
ADA	55%
ACU	30%
AFL-CIO	100%
CCUS	25%

Elections

	1988
General	50%
Primary	79%

Richard H. Bryan (D-Nev.)
Of Carson City • Elected 1988

Born: July 16, 1937, Washington, D.C.
Education: U. of Nevada, B.A. 1959; U. of California, LL.B. 1963.
Military Career: Army, 1959-60.
Occupation: Lawyer.
Family: Wife, Bonnie Fairchild; three children.
Religion: Episcopalian.
Political Career: Nev. Assembly, 1969-73; Nev. Senate, 1973-79; Democratic nominee for Nev. attorney general, 1974; Nev. attorney general, 1979-83; governor, 1983-89.

Capitol Office: 364 Russell Senate Office Building 20510; 224-6244.
Office Staff: Administrative Assistant, Jean Marie Neal; Press Secretary, Jim Mulhall; Scheduler, Anne Manhart.
Committees: Banking, Housing & Urban Affairs; Commerce, Science & Transportation.

Nevada — The statewide vote for George Bush was 59% in 1988.

Dale Bumpers (D-Ark.)
Of Charleston • Elected 1974

Born: August 12, 1925, Charleston, Ark.
Education: U. of Arkansas, 1946-48;
Northwestern U., LL.B. 1951;
Northwestern U., J.D. 1965.
Military Career: Marine Corps, 1943-46.
Occupation: Lawyer; farmer; hardware
company executive.
Family: Wife, Betty Flanagan; three
children.
Religion: Methodist.
Political Career: Governor, 1971-75.

Capitol Office: 229 Dirksen Senate
Office Building 20510; 224-4843.
Office Staff: Administrative Assistant,
Mary Davis; Press Secretary, Melissa
Skolfield; Appointments Secretary, Rosi
Smith.
Committees: Appropriations; Energy &
Natural Resources; Small Business
(Chairman).

Arkansas — The statewide vote for
George Bush was 56% in 1988.

CQ Voting Studies

	1989	1990
Presidential	50%	35%
Party	87%	84%
Participation	99%	98%

Interest Groups

	1988	1989
ADA	80%	90%
ACU	12%	21%
AFL-CIO	79%	90%
CCUS	33%	25%

Elections

	1980	1986
General	59%	62%
Primary	u/o	u/o

CQ Voting Studies

	1989	1990
Presidential	51%	27%
Party	90%	86%
Participation	99%	99%

Interest Groups

	1988	1989
ADA	85%	85%
ACU	16%	11%
AFL-CIO	100%	100%
CCUS	29%	38%

Elections

	1982	1988
General	63%	59%
Primary	u/o	u/o

Quentin N. Burdick (D-N.D.)
Of Fargo • Elected 1960

Born: June 19, 1908, Munich, N.D.
Education: U. of Minnesota, B.A. 1931; U. of Minnesota, LL.B. 1932.
Occupation: Lawyer.
Family: Wife, Jocelyn Birch Peterson; six children.
Religion: United Church of Christ.
Political Career: Candidate for Cass County State's Attorney, 1934; Republican candidate for N.D. Senate, 1936; candidate for Cass County State's Attorney, 1940; Republican nominee for lieutenant governor, 1942; Democratic nominee for governor, 1946; Democratic nominee for U.S. Senate, 1956; U.S. House, 1959-60.

Capitol Office: 511 Hart Senate Office Building 20510; 224-2551.
Office Staff: Administrative Assistant, Mary Wakefield; Press Secretary, Jean Brodshaug; Personal Secretary, Geraldine Gaginis.
Committees: Appropriations; Environment & Public Works (Chairman).

North Dakota — The statewide vote for George Bush was 56% in 1988.

Conrad Burns (R-Mont.)
Of Billings • Elected 1988

Born: January 25, 1935, Gallatin, Mo.
Education: U. of Missouri, 1952-54.
Military Career: Marine Corps, 1955-57.
Occupation: Radio and television broadcaster; auctioneer.
Family: Wife, Phyllis Kuhlmann; two children.
Religion: Lutheran.
Political Career: Yellowstone County commissioner, 1987-89.

Capitol Office: 183 Dirksen Senate Office Building 20510; 224-2644.
Office Staff: Administrative Assistant, Jack Ramirez; Communications Director, Bryce Dustman; Personal Assistant, Patty Deutsche.
Committees: Commerce, Science & Transportation; Energy & Natural Resources; Small Business.

Montana — The statewide vote for George Bush was 52% in 1988.

CQ Voting Studies

	1989	1990
Presidential	86%	81%
Party	92%	92%
Participation	98%	99%

Interest Groups

	1989
ADA	0%
ACU	85%
AFL-CIO	0%
CCUS	88%

Elections

	1988
General	52%
Primary	85%

Robert C. Byrd (D-W.Va.)
Of Sophia • Elected 1958

Born: November 20, 1917, North Wilkesboro, N.C.
Education: Beckley College; Concord College; Morris Harvey College, 1950-51; Marshall College, 1951-52; American U., J.D. 1963.
Occupation: Lawyer.
Family: Wife, Erma Ora James; two children.
Religion: Baptist.
Political Career: W.Va. House, 1947-50; W.Va. Senate, 1951-52; U.S. House, 1953-59.

Capitol Office: 311 Hart Senate Office Building 20510; 224-3954.
Office Staff: Administrative Assistant, Joan Drummond; Press Assistant, Tina Evans; Appointments Secretary, Kathy McNally.
Committees: Appropriations (Chairman); Armed Services; Rules & Administration.

West Virginia — The statewide vote for George Bush was 47% in 1988.

CQ Voting Studies

	1989	1990
Presidential	54%	42%
Party	83%	74%
Participation	100%	100%

Interest Groups

	1988	1989
ADA	55%	60%
ACU	36%	14%
AFL-CIO	86%	100%
CCUS	29%	38%

Elections

	1982	1988
General	69%	65%
Primary	u/o	81%

John H. Chafee (R-R.I.)
Of Warwick • Elected 1976

Born: October 22, 1922, Providence, R.I.
Education: Yale U., B.A. 1947; Harvard U., LL.B. 1950.
Military Career: Marine Corps, 1942-45; Marine Corps, 1951-52.
Occupation: Lawyer.
Family: Wife, Virginia Coates; five children.
Religion: Episcopalian.
Political Career: R.I. House, 1957-63; minority leader, 1959-63; governor, 1963-69; defeated for re-election as governor, 1968; U.S. secretary of the Navy, 1969-72; Republican nominee for U.S. Senate, 1972.

Capitol Office: 567 Dirksen Senate Office Building 20510; 224-2921.
Office Staff: Chief of Staff, David A. Griswold; Press Secretary, Ed Quinlan; Executive Assistant, Hollis Brown Nesbit.
Committees: Environment & Public Works (Ranking); Finance.

Rhode Island — The statewide vote for George Bush was 44% in 1988.

CQ Voting Studies

	1989	1990
Presidential	81%	58%
Party	57%	58%
Participation	100%	96%

Interest Groups

	1988	1989
ADA	90%	35%
ACU	4%	39%
AFL-CIO	86%	30%
CCUS	36%	75%

Elections

	1982	1988
General	51%	55%
Primary	u/o	u/o

CQ Voting Studies

	1989	1990
Presidential	81%	77%
Party	92%	87%
Participation	99%	98%

Interest Groups

	1988	1989
ADA	10%	10%
ACU	92%	86%
AFL-CIO	29%	20%
CCUS	93%	88%

Elections

	1988	1990
General	62%	54%
Primary	u/o	u/o

Daniel R. Coats (R-Ind.)
Of Fort Wayne • Appointed 1989

Born: May 16, 1943, Jackson, Mich.
Education: Wheaton College, B.A. 1965;
Indiana U., J.D. 1971.
Military Career: Army Corps of
Engineers, 1966-68.
Occupation: Lawyer.
Family: Wife, Marcia Anne Crawford;
three children.
Religion: Presbyterian.
Political Career: U.S. House, 1981-89.

Capitol Office: 407 Russell Senate Office
Building 20510; 224-5623.
Office Staff: Administrative Assistant,
Dave Hoppe; Press Secretary, Curt Smith;
Personal Secretary, Karen Parker.
Committees: Armed Services; Labor &
Human Resources.

Indiana — The statewide vote for George
Bush was 60% in 1988.

Thad Cochran (R-Miss.)
Of Byram • Elected 1978

Born: December 7, 1937, Pontotoc, Miss.
Education: U. of Mississippi, B.A. 1959; U. of Mississippi, J.D. 1965.
Military Career: Navy, 1959-61.
Occupation: Lawyer.
Family: Wife, Rose Clayton; two children.
Religion: Baptist.
Political Career: U.S. House, 1973-78.

Capitol Office: 326 Russell Senate Office Building 20510; 224-5054.
Office Staff: Administrative Assistant, Margo Carlisle; Press Secretary, Lynne Moten; Executive Assistant, Ann Copland.
Committees: Agriculture, Nutrition & Forestry; Appropriations; Labor & Human Resources.

Mississippi — The statewide vote for George Bush was 60% in 1988.

CQ Voting Studies

	1989	1990
Presidential		
Party	94%	85%
Participation	85%	83%
	99%	99%

Interest Groups

	1988	1989
ADA	5%	0%
ACU	96%	78%
AFL-CIO	15%	10%
CCUS	100%	75%

Elections

	1984	1990
General	61%	u/o
Primary	u/o	u/o

CQ Voting Studies

	1989	1990
Presidential	74%	44%
Party	52%	47%
Participation	100%	100%

Interest Groups

	1988	1989
ADA	35%	45%
ACU	46%	50%
AFL-CIO	57%	30%
CCUS	57%	75%

Elections

	1984	1990
General	73%	61%
Primary	u/o	u/o

William S. Cohen (R-Maine)
Of Bangor • Elected 1978

Born: August 28, 1940, Bangor, Maine.
Education: Bowdoin College, B.A. 1962; Boston U., LL.B. 1965.
Occupation: Lawyer.
Family: Divorced; two children.
Religion: Unitarian.
Political Career: Bangor City Council, 1969-72; mayor of Bangor, 1971-72; U.S. House, 1973-79.

Capitol Office: 322 Hart Senate Office Building 20510; 224-2523.
Office Staff: Administrative Assistant, Robert Tyrer; Press Secretary, Kathryn Gest; Appointments Secretary, Donna Saucier.
Committees: Armed Services; Governmental Affairs.

Maine — The statewide vote for George Bush was 55% in 1988.

Kent Conrad (D-N.D.)
Of Bismarck • Elected 1986

Born: March 12, 1948, Bismarck, N.D.
Education: U. of Missouri, 1967
Stanford U., B.A. 1971; George
Washington U., M.B.A. 1975.
Occupation: Management and
personnel director.
Family: Wife, Lucy Calautti; two children.
Religion: Unitarian.
Political Career: Candidate N.D. Auditor,
1976; N.D. tax commissioner, 1981-86.

Capitol Office: 361 Dirksen Senate
Office Building 20510; 224-2043.
Office Staff: Chief of Staff, David Haring;
Press Secretary, Laurie L. Boeder;
Executive Assistant/Scheduling Director,
Lisa Jackson.
Committees: Agriculture, Nutrition &
Forestry; Budget; Energy & Natural
Resources.

North Dakota — The statewide vote for
George Bush was 56% in 1988.

CQ Voting Studies

	1989	1990
Presidential	55%	34%
Party	70%	75%
Participation	100%	99%

Interest Groups

	1988	1989
ADA	80%	70%
ACU	24%	29%
AFL-CIO	93%	90%
CCUS	29%	50%

Elections

	1986
General	50%
Primary	u/o

Elections

	1988	1990
General	66%	61%
Primary	u/o	59%

Larry E. Craig (R-Idaho)
Of Midvale • Elected 1990

Born: July 20, 1945, Council, Idaho.
Education: U. of Idaho, B.A. 1969; George Washington U., 1970.
Military Career: National Guard, 1970-72.
Occupation: Farmer; real estate salesman.
Family: Wife, Suzanne Scott; three stepchildren.
Religion: Methodist.
Political Career: Idaho Senate, 1975-81; U.S. House, 1981-91.
Capitol Office: 708 Hart Senate Office Building 20510; 224-2752.
Office Staff: Administrative Assistant, Greg Casey; Press Secretary, David Fish; Executive Assistant, Lynn Dadant.
Committees: Agriculture, Nutrition & Forestry; Energy & Natural Resources.

Idaho — The statewide vote for George Bush was 62% in 1988.

Alan Cranston (D Calif.)
Of Los Angeles • Elected 1968

Born: June 19, 1914, Palo Alto, Calif.
Education: Pomona College, 1932-33; U. of Mexico, 1933; Stanford U., A.B. 1936.
Military Career: Army, 1944-45.
Occupation: Journalist; real estate executive; author.
Family: Divorced; one child.
Religion: Protestant.
Political Career: Calif. controller, 1959-67; sought Democratic nomination for U.S. Senate, 1964; sought Democratic nomination for president, 1984.

Capitol Office: 112 Hart Senate Office Building 20510; 224-3553.
Office Staff: Administrative Assistant, Roy Greenaway; Press Secretary, Murray Flander; Executive Assistant, Mary Lou McNeely.
Committees: Banking, Housing & Urban Affairs; Foreign Relations; Veterans' Affairs (Chairman).

California — The statewide vote for George Bush was 51% in 1988.

CQ Voting Studies

	1989	1990
Presidential	50%	27%
Party	95%	90%
Participation	99%	98%

Interest Groups

	1988	1989
ADA	95%	85%
ACU	0%	4%
AFL-CIO	86%	90%
CCUS	29%	50%

Elections

	1980	1986
General	57%	49%
Primary	80%	81%

CQ Voting Studies

	1989	1990
Presidential	67%	68%
Party	52%	68%
Participation	99%	99%

Interest Groups

	1988	1989
ADA	15%	35%
ACU	80%	48%
AFL-CIO	57%	70%
CCUS	64%	63%

Elections

	1980	1986
General	45%	57%
Primary	56%	u/o

Alfonse M. D'Amato (R-N.Y.)
Of Island Park • Elected 1980
Pronounced dah MAH toe

Born: August 1, 1937, Brooklyn, N.Y.
Education: Syracuse U., B.S. 1959; Syracuse U., J.D. 1961.
Occupation: Lawyer.
Family: Wife, Penny Collenburg; four children.
Religion: Roman Catholic.
Political Career: Nassau County public administrator, 1965-68; receiver of taxes, town of Hempstead, 1969-71; Hempstead town supervisor, 1971-77; Nassau County Board of Supervisors, 1971-80; presiding supervisor, 1977-81.

Capitol Office: 520 Hart Senate Office Building 20510; 224-6542.
Office Staff: Administrative Assistant, Michael T. Kinsella; Press Secretary, Frank Coleman; Executive Assistant, Debbie Evans.
Committees: Appropriations; Banking, Housing & Urban Affairs.

New York — The statewide vote for George Bush was 48% in 1988.

John C. Danforth (R-Mo.)
Of Newburg • Elected 1976

Born: September 5, 1936, St. Louis, Mo.
Education: Princeton U., A.B. 1958; Yale U., B.D. 1963; Yale U., LL.B. 1963.
Occupation: Lawyer; clergyman.
Family: Wife, Sally Dobson; five children.
Religion: Episcopalian.
Political Career: Mo. attorney general, 1969-77; Republican nominee for U.S. Senate, 1970.

Capitol Office: 249 Russell Senate Office Building 20510; 224-6154.
Office Staff: Administrative Assistant, Alexander Netchvolodoff; Press Secretary, Steve Hilton; Executive Secretary, Sherrey Kenney.
Committees: Commerce, Science & Transportation; Finance.

Missouri — The statewide vote for George Bush was 52% in 1988.

CQ Voting Studies

	1989	1990
Presidential	90%	74%
Party	75%	71%
Participation	99%	99%

Interest Groups

	1988	1989
ADA	20%	15%
ACU	72%	71%
AFL-CIO	42%	20%
CCUS	71%	63%

Elections

	1982	1988
General	51%	68%
Primary	74%	u/o

CQ Voting Studies

	1989	1990
Presidential	49%	31%
Party	90%	87%
Participation	99%	99%

Interest Groups

	1988	1989
ADA	85%	80%
ACU	13%	7%
AFL-CIO	93%	90%
CCUS	36%	50%

Elections

	1984	1986
General	57%	52%
Primary	u/o	u/o

Tom Daschle (D-S.D.)
Of Aberdeen • Elected 1986
Pronounced DASH el

Born: December 9, 1947, Aberdeen, S.D.
Education: South Dakota State U., B.A. 1969.
Military Career: Air Force, 1969-72.
Occupation: Congressional aide.
Family: Wife, Linda Hall; three children.
Religion: Roman Catholic.
Political Career: U.S. House, 1979-87.

Capitol Office: 317 Hart Senate Office Building 20510; 224-2321.
Office Staff: Administrative Assistant, Peter Rouse; Press Secretary, Steve Kinsella; Executive Assistant, Anne Foley.
Committees: Agriculture, Nutrition & Forestry; Finance.

South Dakota — The statewide vote for George Bush was 53% in 1988.

Dennis DeConcini (D-Ariz.)
Of Tucson • Elected 1976
Pronounced dee con SEE nee

Born: May 8, 1937, Tucson, Ariz.
Education: U. of Arizona, B.A. 1959; U. of Arizona, LL.B. 1963.
Military Career: Army, 1959-60; Army Reserve, 1960-67.
Occupation: Lawyer.
Family: Wife, Susan Hurley; three children.
Religion: Roman Catholic.
Political Career: Pima County attorney, 1973-76.

Capitol Office: 328 Hart Senate Office Building 20510; 224-4521.
Office Staff: Administrative Assistant, Gene Karp; Press Secretary, Bob Maynes; Executive Assistant, Nancy Suter.
Committees: Appropriations; Judiciary; Rules & Administration; Veterans' Affairs.

Arizona — The statewide vote for George Bush was 60% in 1988.

CQ Voting Studies

	1989	1990
Presidential	61%	40%
Party	64%	74%
Participation	99%	97%

Interest Groups

	1988	1989
ADA	55%	60%
ACU	33%	32%
AFL-CIO	92%	80%
CCUS	21%	50%

Elections

	1982	1988
General	57%	57%
Primary	84%	u/o

CQ Voting Studies

	1989	1990
Presidential	72%	53%
Party	62%	70%
Participation	100%	100%

Interest Groups

	1988	1989
ADA	45%	55%
ACU	44%	32%
AFL-CIO	69%	90%
CCUS	57%	50%

Elections

	1980	1986
General	56%	65%
Primary	67%	85%

Alan J. Dixon (D-Ill.)
Of Belleville • Elected 1980

Born: July 7, 1927, Belleville, Ill.
Education: U. of Illinois, B.S. 1949;
Washington U., LL.B. 1949.
Military Career: Naval Air Cadet, 1945-46.
Occupation: Lawyer.
Family: Wife, Joan Louise Fox; three children.
Religion: Presbyterian.
Political Career: Ill. House, 1951-63; Ill. Senate, 1963-71; Ill. treasurer, 1971-77; Ill. secretary of state, 1977-81.

Capitol Office: 331 Hart Senate Office Building 20510; 224-2854.
Office Staff: Administrative Assistant, Eugene Callahan; Press Secretary, William Adams; Personal Secretary, Britta Brackney.
Committees: Armed Services; Banking, Housing & Urban Affairs; Small Business.

Illinois — The statewide vote for George Bush was 51% in 1988.

Christopher J. Dodd (D-Conn.)
Of East Haddam • Elected 1980

Born: May 27, 1944, Willimantic, Conn.
Education: Providence College, B.A.
1966; U. of Louisville, J.D. 1972.
Military Career: Army Reserve, 1969-75.
Occupation: Lawyer.
Family: Divorced.
Religion: Roman Catholic.
Political Career: U.S. House, 1975-81.

Capitol Office: 444 Russell Senate Office
Building 20510; 224-2823.
Office Staff: Administrative
Assistant/Chief of Staff, Jason Isaacson;
Press Secretary, Julie Rosson; Special
Assistant/Scheduler, Lee Mulvihill.
Committees: Banking, Housing & Urban
Affairs; Budget; Foreign Relations; Labor
& Human Resources; Rules &
Administration.

Connecticut — The statewide vote for
George Bush was 52% in 1988.

CQ Voting Studies

	1989	1990
Presidential	54%	39%
Party	89%	89%
Participation	99%	97%

Interest Groups

	1988	1989
ADA	85%	65%
ACU	8%	22%
AFL-CIO	86%	100%
CCUS	36%	50%

Elections

	1980	1986
General	56%	65%
Primary	u/o	u/o

CQ Voting Studies

	1989	1990
Presidential	94%	80%
Party	89%	86%
Participation	99%	100%

Interest Groups

	1988	1989
ADA	15%	5%
ACU	91%	86%
AFL-CIO	33%	0%
CCUS	91%	88%

Elections

	1980	1986
General	64%	70%
Primary	82%	84%

Bob Dole (R-Kan.)
Of Russell • Elected 1968

Born: July 22, 1923, Russell, Kan.
Education: U. of Kansas, 1941-43; Washburn U., A.B. 1952; Washburn U., LL.B. 1952.
Military Career: Army, 1943-48.
Occupation: Lawyer.
Family: Wife, Mary Elizabeth Hanford; one child.
Religion: Methodist.
Political Career: Kan. House, 1951-53; Russell County attorney, 1953-61; U.S. House, 1961-69; Republican nominee for vice president, 1976; sought Republican nomination for president, 1980.

Capitol Office: 141 Hart Senate Office Building 20510; 224-6521.
Office Staff: Administrative Assistant, James Kevin Wholey; Press Secretary, Walt Riker; Executive Assistant/Personal Secretary, Yvonne Hopkins.
Committees: Agriculture, Nutrition & Forestry; Finance; Rules & Administration.

Kansas — The statewide vote for George Bush was 56% in 1988.

Pete V. Domenici (R-N.M.)

Of Albuquerque • Elected 1972

Pronounced da MEN ah chee

Born: May 7, 1932, Albuquerque, N.M.
Education: U. of Albuquerque, 1950-52;
U. of New Mexico, B.S. 1954; U. of
Denver, LL.B. 1958.
Occupation: Lawyer.
Family: Wife, Nancy Burk; eight children.
Religion: Roman Catholic.
Political Career: Albuquerque City
Commission, 1966-70; chairman and ex-
officio mayor, 1967-70; Republican
nominee for governor, 1970.

Capitol Office: 434 Dirksen Senate
Office Building 20510; 224-6621.
Office Staff: Administrative Assistant,
Paul Gilman; Press Secretary, Ari Fleisher;
Personal Secretary, Angela Raish.
Committees: Appropriations; Budget;
Energy & Natural Resources.

New Mexico — The statewide vote for
George Bush was 52% in 1988.

CQ Voting Studies

	1989	1990
Presidential	90%	67%
Party	74%	69%
Participation	97%	94%

Interest Groups

	1988	1989
ADA	15%	10%
ACU	72%	88%
AFL-CIO	46%	11%
CCUS	79%	88%

Elections

	1984	1990
General	72%	73%
Primary	u/o	u/o

CQ Voting Studies

	1989	1990
Presidential	77%	62%
Party	56%	55%
Participation	97%	95%

Interest Groups

	1988	1989
ADA	60%	40%
ACU	26%	41%
AFL-CIO	77%	30%
CCUS	43%	50%

Elections

	1982	1988
General	53%	56%
Primary	93%	93%

Dave Durenberger (R-Minn.)
Of Minneapolis • Elected 1978

Born: August 19, 1934, St. Cloud, Minn.
Education: St. John's U., B.A. 1955; U. of Minnesota, J.D. 1959.
Military Career: Army Reserve, 1956-63.
Occupation: Lawyer; adhesives manufacturing executive.
Family: Wife, Gilda Beth "Penny" Baran; four children.
Religion: Roman Catholic.
Political Career: No previous office.

Capitol Office: 154 Russell Senate Office Building 20510; 224-3244.
Office Staff: Chief of Staff, Bert McKasy; Communications Director, Steve Moore; Appointments Secretary, Julie Hasler.
Committees: Environment & Public Works; Finance; Labor & Human Resources.

Minnesota — The statewide vote for George Bush was 46% in 1988.

Jim Exon (D-Neb.)
Of Lincoln • Elected 1978

Born: August 9, 1921, Geddes, S.D.
Education: U. of Omaha, 1939-41.
Military Career: Army, 1941-45; Reserve, 1945-49.
Occupation: Office equipment dealer.
Family: Wife, Patricia Ann Pros; three children.
Religion: Episcopalian.
Political Career: Democratic National Committee, 1968-71; governor, 1971-79.

Capitol Office: 528 Hart Senate Office Building 20510; 224-4224.
Office Staff: Chief of Staff, Greg Pallas; Press Secretary, Mark Bowen; Personal Secretary, Adele Hanson.
Committees: Armed Services; Budget; Commerce, Science & Transportation.

Nebraska — The statewide vote for George Bush was 60% in 1988.

CQ Voting Studies

	1989	1990
Presidential	65%	54%
Party	53%	63%
Participation	99%	97%

Interest Groups

	1988	1989
ADA	35%	35%
ACU	48%	36%
AFL-CIO	71%	100%
CCUS	50%	25%

Elections

	1984	1990
General	52%	59%
Primary	u/o	u/o

Wendell H. Ford (D-Ky.)
Of Owensboro • Elected 1974

Born: September 8, 1924, Thruston, Ky.
Education: U. of Kentucky, 1942-43.
Military Career: Army, 1944-46; Army National Guard, 1949-62.
Occupation: Insurance executive.
Family: Wife, Jean Neel; two children.
Religion: Baptist.
Political Career: Ky. Senate, 1965-67; lieutenant governor, 1967-71; governor, 1971-74.

Capitol Office: 173A Russell Senate Office Building 20510; 224-4343.
Office Staff: Administrative Assistant, James T. Fleming; Press Secretary/Communications Director, Phil Norman; Appointments Secretary, Sherry McCabe.
Committees: Commerce, Science & Transportation; Energy & Natural Resources; Rules & Administration (Chairman).

Kentucky — The statewide vote for George Bush was 56% in 1988.

CQ Voting Studies

	1989	1990
Presidential	60%	55%
Party	64%	69%
Participation	99%	99%

Interest Groups

	1988	1989
ADA	65%	45%
ACU	24%	25%
AFL-CIO	93%	100%
CCUS	21%	25%

Elections

	1980	1986
General	65%	74%
Primary	87%	u/o

Wyche Fowler, Jr. (D-Ga.)
Of Atlanta • Elected 1986
Pronouced WHYch

Born: October 6, 1940, Atlanta, Ga.
Education: Davidson College, A.B. 1962; Emory U., J.D. 1969.
Military Career: Army, 1963-65.
Occupation: Lawyer.
Family: Wife, Donna Hulsizer; one child.
Religion: Presbyterian.
Political Career: Atlanta Board of Aldermen, 1970-74; sought Democratic nomination for U.S. House, 1972; president, Atlanta City Council, 1974-77; U.S. House, 1977-87.

Capitol Office: 204 Russell Senate Office Building 20510; 224-3643.
Office Staff: Chief of Staff, Bill Johnstone; Press Secretary, Deborah Matthews; Personal Assistant, Laura Parker.
Committees: Agriculture, Nutrition & Forestry; Appropriations; Budget; Energy & Natural Resources.

Georgia — The statewide vote for George Bush was 60% in 1988.

CQ Voting Studies

	1989	1990
Presidential	61%	43%
Party	72%	84%
Participation	99%	98%

Interest Groups

	1988	1989
ADA	75%	60%
ACU	8%	15%
AFL-CIO	79%	89%
CCUS	43%	50%

Elections

	1984	1986
General	u/o	51%
Primary	64%	50%

Jake Garn (R-Utah)
Of Salt Lake City • Elected 1974

Born: October 12, 1932, Richfield, Utah.
Education: U. of Utah, B.S. 1955.
Military Career: Navy, 1956-60; Air National Guard, 1960-69.
Occupation: Insurance executive.
Family: Wife, Kathleen Brewerton; seven children.
Religion: Mormon.
Political Career: Salt Lake City commissioner, 1968-72; mayor of Salt Lake City, 1972-74.

Capitol Office: 505 Dirksen Senate Office Building 20510; 224-5444.
Office Staff: Chief of Staff/Administrative Assistant, W.P. Skip Glines; Communications Director, Laurie Turner; Executive Assistant, Alvina Wall.
Committees: Appropriations; Banking, Housing & Urban Affairs; Energy & Natural Resources; Rules & Administration.

Utah — The statewide vote for George Bush was 66% in 1988.

CQ Voting Studies

	1989	1990
Presidential	86%	73%
Party	97%	88%
Participation	96%	94%

Interest Groups

	1988	1989
ADA	0%	5%
ACU	96%	96%
AFL-CIO	7%	0%
CCUS	92%	88%

Elections

	1980	1986
General	74%	72%
Primary	u/o	u/o

John Glenn (D-Ohio)
Of Columbus • Elected 1974

Born: July 18, 1921, Cambridge, Ohio.
Education: Muskingum College, B.S. 1962.
Military Career: Marine Corps, 1942-65.
Occupation: Astronaut; soft drink company executive.
Family: Wife, Anna Margaret Castor; two children.
Religion: Presbyterian.
Political Career: Sought Democratic nomination for U.S. Senate, 1970; sought Democratic nomination for president, 1984.

Capitol Office: 503 Hart Senate Office Building 20510; 224-3353.
Office Staff: Administrative Assistant, Mary Jane Veno; Press Secretary, Rebecca Bell; Scheduler, Kathleen Long.
Committees: Armed Services; Governmental Affairs (Chairman).

Ohio — The statewide vote for George Bush was 55% in 1988.

CQ Voting Studies

	1989	1990
Presidential	59%	39%
Party	82%	79%
Participation	98%	100%

Interest Groups

	1988	1989
ADA	80%	65%
ACU	9%	26%
AFL-CIO	79%	100%
CCUS	31%	38%

Elections

	1980	1986
General	69%	62%
Primary	86%	88%

CQ Voting Studies

	1989	1990
Presidential	56%	38%
Party	68%	93%
Participation	89%	99%

Interest Groups

	1988	1989
ADA	60%	55%
ACU	9%	19%
AFL-CIO	83%	88%
CCUS	45%	60%

Elections

	1984	1990
General	61%	68%
Primary	u/o	u/o

Al Gore (D-Tenn.)
Of Carthage • Elected 1984

Born: March 31, 1948, Washington, D.C.
Education: Harvard U., B.A. 1969;
Vanderbilt School of Religion, 1972;
Vanderbilt U. Law School, 1974-76.
Military Career: Army, 1969-71.
Occupation: Journalist; home builder.
Family: Wife, Mary Elizabeth "Tipper"
Aitcheson; four children.
Religion: Baptist.
Political Career: U.S. House, 1977-85;
sought Democratic nomination for
president, 1988.

Capitol Office: 393 Russell Senate Office
Building 20510; 224-4944.
Office Staff: Administrative Assistant,
Roy Neel; Press Secretary, Marla Romash;
Executive Assistant/Scheduler, Beth
Prichard.
Committees: Armed Services;
Commerce, Science & Transportation;
Rules & Administration.

Tennessee — The statewide vote for
George Bush was 58% in 1988.

Slade Gorton (R-Wash.)
Of Seattle • Elected 1980

Born: January 8, 1928, Chicago, Ill.
Education: Dartmouth College, B.A.
1950; Columbia U., LL.B. 1953.
Military Career: Army, 1945-46; Air
Force, 1953-56; Air Force Reserve, 1956-
81.
Occupation: Lawyer.
Family: Wife, Sally Jean Clark; three
children.
Religion: Episcopalian.
Political Career: Wash. House, 1959-69;
majority leader, 1967-69; Wash. attorney
general, 1969-81; defeated for reelection
to Senate, 1986; reelected 1988.

Capitol Office: 730 Hart Senate Office
Building 20510; 224-3441.
Office Staff: Administrative Assistant,
Mike McGavick; Press Secretary, Kraig
Naasz; Office Manager/Scheduler, Vickie
McQuade.
Committees: Agriculture, Nutrition &
Forestry; Armed Services; Commerce,
Science & Transportation.

Washington — The statewide vote for
George Bush was 48% in 1988.

CQ Voting Studies

	1989	1990
Presidential	89%	76%
Party	80%	81%
Participation	100%	100%

Interest Groups

	1989
ADA	15%
ACU	75%
AFL-CIO	20%
CCUS	88%

Elections

	1980	1988
General	54%	51%
Primary	33%	36%

CQ Voting Studies

	1989	1990
Presidential	64%	53%
Party	68%	76%
Participation	99%	99%

Interest Groups

	1988	1989
ADA	55%	50%
ACU	28%	36%
AFL-CIO	71%	100%
CCUS	38%	38%

Elections

	1986
General	55%
Primary	85%

Bob Graham (D-Fla.)
Of Miami Lakes • Elected 1986

Born: November 9, 1936, Miami, Fla.
Education: U. of Florida, B.A. 1959;
Harvard U., LL.B. 1962.
Occupation: Developer.
Family: Wife, Adele Khoury; four
children.
Religion: United Church of Christ.
Political Career: Fla. House, 1967-71; Fla.
Senate, 1971-79; governor, 1979-87.

Capitol Office: 241 Dirksen Senate
Office Building 20510; 224-3041.
Office Staff: Administrative Assistant,
Samuel R. Shorstein; Press Secretary,
Kenneth Klein; Executive Assistant, Becky
Hendrix.
Committees: Banking, Housing & Urban
Affairs; Environment & Public Works;
Veterans' Affairs.

Florida — The statewide vote for George
Bush was 61% in 1988.

Phil Gramm (R-Texas)
Of College Station • Elected 1984

Born: July 8, 1942, Fort Benning, Ga.
Education: U. of Georgia, B.A. 1964; U. of Georgia, Ph.D. 1967.
Occupation: Professor of economics.
Family: Wife, Wendy Lee; two children.
Religion: Episcopalian.
Political Career: Sought Democratic nomination for U.S. Senate, 1976; U.S. House, 1979-85.

Capitol Office: 370 Russell Senate Office Building 20510; 224-2934.
Office Staff: Chief of Staff, Ruth Cymber; Press Secretary, Larry Neal; Scheduler, Meredith White.
Committees: Appropriations; Banking, Housing & Urban Affairs; Budget.

Texas — The statewide vote for George Bush was 56% in 1988.

CQ Voting Studies

	1989	1990
Presidential	86%	78%
Party	91%	88%
Participation	97%	96%

Interest Groups

	1988	1989
ADA	0%	0%
ACU	95%	96%
AFL-CIO	0%	0%
CCUS	92%	88%

Elections

	1984	1990
General	59%	60%
Primary	73%	u/o

Charles E. Grassley (R-Iowa)
Of New Hartford • Elected 1980

Born: September 17, 1933, New Hartford, Iowa.
Education: U. of Northern Iowa, B.A. 1955; U. of Northern Iowa, M.A. 1956; U. of Iowa, 1957-58.
Occupation: Farmer.
Family: Wife, Barbara Ann Speicher; five children.
Religion: Baptist.
Political Career: Iowa House, 1959-75; U.S. House, 1975-81.

Capitol Office: 135 Hart Senate Office Building 20510; 224-3744.
Office Staff: Administrative Assistant, Robert J. Ludwiczak; Press Secretary, Caran Kolbe McKee; Scheduler, Mary Jo Archibold.
Committees: Appropriations; Budget; Judiciary; Small Business.

Iowa — The statewide vote for George Bush was 44% in 1988.

CQ Voting Studies

	1989	1990
Presidential	79%	70%
Party	91%	85%
Participation	100%	99%

Interest Groups

	1988	1989
ADA	5%	25%
ACU	88%	86%
AFL-CIO	21%	10%
CCUS	93%	75%

Elections

	1980	1986
General	54%	66%
Primary	66%	u/o

Tom Harkin (D-Iowa)
Of Cumming • Elected 1984

Born: November 19, 1939, Cumming, Iowa.
Education: Iowa State U., B.S. 1962; Catholic U., J.D. 1972.
Military Career: Navy, 1962-67; Naval Reserve, 1968-74.
Occupation: Lawyer.
Family: Wife, Ruth Raduenz; two children.
Religion: Roman Catholic.
Political Career: Democratic nominee for U.S. House, 1972; U.S. House, 1975-85.

Capitol Office: 316 Hart Senate Office Building 20510; 224-3254.
Office Staff: Administrative Assistant, Donald J. Foley; Press Secretary, Lorraine A. Voles; Scheduling Secretary, Jennifer Marshall.
Committees: Agriculture, Nutrition & Forestry; Appropriations; Labor & Human Resources; Small Business.

Iowa — The statewide vote for George Bush was 44% in 1988.

CQ Voting Studies

	1989	1990
Presidential	38%	22%
Party	77%	85%
Participation	98%	100%

Interest Groups

	1988	1989
ADA	95%	95%
ACU	0%	14%
AFL-CIO	92%	100%
CCUS	36%	38%

Elections

	1984	1990
General	56%	54%
Primary	u/o	u/o

Orrin G. Hatch (R-Utah)
Of Midvale • Elected 1976

Born: March 22, 1934, Pittsburgh, Penn.
Education: Brigham Young U., B.S. 1959;
U. of Pittsburgh, LL.B. 1962.
Occupation: Lawyer.
Family: Wife, Elaine Hansen; six children.
Religion: Mormon.
Political Career: No previous office.

Capitol Office: 135 Russell Senate Office
Building 20510; 224-5251.
Office Staff: Administrative Assistant,
Kevin S. McGuiness; Press Secretary, Paul
Smith; Personal Secretary, Ruth Carroll.
Committees: Judiciary; Labor and Human
Resources (Ranking).

Utah — The statewide vote for George
Bush was 66% in 1988.

CQ Voting Studies

	1989	1990
Presidential	81%	77%
Party	85%	89%
Participation	99%	99%

Interest Groups

	1988	1989
ADA	5%	5%
ACU	96%	93%
AFL-CIO	36%	10%
CCUS	86%	88%

Elections

	1982	1988
General	58%	67%
Primary	u/o	u/o

Mark O. Hatfield (R-Ore.)
Of Tigard • Elected 1966

Born: July 12, 1922, Dallas, Ore.
Education: Willamette U., B.A. 1943;
Stanford U., M.A. 1948.
Military Career: Navy, 1943-46.
Occupation: Professor of political
science.
Family: Wife, Antoinette Kuzmanich;
four children.
Religion: Baptist.
Political Career: Ore. House, 1951-55;
Ore. Senate, 1955-57; Ore. secretary of
state, 1957-59; Ore. governor, 1959-67.

Capitol Office: 711 Hart Senate Office
Building 20510; 224-3753.
Office Staff: Administrative Assistant,
Gerald W. Frank; Press Secretary, Bill
Calder; Personal Secretary, Janet Lamos.
Committees: Appropriations (Ranking);
Energy & Natural Resources; Rules &
Administration.

Oregon — The statewide vote for
George Bush was 47% in 1988.

CQ Voting Studies

	1989	1990
Presidential	69%	38%
Party	39%	31%
Participation	98%	88%

Interest Groups

	1988	1989
ADA	70%	80%
ACU	30%	21%
AFL-CIO	62%	50%
CCUS	57%	63%

Elections

	1984	1990
General	67%	54%
Primary	79%	78%

Howell Heflin (D-Ala.)
Of Tuscumbia • Elected 1978

Born: June 19, 1921, Poulan, Ga.
Education: Birmingham Southern College, B.A. 1942; U. of Alabama, J.D. 1948.
Military Career: Marine Corps, 1942-46.
Occupation: Judge; lawyer; government and political science lecturer.
Family: Wife, Elizabeth Ann Carmichael; one child.
Religion: Methodist.
Political Career: Chief justice, Ala. Supreme Court, 1971-77.
Capitol Office: 728 Hart Senate Office Building 20510; 224-4124.
Office Staff: Administrative Assistant, Stephen Raby; Press Secretary, Tom McMahon; Appointments Secretary, Catherine Hughes.
Committees: Agriculture, Nutrition & Forestry; Judiciary.

Alabama — The statewide vote for George Bush was 59% in 1988.

CQ Voting Studies

	1989	1990
Presidential	71%	60%
Party	39%	53%
Participation	100%	99%

Interest Groups

	1988	1989
ADA	30%	25%
ACU	58%	75%
AFL-CIO	64%	90%
CCUS	50%	63%

Elections

	1984	1990
General	63%	61%
Primary	83%	81%

John Heinz (R-Pa.)
Of Pittsburgh • Elected 1976

Born: October 23, 1938, Pittsburgh, Penn.
Education: Yale U., B.A. 1960; Harvard U., M.B.A. 1963.
Military Career: Air Force, 1963-69.
Occupation: Food industry executive.
Family: Wife, Teresa Simoes-Ferreira; three children.
Religion: Episcopalian.
Political Career: U.S. House, 1971-77.

Capitol Office: 277 Russell Senate Office Building 20510; 224-6324.
Office Staff: Administrative Assistant, Cliff Shannon; Press Secretary, Grant Oliphant; Scheduler, Jeanne Alexander.
Committees: Banking, Housing & Urban Affairs; Finance; Governmental Affairs.

Pennsylvania — The statewide vote for George Bush was 51% in 1988.

CQ Voting Studies

	1989	1990
Presidential	71%	57%
Party	50%	52%
Participation	99%	98%

Interest Groups

	1988	1989
ADA	55%	35%
ACU	41%	54%
AFL-CIO	79%	80%
CCUS	46%	75%

Elections

	1982	1988
General	59%	66%
Primary	u/o	u/o

Jesse Helms (R-N.C.)
Of Raleigh • Elected 1972

Born: October 18, 1921, Monroe, N.C.
Education: Wingate Junior College, 1938-39; Wake Forest College, 1939-40.
Military Career: Navy, 1942-45.
Occupation: Journalist; broadcasting executive; banking executive; congressional aide.
Family: Wife, Dorothy Jane Coble; three children.
Religion: Baptist.
Political Career: Raleigh City Council, 1957-61.
Capitol Office: 403 Dirksen Senate Office Building 20510; 224-6342.
Office Staff: Administrative Assistant, Clint Fuller; Scheduler, Frances Marcus.
Committees: Agriculture, Nutrition & Forestry; Foreign Relations (Ranking); Rules & Administration.

North Carolina — The statewide vote for George Bush was 58% in 1988.

CQ Voting Studies

	1989	1990
Presidential	71%	68%
Party	86%	88%
Participation	98%	99%

Interest Groups

	1988	1989
ADA	5%	5%
ACU	100%	100%
AFL-CIO	23%	20%
CCUS	75%	75%

Elections

	1984	1990
General	52%	53%
Primary	91%	84%

Ernest F. Hollings (D-S.C.)
Of Charleston • Elected 1966

Born: January 1, 1922, Charleston, S.C.
Education: The Citadel, B.A. 1942; U. of
South Carolina, LL.B. 1947.
Military Career: Army, 1942-45.
Occupation: Lawyer.
Family: Wife, Rita "Peatsy" Liddy; four
children.
Religion: Lutheran.
Political Career: S.C. House, 1949-55;
lieutenant governor, 1955-59; governor,
1959-63; sought Democratic nomination
for U.S. Senate, 1962; sought Democratic
nomination for president, 1984.

Capitol Office: 125 Russell Senate Office
Building 20510; 224-6121.
Office Staff: Administrative Assistant,
Ashley O. Thrift; Press Secretary, John
Patterson; Appointments Secretary, Mary
Winton Hughes.
Committees: Appropriations; Budget;
Commerce, Science & Transportation
(Chairman).

South Carolina — The statewide vote for
George Bush was 62% in 1988.

CQ Voting Studies

	1989	1990
Presidential	67%	52%
Party	61%	73%
Participation	100%	100%

Interest Groups

	1988	1989
ADA	55%	45%
ACU	48%	50%
AFL-CIO	86%	80%
CCUS	29%	63%

Elections

	1980	1986
General	70%	63%
Primary	81%	u/o

CQ Voting Studies

	1989	1990
Presidential	60%	45%
Party	83%	84%
Participation	98%	97%

Interest Groups

	1988	1989
ADA	85%	70%
ACU	4%	11%
AFL-CIO	92%	90%
CCUS	38%	50%

Elections

	1980	1986
General	78%	74%
Primary	88%	u/o

Daniel K. Inouye (D-Hawaii)

Of Honolulu • Elected 1962
Pronounced in NO ay

Born: September 7, 1924, Honolulu, Hawaii.
Education: U. of Hawaii, B.A. 1950; George Washington U., J.D. 1952.
Military Career: Army, 1943-47.
Occupation: Lawyer.
Family: Wife, Margaret Shinobu Awamura; one child.
Religion: Methodist.
Political Career: Hawaii Territorial House, majority leader, 1954-58; Hawaii Territorial Senate, 1958-59; U.S. House, 1959-63.

Capitol Office: 722 Hart Senate Office Building 20510; 224-3934.
Office Staff: Administrative Assistant, Patrick DeLeon; Press Secretary, Jennifer Goto; Office Manager, Beverly MacDonald.
Committees: Appropriations; Commerce, Science & Transportation; Rules & Administration.

Hawaii — The statewide vote for George Bush was 45% in 1988.

James M. Jeffords (R-Vt.)
Of Shrewsbury • Elected 1988

Born: May 11, 1934, Rutland, Vt.
Education: Yale U., B.S.I.A. 1956; Harvard U., LL.B. 1962.
Military Career: Navy, 1956-59; Naval Reserve, 1959-present.
Occupation: Lawyer.
Family: Wife, Elizabeth Daley; two children.
Religion: Congregationalist.
Political Career: Vt. Senate, 1967-69; Vt. attorney general, 1969-73; sought Republican nomination for governor, 1972.

Capitol Office: 530 Dirksen Senate Office Building 20510; 224-5141.
Office Staff: Administrative Assistant, Susan Boardman Russ; Press Secretary, Howard Coffin; Scheduler, Trecia Bickford.
Committees: Environment & Public Works; Labor & Human Resources; Veterans' Affairs.

Vermont — The statewide vote for George Bush was 51% in 1988.

CQ Voting Studies

	1989	1990
Presidential	68%	51%
Party	40%	36%
Participation	92%	97%

Interest Groups

	1988	1989
ADA	70%	40%
ACU	21%	44%
AFL-CIO	92%	40%
CCUS	54%	71%

Elections

	1986	1988
General	89%	68%
Primary	u/o	61%

J. Bennett Johnston (D-La.)
Of Shreveport • Elected 1972

Born: June 10, 1932, Shreveport, La.
Education: Washington and Lee U., 1950-51; U.S. Military Academy, 1951-52; Washington and Lee U., 1952-53; Louisiana State U., LL.B. 1956.
Military Career: Army, 1956-59.
Occupation: Lawyer.
Family: Wife, Mary Gunn; four children.
Religion: Baptist.
Political Career: La. House, 1964-68; La. Senate, 1968-72; sought Democratic nomination for governor, 1971.

Capitol Office: 136 Hart Senate Office Building 20510; 224-5824.
Office Staff: Administrative Assistant, James M. Oakes; Press Secretary, Tony Garrett; Scheduler, Cheryl Brignace.
Committees: Appropriations; Budget; Energy & Natural Resources (Chairman).

Louisiana — The statewide vote for George Bush was 54% in 1988.

CQ Voting Studies

	1989	1990
Presidential	70%	53%
Party	71%	65%
Participation	100%	94%

Interest Groups

	1988	1989
ADA	55%	30%
ACU	36%	32%
AFL-CIO	86%	70%
CCUS	50%	63%

Elections

	1984	1990
General	u/o	u/o
Primary	86%	54%

Nancy Landon Kassebaum
(R-Kan.)
Of Burdick • Elected 1978

Born: July 29, 1932, Topeka, Kan.
Education: U. of Kansas, B.A. 1954; U. of Michigan, M.A. 1956.
Occupation: Broadcasting executive.
Family: Divorced; four children.
Religion: Episcopalian.
Political Career: Maize School Board, 1973-75.

Capitol Office: 302 Russell Senate Office Building 20510; 224-4774.
Office Staff: Administrative Assistant, Dave Bartel; Press Secretary, Larry Shainman; Executive Assistant, Ann Shirley.
Committees: Banking, Housing & Urban Affairs; Foreign Relations; Labor & Human Resources.

Kansas — The statewide vote for George Bush was 56% in 1988.

CQ Voting Studies

	1989	1990
Presidential	85%	68%
Party	71%	67%
Participation	99%	98%

Interest Groups

	1988	1989
ADA	30%	20%
ACU	61%	57%
AFL-CIO	23%	0%
CCUS	71%	63%

Elections

	1984	1990
General	76%	74%
Primary	u/o	87%

CQ Voting Studies

	1989	1990
Presidential	85%	71%
Party	90%	80%
Participation	99%	100%

Interest Groups

	1988	1989
ADA	10%	10%
ACU	84%	89%
AFL-CIO	43%	20%
CCUS	71%	88%

Elections

	1980	1986
General	50%	51%
Primary	37%	u/o

Bob Kasten (R-Wis.)
Of Milwaukee • Elected 1980

Born: June 19, 1942, Milwaukee, Wis.
Education: U. of Arizona, B.A. 1964;
Columbia U., M.B.A. 1966.
Military Career: Air National Guard,
1967-72.
Occupation: Shoe company executive.
Family: Wife, Eva Jean Nimmons; one
child.
Religion: Presbyterian.
Political Career: Republican nominee for
Wis. Assembly, 1970; Wis. Senate, 1973-
75; U.S. House, 1975-79; sought
Republican nomination for governor,
1978.

Capitol Office: 110 Hart Senate Office
Building 20510; 224-5323.
Office Staff: Administrative Assistant, Jim
Sims; Press Secretary, Kirsten Fedewa;
Personal Secretary, Jean Sybeldon.
Committees: Appropriations; Budget;
Commerce, Science & Transportation;
Small Business (Ranking).

Wisconsin — The statewide vote for
George Bush was 48% in 1988.

Edward M. Kennedy (D-Mass.)
Of Boston • Elected 1962

Born: February 22, 1932, Boston, Mass.
Education: Harvard U., B.A. 1956;
International Law School, The Hague,
The Netherlands, 1958; U. of Virginia,
LL.B. 1959.
Military Career: Army, 1951-53.
Occupation: Lawyer.
Family: Divorced; three children.
Religion: Roman Catholic.
Political Career: Suffolk County assistant
district attorney, 1961-62; sought
Democratic nomination for president,
1980.

Capitol Office: 315 Russell Senate Office
Building 20510; 224-4543.
Office Staff: Administrative Assistant,
Ranny Cooper; Press Secretary, Paul
Donovan; Appointments Secretary, Beth
Cummings.
Committees: Armed Services; Judiciary;
Labor & Human Resources (Chairman).

Massachusetts — The statewide vote for
George Bush was 45% in 1988.

CQ Voting Studies

	1989	1990
Presidential	48%	25%
Party	90%	89%
Participation	98%	96%

Interest Groups

	1988	1989
ADA	95%	85%
ACU	0%	7%
AFL-CIO	100%	90%
CCUS	27%	29%

Elections

	1982	1988
General	61%	65%
Primary	u/o	u/o

CQ Voting Studies

	1989	1990
Presidential	51%	40%
Party	88%	84%
Participation	100%	99%

Interest Groups

	1989
ADA	80%
ACU	11%
AFL-CIO	100%
CCUS	50%

Elections

	1988
General	57%
Primary	91%

Bob Kerrey (D-Neb.)
Of Lincoln • Elected 1988

Born: August 27, 1943, Lincoln, Neb.
Education: U. of Nebraska, B.S. 1966.
Military Career: Navy, 1966-69.
Occupation: Restaurateur.
Family: Divorced; two children.
Religion: Congregationalist.
Political Career: Governor, 1983-87.

Capitol Office: 302 Hart Senate Office Building 20510; 224-6551.
Office Staff: Chief of Staff, Bill Shore; Press Secretary, Steve Jarding; Scheduler, Cindy Dwyer.
Committees: Agriculture, Nutrition & Forestry; Appropriations.

Nebraska — The statewide vote for George Bush was 60% in 1988.

John Kerry (D Mass.)
Of Boston • Elected 1984

Born: December 22, 1943, Denver, Colo.
Education: Yale U., B.A. 1966; Boston
College, J.D. 1976.
Military Career: Navy, 1968-69.
Occupation: Lawyer.
Family: Divorced; two children.
Religion: Roman Catholic.
Political Career: Lieutenant governor,
1982-84; Democratic nominee for U.S.
House, 1972.

Capitol Office: 421 Russell Senate Office
Building 20510; 224-2742.
Office Staff: Administrative Assistant,
Frances Zwenig; Press Secretary, Larry
Carpman; Appointments Secretary, Pat
Gray.
Committees: Banking, Housing & Urban
Affairs; Commerce, Science &
Transportation; Foreign Relations; Small
Business.

Massachusetts — The statewide vote for
George Bush was 45% in 1988.

CQ Voting Studies

	1989	1990
Presidential	47%	25%
Party	86%	85%
Participation	100%	96%

Interest Groups

	1988	1989
ADA	90%	95%
ACU	0%	11%
AFL-CIO	93%	100%
CCUS	36%	50%

Elections

	1984	1990
General	55%	57%
Primary	41%	u/o

Herb Kohl (D-Wis.)
Of Milwaukee • Elected 1988

Born: February 7, 1935, Milwaukee, Wis.
Education: U. of Wisconsin, B.A. 1956; Harvard U., M.B.A. 1958.
Military Career: Army Reserve, 1958-64.
Occupation: Businessman; professional basketball team owner.
Family: Single.
Religion: Jewish.
Political Career: Wis. Democratic Party chairman, 1975-77.

Capitol Office: 330 Hart Senate Office Building 20510; 224-5653.
Office Staff: Chief of Staff, Bob Seltzer; Press Secretary, Kristy Schantz; Executive Assistant, Arlene Branca.
Committees: Governmental Affairs; Judiciary.

Wisconsin — The statewide vote for George Bush was 48% in 1988.

CQ Voting Studies

	1989	1990
Presidential	47%	25%
Party	87%	86%
Participation	99%	99%

Interest Groups

	1989
ADA	95%
ACU	11%
AFL-CIO	90%
CCUS	25%

Elections

	1988
General	52%
Primary	47%

Frank R. Lautenberg (D-N.J.)
Of Montclair • Elected 1982

Born: January 23, 1924, Paterson, N.J.
Education: Columbia U., B.S. 1949.
Military Career: Army, 1942-46.
Occupation: Computer firm executive.
Family: Wife, Lois Levinson; four children.
Religion: Jewish.
Political Career: No previous office.

Capitol Office: 717 Hart Senate Office Building 20510; 224-4744.
Office Staff: Administrative Assistant, Eve Lubalin; Press Secretary, Steven Schlein; Scheduler, Jack Way.
Committees: Appropriations; Budget; Environment & Public Works.

New Jersey — The statewide vote for George Bush was 56% in 1988.

CQ Voting Studies

	1989	1990
Presidential	49%	25%
Party	87%	88%
Participation	98%	100%

Interest Groups

	1988	1989
ADA	90%	80%
ACU	0%	7%
AFL-CIO	100%	90%
CCUS	17%	29%

Elections

	1982	1988
General	51%	54%
Primary	26%	78%

CQ Voting Studies

	1989	1990
Presidential	47%	32%
Party	96%	93%
Participation	99%	100%

Interest Groups

	1988	1989
ADA	100%	100%
ACU	0%	0%
AFL-CIO	86%	100%
CCUS	36%	38%

Elections

	1980	1986
General	50%	63%
Primary	u/o	u/o

Patrick J. Leahy (D-Vt.)
Of Middlesex • Elected 1974

Born: March 31, 1940, Montpelier, Vt.
Education: St. Michael's College, B.A. 1961; Georgetown U., J.D. 1964.
Occupation: Lawyer.
Family: Wife, Marcelle Pomerleau; three children.
Religion: Roman Catholic.
Political Career: Chittenden County state's attorney, 1967-75.

Capitol Office: 433 Russell Senate Office Building 20510; 224-4242.
Office Staff: Administrative Assistant, Ellen McCulloch-Lovell; Press Secretary, Joe Jamele; Scheduler, Kevin McDonald.
Committees: Agriculture, Nutrition & Forestry (Chairman); Appropriations; Judiciary.

Vermont — The statewide vote for George Bush was 51% in 1988.

Carl Levin (D-Mich.)
Of Detroit • Elected 1978

Born: June 28, 1934, Detroit, Mich.
Education: Swarthmore College, B.A. 1956; Harvard U., LL.B. 1959.
Occupation: Lawyer.
Family: Wife, Barbara Halpern; three children.
Religion: Jewish.
Political Career: Detroit City Council, 1970-73; president, 1974-77.

Capitol Office: 459 Russell Senate Office Building 20510; 224-6221.
Office Staff: Administrative Assistant, Gordon Kerr; Press Secretary, Willie Blacklow; Personal Secretary, Helen Galen.
Committees: Armed Services; Governmental Affairs; Small Business.

Michigan — The statewide vote for George Bush was 54% in 1988.

CQ Voting Studies

	1989	1990
Presidential	50%	33%
Party	80%	82%
Participation	99%	99%

Interest Groups

	1988	1989
ADA	80%	80%
ACU	0%	14%
AFL-CIO	92%	100%
CCUS	21%	25%

Elections

	1984	1990
General	52%	58%
Primary	u/o	u/o

CQ Voting Studies

	1989	1990
Presidential	56%	37%
Party	81%	86%
Participation	100%	99%

Interest Groups

	1989
ADA	75%
ACU	32%
AFL-CIO	90%
CCUS	38%

Elections

	1988
General	50%
Primary	u/o

Joseph I. Lieberman (D-Conn.)
Of New Haven • Elected 1988

Born: February 24, 1942, Stamford, Conn.
Education: Yale U., B.A. 1964; Yale U., LL.B. 1967.
Occupation: Lawyer.
Family: Wife, Hadassah Freilich; four children.
Religion: Jewish.
Political Career: Conn. Senate, 1971-81; majority leader, 1975-81; sought Democratic nomination for U.S House, 1980; Conn. attorney general, 1983-89.

Capitol Office: 502 Hart Senate Office Building 20510; 224-4041.
Office Staff: Administrative Assistant, Michael Lewan; Press Secretary, Jim Kennedy; Executive Assistant/Scheduler, Carleen Overstreet.
Committees: Environment & Public Works; Governmental Affairs; Small Business.

Connecticut — The statewide vote for George Bush was 52% in 1988.

Trent Lott (R-Miss.)
Of Pascagoula • Elected 1988

Born: October 9, 1941, Grenada County, Miss.
Education: U. of Mississippi, B.P.A. 1963; U. of Mississippi, J.D. 1967.
Occupation: Lawyer.
Family: Wife, Patricia Elizabeth Thompson; two children.
Religion: Baptist.
Political Career: U.S. House, 1973-89.

Capitol Office: 487 Russell Senate Office Building 20510; 224-6253.
Office Staff: Chief of Staff, Prentiss W. Bolen; Press Secretary, Bruce Lott; Appointments Secretary, Susan Wells.
Committees: Armed Services; Commerce, Science & Transportation; Small Business.

Mississippi — The statewide vote for George Bush was 60% in 1988.

CQ Voting Studies

	1989	1990
Presidential	82%	76%
Party	92%	82%
Participation	96%	98%

Interest Groups

	1988	1989
ADA	5%	5%
ACU	95%	96%
AFL-CIO	33%	20%
CCUS	82%	88%

Elections

	1986	1988
General	82%	54%
Primary	u/o	u/o

CQ Voting Studies

	1989	1990
Presidential	93%	86%
Party	83%	86%
Participation	97%	99%

Interest Groups

	1988	1989
ADA	10%	10%
ACU	88%	75%
AFL-CIO	21%	0%
CCUS	92%	100%

Elections

	1982	1988
General	54%	68%
Primary	u/o	u/o

Richard G. Lugar (R-Ind.)
Of Indianapolis • Elected 1976

Born: April 4, 1932, Indianapolis, Ind.
Education: Denison U., B.A. 1954; Oxford U., B.A., M.A. 1956.
Military Career: Navy, 1957-60.
Occupation: Agricultural industries executive.
Family: Wife, Charlene Smeltzer; four children.
Religion: Methodist.
Political Career: Indianapolis School Board, 1964-67; mayor of Indianapolis, 1968-75; Republican nominee for U.S. Senate, 1974.

Capitol Office: 306 Hart Senate Office Building 20510; 224-4814.
Office Staff: Administrative Assistant, Marty Morris; Press Secretary, Kevin Kellems; Scheduler, Sally Quilhot.
Committees: Agriculture, Nutrition & Forestry (Ranking); Foreign Relations.

Indiana — The statewide vote for George Bush was 60% in 1988.

Connie Mack (R-Fla.)

Of Cape Coral • Elected 1988

Born: October 29, 1940, Philadelphia, Penn.
Education: U. of Florida, B.S. 1966.
Occupation: Banker.
Family: Wife, Priscilla Hobbs; two children.
Religion: Roman Catholic.
Political Career: U.S. House, 1983-89.

Capitol Office: 517 Hart Senate Office Building 20510; 224-5274.
Office Staff: Administrative Assistant, Mitch Bainwol; Press Secretary, Marty Filipowski; Scheduler, Elizabeth Walker.
Committees: Banking, Housing & Urban Affairs; Foreign Relations.

Florida — The statewide vote for George Bush was 61% in 1988.

CQ Voting Studies

	1989	1990
Presidential		
Party	86%	88%
Participation	90%	86%
	99%	99%

Interest Groups

	1988	1989
ADA	0%	5%
ACU	100%	96%
AFL-CIO	0%	10%
CCUS	86%	88%

Elections

	1986	1988
General	75%	50%
Primary	u/o	62%

John McCain (R-Ariz.)
Of Phoenix • Elected 1986

Born: August 29, 1936, Panama Canal Zone.
Education: U.S. Naval Academy, B.S. 1958; National War College, 1973-74.
Military Career: Navy, 1958-81.
Occupation: Naval officer; beer distributor.
Family: Wife, Cindy Lou Hensley; six children.
Religion: Episcopalian.
Political Career: U.S. House, 1983-87.

Capitol Office: 111 Russell Senate Office Building 20510; 224-2235.
Office Staff: Administrative Assistant, Jim Weber; Press Secretary, Scott Celley; Appointments Secretary, Diane McClellan.
Committees: Armed Services; Commerce, Science & Transportation.

Arizona — The statewide vote for George Bush was 60% in 1988.

CQ Voting Studies

	1989	1990
Presidential	91%	74%
Party	85%	78%
Participation	97%	98%

Interest Groups

	1988	1989
ADA	10%	5%
ACU	80%	93%
AFL-CIO	14%	0%
CCUS	64%	88%

Elections

	1984	1986
General	78%	61%
Primary	u/o	u/o

Mitch McConnell (R-Ky.)
Of Louisville • Elected 1984

Born: February 20, 1942, Sheffield, Ala.
Education: U. of Louisville, B.A. 1964; U. of Kentucky, J.D. 1967.
Occupation: Lawyer.
Family: Divorced; three children.
Religion: Baptist.
Political Career: Jefferson County judge/executive, 1978-85.

Capitol Office: 120 Russell Senate Office Building 20510; 224-2541.
Office Staff: Administrative Assistant, Niels C. Holch; Press Secretary, Mary Jane M.J. Fingland; Personal Secretary, Mary Barham.
Committees: Agriculture, Nutrition & Forestry; Foreign Relations; Rules & Administration.

Kentucky — The statewide vote for George Bush was 56% in 1988.

CQ Voting Studies

	1989	1990
Presidential	82%	78%
Party	94%	84%
Participation	100%	99%

Interest Groups

	1988	1989
ADA	5%	10%
ACU	92%	89%
AFL-CIO	29%	20%
CCUS	93%	75%

Elections

	1984	1990
General	50%	52%
Primary	79%	89%

Howard M. Metzenbaum
(D-Ohio)
Of Lyndhurst • Elected 1976

Born: June 4, 1917, Lyndhurst, Ohio.
Education: Ohio State U., B.A. 1939;
Ohio State U., LL.B. 1941.
Occupation: Lawyer; newspaper
publisher; parking lot executive.
Family: Wife, Shirley Turoff; four
children.
Religion: Jewish.
Political Career: Ohio House, 1943-47;
Ohio Senate, 1947-51; Democratic
nominee for U.S. Senate, 1974; served in
Senate by appointment, 1974.

Capitol Office: 140 Russell Senate Office
Building 20510; 224-2315.
Office Staff: Administrative Assistant,
Joel Johnson; Communications Director,
Nancy Coffey; Appointments Secretary,
Sheri Sweitzer.
Committees: Environment & Public
Works; Judiciary; Labor & Human
Resources.

Ohio — The statewide vote for George
Bush was 55% in 1988.

CQ Voting Studies

	1989	1990
Presidential	39%	27%
Party	92%	85%
Participation	99%	97%

Interest Groups

	1988	1989
ADA	80%	95%
ACU	4%	7%
AFL-CIO	100%	100%
CCUS	15%	25%

Elections

	1982	1988
General	57%	57%
Primary	83%	84%

Barbara A. Mikulski (D-Md.)
Of Baltimore • Elected 1986

Born: July 20, 1936, Baltimore, Md.
Education: Mount Saint Agnes College, B.A. 1958; U. of Maryland, M.S.W. 1965.
Occupation: Social worker.
Family: Single.
Religion: Roman Catholic.
Political Career: Baltimore City Council, 1971-77; Democratic nominee for U.S. Senate, 1974; U.S. House, 1977-87.

Capitol Office: 320 Hart Senate Office Building 20510; 224-4654.
Office Staff: Chief of Staff, Maggie McIntosh; Press Secretary, Linda Marson; Appointments Secretary, Brenda Beitzell.
Committees: Appropriations; Labor & Human Resources; Small Business.

Maryland — The statewide vote for George Bush was 51% in 1988.

CQ Voting Studies

	1989	1990
Presidential	41%	26%
Party	94%	89%
Participation	98%	97%

Interest Groups

	1988	1989
ADA	95%	90%
ACU	0%	8%
AFL-CIO	100%	100%
CCUS	29%	38%

Elections

	1984	1986
General	68%	61%
Primary	90%	50%

CQ Voting Studies

	1989	1990
Presidential	57%	34%
Party	86%	89%
Participation	100%	100%

Interest Groups

	1988	1989
ADA	95%	80%
ACU	0%	11%
AFL-CIO	100%	100%
CCUS	21%	50%

Elections

	1982	1988
General	61%	81%
Primary	u/o	u/o

George J. Mitchell (D-Maine)
Of Portland • Appointed 1980

Born: August 20, 1933, Waterville, Maine.
Education: Bowdoin College, B.A. 1954;
Georgetown U., LL.B. 1960.
Military Career: Army, 1954-56.
Occupation: Lawyer; judge.
Family: Divorced; one child.
Religion: Roman Catholic.
Political Career: Maine Democratic Party
chairman, 1966-68; Democratic National
Committee, 1969-77; assistant county
attorney, 1971-77; Democratic nominee
for governor, 1974; U.S. attorney, 1977-
79; U.S. District Court Judge, 1979-80.

Capitol Office: 176 Russell Senate Office
Building 20510; 224-5344.
Office Staff: Chief of Staff, John Hilley;
Press Secretary, Diane Dewhirst;
Executive Assistant, Pat Sarcone.
Committees: Environment & Public
Works; Finance; Veterans' Affairs.

Maine — The statewide vote for George
Bush was 55% in 1988.

Daniel Patrick Moynihan
(D-N.Y.)
Of Pindars Corners • Elected 1976

Born: March 16, 1927, Tulsa, Okla.
Education: City College, N.Y., 1943; Tufts U., B.N.S. 1946; Tufts U., B.A. 1948; Fletcher School of Law and Diplomacy, M.A. 1949; Fletcher School of Law and Diplomacy, Ph.D. 1961.
Military Career: Navy, 1944-47.
Occupation: Professor of government; writer.
Family: Wife, Elizabeth Brennan; three children.
Religion: Roman Catholic.
Political Career: Sought Democratic nomination for N.Y. City Council president, 1965.
Capitol Office: 464 Russell Senate Office Building 20510; 224-4451.
Office Staff: Administrative Assistant, Laurence O'Donnell; Press Secretary, Brian Connolly; Personal Secretary, Eleanor Suntum.
Committees: Environment & Public Works; Finance; Foreign Relations; Rules & Administration.

New York — The statewide vote for George Bush was 48% in 1988.

CQ Voting Studies

	1989	1990
Presidential	52%	31%
Party	90%	89%
Participation	98%	98%

Interest Groups

	1988	1989
ADA	90%	75%
ACU	8%	4%
AFL-CIO	93%	100%
CCUS	31%	38%

Elections

	1982	1988
General	65%	67%
Primary	85%	u/o

Frank H. Murkowski (R-Alaska)
Of Fairbanks • Elected 1980

Born: March 28, 1933, Seattle, Wash.
Education: Santa Clara U., 1951-53;
Seattle U., B.A. 1955.
Military Career: Coast Guard, 1955-56.
Occupation: Banker.
Family: Wife, Nancy Gore; six children.
Religion: Roman Catholic.
Political Career: Alaska commissioner of
economic development, 1966-70;
Republican nominee for U.S. House,
1970.

Capitol Office: 709 Hart Senate Office
Building 20510; 224-6665.
Office Staff: Administrative Assistant,
Gregg Renkes; Communications
Director, Bill Woolf; Personal Secretary,
Carol Elliott.
Committees: Energy & Natural
Resources; Foreign Relations; Veterans'
Affairs (Ranking).

Alaska — The statewide vote for George
Bush was 60% in 1988.

CQ Voting Studies

	1989	1990
Presidential	85%	75%
Party	87%	85%
Participation	96%	98%

Interest Groups

	1988	1989
ADA	15%	5%
ACU	79%	81%
AFL-CIO	23%	10%
CCUS	85%	75%

Elections

	1980	1986
General	54%	54%
Primary	59%	u/o

Don Nickles (R-Okla.)
Of Ponca City • Elected 1980

Born: December 6, 1948, Ponca City, Okla.

Education: Oklahoma State U., B.B.A. 1971.

Military Career: Army National Guard, 1970-76.

Occupation: Machine company executive.

Family: Wife, Linda Lou Morrison; four children.

Religion: Roman Catholic.

Political Career: Okla. Senate, 1979-81.

Capitol Office: 713 Hart Senate Office Building 20510; 224-5754.

Office Staff: Administrative Assistant, Les Brorsen; Press Secretary, Judy Gorman; Scheduler, Debbie Price.

Committees: Appropriations; Budget; Energy & Natural Resources.

Oklahoma — The statewide vote for George Bush was 58% in 1988.

CQ Voting Studies

	1989	1990
Presidential	86%	83%
Party	96%	91%
Participation	99%	98%

Interest Groups

	1988	1989
ADA	0%	0%
ACU	92%	96%
AFL-CIO	7%	0%
CCUS	86%	88%

Elections

	1980	1986
General	54%	55%
Primary	35%	u/o

Sam Nunn   (D-Ga.)
Of Perry • *Elected 1972*

Born: September 8, 1938, Perry, Ga.
Education: Georgia Institute of
Technology, 1956-59; Emory U., A.B.
1961; Emory U., LL.B. 1962.
Military Career: Coast Guard, 1959-60;
Coast Guard Reserve, 1960-68.
Occupation: Farmer; lawyer.
Family: Wife, Colleen Ann O'Brien.
Religion: Methodist.
Political Career: Ga. House, 1969-72.

Capitol Office: 303 Dirksen Senate
Office Building 20510; 224-3521.
Office Staff: Administrative Assistant,
Charles E. Harman; Press Secretary, Scott
Williams; Office Administrator/Personal
Secretary, Rose Johnson.
Committees: Armed Services (Chairman);
Governmental Affairs; Small Business.

Georgia — The statewide vote for
George Bush was 60% in 1988.

CQ Voting Studies

	1989	1990
Presidential	72%	57%
Party	68%	70%
Participation	99%	98%

Interest Groups

	1988	1989
ADA	40%	35%
ACU	42%	37%
AFL-CIO	54%	80%
CCUS	50%	63%

Elections

	1984	1990
General	80%	u/o
Primary	90%	u/o

Bob Packwood (R-Ore.)
Of Portland • Elected 1968

Born: September 11, 1932, Portland, Ore.
Education: Willamette U., B.A. 1954; New York U., LL.B. 1957.
Occupation: Lawyer.
Family: Divorced; two children.
Religion: Unitarian.
Political Career: Ore. House, 1963-69.

Capitol Office: 259 Russell Senate Office Building 20510; 224-5244.
Office Staff: Chief of Staff, Elaine Franklin; Communications Director, Julia Brim-Edwards; Appointments Secretary, Pam Salling.
Committees: Commerce, Science & Transportation; Finance (Ranking).

Oregon — The statewide vote for George Bush was 47% in 1988.

CQ Voting Studies

	1989	1990
Presidential	79%	56%
Party	55%	45%
Participation	98%	95%

Interest Groups

	1988	1989
ADA	55%	30%
ACU	40%	61%
AFL-CIO	64%	60%
CCUS	57%	57%

Elections

	1980	1986
General	52%	63%
Primary	62%	58%

Claiborne Pell (D-R.I.)
Of Newport • Elected 1960

Born: November 22, 1918, New York, N.Y.
Education: Princeton U., A.B. 1940; Columbia U., A.M. 1946.
Military Career: Coast Guard, 1941-45.
Occupation: Investment executive.
Family: Wife, Nuala O'Donnell; four children.
Religion: Episcopalian.
Political Career: No previous office.

Capitol Office: 335 Russell Senate Office Building 20510; 224-4642.
Office Staff: Chief of Staff, Thomas G. Hughes; Press Secretary, William Bryant; Appointments Secretary, Susan Cameron.
Committees: Foreign Relations (Chairman); Labor & Human Resources; Rules & Administration.

Rhode Island — The statewide vote for George Bush was 44% in 1988.

CQ Voting Studies

	1989	1990
Presidential	49%	25%
Party	85%	86%
Participation	96%	96%

Interest Groups

	1988	1989
ADA	100%	85%
ACU	0%	4%
AFL-CIO	100%	80%
CCUS	36%	43%

Elections

	1984	1990
General	73%	62%
Primary	u/o	u/o

Larry Pressler (R-S.D.)
Of Humboldt • Elected 1978

Born: March 29, 1942, Humboldt, S.D.
Education: U. of South Dakota, B.A. 1964; Oxford U., 1965; Harvard U., M.A. 1971; Harvard U., J.D. 1971.
Military Career: Army, 1966-68.
Occupation: Lawyer.
Family: Wife, Harriet Dent; one stepchild.
Religion: Roman Catholic.
Political Career: U.S. House, 1975-79.

Capitol Office: 133 Hart Senate Office Building 20510; 224-5842.
Office Staff: Chief of Staff, Kevin V. Schieffer; Communications Director, Kristi Sommers; Appointments Secretary, Ramona Lessen.
Committees: Banking, Housing & Urban Affairs; Commerce, Science & Transportation; Foreign Relations; Small Business.

South Dakota — The statewide vote for George Bush was 53% in 1988.

CQ Voting Studies

	1989	1990
Presidential	59%	58%
Party	75%	74%
Participation	100%	96%

Interest Groups

	1988	1989
ADA	0%	35%
ACU	96%	75%
AFL-CIO	29%	40%
CCUS	79%	63%

Elections

	1984	1990
General	74%	52%
Primary	u/o	u/o

CQ Voting Studies

	1989	1990
Presidential	53%	34%
Party	80%	85%
Participation	98%	97%

Interest Groups

	1988	1989
ADA	75%	80%
ACU	16%	27%
AFL-CIO	79%	89%
CCUS	43%	25%

Elections

	1984	1990
General	57%	u/o
Primary	u/o	u/o

David Pryor (D-Ark.)
Of Little Rock • Elected 1978

Born: August 29, 1934, Camden, Ark.
Education: U. of Arkansas, B.A. 1957; U. of Arkansas, LL.B. 1964.
Occupation: Lawyer; newspaper publisher.
Family: Wife, Barbara Lunsford; three children.
Religion: Presbyterian.
Political Career: Ark. House, 1961-67; U.S. House, 1967-73; sought Democratic nomination for U.S. Senate, 1972; governor, 1975-79.

Capitol Office: 267 Russell Senate Office Building 20510; 224-2353.
Office Staff: Administrative Assistant, Don Harrell; Press Secretary, Damon Thompson; Appointments Secretary, Leslie Chalmers.
Committees: Agriculture, Nutrition & Forestry; Finance; Governmental Affairs.

Arkansas — The statewide vote for George Bush was 56% in 1988.

Harry Reid (D Nev.)
Of Searchlight • Elected 1986

Born: December 2, 1939, Searchlight, Nev.
Education: Southern Utah State College, A.S. 1959; Utah State U., B.A. 1961; George Washington U., J.D. 1964.
Occupation: Lawyer.
Family: Wife, Landra Gould; five children.
Religion: Mormon.
Political Career: Nev. Assembly, 1969-71; lieutenant governor, 1971-75; Democratic nominee for U.S. Senate, 1974; candidate for mayor of Las Vegas, 1975; U.S. House, 1983-87.

Capitol Office: 324 Hart Senate Office Building 20510; 224-3542.
Office Staff: Chief of Staff, Reynaldo Martinez; Press Secretary, Craig L. Varoga; Appointments Secretary, Margaret Stout.
Committees: Appropriations; Environment & Public Works.

Nevada — The statewide vote for George Bush was 59% in 1988.

CQ Voting Studies

	1989	1990
Presidential	63%	44%
Party	71%	79%
Participation	99%	99%

Interest Groups

	1988	1989
ADA	55%	65%
ACU	28%	21%
AFL-CIO	92%	100%
CCUS	29%	38%

Elections

	1984	1986
General	56%	50%
Primary	u/o	83%

CQ Voting Studies

	1989	1990
Presidential	45%	30%
Party	93%	85%
Participation	96%	95%

Interest Groups

	1988	1989
ADA	90%	85%
ACU	4%	12%
AFL-CIO	93%	100%
CCUS	36%	38%

Elections

	1982	1988
General	58%	60%
Primary	u/o	u/o

Donald W. Riegle, Jr.
(D-Mich.)
Of Flint • Elected 1976

Born: February 4, 1938, Flint, Mich.
Education: Flint Junior College, 1956-57; Western Michigan U., 1957-58; U. of Michigan, B.A. 1960; Michigan State U., M.B.A. 1961; Harvard U. Business School, 1964-66.
Occupation: Business executive; professor.
Family: Wife, Lori Hansen; four children.
Religion: Methodist.
Political Career: U.S. House, 1967-77; served as Republican, 1967-73.

Capitol Office: 105 Dirksen Senate Office Building 20510; 224-4822.
Office Staff: Administrative Assistant, David Krawitz; Press Secretary, Karolyn Wallace; Scheduler, Byronie Byers.
Committees: Banking, Housing & Urban Affairs (Chairman); Budget; Finance.

Michigan — The statewide vote for George Bush was 54% in 1988.

Charles S. Robb (D-Va.)
Of McLean • Elected 1988

Born: June 26, 1939, Phoenix, Ariz.
Education: Cornell U., 1957-58; U. of Wisconsin, B.B.A. 1961; U. of Virginia, J.D. 1973.
Military Career: Marine Corps, 1961-70.
Occupation: Lawyer.
Family: Wife, Lynda Bird Johnson; three children.
Religion: Episcopalian.
Political Career: Lieutenant governor, 1978-82; governor, 1982-86.

Capitol Office: 493 Russell Senate Office Building 20510; 224-4024.
Office Staff: Administrative Assistant, David K. McCloud; Press Secretary, Steven Johnson; Scheduler, Sheila M. Dwyer.
Committees: Budget; Commerce, Science & Transportation; Foreign Relations.

Virginia — The statewide vote for George Bush was 60% in 1988.

CQ Voting Studies

	1989	1990
Presidential	73%	55%
Party	69%	73%
Participation	100%	100%

Interest Groups

	1989
ADA	45%
ACU	36%
AFL-CIO	80%
CCUS	63%

Elections

	1988
General	71%
Primary	u/o

John D. Rockefeller IV
(D-W.Va.)
Of Charleston • Elected 1984

Born: June 18, 1937, New York, N.Y.
Education: International Christian U.,
Tokyo, Japan, 1957-60; Harvard U., A.B.
1961.
Occupation: Public official.
Family: Wife, Sharon Percy; four
children.
Religion: Presbyterian.
Political Career: W.Va. House, 1967-69;
W.Va. Secretary of State, 1969-73;
Democratic nominee for governor, 1972;
governor, 1977-85.

Capitol Office: 724 Hart Senate Office
Building 20510; 224-6472.
Office Staff: Administrative Assistant, R.
Lane Bailey; Press Secretary, Marisa
Spatafore; Scheduler, Kathy Kellogg.
Committees: Commerce, Science &
Transportation; Finance; Veterans' Affairs.

West Virginia — The statewide vote for
George Bush was 47% in 1988.

CQ Voting Studies

	1989	1990
Presidential	51%	26%
Party	78%	86%
Participation	99%	99%

Interest Groups

	1988	1989
ADA	70%	80%
ACU	16%	14%
AFL-CIO	86%	90%
CCUS	36%	38%

Elections

	1984	1990
General	52%	68%
Primary	66%	85%

William V. Roth, Jr. (R-Del.)

Of Wilmington • Elected 1970

Born: July 22, 1921, Great Falls, Mont.
Education: U. of Oregon, B.A. 1944;
Harvard U., M.B.A. 1947; Harvard U.,
LL.B. 1949.
Military Career: Army, 1943-46.
Occupation: Lawyer.
Family: Wife, Jane Richards; two
children.
Religion: Episcopalian.
Political Career: Republican nominee for
lieutenant governor, 1960; U.S. House,
1967-71.

Capitol Office: 104 Hart Senate Office
Building 20510; 224-2441.
Office Staff: Administrative Assistant,
John M. Duncan; Press Secretary, Verna
Wilkins; Appointments Secretary, Betty
Martin.
Committees: Banking, Housing & Urban
Affairs; Finance; Governmental Affairs.

Delaware — The statewide vote for
George Bush was 56% in 1988.

CQ Voting Studies

	1989	1990
Presidential	94%	72%
Party	85%	80%
Participation	97%	99%

Interest Groups

	1988	1989
ADA	20%	0%
ACU	60%	81%
AFL-CIO	43%	0%
CCUS	57%	88%

Elections

	1982	1988
General	55%	62%
Primary	u/o	u/o

Warren B. Rudman (R-N.H.)
Of Nashua • Elected 1980

Born: May 18, 1930, Boston, Mass.
Education: Syracuse U., B.S. 1952; Boston College, LL.B. 1960.
Military Career: Army, 1952-54.
Occupation: Lawyer.
Family: Wife, Shirley Wahl; three children.
Religion: Jewish.
Political Career: N.H. attorney general (appointed), 1970-76.

Capitol Office: 530 Hart Senate Office Building 20510; 224-3324.
Office Staff: Administrative Assistant, G. Allan Walker; Press Secretary, Paul E. Jacobson; Scheduling Assistant, Kathy Gowen.
Committees: Appropriations; Budget; Governmental Affairs.

New Hampshire — The statewide vote for George Bush was 62% in 1988.

CQ Voting Studies

	1989	1990
Presidential	80%	74%
Party	62%	73%
Participation	99%	94%

Interest Groups

	1988	1989
ADA	15%	25%
ACU	68%	70%
AFL-CIO	29%	10%
CCUS	93%	75%

Elections

	1980	1986
General	52%	63%
Primary	20%	u/o

Terry Sanford (D-N.C.)
Of Durham • Elected 1986

Born: August 20, 1917, Laurinburg, N.C.
Education: Presbyterian Junior College;
U. of North Carolina, A.B. 1939; U. of
North Carolina, J.D. 1946.
Military Career: Army parachute
infantry, 1942-46; N.C. National Guard,
1948-60.
Occupation: University president;
lawyer; FBI agent.
Family: Wife, Margaret Rose Knight; two
children.
Religion: Methodist.
Political Career: N.C. Senate, 1953-55;
governor, 1961-65; sought Democratic
nomination for president, 1972; sought
Democratic nomination for president,
1976.

Capitol Office: 716 Hart Senate Office
Building 20510; 224-3154.
Office Staff: Administrative Assistant,
Samuel H. Poole; Press Secretary, Ken
Friedlein; Executive Assistant, Christy
Russell.
Committees: Banking, Housing & Urban
Affairs; Budget; Foreign Relations.

North Carolina — The statewide vote for
George Bush was 58% in 1988.

CQ Voting Studies

	1989	1990
Presidential	56%	41%
Party	85%	81%
Participation	95%	97%

Interest Groups

	1988	1989
ADA	90%	65%
ACU	4%	19%
AFL-CIO	85%	100%
CCUS	43%	50%

Elections

	1986
General	52%
Primary	60%

Paul S. Sarbanes   (D-Md.)
Of Baltimore • Elected 1976

Born: February 3, 1933, Salisbury, Md.
Education: Princeton U., A.B. 1954;
Oxford U., B.A. 1957; Harvard U., LL.B.
1960.
Occupation: Lawyer.
Family: Wife, Christine Dunbar; three
children.
Religion: Greek Orthodox.
Political Career: Md. House, 1967-71;
U.S. House, 1971-77.

Capitol Office: 332 Dirksen Senate
Office Building 20510; 224-4524.
Office Staff: Administrative Assistant,
Marvin Moss; Press Secretary, Bruce
Frame; Executive Assistant, Elise Gillette.
Committees: Banking, Housing & Urban
Affairs; Foreign Relations.

Maryland — The statewide vote for
George Bush was 51% in 1988.

CQ Voting Studies

	1989	1990
Presidential	45%	31%
Party	95%	93%
Participation	99%	100%

Interest Groups

	1988	1989
ADA	90%	85%
ACU	4%	7%
AFL-CIO	100%	100%
CCUS	29%	25%

Elections

	1982	1988
General	64%	62%
Primary	81%	86%

Jim Sasser (D-Tenn.)
Of Nashville • *Elected 1976*

Born: September 30, 1936, Memphis, Tenn.
Education: U. of Tennessee, 1954-55; Vanderbilt U., B.A. 1958; Vanderbilt U., J.D. 1961.
Military Career: Marine Corps Reserve, 1957-63.
Occupation: Lawyer.
Family: Wife, Mary Gorman; two children.
Religion: Methodist.
Political Career: No previous office.

Capitol Office: 363 Russell Senate Office Building 20510; 224-3344.
Office Staff: Chief of Staff, Craven Crowell; Press Secretary, James Pratt; Personal Secretary, Linda K. Graham.
Committees: Appropriations; Banking, Housing & Urban Affairs; Budget (Chairman); Governmental Affairs.

Tennessee — The statewide vote for George Bush was 58% in 1988.

CQ Voting Studies

	1989	1990
Presidential	55%	33%
Party	89%	90%
Participation	96%	99%

Interest Groups

	1988	1989
ADA	75%	85%
ACU	9%	8%
AFL-CIO	86%	100%
CCUS	43%	57%

Elections

	1982	1988
General	62%	65%
Primary	89%	u/o

John Seymour   (R-Calif.)
Of Anaheim • Appointed 1991
Pronounced SEE more

Born: December 3, 1937, Chicago, Ill.
Education: U.C.L.A., B.S. 1962.
Military Career: Marine Corps, 1955-59.
Occupation: Real estate broker.
Family: Wife, Judy Thacker; six children.
Religion: Protestant.
Political Career: Anaheim City Council, 1974-78; mayor of Anaheim, 1978-82; Calif. Senate, 1982-91.

Capitol Office: 720 Hart Senate Office Building 20510; 224-3841.
Office Staff: Administrative Assistant, Alex Matthews
Committees: Agriculture, Nutrition & Forestry; Energy & Natural Resources

California — The statewide vote for George Bush was 51% in 1988.

Richard C. Shelby (D-Ala.)
Of Tuscaloosa • Elected 1986

Born: May 6, 1934, Birmingham, Ala.
Education: U. of Alabama, A.B. 1957; U. of Alabama, LL.B. 1963.
Occupation: Lawyer.
Family: Wife, Annette Nevin; two children.
Religion: Presbyterian.
Political Career: Ala. Senate, 1971-79; U.S. House, 1979-87.

Capitol Office: 313 Hart Senate Office Building 20510; 224-5744.
Office Staff: Administrative Assistant, Tom Young; Communications Director/Press Secretary, Tricia Primrose; Office Manager, Anne Caldwell.
Committees: Armed Services; Banking, Housing & Urban Affairs; Energy & Natural Resources.

Alabama — The statewide vote for George Bush was 59% in 1988.

CQ Voting Studies

	1989	1990
Presidential	68%	55%
Party	46%	59%
Participation	100%	100%

Interest Groups

	1988	1989
ADA	35%	25%
ACU	60%	57%
AFL-CIO	71%	90%
CCUS	57%	63%

Elections

	1984	1986
General	97%	50%
Primary	u/o	51%

CQ Voting Studies

	1989	1990
Presidential	41%	20%
Party	86%	90%
Participation	98%	99%

Interest Groups

	1988	1989
ADA	85%	100%
ACU	0%	14%
AFL-CIO	91%	90%
CCUS	42%	25%

Elections

	1984	1990
General	50%	65%
Primary	36%	u/o

Paul Simon (D-Ill.)

Of Makanda • Elected 1984

Born: November 29, 1928, Eugene, Ore.
Education: U. of Oregon, 1945-46; Dana College, 1946-48.
Military Career: Army, 1951-53.
Occupation: Author; newspaper editor and publisher.
Family: Wife, Jeanne Hurley; two children.
Religion: Lutheran.
Political Career: Ill. House, 1955-63; Ill. Senate, 1963-69; lieutenant governor, 1969-73; sought Democratic nomination for governor, 1972; U.S. House, 1975-85; sought Democratic nomination for president, 1988.

Capitol Office: 462 Dirksen Senate Office Building 20510; 224-2152.
Office Staff: Administrative Assistant, Floyd Fithian; Press Secretary, David Carle; Appointments Secretary, Kathleen Crowell.
Committees: Budget; Foreign Relations; Judiciary; Labor & Human Resources.

Illinois — The statewide vote for George Bush was 51% in 1988.

Alan K. Simpson   (R-Wyo.)
Of Cody • Elected 1978

Born: September 2, 1931, Denver, Colo.
Education: U. of Wyoming, B.S.L. 1954;
U. of Wyoming, LL.B. 1958.
Military Career: Army, 1954-56.
Occupation: Lawyer.
Family: Wife, Ann Schroll; three
children.
Religion: Episcopalian.
Political Career: Cody City attorney,
1959-69; Wyo. House, 1965-77.

Capitol Office: 261 Dirksen Senate
Office Building 20510; 224-3424.
Office Staff: Administrative Assistant,
Don Hardy; Press Secretary, Stan Cannon;
Deputy Administrative Assistant, Laurie
Goodman; Scheduling Secretary, Laurie
Rosen.
Committees: Environment & Public
Works; Judiciary; Veterans' Affairs.

Wyoming — The statewide vote for
George Bush was 61% in 1988.

CQ Voting Studies

	1989	1990
Presidential	84%	80%
Party	81%	86%
Participation	96%	95%

Interest Groups

	1988	1989
ADA	15%	10%
ACU	92%	70%
AFL-CIO	21%	0%
CCUS	86%	88%

Elections

	1984	1990
General	78%	64%
Primary	88%	84%

Robert C. Smith (R-N.H.)
Of Tuftonboro • Elected 1990

Born: March 30, 1941, Trenton, N.J.
Education: Lafayette College, B.A. 1965.
Military Career: Navy, 1965-67.
Occupation: Real estate broker; teacher.
Family: Wife, Mary Jo Hutchinson; three children.
Religion: Roman Catholic.
Political Career: Gov. Wentworth Regional School Board (Wolfeboro, N.H.), 1978-84; sought Republican nomination for U.S. House, 1980; Republican nominee for U.S. House, 1982; U.S. House, 1985-90.

Capitol Office: 825-A Hart Senate Office Building 20510; 224-2841.
Office Staff: Administrative Assistant, Patrick Pettey; Press Secretary, Lisa Stocklan; Personal Secretary/N.H. Scheduler, Kimberly Estes.
Committees: Armed Services; Environment & Public Works.

New Hampshire — The statewide vote for George Bush was 62% in 1988.

Elections

	1988	1990
General	60%	65%
Primary	u/o	65%

Arlen Specter (R-Pa.)

Of Philadelphia • Elected 1980

Born: February 12, 1930, Wichita, Kan.
Education: U. of Pennsylvania, B.A. 1951;
Yale U., LL.B. 1956.
Military Career: Air Force, 1951-53.
Occupation: Lawyer; professor of law.
Family: Wife, Joan Levy; two children.
Religion: Jewish.
Political Career: Philadelphia district
attorney, 1966-74; Republican nominee
for mayor of Philadelphia, 1967; defeated
for re-election as district attorney, 1973;
sought Republican nomination for U.S.
Senate, 1976; sought Republican
nomination for governor, 1978.

Capitol Office: 303 Hart Senate Office
Building 20510; 224-4254.
Office Staff: Administrative Assistant,
Carl Feldbaum; Press Secretary, Dan
McKenna; Scheduler, Sylvia Nolde.
Committees: Appropriations; Judiciary;
Veterans' Affairs.

Pennsylvania — The statewide vote for
George Bush was 51% in 1988.

CQ Voting Studies

	1989	1990
Presidential	66%	58%
Party	55%	53%
Participation	100%	99%

Interest Groups

	1988	1989
ADA	60%	40%
ACU	33%	57%
AFL-CIO	83%	50%
CCUS	62%	75%

Elections

	1980	1986
General	51%	56%
Primary	36%	76%

Ted Stevens (R-Alaska)
Of Girdwood • Elected 1970

Born: November 18, 1923, Indianapolis, Ind.

Education: U.C.L.A., B.A. 1947; Harvard U., LL.B. 1950.

Military Career: Army Air Corps, 1943-46.

Occupation: Lawyer.

Family: Wife, Catherine Chandler; six children.

Religion: Episcopalian.

Political Career: Republican nominee for U.S. Senate, 1962; Alaska House, 1965-68; majority leader and speaker pro tempore, 1967-68; sought Republican nomination for U.S. Senate, 1968.

Capitol Office: 522 Hart Senate Office Building 20510; 224-3004.

Office Staff: Chief of Staff, Greg Chapados; Press Secretary, Jane Robbins; Appointments Secretary, DeLynn Henry.

Committees: Appropriations; Commerce, Science & Transportation; Governmental Affairs; Rules & Administration; Small Business.

Alaska — The statewide vote for George Bush was 60% in 1988.

CQ Voting Studies

	1989	1990
Presidential	87%	72%
Party	73%	66%
Participation	99%	96%

Interest Groups

	1988	1989
ADA	25%	20%
ACU	64%	64%
AFL-CIO	36%	40%
CCUS	69%	75%

Elections

	1984	1990
General	71%	66%
Primary	u/o	59%

Steve Symms (R-Idaho)
Of Caldwell • Elected 1980

Born: April 23, 1938, Nampa, Idaho.
Education: U. of Idaho, B.S. 1960.
Military Career: Marine Corps, 1960-63.
Occupation: Fruit grower; fitness club owner.
Family: Wife, Frances E. Stockdale; four children.
Religion: Methodist.
Political Career: U.S. House, 1973-81.

Capitol Office: 509 Hart Senate Office Building 20510; 224-6142.
Office Staff: Administrative Assistant, Phil Ufholz; Press Secretary, Dave Pearson; Executive Assistant, Gaye Bennett.
Committees: Budget; Environment & Public Works; Finance.

Idaho — The statewide vote for George Bush was 62% in 1988.

CQ Voting Studies

	1989	1990
Presidential	82%	74%
Party	94%	93%
Participation	97%	97%

Interest Groups

	1988	1989
ADA	0%	0%
ACU	100%	96%
AFL-CIO	0%	0%
CCUS	86%	88%

Elections

	1980	1986
General	50%	52%
Primary	u/o	u/o

Strom Thurmond (R-S.C.)
Of Aiken • Elected 1954

Born: December 5, 1902, Edgefield, S.C.
Education: Clemson College, B.S. 1923.
Military Career: Army, 1942-46; Army Reserve, 1924-60.
Occupation: Lawyer; teacher; coach; education administration.
Family: Wife, Nancy Moore; four children.
Religion: Baptist.
Political Career: Edgefield Superintendent of Education, 1929-33; S.C. Senate, 1933-38; U.S. Circuit Court, 1938-46; governor, 1947-51; States' Rights nominee for president, 1948; sought Democratic nomination for U.S. Senate, 1950.

Capitol Office: 217 Russell Senate Office Building 20510; 224-5972.
Office Staff: Chief of Staff/Administrative Assistant, R.J. Duke Short; Press Secretary, Susan Pelter; Executive Assistant, Holly Richardson.
Committees: Armed Services; Judiciary (Ranking); Labor & Human Resources; Veterans' Affairs.

South Carolina — The statewide vote for George Bush was 62% in 1988.

CQ Voting Studies

	1989	1990
Presidential	90%	78%
Party	98%	89%
Participation	100%	99%

Interest Groups

	1988	1989
ADA	0%	5%
ACU	92%	96%
AFL-CIO	21%	0%
CCUS	93%	88%

Elections

	1984	1990
General	67%	64%
Primary	94%	u/o

Malcolm Wallop (R-Wyo.)
Of Big Horn • Elected 1976

Born: February 27, 1933, New York, N.Y.
Education: Yale U., B.A. 1954.
Military Career: Army, 1955-57.
Occupation: Rancher; meatpacking executive.
Family: Wife, French Carter Gamble; four children, one stepchild.
Religion: Episcopalian.
Political Career: Wyo. House, 1969-73; Wyo. Senate, 1973-77; sought Republican nomination for governor, 1974.

Capitol Office: 237 Russell Senate Office Building 20510; 224-6441.
Office Staff: Administrative Assistant, Rob Wallace; Press Secretary, Janis Budge; Appointments Secretary, Kathi Wise.
Committees: Armed Services; Energy & Natural Resources; Small Business.

Wyoming — The statewide vote for George Bush was 61% in 1988.

CQ Voting Studies

	1989	1990
Presidential	78%	76%
Party	91%	88%
Participation	94%	90%

Interest Groups

	1988	1989
ADA	0%	0%
ACU	100%	100%
AFL-CIO	11%	0%
CCUS	91%	100%

Elections

	1982	1988
General	57%	50%
Primary	81%	83%

John W. Warner (R-Va.)
Of Middleburg • Elected 1978

Born: February 18, 1927, Washington, D.C.
Education: Washington and Lee U., B.S. 1949; U. of Virginia, LL.B. 1953.
Military Career: Navy, 1944-46; Marine Corps, 1950-52.
Occupation: Lawyer; farmer.
Family: Divorced; three children.
Religion: Episcopalian.
Political Career: No previous office.

Capitol Office: 225 Russell Senate Office Building 20510; 224-2023.
Office Staff: Administrative Assistant, Susan Aheron Magill; Press Secretary, Phil Smith; Executive Assistant/Scheduler, Kathleen Dorn.
Committees: Armed Services (Ranking); Environment & Public Works.

Virginia — The statewide vote for George Bush was 60% in 1988.

CQ Voting Studies

	1989	1990
Presidential	86%	78%
Party	81%	69%
Participation	99%	99%

Interest Groups

	1988	1989
ADA	5%	5%
ACU	87%	89%
AFL-CIO	36%	10%
CCUS	86%	88%

Elections

	1984	1990
General	70%	81%
Primary	u/o	u/o

Paul Wellstone (D-Minn.)
Of Northfield • Elected 1990

Born: July 21, 1944, Washington, D.C.
Education: U. of North Carolina, B.A.
1965; U. of North Carolina, Ph.D. 1969.
Occupation: College professor.
Family: Wife, Sheila Ison; three children.
Religion: Jewish.
Political Career: Democratic nominee
for state auditor, 1982; Democratic
National Committee, 1984-91; Minn. co-
chairman, Jesse Jackson for President,
1988; Minn. co-chairman, Michael S.
Dukakis for President, 1988.

Capitol Office: 123 Hart Senate Office
Building 20510; 224-5641.
Office Staff: Administrative Assistant,
John Blackshaw; Press Secretary, Doug
Stone; Scheduler, Keri Dziedzic.
Committees: Energy & Natural
Resources; Labor & Human Resources.

Minnesota — The statewide vote for
George Bush was 46% in 1988.

Elections

	1990
General	52%
Primary	60%

CQ Voting Studies

	1989	1990
Presidential	56%	37%
Party	85%	88%
Participation	99%	98%

Interest Groups

	1988	1989
ADA	95%	95%
ACU	0%	7%
AFL-CIO	79%	90%
CCUS	36%	57%

Elections

	1984	1986
General	53%	50%
Primary	u/o	u/o

Tim Wirth (D-Colo.)
Of Boulder • Elected 1986

Born: September 22, 1939, Santa Fe, N.M.
Education: Harvard U., A.B. 1961; Harvard U., M.Ed. 1964; Stanford U., Ph.D. 1973.
Military Career: Army Reserve, 1961-67.
Occupation: Education official.
Family: Wife, Wren Winslow; two children.
Religion: Episcopalian.
Political Career: U.S. House, 1975-87.

Capitol Office: 380 Russell Senate Office Building 20510; 224-5852.
Office Staff: Chief of Staff, John Lynn; Press Secretary, Lisa Caputo; Executive Assistant, Roxie Lopez.
Committees: Armed Services; Banking, Housing & Urban Affairs; Budget; Energy & Natural Resources.

Colorado — The statewide vote for George Bush was 53% in 1988.

U.S. Representatives

Neil Abercrombie (D-Hawaii)
Of Honolulu • Elected 1990

Born: June 26, 1938, Buffalo, N.Y.
Education: Union College, B.A. 1959; U. of Hawaii, M.A. 1964; U. of Hawaii, Ph.D. 1974.
Occupation: Community activist.
Family: Wife, Nancie Caraway.
Religion: Not specified.
Political Career: Hawaii House, 1974-78; Hawaii Senate, 1978-86; U.S. House, 1986-87; sought Democratic nomination for U.S. House, 1986; Honolulu City Council, 1988-90.

Capitol Office: 1440 Longworth House Office Building 20515; 225-2576.
Office Staff: Administrative Assistant, Skip Roberts; Press Secretary, Michael Slackman.
Committees: Armed Services; Merchant Marine & Fisheries.

Hawaii 1st — Honolulu. The district vote for George Bush was 45% in 1988.

Elections

	1990
General	61%
Primary	45%

Gary L. Ackerman (D-N.Y.)
Of Queens • Elected 1983

Born: November 19, 1942, Brooklyn, N.Y.
Education: Queens College, B.A. 1965.
Occupation: Teacher; publisher and editor; advertising executive.
Family: Wife, Rita Gail Tewel; three children.
Religion: Jewish.
Political Career: Sought Democratic nomination for N.Y. City Council at large, 1977; N.Y. Senate, 1979-83.

Capitol Office: 238 Cannon House Office Building 20515; 225-2601.
Office Staff: Administrative Assistant, Jedd Moskowitz; Press Secretary, Howard Doyle; Personal Secretary, Betsy Francisco.
Committees: Banking, Finance & Urban Affairs; Foreign Affairs; Post Office & Civil Service.

New York 7th — Central Queens — Hollis; Kew Gardens. The district vote for George Bush was 39% in 1988.

CQ Voting Studies

	1989	1990
Presidential	27%	14%
Party	92%	92%
Participation	93%	92%

Interest Groups

	1988	1989
ADA	95%	90%
ACU	0%	0%
AFL-CIO	100%	100%
CCUS	23%	40%

Elections

	1988	1990
General	u/o	u/o
Primary	u/o	u/o

Bill Alexander (D-Ark.)
Of Osceola • Elected 1968

Born: January 16, 1934, Memphis, Tenn.
Education: Southwestern at Memphis, B.A. 1957; Vanderbilt U., LL.B. 1960.
Military Career: Army, 1951-53.
Occupation: Lawyer.
Family: Divorced; one child.
Religion: Episcopalian.
Political Career: No previous office.

Capitol Office: 233 Cannon House Office Building 20515; 225-4076.
Office Staff: Administrative Assistant, Gary Johnson; Press Secretary, Philip Launius; Office Manager/Executive Secretary, Julia Smith.
Committees: Appropriations.

Arkansas 1st — East — Jonesboro. The district vote for George Bush was 51% in 1988.

CQ Voting Studies

	1989	1990
Presidential	34%	27%
Party	88%	72%
Participation	96%	85%

Interest Groups

	1988	1989
ADA	80%	60%
ACU	5%	22%
AFL-CIO	100%	91%
CCUS	17%	30%

Elections

	1988	1990
General	u/o	64%
Primary	67%	54%

Wayne Allard (R-Colo.)
Of Loveland • Elected 1990

Born: December 2, 1943, Fort Collins, Colo.
Education: Colorado State U., D.V.M. 1968.
Occupation: Veterinarian.
Family: Wife, Joan Malcolm; two children.
Religion: Protestant.
Political Career: Colo. Senate, 1983-90.

Capitol Office: 513 Cannon House Office Building 20515; 225-4676.
Office Staff: Administrative Assistant, Roy Palmer; Press Secretary, Doug Benevento; Appointments Secretary, Doris Wilson.
Committees: Agriculture; Interior & Insular Affairs; Small Business.

Colorado 4th — North and East — Fort Collins; Greeley. The district vote for George Bush was 55% in 1988.

Elections

	1990
General	54%
Primary	56%

Glenn M. Anderson   (D-Calif.)
Of San Pedro • Elected 1968

Born: February 21, 1913, Hawthorne, Calif.
Education: U.C.L.A., B.A. 1936.
Military Career: Army, 1943-45.
Occupation: Banker; home builder.
Family: Wife, Lee Dutton; three children.
Religion: Episcopalian.
Political Career: Mayor of Hawthorne, 1941-43; Calif. Assembly, 1943-51; Democratic nominee for Calif. Senate, 1950; lieutenant governor, 1959-67; defeated for re-election, 1966.

Capitol Office: 2329 Rayburn House Office Building 20515; 225-6676.
Office Staff: Administrative Assistant/Press Secretary, Jeremiah Bresnahan; Appointments Secretary, Jessica Kleppinger.
Committees: Merchant Marine & Fisheries; Public Works & Transportation.

California 32nd — San Pedro; Long Beach. The district vote for George Bush was 50% in 1988.

CQ Voting Studies

	1989	1990
Presidential	36%	18%
Party	85%	93%
Participation	95%	99%

Interest Groups

	1988	1989
ADA	70%	65%
ACU	10%	27%
AFL-CIO	92%	82%
CCUS	0%	50%

Elections

	1988	1990
General	67%	62%
Primary	u/o	u/o

Michael A. Andrews (D-Texas)
Of Houston • Elected 1982

Born: February 7, 1944, Houston, Texas.
Education: U. of Texas, B.A. 1967;
Southern Methodist U., J.D. 1970.
Occupation: Lawyer.
Family: Wife, Ann Bowman; two
children.
Religion: Episcopalian.
Political Career: Democratic nominee
for U.S House, 1980.

Capitol Office: 303 Cannon House
Office Building 20515; 225-7508.
Office Staff: Administrative Assistant,
Ann M. Rowan; Press Secretary, Jeff
Patterson; Executive Assistant/Office
Manager, Lori Kenyon Huffman.
Committees: Ways & Means.

Texas 25th — South Houston and
Southeast Suburbs. The district vote for
George Bush was 47% in 1988.

CQ Voting Studies

	1989	1990
Presidential	45%	32%
Party	78%	79%
Participation	98%	99%

Interest Groups

	1988	1989
ADA	75%	35%
ACU	29%	48%
AFL-CIO	86%	45%
CCUS	62%	50%

Elections

	1988	1990
General	71%	u/o
Primary	u/o	u/o

Robert E. Andrews (D-N.J.)
Of Bellmawr • Elected 1990

Born: August 4, 1957, Camden, N.J.
Education: Bucknell U., B.A. 1979;
Cornell U., J.D. 1982.
Occupation: Law professor.
Family: Single.
Religion: Episcopalian.
Political Career: Camden County Board
of Chosen Freeholders, 1987-90; director
of freeholders, 1988-90.

Capitol Office: 1005 Longworth House
Office Building 20515; 225-6501.
Office Staff: Administrative
Assistant/Press Secretary, Fran Callanan.
Committees: Education & Labor; Small
Business.

New Jersey 1st — Southwest — Camden.
The district vote for George Bush was
52% in 1988.

Elections

	1990
General	54%
Primary	53%

Elections

	1990
General	60%
Primary	36%

Thomas H. Andrews (D-Maine)
Of Portland • Elected 1990

Born: March 22, 1953, North Easton, Mass.
Education: Bowdoin College, B.A. 1976.
Occupation: Association director, political activist.
Family: Wife, Debra Johnson.
Religion: Unitarian.
Political Career: Maine House, 1983-85; Maine Senate, 1985-90.

Capitol Office: 1724 Longworth House Office Building 20515; 225-6116.
Office Staff: Administrative Assistant, Craig S. Brown; Press Secretary, Dennis Bailey.
Committees: Armed Services; Small Business.

Maine 1st — South — Portland; Augusta. The district vote for George Bush was 56% in 1988.

Frank Annunzio (D-Ill.)
Of Chicago • Elected 1964

Born: January 12, 1915, Chicago, Ill.
Education: DePaul U., B.S. 1940; DePaul U., M.A. 1942.
Occupation: High school teacher; labor official.
Family: Wife, Angeline Alesia; three children.
Religion: Roman Catholic.
Political Career: Ill. labor director, 1949-52.

Capitol Office: 2303 Rayburn House Office Building 20515; 225-6661.
Office Staff: Administrative Assistant, Anna Azhderian.
Committees: House Administration; Banking, Finance & Urban Affairs.

Illinois 11th — Northwest Chicago and Suburbs. The district vote for George Bush was 54% in 1988.

CQ Voting Studies

	1989	1990
Presidential	37%	35%
Party	89%	83%
Participation	97%	97%

Interest Groups

	1988	1989
ADA	75%	75%
ACU	17%	7%
AFL-CIO	100%	100%
CCUS	25%	44%

Elections

	1988	1990
General	65%	54%
Primary	u/o	u/o

CQ Voting Studies

	1989	1990
Presidential	38%	27%
Party	79%	85%
Participation	92%	96%

Interest Groups

	1988	1989
ADA	80%	60%
ACU	16%	23%
AFL-CIO	92%	70%
CCUS	46%	44%

Elections

	1988	1990
General	69%	72%
Primary	u/o	u/o

Beryl Anthony, Jr. (D-Ark.)
Of El Dorado • Elected 1978

Born: February 21, 1938, El Dorado, Ark.
Education: U. of Arkansas, B.S., B.A. 1961;
U. of Arkansas, J.D. 1963.
Occupation: Lawyer.
Family: Wife, Sheila Foster; two children.
Religion: Episcopalian.
Political Career: Prosecuting attorney,
Ark. 13th Judicial District, 1971-77.

Capitol Office: 1212 Longworth House
Office Building 20515; 225-3772.
Office Staff: Administrative Assistant,
Mark Lowman; Press Secretary, Vacant;
Personal Secretary, Carol Kiernan.
Committees: Ways & Means.

Arkansas 4th — South — Pine Bluff. The
district vote for George Bush was 52% in
1988.

Douglas Applegate (D-Ohio)
Of Steubenville • Elected 1976

Born: March 27, 1928, Steubenville, Ohio.
Education: Steubenville H.S., graduated 1947.
Occupation: Real estate broker.
Family: Wife, Betty Engstrom; two children.
Religion: Presbyterian.
Political Career: Ohio House, 1961-69; Ohio Senate, 1969-76.

Capitol Office: 2183 Rayburn House Office Building 20515; 225-6265.
Office Staff: Administrative Assistant/Press Secretary, James Hart; Personal Secretary/Scheduler, Wendy Conrad.
Committees: Public Works & Transportation; Veterans' Affairs.

Ohio 18th — East — Steubenville. The district vote for George Bush was 47% in 1988.

CQ Voting Studies

	1989	1990
Presidential	45%	30%
Party	67%	73%
Participation	96%	98%

Interest Groups

	1988	1989
ADA	70%	70%
ACU	24%	33%
AFL-CIO	100%	83%
CCUS	29%	50%

Elections

	1988	1990
General	77%	74%
Primary	u/o	88%

Bill Archer (R-Texas)
Of Houston • Elected 1970

Born: March 22, 1928, Houston, Texas.
Education: Rice U., 1945-46; U. of Texas, B.B.A. 1949; U. of Texas, LL.B. 1951.
Military Career: Air Force, 1951-53.
Occupation: Lawyer; feed company executive.
Family: Wife, Sharon Sawyer; five children, two stepchildren.
Religion: Roman Catholic.
Political Career: Hunters Creek Village Council, 1955-62; Texas House, 1967-71.

Capitol Office: 1236 Longworth House Office Building 20515; 225-2571.
Office Staff: Administrative Assistant, Don Carlson; Press Secretary, Maureen Mulqueeny; Personal Secretary, Linda Figura.
Committees: Ways & Means (Ranking).

Texas 7th — Western Houston and Suburbs. The district vote for George Bush was 75% in 1988.

CQ Voting Studies

	1989	1990
Presidential	81%	84%
Party	75%	86%
Participation	97%	98%

Interest Groups

	1988	1989
ADA	0%	0%
ACU	100%	88%
AFL-CIO	0%	0%
CCUS	100%	90%

Elections

	1988	1990
General	79%	u/o
Primary	u/o	u/o

Dick Armey (R-Texas)
Of Copper Canyon • Elected 1984

Born: July 7, 1940, Cando, N.D.
Education: Jamestown College, B.A.
1963; U. of North Dakota, M.A. 1964; U.
of Oklahoma, Ph.D. 1969.
Occupation: Economist.
Family: Wife, Susan K. Byrd; five
children.
Religion: Presbyterian.
Political Career: No previous office.

Capitol Office: 130 Cannon House
Office Building 20515; 225-7772.
Office Staff: Administrative Assistant,
Kerry Knott; Press Secretary, Ed Gillespie;
Scheduler, Charla Worsham.
Committees: Budget; Education & Labor.

Texas 26th — Fort Worth Suburbs —
Arlington; Denton. The district vote for
George Bush was 69% in 1988.

CQ Voting Studies

	1989	1990
Presidential	76%	81%
Party	94%	95%
Participation	97%	99%

Interest Groups

	1988	1989
ADA	0%	0%
ACU	100%	96%
AFL-CIO	0%	0%
CCUS	100%	90%

Elections

	1988	1990
General	69%	70%
Primary	u/o	u/o

Les Aspin (D-Wis.)
Of East Troy • Elected 1970

Born: July 21, 1938, Milwaukee, Wis.
Education: Yale U., B.A. 1960; Oxford U.,
M.A. 1962; Massachusetts Institute of
Technology, Ph.D. 1965.
Military Career: Army, 1966-68.
Occupation: Professor of economics.
Family: Divorced.
Religion: Episcopalian.
Political Career: Sought Democratic
nomination for Wis. treasurer, 1968.

Capitol Office: 2336 Rayburn House
Office Building 20515; 225-3031.
Office Staff: Administrative Assistant,
Ted Bornstein; Press Secretary, Lauren
Ariker; Office Manager/Personal
Secretary, Judy Berman.
Committees: Armed Services (Chairman).

Wisconsin 1st — Southeast — Racine;
Kenosha. The district vote for George
Bush was 48% in 1988.

CQ Voting Studies

	1989	1990
Presidential	41%	24%
Party	70%	83%
Participation	83%	91%

Interest Groups

	1988	1989
ADA	75%	65%
ACU	4%	8%
AFL-CIO	100%	82%
CCUS	27%	40%

Elections

	1988	1990
General	76%	u/o
Primary	u/o	86%

Chester G. Atkins (D Mass.)
Of Concord • Elected 1984

Born: April 14, 1948, Geneva,
Switzerland.
Education: Antioch College, B.A. 1970.
Occupation: Public official.
Family: Wife, Corinne Hobbs; two
children.
Religion: Unitarian.
Political Career: Mass. House, 1971-73;
Mass. Senate, 1973-85.

Capitol Office: 123 Cannon House
Office Building 20515; 225-3411.
Office Staff: Administrative Assistant,
Linda Hartke; Press Secretary, Mark
Provost; Office Manager, Linda
Eisenstadt.
Committees: Appropriations.

**Massachusetts 5th — North — Lowell;
Lawrence.** The district vote for George
Bush was 51% in 1988.

CQ Voting Studies

	1989	1990
Presidential	30%	20%
Party	95%	93%
Participation	96%	97%

Interest Groups

	1988	1989
ADA	100%	100%
ACU	0%	0%
AFL-CIO	100%	92%
CCUS	23%	30%

Elections

	1988	1990
General	84%	52%
Primary	u/o	u/o

Les AuCoin (D-Ore.)
Of Portland • Elected 1974
Pronounced oh COIN

Born: October 21, 1942, Redmond, Ore.
Education: Pacific U., B.A. 1969.
Military Career: Army, 1961-64.
Occupation: Journalist; public relations executive.
Family: Wife, Susan Swearingen; two children.
Religion: Protestant.
Political Career: Ore. House, 1971-75; majority leader, 1973-75.

Capitol Office: 2159 Rayburn House Office Building 20515; 225-0855.
Office Staff: Administrative Assistant, Bob Crane; Press Secretary, Rachel Gorlin; Office Manager, Lori Kannier.
Committees: Appropriations.

Oregon 1st — Western Portland and Suburbs. The district vote for George Bush was 47% in 1988.

CQ Voting Studies

	1989	1990
Presidential	26%	20%
Party	84%	81%
Participation	91%	88%

Interest Groups

	1988	1989
ADA	95%	85%
ACU	8%	8%
AFL-CIO	86%	100%
CCUS	43%	30%

Elections

	1988	1990
General	70%	63%
Primary	u/o	u/o

Jim Bacchus (D-Fla.)
Of Belle Isle • Elected 1990
Pronounced BACK us

Born: June 21, 1949, Nashville, Tenn.
Education: Vanderbilt U., B.A. 1971; Yale U., M.A. 1973; Florida State U., J.D. 1978.
Military Career: Army Reserve, 1971-77.
Occupation: Lawyer; journalist.
Family: Wife, Rebecca McMillan; one child.
Religion: Presbyterian.
Political Career: No previous office.

Capitol Office: 431 Cannon House Office Building 20515; 225-3671.
Office Staff: Administrative Assistant, Linda Hennessee; Press Secretary, Daniel Sallick; Appointments Secretary, Liz D'Amato.
Committees: Banking, Finance & Urban Affairs; Science, Space & Technology.

Florida 11th — East — Melbourne; Part of Orange County. The district vote for George Bush was 70% in 1988.

Elections

	1990
General	52%
Primary	u/o

CQ Voting Studies

	1989	1990
Presidential	70%	69%
Party	87%	81%
Participation	96%	91%

Interest Groups

	1988	1989
ADA	5%	5%
ACU	100%	79%
AFL-CIO	15%	17%
CCUS	100%	90%

Elections

	1988	1990
General	u/o	u/o
Primary	u/o	u/o

Richard H. Baker (R-La.)
Of Baton Rouge • Elected 1986

Born: May 22, 1948, New Orleans, La.
Education: Louisiana State U., B.A. 1971.
Occupation: Real estate broker.
Family: Wife, Kay Carpenter; two children.
Religion: Methodist.
Political Career: La. House, 1973-87; candidate for La. Senate, 1980.

Capitol Office: 404 Cannon House Office Building 20515; 225-3901.
Office Staff: Administrative Assistant, Tim Carpenter; Communications Director, Jessica Guttry; Office Manager/Personal Secretary, Earline Sims.
Committees: Banking, Finance & Urban Affairs; Small Business.

Louisiana 6th — East Central — Baton Rouge. The district vote for George Bush was 60% in 1988.

Cass Ballenger (R-N.C.)
Of Hickory • Elected 1986

Born: December 6, 1926, Hickory, N.C.
Education: U. of North Carolina, 1944-45; Amherst College, B.A. 1948.
Military Career: Navy Air Corps, 1944-45.
Occupation: President of plastics packaging company.
Family: Wife, Donna Davis; three children.
Religion: Episcopalian.
Political Career: Catawba County Board of Commissioners, 1966-74; chairman, 1970-74; N.C. House, 1975-77; N.C. Senate, 1977-87.

Capitol Office: 328 Cannon House Office Building 20515; 225-2576.
Office Staff: Administrative Assistant, Patrick Murphy; Press Secretary, David O. Murray; Executive Assistant/Scheduler, Stephanie Bridges.
Committees: Education & Labor; Public Works & Transportation.

North Carolina 10th — West -- Gastonia; Hickory. The district vote for George Bush was 65% in 1988.

CQ Voting Studies

	1989	1990
Presidential	79%	73%
Party	93%	90%
Participation	98%	97%

Interest Groups

	1988	1989
ADA	10%	10%
ACU	92%	96%
AFL-CIO	14%	9%
CCUS	100%	100%

Elections

	1988	1990
General	61%	62%
Primary	u/o	87%

Doug Barnard, Jr. (D-Ga.)
Of Augusta • Elected 1976

Born: March 20, 1922, Augusta, Ga.
Education: Mercer U., B.A. 1942; Mercer U., LL.B. 1948.
Military Career: Army, 1943-45.
Occupation: Banker.
Family: Wife, Naomi Elizabeth Holt; three children.
Religion: Baptist.
Political Career: No previous office.

Capitol Office: 2227 Rayburn House Office Building 20515; 225-4101.
Office Staff: Administrative Assistant, Beverly Bell; Executive Assistant, Sandra Swank.
Committees: Banking, Finance & Urban Affairs; Government Operations.

Georgia 10th — North Central — Athens; Augusta. The district vote for George Bush was 65% in 1988.

CQ Voting Studies

	1989	1990
Presidential	67%	49%
Party	56%	52%
Participation	92%	87%

Interest Groups

	1988	1989
ADA	25%	10%
ACU	64%	79%
AFL-CIO	54%	18%
CCUS	67%	90%

Elections

	1988	1990
General	64%	58%
Primary	u/o	71%

Bill Barrett   (R-Neb.)
Of Lexington • Elected 1990

Born: February 9, 1929, Lexington, Neb.
Education: Hastings College, B.A. 1951.
Military Career: Navy, 1951-52.
Occupation: Insurance and real estate company owner.
Family: Wife, Elsie Carlson; four children.
Religion: Presbyterian.
Political Career: Neb. Legislature, 1979-91; Speaker, 1987-91.

Capitol Office: 1607 Longworth House Office Building 20515; 225-6435.
Office Staff: Administrative Assistant, Jeri Finke; Press Secretary, Michele Dishong; Appointments Secretary, Jim Brouillette.
Committees: Agriculture; Education & Labor.

Nebraska 3rd — Central and West — Grand Island. The district vote for George Bush was 67% in 1988.

Elections

	1990
General	51%
Primary	30%

Steve Bartlett (R-Texas)
Of Dallas • Elected 1982

Born: September 19, 1947, Los Angeles, Calif.
Education: U. of Texas, B.A. 1971.
Occupation: Owner of tool and plastics company.
Family: Wife, Gail Coke; three children.
Religion: Presbyterian.
Political Career: Dallas City Council, 1977-81.

Capitol Office: 1113 Longworth House Office Building 20515; 225-4201.
Office Staff: Administrative Assistant, Mary Jane Maddox; Communications Director, Teresa Garland; Office Manager/Scheduler, Mitchell Dedert.
Committees: Banking, Finance & Urban Affairs; Education & Labor.

Texas 3rd — North Dallas; Northern Suburbs. The district vote for George Bush was 75% in 1988.

CQ Voting Studies

	1989	1990
Presidential	80%	78%
Party	69%	79%
Participation	98%	99%

Interest Groups

	1988	1989
ADA	10%	10%
ACU	96%	93%
AFL-CIO	0%	8%
CCUS	100%	100%

Elections

	1988	1990
General	82%	u/o
Primary	u/o	u/o

Joe L. Barton (R-Texas)
Of Ennis • Elected 1984

Born: September 15, 1949, Waco, Texas.
Education: Texas A&M U., B.S. 1972;
Purdue U., M.S. 1973.
Occupation: Engineering consultant.
Family: Wife, Janet Sue Winslow; three
children.
Religion: Methodist.
Political Career: No previous office.

Capitol Office: 1225 Longworth House
Office Building 20515; 225-2002.
Office Staff: Administrative Assistant,
Cathy Gillespie; Press Secretary, Craig
Murphy; Office Manager, Ellen Gober.
Committees: Energy & Commerce;
Science, Space & Technology.

Texas 6th — Suburban Dallas-Fort Worth
and Houston; Bryan. The district vote for
George Bush was 62% in 1988.

CQ Voting Studies

	1989	1990
Presidential	67%	68%
Party	88%	86%
Participation	93%	94%

Interest Groups

	1988	1989
ADA	5%	10%
ACU	96%	89%
AFL-CIO	0%	8%
CCUS	100%	90%

Elections

	1988	1990
General	68%	66%
Primary	u/o	u/o

Herbert H. Bateman (R-Va.)
Of Newport News • Elected 1982

Born: August 7, 1928, Elizabeth City, N.C.
Education: College of William and Mary, B.A. 1949; Georgetown U., J.D. 1956.
Military Career: Air Force, 1951-53.
Occupation: Lawyer.
Family: Wife, Laura Yacobi; two children.
Religion: Protestant.
Political Career: Va. Senate, 1968-82; sought Republican nomination for lieutenant governor, 1981.

Capitol Office: 1030 Longworth House Office Building 20515; 225-4261.
Office Staff: Administrative Assistant, Jack Brooks; Communications Director, Don Scandling; Office Manager/Personal Secretary, Peggy Haar.
Committees: Armed Services; Merchant Marine & Fisheries.

Virginia 1st — East — Newport News; Hampton. The district vote for George Bush was 60% in 1988.

CQ Voting Studies

	1989	1990
Presidential	74%	69%
Party	61%	63%
Participation	90%	98%

Interest Groups

	1988	1989
ADA	20%	0%
ACU	84%	81%
AFL-CIO	14%	17%
CCUS	85%	100%

Elections

	1988	1990
General	73%	51%
Primary	u/o	u/o

Anthony C. Beilenson
(D-Calif.)
Of Los Angeles • Elected 1976
Pronounced BEE lin son

Born: October 26, 1932, New Rochelle, N.Y.
Education: Harvard U., A.B. 1954; Harvard U., LL.B. 1957.
Occupation: Lawyer.
Family: Wife, Dolores Martin; three children.
Religion: Jewish.
Political Career: Calif. Assembly, 1963-67; Calif. Senate, 1967-77; sought Democratic nomination for U.S. Senate, 1968.

Capitol Office: 1025 Longworth House Office Building 20515; 225-5911.
Office Staff: Administrative Assistant, Jan Faulstich; Scheduler, Anita Lawson.
Committees: Budget; Rules.

California 23rd — Beverly Hills; Part of San Fernando Valley. The district vote for George Bush was 43% in 1988.

CQ Voting Studies

	1989	1990
Presidential	33%	26%
Party	84%	89%
Participation	94%	97%

Interest Groups

	1988	1989
ADA	95%	85%
ACU	8%	4%
AFL-CIO	77%	67%
CCUS	50%	30%

Elections

	1988	1990
General	63%	62%
Primary	84%	u/o

CQ Voting Studies

	1989	1990
Presidential	43%	33%
Party	80%	68%
Participation	100%	99%

Interest Groups

	1988	1989
ADA	65%	70%
ACU	28%	46%
AFL-CIO	79%	75%
CCUS	43%	60%

Elections

	1988	1990
General	u/o	73%
Primary	u/o	u/o

Charles E. Bennett (D-Fla.)
Of Jacksonville • Elected 1948

Born: December 2, 1910, Canton, N.Y.
Education: U. of Florida, B.A. 1934; U. of Florida, J.D. 1934.
Military Career: Army, 1942-47.
Occupation: Lawyer.
Family: Wife, Jean Fay; three children.
Religion: Disciples of Christ.
Political Career: Fla. House, 1941.

Capitol Office: 2107 Rayburn House Office Building 20515; 225-2501.
Office Staff: Administrative Assistant, James Pearthree; Appointments Secretary, Darla Smallwood.
Committees: Armed Services; Merchant Marine & Fisheries.

Florida 3rd — Northeast — Jacksonville. The district vote for George Bush was 60% in 1988.

Helen Delich Bentley   (R-Md.)
Of Lutherville • Elected 1984

Born: November 28, 1923, Ruth, Nev.
Education: U. of Nevada, 1941-42;
George Washington U., 1943; U. of
Missouri, B.A. 1944.
Occupation: International trade
consultant; federal official; journalist.
Family: Husband, William Roy Bentley.
Religion: Greek Orthodox.
Political Career: Republican nominee for
U.S. House, 1980; Republican nominee
for U.S. House, 1982.

Capitol Office: 1610 Longworth House
Office Building 20515; 225-3061.
Office Staff: Administrative
Assistant/Press Secretary, Pat Wait;
Appointments Secretary/Scheduler,
Diane Baker.
Committees: Budget; Public Works &
Transportation.

Maryland 2nd — Baltimore Suburbs. The
district vote for George Bush was 62% in
1988.

CQ Voting Studies

	1989	1990
Presidential	51%	61%
Party	74%	76%
Participation	92%	95%

Interest Groups

	1988	1989
ADA	10%	20%
ACU	86%	86%
AFL-CIO	69%	50%
CCUS	79%	90%

Elections

	1988	1990
General	71%	74%
Primary	u/o	u/o

CQ Voting Studies

	1989	1990
Presidential	69%	62%
Party	58%	73%
Participation	99%	99%

Interest Groups

	1988	1989
ADA	20%	15%
ACU	76%	61%
AFL-CIO	57%	33%
CCUS	93%	80%

Elections

	1988	1990
General	67%	65%
Primary	u/o	u/o

Doug Bereuter   (R-Neb.)
Of Utica • Elected 1978
Pronounced BEE right er

Born: October 6, 1939, York, Neb.
Education: U. of Nebraska, B.A. 1961;
Harvard U., M.C.P. 1963; Harvard U.,
M.P.A. 1973.
Military Career: Army, 1963-65.
Occupation: City planner; associate
professor of planning.
Family: Wife, Louise Anna Meyer; two
children.
Religion: Lutheran.
Political Career: Neb. Legislature, 1975-
79.

Capitol Office: 2348 Rayburn House
Office Building 20515; 225-4806.
Office Staff: Administrative Assistant,
Susan Olson; Press Secretary, Carol
Lawrence; Personal Secretary, Marcia
Smith.
Committees: Banking, Finance & Urban
Affairs; Foreign Affairs; Select
Intelligence.

Nebraska 1st — East Central — Lincoln.
The district vote for George Bush was
56% in 1988.

Howard L. Berman (D-Calif.)
Of Panorama City • Elected 1982

Born: April 15, 1941, Los Angeles, Calif.
Education: U.C.L.A., B.A. 1962; U.C.L.A., LL.B. 1965.
Occupation: Lawyer.
Family: Wife, Janis Schwartz; two children.
Religion: Jewish.
Political Career: Calif. Assembly, 1973-83.

Capitol Office: 137 Cannon House Office Building 20515; 225-4695.
Office Staff: Administrative Assistant, Gene Smith; Press Secretary, Graham Cannon; Office Manager, Nancy Milburn.
Committees: Budget; Foreign Affairs; Judiciary.

California 26th — Santa Monica Mountains; Central San Fernando Valley. The district vote for George Bush was 44% in 1988.

CQ Voting Studies

	1989	1990
Presidential	31%	20%
Party	90%	93%
Participation	93%	96%

Interest Groups

	1988	1989
ADA	95%	95%
ACU	4%	4%
AFL-CIO	85%	100%
CCUS	36%	30%

Elections

	1988	1990
General	70%	61%
Primary	u/o	86%

CQ Voting Studies

	1989	1990
Presidential	52%	42%
Party	70%	71%
Participation	98%	96%

Interest Groups

	1988	1989
ADA	45%	40%
ACU	50%	39%
AFL-CIO	100%	70%
CCUS	46%	44%

Elections

	1988	1990
General	96%	u/o
Primary	u/o	u/o

Tom Bevill (D-Ala.)
Of Jasper • Elected 1966

Born: March 27, 1921, Townley, Ala.
Education: U. of Alabama, B.S. 1943; U. of Alabama, LL.B. 1948.
Military Career: Army, 1943-46.
Occupation: Lawyer.
Family: Wife, Lou Betts; three children.
Religion: Baptist.
Political Career: Ala. House, 1959-67; sought Democratic nomination for U.S. House, 1964.

Capitol Office: 2302 Rayburn House Office Building 20515; 225-4876.
Office Staff: Administrative Assistant, Don Smith; Press Secretary, Olivia Barton; Office Manager/Executive Secretary, Gayle Woody.
Committees: Appropriations.

Alabama 4th — North Central — Gadsden. The district vote for George Bush was 57% in 1988.

James Bilbray (D-Nev.)
Of Las Vegas • Elected 1986

Born: May 19, 1938, Las Vegas, Nev.
Education: American U., B.A. 1962;
Washington College of Law, J.D. 1964.
Military Career: National Guard, 1955-
63; Reserve, 1963-present.
Occupation: Lawyer.
Family: Wife, Michaelene Mercer; three
children.
Religion: Roman Catholic.
Political Career: Democratic nominee
for U.S. House, 1972; Nev. Senate, 1981-
87.

Capitol Office: 319 Cannon House
Office Building 20515; 225-5965.
Office Staff: Administrative Assistant,
John Fadgen; Press Secretary, Mark
Fierro; Appointments Secretary, Tina
Morris.
Committees: Armed Services; Small
Business.

Nevada 1st — South — Las Vegas. The
district vote for George Bush was 56% in
1988.

CQ Voting Studies

	1989	1990
Presidential	45%	33%
Party	83%	83%
Participation	97%	98%

Interest Groups

	1988	1989
ADA	60%	55%
ACU	44%	25%
AFL-CIO	93%	75%
CCUS	43%	50%

Elections

	1988	1990
General	64%	61%
Primary	u/o	86%

Michael Bilirakis (R-Fla.)
Of Palm Harbor • *Elected 1982*
Pronounced bill a RACK us

Born: July 16, 1930, Tarpon Springs, Fla.
Education: U. of Pittsburgh, B.S. 1959;
George Washington U., 1959-60; U. of
Florida, J.D. 1963.
Military Career: Air Force, 1951-55.
Occupation: Lawyer; restaurant owner.
Family: Wife, Evelyn Miaoulis; two
children.
Religion: Greek Orthodox.
Political Career: No previous office.

Capitol Office: 2432 Rayburn House
Office Building 20515; 225-5755.
Office Staff: Administrative Assistant,
Robert Meyers; Press Secretary, David
White; Appointments Secretary, Ellen
Stavros.
Committees: Energy & Commerce;
Veterans' Affairs.

Florida 9th — West — Clearwater; Parts
of Pasco and Hillsborough Counties. The
district vote for George Bush was 60% in
1988.

CQ Voting Studies

	1989	1990
Presidential	60%	51%
Party	86%	70%
Participation	97%	84%

Interest Groups

	1988	1989
ADA	10%	10%
ACU	96%	86%
AFL-CIO	14%	25%
CCUS	93%	100%

Elections

	1988	1990
General	u/o	58%
Primary	u/o	83%

Thomas J. Bliley, Jr. (R Va.)
Of Richmond • Elected 1980

Born: January 28, 1932, Chesterfield County, Va.
Education: Georgetown U., B.A. 1952.
Military Career: Navy, 1952-55.
Occupation: Funeral director.
Family: Wife, Mary Virginia Kelley; two children.
Religion: Roman Catholic.
Political Career: Richmond City Council, 1968-77; mayor, 1970-77.

Capitol Office: 2441 Rayburn House Office Building 20515; 225-2815.
Office Staff: Administrative Assistant, Jeff Schlagenhauf; Press Secretary, Elizabeth Frazee; Personal Secretary, Phyllis Troy.
Committees: District of Columbia (Ranking); Energy & Commerce.

Virginia 3rd — Richmond and Suburbs. The district vote for George Bush was 63% in 1988.

CQ Voting Studies

	1989	1990
Presidential	80%	66%
Party	88%	84%
Participation	98%	98%

Interest Groups

	1988	1989
ADA	10%	0%
ACU	96%	96%
AFL-CIO	21%	8%
CCUS	93%	100%

Elections

	1988	1990
General	u/o	65%
Primary	u/o	u/o

CQ Voting Studies

	1989	1990
Presidential	51%	40%
Party	46%	47%
Participation	96%	99%

Interest Groups

	1988	1989
ADA	65%	65%
ACU	24%	43%
AFL-CIO	86%	75%
CCUS	64%	70%

Elections

	1988	1990
General	u/o	84%
Primary	u/o	u/o

Sherwood Boehlert (R-N.Y.)
Of New Hartford • Elected 1982
Pronounced BO lert

Born: September 28, 1936, Utica, N.Y.
Education: Utica College, A.B. 1961.
Military Career: Army, 1956-58.
Occupation: Congressional aide; public-relations manager.
Family: Wife, Marianne Willey; four children.
Religion: Roman Catholic.
Political Career: Sought Republican nomination for U.S. House, 1972; Oneida County executive, 1979-82.

Capitol Office: 1127 Longworth House Office Building 20515; 225-3665.
Office Staff: Administrative Assistant, Dan Costello; Press Secretary, Hank Price; Executive Assistant, Dorothy Vagnozzi.
Committees: Public Works & Transportation; Science, Space & Technology.

New York 25th — Central — Rome; Utica. The district vote for George Bush was 54% in 1988.

John A. Boehner (R-Ohio)
Of West Chester • Elected 1990
Pronounced BAY ner

Born: November 17, 1949, Cincinnati, Ohio.
Education: Xavier U., B.S. 1977.
Military Career: U.S. Navy, 1969.
Occupation: Plastics and packaging sales company president.
Family: Wife, Debbie Gunlack; two children.
Religion: Roman Catholic.
Political Career: Ohio House, 1985-91.

Capitol Office: 1020 Longworth House Office Building 20515; 225-6205.
Office Staff: Administrative Assistant/Press Secretary, Barry Jackson; Scheduler, Connie Valen.
Committees: Agriculture; Education & Labor; Small Business.

Ohio 8th — Southwest — Middletown; Hamilton. The district vote for George Bush was 69% in 1988.

Elections

	1990
General	61%
Primary	49%

David E. Bonior (D-Mich.)
Of Mount Clemens • Elected 1976
Pronounced BON yer

Born: June 6, 1945, Detroit, Mich.
Education: U. of Iowa, B.A. 1967;
Chapman College, M.A. 1972.
Military Career: Air Force, 1968-72.
Occupation: Probation officer.
Family: Divorced; two children.
Religion: Roman Catholic.
Political Career: Mich. House, 1973-77.

Capitol Office: 2242 Rayburn House
Office Building 20515; 225-2106.
Office Staff: Administrative Assistant,
Sarah Dufendach; Press Secretary, Nathan
Blain; Executive Secretary, Paula Short.
Committees: Rules.

Michigan 12th — Southeast — Macomb
County; Port Huron. The district vote for
George Bush was 60% in 1988.

CQ Voting Studies

	1989	1990
Presidential	36%	18%
Party	92%	95%
Participation	98%	98%

Interest Groups

	1988	1989
ADA	95%	95%
ACU	4%	4%
AFL-CIO	100%	100%
CCUS	21%	30%

Elections

	1988	1990
General	54%	66%
Primary	u/o	86%

Robert A. Borski (D-Pa.)
Of Philadelphia • Elected 1982

Born: October 20, 1948, Philadelphia, Penn.
Education: U. of Baltimore, B.A. 1971.
Occupation: Stockbroker.
Family: Divorced; three children.
Religion: Roman Catholic.
Political Career: Pa. House, 1977-83.

Capitol Office: 407 Cannon House Office Building 20515; 225-8251.
Office Staff: Administrative Assistant, Kay Arndorfer; Office Manager/Scheduler, Erin Manning.
Committees: Merchant Marine & Fisheries; Public Works & Transportation.

Pennsylvania 3rd — Northeast Philadelphia. The district vote for George Bush was 52% in 1988.

CQ Voting Studies

	1989	1990
Presidential	41%	27%
Party	87%	90%
Participation	97%	98%

Interest Groups

	1988	1989
ADA	80%	75%
ACU	12%	7%
AFL-CIO	100%	92%
CCUS	23%	50%

Elections

	1988	1990
General	63%	59%
Primary	91%	u/o

CQ Voting Studies

	1989	1990
Presidential	27%	20%
Party	88%	90%
Participation	91%	95%

Interest Groups

	1988	1989
ADA	75%	80%
ACU	9%	8%
AFL-CIO	100%	73%
CCUS	29%	30%

Elections

	1988	1990
General	63%	97%
Primary	u/o	u/o

Rick Boucher (D-Va.)
Of Abingdon • Elected 1982
Pronounced BOUGH cher

Born: August 1, 1946, Abingdon, Va.
Education: Roanoke College, B.A. 1968;
U. of Virginia, J.D. 1971.
Occupation: Lawyer.
Family: Single.
Religion: Methodist.
Political Career: Va. Senate, 1975-82.

Capitol Office: 405 Cannon House
Office Building 20515; 225-3861.
Office Staff: Administrative Assistant,
Kevin Burke; Press Secretary, Sarah
Broadwater; Personal Secretary,
Catherine Elliott.
Committees: Energy & Commerce;
Judiciary; Science, Space & Technology.

Virginia 9th — Southwest — Blacksburg;
Bristol. The district vote for George Bush
was 54% in 1988.

Barbara Boxer (D-Calif.)
Of Greenbrae • Elected 1982

Born: November 11, 1940, Brooklyn, N.Y.
Education: Brooklyn College, B.A. 1962.
Occupation: Stockbroker; journalist.
Family: Husband, Stewart Boxer; two children.
Religion: Jewish.
Political Career: Candidate for Marin County Board of Supervisors, 1972; Marin County Board of Supervisors, 1977-83.

Capitol Office: 307 Cannon House Office Building 20515; 225-5161.
Office Staff: Administrative Assistant, Andrew Littman; Communications Director, Rob Alexander; Office Manager/Scheduler, Betty McArthur.
Committees: Armed Services; Government Operations.

California 6th — Northwest San Francisco; Marin County; parts of Sonoma and Solano counties. The district vote for George Bush was 35% in 1988.

CQ Voting Studies

	1989	1990
Presidential	26%	14%
Party	95%	86%
Participation	96%	89%

Interest Groups

	1988	1989
ADA	80%	100%
ACU	5%	0%
AFL-CIO	93%	91%
CCUS	27%	30%

Elections

	1988	1990
General	73%	68%
Primary	u/o	u/o

Bill Brewster (D-Okla.)
Of Marietta • Elected 1990

Born: November 8, 1941, Ardmore, Okla.
Education: Southwestern Oklahoma State U., B.S. 1964.
Military Career: Army Reserve, 1966-71.
Occupation: Pharmacist; rancher; real estate company owner.
Family: Wife, Suzie Nelson; one child.
Religion: Baptist.
Political Career: Okla. House, 1983-91.

Capitol Office: 1407 Longworth House Office Building 20515; 225-4565.
Office Staff: Administrative Assistant (Appointments), Phyllis Kreis; Press Secretary, Jim Pate.
Committees: Public Works & Transportation; Veterans' Affairs.

Oklahoma 3rd — Southeast — Little Dixie. The district vote for George Bush was 50% in 1988.

Elections

	1990
General	80%
Primary	51%

Jack Brooks (D-Texas)
Of Beaumont • Elected 1952

Born: December 18, 1922, Crowley, La.
Education: Lamar Junior College, 1939-41; U. of Texas, B.J. 1943; U. of Texas, J.D. 1949.
Military Career: Marine Corps, 1942-45; Marine Corps Reserve, 1945-72.
Occupation: Lawyer.
Family: Wife, Charlotte Collins; three children.
Religion: Methodist.
Political Career: Texas House, 1947-51.

Capitol Office: 2449 Rayburn House Office Building 20515; 225-6565.
Office Staff: Administrative Assistant, Sharon Matts; Appointments Secretary, Pamela Mays.
Committees: Judiciary (Chairman).

Texas 9th — Southeast — Beaumont; Galveston. The district vote for George Bush was 46% in 1988.

CQ Voting Studies

	1989	1990
Presidential	16%	18%
Party	69%	87%
Participation	72%	92%

Interest Groups

	1988	1989
ADA	75%	65%
ACU	9%	17%
AFL-CIO	100%	73%
CCUS	23%	40%

Elections

	1988	1990
General	u/o	58%
Primary	u/o	72%

William S. Broomfield
(R-Mich.)
Of Lake Orion • Elected 1956

Born: April 28, 1922, Royal Oak, Mich.
Education: Michigan State U., 1951.
Military Career: Army Air Corps, 1942.
Occupation: Insurance executive.
Family: Wife, Jane Smith Thompson;
three children.
Religion: Presbyterian.
Political Career: Mich. House, 1949-55;
Mich. Senate, 1955-57.

Capitol Office: 2306 Rayburn House
Office Building 20515; 225-6135.
Office Staff: Administrative Assistant,
Jack Sinclair; Press Secretary, Terri
Hauser; Executive Assistant, Nancy
Moore.
Committees: Foreign Affairs (Ranking);
Small Business.

Michigan 18th — Oakland County. The
district vote for George Bush was 71% in
1988.

CQ Voting Studies

	1989	1990
Presidential	74%	72%
Party	62%	76%
Participation	94%	95%

Interest Groups

	1988	1989
ADA	30%	20%
ACU	84%	88%
AFL-CIO	36%	9%
CCUS	92%	100%

Elections

	1988	1990
General	76%	66%
Primary	u/o	u/o

John Bryant   (D-Texas)
Of Dallas • Elected 1982

Born: February 22, 1947, Lake Jackson, Texas.
Education: Southern Methodist U., B.A. 1969; Southern Methodist U., J.D. 1972.
Occupation: Lawyer.
Family: Wife, Janet Elizabeth Watts; three children.
Religion: Methodist.
Political Career: Texas House, 1974-83.

Capitol Office: 208 Cannon House Office Building 20515; 225-2231.
Office Staff: Administrative Assistant, Randy White; Press Secretary, Carlton Carl; Office Manager, Carol Jordan.
Committees: Budget; Energy & Commerce; Judiciary.

Texas 5th — Downtown Dallas; Eastern and Southern Suburbs. The district vote for George Bush was 50% in 1988.

Glen Browder   (D-Ala.)
Of Jacksonville • Elected 1989
Pronounced BROW der

Born: January 15, 1943, Sumter, S.C.
Education: Presbyterian College, B.A. 1965; Emory U., M.A. 1971; Emory U., Ph.D. 1971.
Occupation: Professor of political science.
Family: Wife, Rebecca Moore; one child.
Religion: Methodist.
Political Career: Ala. House, 1983-86; Ala. secretary of state, 1987-89.

Capitol Office: 1221 Longworth House Office Building 20515; 225-3261.
Office Staff: Administrative Assistant, Ray Minter; Press Secretary, Marti Thomas; Personal Secretary, Debby McBride.
Committees: Armed Services; Science, Space & Technology.

Alabama 3rd — East — Annistan; Auburn. The district vote for George Bush was 60% in 1988.

CQ Voting Studies

	1989	1990
Presidential	54%	41%
Party	68%	74%
Participation	98%	99%

Interest Groups

	1988	1989
ADA		44%
ACU		58%
AFL-CIO		63%
CCUS		70%

Elections

	1989*	1990
General	65%	74%
Primary	63%	u/o

*Special election.

George E. Brown, Jr.   (D-Calif.)
Of Riverside • Elected 1962

Born: March 6, 1920, Holtville, Calif.
Education: El Centro Junior College, 1938; U.C.L.A., B.A. 1946.
Military Career: Army, 1942-46.
Occupation: Management consultant; physicist.
Family: Widowed; four children.
Religion: Methodist.
Political Career: Monterey Park City Council, 1954-55; mayor of Monterey Park, 1955-58; Calif. Assembly, 1959-63; sought Democratic nomination for U.S. Senate, 1970; reelected to House, 1972.

Capitol Office: 2188 Rayburn House Office Building 20515; 225-6161.
Office Staff: Administrative Assistant, Pete Didisheim; Press Secretary, Maria Padian; Office Manager/Appointments Secretary, Ruth Hogue.
Committees: Agriculture; Science, Space & Technology (Chairman).

California 36th — San Bernadino; Riverside. The district vote for George Bush was 51% in 1988.

CQ Voting Studies

	1989	1990
Presidential	31%	19%
Party	87%	79%
Participation	91%	87%

Interest Groups

	1988	1989
ADA	80%	75%
ACU	5%	0%
AFL-CIO	100%	100%
CCUS	25%	40%

Elections

	1988	1990
General	54%	53%
Primary	82%	u/o

Terry L. Br
Of Olney • El(

Born: March ;
Education: U.
Illinois, J.D. 19(
Occupation: L
Family: Wife, (
children.
Religion: Metr
Political Caree
Democratic no
1978.

Capitol Office:
Office Building .
Office Staff: Co
Co-Director, Mi
Secretary, Mike
Denise Shotwell.
Committees: En(
Science, Space &

Illinois 19th — S(
Champaign-Urba
George Bush was

CQ Voting Studies

	1989	19
Presidential	24%	1;
Party	70%	8!
Participation	72%	9

Interest Groups

	1988	1!
ADA	85%	7
ACU	9%	1
AFL-CIO	100%	9
CCUS	27%	3

Elections

	1988	1
General	61%	6
Primary	u/o	

Jim Bunning (R-Ky.)
Of Fort Thomas • Elected 1986

Born: October 23, 1931, Campbell
County, Ky.
Education: Xavier U., B.S. 1953.
Occupation: Professional baseball player;
investment broker.
Family: Wife, Mary Catherine Theis; nine
children.
Religion: Roman Catholic.
Political Career: Fort Thomas City
Council, 1977-79; Ky. Senate, 1979-83;
Republican nominee for governor, 1983.

Capitol Office: 116 Cannon House
Office Building 20515; 225-3465.
Office Staff: Administrative Assistant,
David A. York; Press Secretary, Richard
Robinson; Office Manager/Executive
Secretary, Joan L. Manning.
Committees: Ways & Means.

Kentucky 4th — Louisville Suburbs;
Covington; Newport. The district vote for
George Bush was 65% in 1988.

CQ Voting Studies

	1989	1990
Presidential	78%	71%
Party	95%	94%
Participation	98%	97%

Interest Groups

	1988	1989
ADA	0%	5%
ACU	100%	96%
AFL-CIO	8%	17%
CCUS	100%	100%

Elections

	1988	1990
General	74%	69%
Primary	u/o	u/o

Dan Burton (R-Ind.)
Of Indianapolis • Elected 1982

Born: June 21, 1938, Indianapolis, Ind.
Education: Indiana U., 1958-59; Cincinnati Bible Seminary, 1959-60.
Military Career: Army, 1956-57; Army Reserve, 1957-62.
Occupation: Real estate and insurance agent.
Family: Wife, Barbara Logan; three children.
Religion: Protestant.
Political Career: Ind. House, 1967-69; Ind. Senate, 1969-71; Republican nominee for U.S. House, 1970; sought Republican nomination for U.S. House, 1972; Ind. House, 1977-81; Ind. Senate, 1981-83.

Capitol Office: 120 Cannon House Office Building 20515; 225-2276.
Office Staff: Administrative Assistant, Jim Atterholt; Press Secretary, Kevin Binger; Executive Assistant/Scheduler, Leah Tolson.
Committees: Foreign Affairs; Post Office & Civil Service; Veterans' Affairs.

Indiana 6th — Northern Indianapolis; Anderson. The district vote for George Bush was 69% in 1988.

CQ Voting Studies

	1989	1990
Presidential	60%	77%
Party	85%	95%
Participation	92%	97%

Interest Groups

	1988	1989
ADA	0%	5%
ACU	100%	96%
AFL-CIO	0%	17%
CCUS	93%	90%

Elections

	1988	1990
General	73%	63%
Primary	u/o	u/o

Albert G. Bustamante (D-Texas)

Of San Antonio • Elected 1984

Born: April 8, 1935, Asherton, Texas.
Education: Sul Ross State College, B.A.
1961.
Military Career: Army, 1954-56.
Occupation: Teacher.
Family: Wife, Rebecca Pounders; three
children.
Religion: Roman Catholic.
Political Career: Bexar County
commissioner, 1972-78; Bexar County
judge, 1978-83.

Capitol Office: 1116 Longworth House
Office Building 20515; 225-4511.
Office Staff: Administrative Assistant, Ella
Wong-Rusinko; Press Secretary,
Benjamin Harrison; Office Manager, Rose
Ann Felty.
Committees: Armed Services;
Government Operations.

Texas 23rd — Southwest — San Antonio
Suburbs; Laredo. The district vote for
George Bush was 50% in 1988.

CQ Voting Studies

	1989	1990
Presidential	40%	25%
Party	86%	85%
Participation	92%	91%

Interest Groups

	1988	1989
ADA	70%	80%
ACU	8%	4%
AFL-CIO	100%	100%
CCUS	21%	30%

Elections

	1988	1990
General	65%	63%
Primary	u/o	u/o

CQ Voting Studies

	1989	1990
Presidential	71%	48%
Party	54%	59%
Participation	98%	94%

Interest Groups

	1988	1989
ADA	30%	15%
ACU	68%	64%
AFL-CIO	77%	25%
CCUS	69%	100%

Elections

	1988	1990
General	75%	65%
Primary	81%	64%

Beverly B. Byron (D-Md.)
Of Frederick • Elected 1978

Born: July 27, 1932, Baltimore, Md.
Education: Hood College, 1963-64.
Occupation: Civic leader.
Family: Husband, Kirk Walsh; three children.
Religion: Episcopalian.
Political Career: No previous office.

Capitol Office: 2430 Rayburn House Office Building 20515; 225-2721.
Office Staff: Administrative Assistant, Brent Ayer; Press Secretary, Beau Wright; Executive Assistant/Intern Coordinator, Etta Becker.
Committees: Armed Services; Interior & Insular Affairs.

Maryland 6th — West — Hagerstown; Cumberland. The district vote for George Bush was 65% in 1988.

Sonny Callahan (R-Ala.)
Of Mobile • Elected 1984

Born: September 11, 1932, Mobile, Ala.
Education: McGill High School, Mobile, graduated 1950.
Military Career: Navy, 1952-54.
Occupation: Moving and storage company executive.
Family: Wife, Karen Reed; six children.
Religion: Roman Catholic.
Political Career: Ala. House, served as Democrat, 1971-79; Ala. Senate, served as Democrat, 1979-83; sought Democratic nomination for lieutenant governor, 1982.

Capitol Office: 1330 Longworth House Office Building 20515; 225-4931.
Office Staff: Administrative Assistant/Press Secretary, Jo Bonner; Appointments Secretary, Billie LaBarbera.
Committees: Energy & Commerce; Merchant Marine & Fisheries.

Alabama 1st — Southwest — Mobile. The district vote for George Bush was 62% in 1988.

CQ Voting Studies

	1989	1990
Presidential	73%	63%
Party	73%	73%
Participation	96%	94%

Interest Groups

	1988	1989
ADA	10%	0%
ACU	96%	93%
AFL-CIO	29%	9%
CCUS	93%	100%

Elections

	1988	1990
General	59%	u/o
Primary	u/o	u/o

Dave Camp (R-Mich.)
Of Midland • Elected 1990

Born: July 9, 1953, Midland, Mich.
Education: Albion College, B.A. 1975; U. of California, San Diego, J.D. 1978.
Occupation: Congressional aide; lawyer.
Family: Single.
Religion: Roman Catholic.
Political Career: Mich. House, 1989-91.

Capitol Office: 511 Cannon House Office Building 20515; 225-3561.
Office Staff: Administrative Assistant, John Guzik; Press Secretary, Rob Rehg; Scheduler, Lyle Hagan.
Committees: Agriculture; Small Business.

Michigan 10th — North Central — Midland. The district vote for George Bush was 58% in 1988.

Elections

	1990
General	66%
Primary	33%

Ben Nighthorse Campbell
(D-Colo.)
Of Ignacio • Elected 1986

Born: April 13, 1933, Auburn, Calif.
Education: San Jose State, B.A. 1957;
Meiji U., Tokyo, 1960-64.
Military Career: Air Force, 1951-53.
Occupation: Jewelry designer; rancher;
horse trainer; teacher.
Family: Wife, Linda Price; two children.
Religion: Unspecified.
Political Career: Colo. House, 1983-87.

Capitol Office: 1530 Longworth House
Office Building 20515; 225-4761.
Office Staff: Administrative Assistant,
Ken Lane; Press Secretary, Carol Knight;
Executive Assistant/Scheduler, Jane
Wilson.
Committees: Agriculture; Interior &
Insular Affairs.

Colorado 3rd — Western Slope; Pueblo.
The district vote for George Bush was
52% in 1988.

CQ Voting Studies

	1989	1990
Presidential	45%	35%
Party	70%	72%
Participation	94%	95%

Interest Groups

	1988	1989
ADA	65%	50%
ACU	21%	36%
AFL-CIO	92%	64%
CCUS	43%	60%

Elections

	1988	1990
General	78%	70%
Primary	u/o	u/o

Tom Campbell (R-Calif.)
Of Stanford • Elected 1988

Born: August 14, 1952, Chicago, Ill.
Education: U. of Chicago, B.A., M.A.
1973; Harvard U., J.D. 1976; U. of
Chicago, Ph.D. 1980.
Occupation: Economist; professor.
Family: Wife, Susanne Martin.
Religion: Roman Catholic.
Political Career: No previous office.

Capitol Office: 313 Cannon House
Office Building 20515; 225-5411.
Office Staff: Chief of Staff, Karin
Miranda; Press Secretary, Greg Stohr;
Executive Assistant, Lisa Colvin Schmidt.
Committees: Banking, Finance & Urban
Affairs; Judiciary; Science, Space &
Technology.

California 12th — Parts of San Mateo and
Santa Clara Counties. The district vote for
George Bush was 49% in 1988.

CQ Voting Studies

	1989	1990
Presidential	56%	50%
Party	47%	69%
Participation	99%	97%

Interest Groups

	1989
ADA	40%
ACU	50%
AFL-CIO	17%
CCUS	100%

Elections

	1988	1990
General	52%	61%
Primary	58%	u/o

Benjamin L. Cardin   (D-Md.)
Of Baltimore • Elected 1986

Born: October 5, 1943, Baltimore, Md.
Education: U. of Pittsburgh, B.A. 1964; U. of Maryland, LL.B. 1967.
Occupation: Lawyer.
Family: Wife, Myrna Edelman; two children.
Religion: Jewish.
Political Career: Md. House, 1967-87; Speaker, 1979-87.

Capitol Office: 117 Cannon House Office Building 20515; 225-4016.
Office Staff: Administrative Assistant, David Koshgarian; Press Secretary, Dawana Merritt; Office Manager/Scheduler, Marli Heimann.
Committees: Ways & Means.

Maryland 3rd — Baltimore; Northern and Southern Suburbs. The district vote for George Bush was 45% in 1988.

CQ Voting Studies

	1989	1990
Presidential	36%	21%
Party	94%	95%
Participation	98%	99%

Interest Groups

	1988	1989
ADA	90%	90%
ACU	4%	7%
AFL-CIO	93%	100%
CCUS	36%	30%

Elections

	1988	1990
General	73%	70%
Primary	86%	83%

CQ Voting Studies

	1989	1990
Presidential	41%	23%
Party	85%	88%
Participation	99%	99%

Interest Groups

	1988	1989
ADA	75%	80%
ACU	24%	21%
AFL-CIO	77%	83%
CCUS	64%	50%

Elections

	1988	1990
General	68%	67%
Primary	u/o	90%

Thomas R. Carper (D-Del.)
Of Wilmington • Elected 1982

Born: January 23, 1947, Beckley, W.Va.
Education: Ohio State U., B.A. 1968; U. of Delaware, M.B.A. 1975.
Military Career: Navy, 1968-73; Naval Reserve, 1973-present.
Occupation: Public official.
Family: Wife, Martha Ann Stacy; one child.
Religion: Presbyterian.
Political Career: Del. treasurer, 1977-83.

Capitol Office: 131 Cannon House Office Building 20515; 225-4165.
Office Staff: Administrative Assistant, Ed Freel; Communications Director, Jeff Bullock; Office Manager, Heidi Glenn.
Committees: Banking, Finance & Urban Affairs; Merchant Marine & Fisheries.

Delaware — At Large. The district vote for George Bush was 56% in 1988.

Bob Carr (D-Mich.)
Of East Lansing • Elected 1974

Born: March 27, 1943, Janesville, Wis.
Education: U. of Wisconsin, B.S. 1965; U. of Wisconsin, J.D. 1968.
Occupation: Lawyer.
Family: Divorced.
Religion: Baptist.
Political Career: Democratic nominee for U.S. House, 1972; Democratic nominee for U.S. House, 1980; reelected, 1982.

Capitol Office: 2439 Rayburn House Office Building 20515; 225-4872.
Office Staff: Chief of Staff, Diane Blagman; Press Secretary, Mark Folse; Executive Assistant/Office Manager, Beverly Swain.
Committees: Appropriations.

Michigan 6th — Central — Lansing; Pontiac. The district vote for George Bush was 57% in 1988.

CQ Voting Studies

	1989	1990
Presidential	30%	29%
Party	80%	81%
Participation	94%	96%

Interest Groups

	1988	1989
ADA	80%	85%
ACU	21%	25%
AFL-CIO	93%	67%
CCUS	46%	50%

Elections

	1988	1990
General	59%	u/o
Primary	u/o	u/o

Rod D. Chandler (R-Wash.)
Of Bellevue • Elected 1982

Born: July 13, 1942, La Grande, Ore.
Education: Eastern Oregon State College, 1961-62; Oregon State U., B.S. 1968.
Military Career: Oregon National Guard, 1959-64.
Occupation: Public relations consultant; banker; television newscaster.
Family: Wife, Joyce Elaine Laremore; two children.
Religion: Unspecified.
Political Career: Wash. House, 1975-83.

Capitol Office: 223 Cannon House Office Building 20515; 225-7761.
Office Staff: Chief of Staff, Steve Tupper; Press Secretary, Steve Witter; Appointments Secretary, Linda Suter.
Committees: Post Office & Civil Service; Ways & Means.

Washington 8th — Seattle Suburbs — Bellevue. The district vote for George Bush was 55% in 1988.

CQ Voting Studies

	1989	1990
Presidential	62%	59%
Party	71%	71%
Participation	97%	95%

Interest Groups

	1988	1989
ADA	45%	15%
ACU	56%	70%
AFL-CIO	29%	9%
CCUS	93%	100%

Elections

	1988	1990
General	71%	56%
Primary	70%	58%

Jim Chapman (D-Texas)
Of Sulphur Springs • Elected 1985

Born: March 8, 1945, Washington, D.C.
Education: U. of Texas, B.A. 1968;
Southern Methodist U., J.D. 1970.
Occupation: Lawyer.
Family: Wife, Betty Brice; two children.
Religion: Methodist.
Political Career: District attorney, 8th
Judicial District of Texas, 1977-85; sought
Democratic nomination for Texas Senate,
1984.

Capitol Office: 236 Cannon House
Office Building 20515; 225-3035.
Office Staff: Administrative Assistant,
Billy Moore; Press Secretary, Sara
Anderson; Executive
Assistant/Scheduler, Leslie Schindel.
Committees: Appropriations.

Texas 1st — Northeast — Texarkana. The
district vote for George Bush was 53% in
1988.

CQ Voting Studies

	1989	1990
Presidential	49%	34%
Party	70%	71%
Participation	93%	92%

Interest Groups

	1988	1989
ADA	50%	50%
ACU	52%	39%
AFL-CIO	71%	50%
CCUS	64%	60%

Elections

	1988	1990
General	62%	61%
Primary	u/o	u/o

William L. Clay (D-Mo.)
Of St. Louis • Elected 1968

Born: April 30, 1931, St. Louis, Mo.
Education: St. Louis U., B.S. 1953.
Military Career: Army, 1953-55.
Occupation: Real estate broker; insurance executive.
Family: Wife, Carol Ann Johnson; three children.
Religion: Roman Catholic.
Political Career: St. Louis Board of Aldermen, 1959-64; St. Louis Democratic Committee member, 1964-67.

Capitol Office: 2470 Rayburn House Office Building 20515; 225-2406.
Office Staff: Administrative Assistant/Press Secretary, Jerome Williams.
Committees: House Administration; Education & Labor; Post Office & Civil Service (Chairman).

Missouri 1st — North St. Louis; Northeast St. Louis County. The district vote for George Bush was 27% in 1988.

CQ Voting Studies

	1989	1990
Presidential	28%	16%
Party	71%	75%
Participation	91%	89%

Interest Groups

	1988	1989
ADA	90%	95%
ACU	0%	0%
AFL-CIO	100%	92%
CCUS	18%	33%

Elections

	1988	1990
General	72%	61%
Primary	u/o	u/o

Bob Clement (D-Tenn.)
Of Nashville • Elected 1988

Born: September 23, 1943, Nashville, Tenn.
Education: U. of Tennessee, B.S. 1967; Memphis State U., M.B.A. 1968.
Military Career: Army, 1969-71; Tenn. Army National Guard, 1971-present.
Occupation: Former college president.
Family: Wife, Mary Carson; four children.
Religion: Methodist.
Political Career: Tenn. Public Service Commission, 1973-79; sought Democratic nomination for governor, 1978; Democratic nominee for U.S. House, 1982.

Capitol Office: 325 Cannon House Office Building 20515; 225-4311.
Office Staff: Administrative Assistant, David Flanders; Press Secretary, Bart Herbison; Executive Assistant, Carolyn Waugh.
Committees: Merchant Marine & Fisheries; Public Works & Transportation.

Tennessee 5th — Nashville. The district vote for George Bush was 52% in 1988.

CQ Voting Studies

	1989	1990
Presidential	42%	25%
Party	74%	85%
Participation	96%	98%

Interest Groups

	1988	1989
ADA	75%	60%
ACU	20%	19%
AFL-CIO	93%	64%
CCUS	36%	50%

Elections

	1988	1990
General	u/o	72%
Primary	u/o	u/o

William F. Clinger   (R-Pa.)
Of Warren • Elected 1978

Born: April 4, 1929, Warren, Penn.
Education: Johns Hopkins U., B.A. 1951;
U. of Virginia, LL.B. 1965.
Military Career: Navy, 1951-55.
Occupation: Lawyer.
Family: Wife, Julia Whitla; four children.
Religion: Presbyterian.
Political Career: No previous office.

Capitol Office: 2160 Rayburn House
Office Building 20515; 225-5121.
Office Staff: Administrative Assistant, Jim
Clarke; Press Secretary, David Fuscus;
Personal Secretary, Nancy Scott.
Committees: Government Operations;
Public Works & Transportation.

Pennsylvania 23rd — Northwest, Central
— State College. The district vote for
George Bush was 56% in 1988.

CQ Voting Studies

	1989	1990
Presidential	78%	66%
Party	66%	65%
Participation	99%	95%

Interest Groups

	1988	1989
ADA	25%	20%
ACU	63%	64%
AFL-CIO	62%	17%
CCUS	86%	100%

Elections

	1988	1990
General	62%	59%
Primary	u/o	u/o

Howard Coble (R-N.C.)
Of Greensboro • Elected 1984

Born: March 18, 1931, Greensboro, N.C.
Education: Appalachian State U., 1949-50; Guilford College, A.B. 1958; U. of North Carolina, J.D. 1962.
Military Career: Coast Guard, 1952-56; Coast Guard Reserve, 1960-82.
Occupation: Lawyer; insurance agent.
Family: Single.
Religion: Presbyterian.
Political Career: Guilford County assistant attorney, 1967-69; N.C. House, 1969; assistant U.S. attorney, 1969-73; commissioner, N.C. Department of Revenue, 1973-77; Republican nominee for N.C. treasurer, 1976; N.C. House, 1979-83.

Capitol Office: 430 Cannon House Office Building 20515; 225-3065.
Office Staff: Administrative Assistant/Press Secretary, Edward McDonald; Executive Assistant, Rochelle Goldman.
Committees: Judiciary; Merchant Marine & Fisheries.

North Carolina 6th — Central — Greensboro; High Point. The district vote for George Bush was 61% in 1988.

CQ Voting Studies

	1989	1990
Presidential	81%	68%
Party	94%	92%
Participation	99%	99%

Interest Groups

	1988	1989
ADA	10%	10%
ACU	92%	82%
AFL-CIO	21%	8%
CCUS	93%	100%

Elections

	1988	1990
General	62%	67%
Primary	u/o	u/o

Ronald D. Coleman (D-Texas)
Of El Paso • Elected 1982

Born: November 29, 1941, El Paso, Texas.
Education: U. of Texas, El Paso, B.A. 1963;
U. of Texas, Austin, J.D. 1967.
Military Career: Army, 1967-69.
Occupation: Lawyer.
Family: Divorced; two children.
Religion: Presbyterian.
Political Career: Texas House, 1973-83.

Capitol Office: 440 Cannon House
Office Building 20515; 225-4831.
Office Staff: Administrative
Assistant/Press Secretary, Paul Rogers;
Personal Secretary, Karen Brooke.
Committees: Appropriations.

Texas 16th — West — El Paso. The
district vote for George Bush was 48% in
1988.

CQ Voting Studies

	1989	1990
Presidential	35%	20%
Party	90%	90%
Participation	96%	97%

Interest Groups

	1988	1989
ADA	80%	75%
ACU	17%	18%
AFL-CIO	93%	91%
CCUS	29%	22%

Elections

	1988	1990
General	u/o	96%
Primary	u/o	u/o

Tom Coleman (R-Mo.)

Of Kansas City • Elected 1976

Born: May 29, 1943, Kansas City, Mo.
Education: William Jewell College, A.B. 1965; New York U., M.P.A. 1966; Washington U., J.D. 1969.
Occupation: Lawyer.
Family: Wife, Marilyn Anderson; three children.
Religion: Protestant.
Political Career: Assistant attorney general, 1969-72; candidate for Clay County clerk, 1970; Mo. House, 1973-77.

Capitol Office: 2468 Rayburn House Office Building 20515; 225-7041.
Office Staff: Executive Assistant, Dennis Lambert; Press Secretary, Craig Orfield; Office Manager, Lyn Gunsalus.
Committees: Agriculture; Education & Labor.

Missouri 6th — Northwest — St. Joseph. The district vote for George Bush was 50% in 1988.

CQ Voting Studies

	1989	1990
Presidential	67%	64%
Party	70%	75%
Participation	95%	98%

Interest Groups

	1988	1989
ADA	25%	5%
ACU	76%	78%
AFL-CIO	64%	25%
CCUS	93%	100%

Elections

	1988	1990
General	59%	52%
Primary	90%	84%

Elections

	1990
General	88%
Primary	34%

Barbara-Rose Collins (D-Mich.)
Of Detroit • Elected 1990

Born: April 13, 1939, Detroit, Mich.
Education: Wayne State U., attended.
Occupation: Public official.
Family: Widowed; two children.
Religion: Shrine of the Black Madonna (Pan-African Orthodox Christian).
Political Career: Detroit Public School Board, 1971-73; Mich. House, 1975-81; Detroit City Council, 1982-91.

Capitol Office: 1541 Longworth House Office Building 20515; 225-2261.
Office Staff: Administrative Assistant, Marvin McGraw.
Committees: Public Works & Transportation; Science, Space & Technology.

Michigan 13th — Downtown Detroit. The district vote for George Bush was 14% in 1988.

Cardiss Collins (D-Ill.)
Of Chicago • Elected 1973

Born: September 24, 1931, St. Louis, Mo.
Education: Northwestern U., 1949-50.
Occupation: Auditor.
Family: Widow of Rep. George W. Collins; one child.
Religion: National Baptist.
Political Career: No previous office.

Capitol Office: 2264 Rayburn House Office Building 20515; 225-5006.
Office Staff: Administrative Assistant, Bud Myers; Executive Assistant, Gerri Houston.
Committees: Energy & Commerce; Government Operations.

Illinois 7th — Chicago — Downtown; West Side. The district vote for George Bush was 22% in 1988.

CQ Voting Studies

	1989	1990
Presidential	14%	10%
Party	51%	87%
Participation	52%	88%

Interest Groups

	1988	1989
ADA	90%	40%
ACU	0%	0%
AFL-CIO	100%	100%
CCUS	21%	57%

Elections

	1988	1990
General	u/o	80%
Primary	89%	82%

CQ Voting Studies

	1989	1990
Presidential	85%	78%
Party	73%	82%
Participation	100%	98%

Interest Groups

	1988	1989
ADA	0%	0%
ACU	92%	96%
AFL-CIO	21%	0%
CCUS	93%	90%

Elections

	1988	1990
General	68%	u/o
Primary	u/o	u/o

Larry Combest (R-Texas)
Of Lubbock • Elected 1984

Born: March 20, 1945, Memphis, Texas.
Education: West Texas State U., B.B.A. 1969.
Occupation: Farmer, stockman, agriculture specialist; congressional aide; electronics wholesaler.
Family: Wife, Sharon McCurry; two children.
Religion: Methodist.
Political Career: Republican Party county chairman, 1970-71.

Capitol Office: 1527 Longworth House Office Building 20515; 225-4005.
Office Staff: Administrative Assistant, Trudi L. Boyd; Press Secretary, Keith Williams; Office Manager, Lynn Cowart.
Committees: Agriculture; District of Columbia; Select Intelligence; Small Business.

Texas 19th — Northwest — Lubbock; Odessa. The district vote for George Bush was 67% in 1988.

Gary Condit   (D-Calif.)
Of Ceres • Elected 1989

Born: April 21, 1948, Salina, Okla.
Education: Modesto Junior College; California State College, Stanislaus, B.A. 1972.
Occupation: Public official.
Family: Wife, Carolyn Berry; two children.
Religion: Baptist.
Political Career: Ceres City Council, 1972-76; mayor of Ceres, 1974-76; Stanislaus County Board of Supervisors, 1976-82; chairman, 1980; Calif. Assembly, 1983-89.

Capitol Office: 1529 Longworth House Office Building 20515; 225-6131.
Office Staff: Administrative Assistant, Tony Corbo; Press Secretary, Wendy Kandarian; Personal Secretary, Camille Johnson.
Committees: Agriculture; Government Operations.

California 15th — Mid-San Joaquin Valley — Modesto. The district vote for George Bush was 52% in 1988.

CQ Voting Studies

	1989	1990
Presidential	35%	25%
Party	83%	70%
Participation	96%	95%

Interest Groups

	1988	1989
ADA		n/a
ACU		33%
AFL-CIO		100%
CCUS		50%

Elections

	1989*	1990
General	57%	66%
Primary		u/o

*Special election.

CQ Voting Studies

	1989	1990
Presidential	43%	31%
Party	24%	27%
Participation	98%	97%

Interest Groups

	1988	1989
ADA	90%	75%
ACU	8%	32%
AFL-CIO	93%	92%
CCUS	46%	40%

Elections

	1988	1990
General	83%	78%
Primary	u/o	u/o

Silvio O. Conte (R-Mass.)
Of Pittsfield • Elected 1958

Born: November 9, 1921, Pittsfield, Mass.
Education: Boston College, LL.B. 1949.
Military Career: Navy, 1942-44.
Occupation: Lawyer.
Family: Wife, Corinne Duval; four children.
Religion: Roman Catholic.
Political Career: Mass. Senate, 1951-59.

Capitol Office: 2300 Rayburn House Office Building 20515; 225-5335.
Office Staff: Office Manager, Marjorie Kelaher; Press Secretary, John Larkin; Appointments Secretary, Nancy Fox.
Committees: Appropriations (Ranking); Small Business.

Massachusetts 1st — West — Berkshire Hills; Pioneer Valley. The district vote for George Bush was 41% in 1988.

John Conyers, Jr. (D-Mich.)
Of Detroit • Elected 1964

Born: May 16, 1929, Detroit, Mich.
Education: Wayne State U., B.A. 1957;
Wayne State U., LL.B. 1958.
Military Career: National Guard, 1948-
52; Army, 1952-53; Army Reserve, 1953-
57.
Occupation: Lawyer.
Family: Single.
Religion: Baptist.
Political Career: Candidate for mayor of
Detroit, 1989.

Capitol Office: 2426 Rayburn House
Office Building 20515; 225-5126.
Office Staff: Administrative
Assistant/Office Manager, Joann E.
Wright; Press Secretary, Robert S.
Weiner; Scheduler, Terri Holloman.
Committees: Government Operations
(Chairman); Judiciary; Small Business.

Michigan 1st — Detroit — North
Central; Highland Park. The district vote
for George Bush was 9% in 1988.

CQ Voting Studies

	1989	1990
Presidential	14%	16%
Party	72%	86%
Participation	68%	89%

Interest Groups

	1988	1989
ADA	90%	90%
ACU	0%	5%
AFL-CIO	100%	88%
CCUS	21%	30%

Elections

	1988	1990
General	91%	91%
Primary	u/o	u/o

Jim Cooper (D-Tenn.)
Of Shelbyville • Elected 1982

Born: June 19, 1954, Shelbyville, Tenn.
Education: U. of North Carolina, B.A. 1975; Oxford U., B.A. 1977; Oxford U., M.A. 1977; Harvard U., J.D. 1980.
Occupation: Lawyer.
Family: Wife, Martha Hays.
Religion: Episcopalian.
Political Career: No previous office.

Capitol Office: 125 Cannon House Office Building 20515; 225-6831.
Office Staff: Administrative Assistant, David Withrow; Personal Secretary, Vera Lou Durigon.
Committees: Budget; Energy & Commerce.

Tennessee 4th — Northeast and South Central. The district vote for George Bush was 57% in 1988.

CQ Voting Studies

	1989	1990
Presidential	48%	37%
Party	78%	74%
Participation	96%	99%

Interest Groups

	1988	1989
ADA	70%	60%
ACU	28%	21%
AFL-CIO	79%	58%
CCUS	69%	60%

Elections

	1988	1990
General	u/o	67%
Primary	u/o	u/o

Jerry F. Costello (D-Ill.)
Of Belleville • Elected 1988

Born: September 25, 1949, East St. Louis, Ill.

Education: Belleville Area College, A.A. 1970; Maryville College of the Sacred Heart, B.A. 1972.

Occupation: Law enforcement administrator.

Family: Wife, Georgia Cockrum; three children.

Religion: Roman Catholic.

Political Career: St. Clair County Board chairman, 1980-88.

Capitol Office: 119 Cannon House Office Building 20515; 225-5661.

Office Staff: Administrative Assistant, Matt Melucci; Press Secretary, Brian Lott; Scheduler, Cindy O'Flaherty.

Committees: Public Works & Transportation; Science, Space & Technology.

Illinois 21st — Southwest — East St. Louis; Alton. The district vote for George Bush was 46% in 1988.

CQ Voting Studies

	1989	1990
Presidential	36%	26%
Party	79%	86%
Participation	98%	99%

Interest Groups

	1988	1989
ADA	n/a	70%
ACU	57%	18%
AFL-CIO	100%	92%
CCUS	n/a	40%

Elections

	1988	1990
General	53%	66%
Primary	46%	u/o

CQ Voting Studies

	1989	1990
Presidential	69%	58%
Party	67%	68%
Participation	97%	96%

Interest Groups

	1988	1989
ADA	50%	30%
ACU	48%	57%
AFL-CIO	64%	17%
CCUS	79%	90%

Elections

	1988	1990
General	67%	60%
Primary	u/o	u/o

Lawrence Coughlin (R-Pa.)
Of Plymouth Meeting • Elected 1968
Pronounced COFF lin

Born: April 11, 1929, Wilkes-Barre, Penn.
Education: Yale U., B.A. 1950; Harvard U., M.B.A. 1954; Temple U., LL.B. 1958.
Military Career: Marine Corps Reserve, 1948-58; Marine Corps Reserve, active duty, 1951-52.
Occupation: Lawyer.
Family: Wife, Susan MacGregor; four children.
Religion: Episcopalian.
Political Career: Pa. House, 1965-67; Pa. Senate, 1967-69.

Capitol Office: 2309 Rayburn House Office Building 20515; 225-6111.
Office Staff: Administrative Assistant, Lorraine Howerton; Press Secretary, Peter Holran; Scheduler, Peter Holran.
Committees: Appropriations.

Pennsylvania 13th — Northwest Philadelphia Suburbs — The Main Line. The district vote for George Bush was 56% in 1988.

C. Christopher Cox (R-Calif.)
Of Newport Beach • Elected 1988

Born: October 16, 1952, St. Paul, Minn.
Education: U. of Southern California,
B.A. 1973; Harvard U., M.B.A. 1977;
Harvard U., J.D. 1977.
Occupation: White House counsel.
Family: Single.
Religion: Roman Catholic.
Political Career: No previous office.

Capitol Office: 412 Cannon House
Office Building 20515; 225-5611.
Office Staff: Chief of Staff, Jan Fujiwara;
Press Secretary, Peter Slen; Personal
Assistant, Linda Hansen.
Committees: Government Operations;
Public Works & Transportation.

California 40th — Coastal and Central
Orange County. The district vote for
George Bush was 68% in 1988.

CQ Voting Studies

	1989	1990
Presidential	71%	75%
Party	85%	86%
Participation	97%	95%

Interest Groups

	1989
ADA	5%
ACU	96%
AFL-CIO	8%
CCUS	90%

Elections

	1988	1990
General	67%	68%
Primary	31%	u/o

John W. Cox, Jr. (D-Ill.)
Of Galena • Elected 1990

Born: July 10, 1947, Hazel Green, Wis.
Education: U. of Wisconsin, Platteville, B.S. 1969; John Marshall School of Law, J.D. 1975.
Military Career: Army, 1969-70.
Occupation: Lawyer.
Family: Wife, Bonnie Aide; three children.
Religion: Roman Catholic.
Political Career: Jo Daviess County state's attorney, 1977-85.

Capitol Office: 501 Cannon House Office Building 20515; 225-5676.
Office Staff: Administrative Assistant, Joan Mooney; Press Secretary, Mary Anne Presman; Scheduler, Lonna Hamilton.
Committees: Banking, Finance & Urban Affairs; Government Operations.

Illinois 16th — Northwest — Rockford. The district vote for George Bush was 58% in 1988.

Elections

	1990
General	55%
Primary	33%

William J. Coyne (D-Pa.)
Of Pittsburgh • Elected 1980

Born: August 24, 1936, Pittsburgh, Penn.
Education: Robert Morris College, B.S.
1965.
Military Career: Army, 1955-57.
Occupation: Accountant.
Family: Single.
Religion: Roman Catholic.
Political Career: Pa. House, 1971-73;
sought Democratic nomination for Pa.
Senate, 1972; Pittsburgh City Council,
1974-81.

Capitol Office: 2455 Rayburn House
Office Building 20515; 225-2301.
Office Staff: Administrative Assistant,
Coleman J. Conroy; Press Secretary, Paul
Gordon; Appointments
Secretary/Receptionist, Elisa Howie.
Committees: Ways & Means.

Pennsylvania 14th — Pittsburgh. The
district vote for George Bush was 26% in
1988.

CQ Voting Studies

	1989	1990
Presidential	30%	17%
Party	96%	93%
Participation	97%	95%

Interest Groups

	1988	1989
ADA	95%	100%
ACU	0%	4%
AFL-CIO	100%	100%
CCUS	31%	10%

Elections

	1988	1990
General	79%	72%
Primary	u/o	u/o

Bud Cramer (D-Ala.)
Of Huntsville • Elected 1990

Born: August 22, 1947, Huntsville, Ala.
Education: U. of Alabama, B.A. 1969; U. of Alabama, J.D. 1972.
Occupation: Lawyer.
Family: Widowed; one child.
Religion: Methodist.
Political Career: Madison County district attorney, 1981-91.

Capitol Office: 1431 Longworth House Office Building 20515; 225-4801.
Office Staff: Administrative Assistant/Press Secretary, Mike Adcock; Scheduler, Wendy Conrad.
Committees: Public Works & Transportation; Science, Space & Technology.

Alabama 5th — North — Huntsville. The district vote for George Bush was 59% in 1988.

Elections

	1990
General	67%
Primary	60%

Philip M. Crane (R-Ill.)
Of McHenry • Elected 1969

Born: November 3, 1930, Chicago, Ill.
Education: DePauw U., 1948-50; Hillsdale College, B.A. 1951; U. of Michigan, 1952-54; U. of Vienna, Austria, 1953; U. of Vienna, Austria, 1956; Indiana U., M.A. 1961; Indiana U., Ph.D. 1963.
Military Career: Army, 1954-56.
Occupation: Professor of history; author; advertising manager.
Family: Wife, Arlene Catherine Johnson; eight children.
Religion: Protestant.
Political Career: Sought Republican nomination for president, 1980.

Capitol Office: 1035 Longworth House Office Building 20515; 225-3711.
Office Staff: Administrative Assistant, Robert C. Coleman; Press Secretary, Robert Foster; Executive Assistant, Kathy Bell.
Committees: Ways & Means.

Illinois 12th — Far Northwest Cook County Suburbs — Palatine. The district vote for George Bush was 71% in 1988.

CQ Voting Studies

	1989	1990
Presidential	63%	84%
Party	86%	89%
Participation	90%	91%

Interest Groups

	1988	1989
ADA	0%	5%
ACU	100%	100%
AFL-CIO	0%	0%
CCUS	93%	90%

Elections

	1988	1990
General	75%	82%
Primary	u/o	u/o

Randy ''Duke'' Cunningham
(R-Calif.)
Of Chula Vista • Elected 1990

Born: December 8, 1941, Los Angeles, Calif.
Education: U. of Missouri, B.A. 1964; National U., M.B.A. 1985; U. of Missouri, M.A. 1979.
Military Career: Navy, 1967-87.
Occupation: Computer software executive.
Family: Wife, Nancy Jones; three children.
Religion: Christian.
Political Career: No previous office.

Capitol Office: 1017 Longworth House Office Building 20515; 225-5452.
Office Staff: Administrative Assistant, Frank Collins.
Committees: Armed Services; Merchant Marine & Fisheries.

California 44th — Central San Diego. The district vote for George Bush was 47% in 1988.

Elections

	1990
General	46%
Primary	45%

William E. Dannemeyer
(R-Calif.)
Of Fullerton • Elected 1978

Born: September 22, 1929, South Gate, Calif.
Education: Santa Maria Junior College, 1946-47; Valparaiso U., B.A. 1950; U. of California, J.D. 1952.
Military Career: Army, 1952-54.
Occupation: Lawyer.
Family: Wife, Evelyn Hoemann; three children.
Religion: Lutheran.
Political Career: Calif. Assembly, served as a Democrat, 1963-67; Democratic nominee for Calif. Senate, 1966; Republican nominee for Calif. Senate, 1972; Calif. Assembly, 1976-77.

Capitol Office: 2351 Rayburn House Office Building 20515; 225-4111.
Office Staff: Administrative Assistant, Linda O'Connor; Press Secretary, Paul Mero; Executive Assistant, Emily Schruhl.
Committees: Budget; Energy & Commerce.

California 39th — Northern Orange County — Anaheim; Fullerton. The district vote for George Bush was 71% in 1988.

CQ Voting Studies

	1989	1990
Presidential	70%	75%
Party	87%	93%
Participation	92%	96%

Interest Groups

	1988	1989
ADA	0%	5%
ACU	100%	100%
AFL-CIO	0%	0%
CCUS	92%	89%

Elections

	1988	1990
General	74%	65%
Primary	85%	u/o

George "Buddy" Darden
(D-Ga.)
Of Marietta • Elected 1983

Born: November 22, 1943, Hancock Co., Ga.
Education: U. of Georgia, B.A. 1965; U. of Georgia, J.D. 1967.
Occupation: Lawyer.
Family: Wife, Lillian Budd; two children.
Religion: Methodist.
Political Career: Cobb County district attorney, 1973-77; Ga. House, 1981-83.

Capitol Office: 228 Cannon House Office Building 20515; 225-2931.
Office Staff: Office Manager, Dotti Mavromatis; Press Secretary, Eric Johnson.
Committees: Armed Services; Interior & Insular Affairs.

Georgia 7th — Northwest — Rome; Marietta. The district vote for George Bush was 70% in 1988.

CQ Voting Studies

	1989	1990
Presidential	56%	43%
Party	72%	75%
Participation	99%	99%

Interest Groups

	1988	1989
ADA	45%	35%
ACU	50%	43%
AFL-CIO	64%	50%
CCUS	64%	90%

Elections

	1988	1990
General	65%	60%
Primary	u/o	u/o

Robert W. Davis (R-Mich.)
Of Gaylord • Elected 1978

Born: July 31, 1932, Marquette, Mich.
Education: Northern Michigan U., 1950-52; Hillsdale College, 1951-52; Wayne State U. College of Mortuary Science, B.S. 1954.
Occupation: Funeral director.
Family: Separated; four children.
Religion: Episcopalian.
Political Career: St. Ignace City Council, 1964-66; Mich. House, 1967-71; Mich. Senate, 1971-79; Senate Republican leader, 1974-79.

Capitol Office: 2417 Rayburn House Office Building 20515; 225-4735.
Office Staff: Administrative Assistant, Pat White; Press Secretary, Bill Blaul; Office Manager/Personal Secretary, Cindy Harrington.
Committees: Armed Services; Merchant Marine & Fisheries (Ranking).

Michigan 11th — Upper Peninsula; Northern Lower Peninsula. The district vote for George Bush was 52% in 1988.

CQ Voting Studies

	1989	1990
Presidential	52%	44%
Party	41%	46%
Participation	88%	95%

Interest Groups

	1988	1989
ADA	60%	40%
ACU	42%	54%
AFL-CIO	100%	82%
CCUS	29%	60%

Elections

	1988	1990
General	60%	61%
Primary	u/o	u/o

E. "Kika" de la Garza (D-Texas)
Of Mission • Elected 1964

Born: September 22, 1927, Mercedes, Texas.
Education: St. Mary's U. of San Antonio, LL.B. 1952.
Military Career: Navy, 1945-46; Army, 1950-52.
Occupation: Lawyer.
Family: Wife, Lucille Alamia; three children.
Religion: Roman Catholic.
Political Career: Texas House, 1953-65.

Capitol Office: 1401 Longworth House Office Building 20515; 225-2531.
Office Staff: Administrative Assistant, Bernice McGuire; Press Secretary, James A. Davis; Scheduler, Rika Spangler.
Committees: Agriculture (Chairman).

Texas 15th — South — McAllen. The district vote for George Bush was 37% in 1988.

CQ Voting Studies

	1989	1990
Presidential	43%	24%
Party	74%	84%
Participation	91%	92%

Interest Groups

	1988	1989
ADA	50%	50%
ACU	20%	21%
AFL-CIO	73%	73%
CCUS	50%	56%

Elections

	1988	1990
General	94%	u/o
Primary	u/o	u/o

Peter A. DeFazio (D-Ore.)
Of Springfield • Elected 1986
Pronounced da FAH zee oh

Born: May 27, 1947, Needham, Mass.
Education: Tufts U., B.A. 1969; U. of Oregon, 1969-71; U. of Oregon, M.S. 1977.
Military Career: Air Force, 1967-71.
Occupation: Congressional aide.
Family: Wife, Myrnie L. Daut.
Religion: Roman Catholic.
Political Career: Lane County commissioner, 1982-86.

Capitol Office: 1233 Longworth House Office Building 20515; 225-6416.
Office Staff: Administrative Assistant, Doug Marker; Press Secretary, Bob Hennessey; Executive Assistant/Scheduler, John Avina.
Committees: Interior & Insular Affairs; Public Works & Transportation.

Oregon 4th — Southwest — Eugene. The district vote for George Bush was 44% in 1988.

CQ Voting Studies

	1989	1990
Presidential	23%	19%
Party	89%	86%
Participation	97%	95%

Interest Groups

	1988	1989
ADA	80%	95%
ACU	13%	7%
AFL-CIO	86%	92%
CCUS	25%	40%

Elections

	1988	1990
General	72%	86%
Primary	u/o	u/o

Rosa DeLauro (D-Conn.)
Of New Haven • Elected 1990
Pronounced da LAUR oh

Born: March 2, 1943, New Haven, Conn.
Education: London School of Economics, 1962-63; Marymount College, B.A. 1964; Columbia U., M.A. 1966.
Occupation: Political activist.
Family: Husband, Stanley Greenberg; three children.
Religion: Roman Catholic.
Political Career: No previous office.

Capitol Office: 327 Cannon House Office Building 20515; 225-3661.
Office Staff: Administrative Assistant, Paul Frick; Press Secretary, David Eichenbaum; Appointments Secretary, Nancy Mulry.
Committees: Government Operations; Public Works & Transportation.

Connecticut 3rd — South — New Haven. The district vote for George Bush was 50% in 1988.

Elections

	1990
General	52%
Primary	u/o

Tom DeLay (R-Texas)
Of Sugar Land • Elected 1984

Born: April 8, 1947, Laredo, Texas.
Education: Baylor U., 1965-67; U. of Houston, B.S. 1970.
Occupation: Pest control company owner.
Family: Wife, Christine Ann Furrh; one child.
Religion: Baptist.
Political Career: Texas House, 1979-85.

Capitol Office: 308 Cannon House Office Building 20515; 225-5951.
Office Staff: Administrative Assistant, Ken Carroll; Press Secretary, Trish Brink; Office Manager, Lori Soika.
Committees: Appropriations.

Texas 22nd — Southwest Houston and Suburbs; Fort Bend and Brazoria Counties. The district vote for George Bush was 62% in 1988.

CQ Voting Studies

	1989	1990
Presidential	79%	83%
Party	87%	91%
Participation	95%	98%

Interest Groups

	1988	1989
ADA	0%	0%
ACU	100%	96%
AFL-CIO	0%	0%
CCUS	92%	80%

Elections

	1988	1990
General	67%	71%
Primary	u/o	u/o

CQ Voting Studies

	1989	1990
Presidential	23%	15%
Party	93%	87%
Participation	95%	95%

Interest Groups

	1988	1989
ADA	100%	100%
ACU	0%	0%
AFL-CIO	100%	100%
CCUS	23%	20%

Elections

	1988	1990
General	67%	61%
Primary	u/o	u/o

Ronald V. Dellums   (D-Calif.)
Of Oakland • Elected 1970

Born: November 24, 1935, Oakland, Calif.
Education: San Francisco State College,
B.A. 1960; U. of California, M.S.W. 1962.
Military Career: Marine Corps, 1954-56.
Occupation: Psychiatric social worker.
Family: Wife, Leola Roscoe Higgs; three
children.
Religion: Protestant.
Political Career: Berkeley City Council,
1967-71.

Capitol Office: 2136 Rayburn House
Office Building 20515; 225-2661.
Office Staff: Administrative Assistant,
Carlottia Scott; Press Secretary, Max
Miller; Staff Assistant, Denise Lewis.
Committees: Armed Services; District of
Columbia (Chairman).

California 8th — Northern Alameda
County — Oakland; Berkeley. The
district vote for George Bush was 29% in
1988.

Butler Derrick (D-S.C.)
Of Edgefield • Elected 1974

Born: September 30, 1936, Springfield, Mass.
Education: U. of South Carolina, 1954-58; U. of Georgia, LL.B. 1965.
Occupation: Lawyer.
Family: Wife, Beverly Grantham; four children.
Religion: Episcopalian.
Political Career: S.C. House, 1969-75.

Capitol Office: 201 Cannon House Office Building 20515; 225-5301.
Office Staff: Administrative Assistant, Leo Coco; Press Secretary, Carrie Rowell; Executive Assistant, Connie Jameson.
Committees: Rules.

South Carolina 3rd — West — Anderson; Aiken. The district vote for George Bush was 66% in 1988.

CQ Voting Studies

	1989	1990
Presidential	43%	31%
Party	79%	81%
Participation	97%	97%

Interest Groups

	1988	1989
ADA	70%	35%
ACU	36%	43%
AFL-CIO	71%	50%
CCUS	54%	80%

Elections

	1988	1990
General	54%	58%
Primary	u/o	u/o

CQ Voting Studies

	1989	1990
Presidential	71%	66%
Party	80%	82%
Participation	92%	94%

Interest Groups

	1988	1989
ADA	20%	5%
ACU	92%	85%
AFL-CIO	38%	17%
CCUS	100%	100%

Elections

	1988	1990
General	94%	51%
Primary	u/o	u/o

Bill Dickinson (R-Ala.)
Of Montgomery • Elected 1964

Born: June 5, 1925, Opelika, Ala.
Education: U. of Alabama, LL.B. 1950.
Military Career: Navy, 1943-46; Air Force Reserve.
Occupation: Railroad executive; judge; lawyer.
Family: Wife, Barbara Edwards; four children.
Religion: Methodist.
Political Career: Opelika city judge, 1951-53; Lee County Court of Common Pleas and Juvenile Court judge, 1953-59; 5th Judicial Circuit judge, 1959-63.

Capitol Office: 2406 Rayburn House Office Building 20515; 225-2901.
Office Staff: Administrative Assistant, Clay Swanzy; Press Secretary, Mike Lewis; Appointments Secretary, Wendy Craine.
Committees: House Administration; Armed Services (Ranking).

Alabama 2nd — Southeast — Montgomery; Dothan. The district vote for George Bush was 62% in 1988.

Norm Dicks (D-Wash.)
Of Bremerton • Elected 1976

Born: December 16, 1940, Bremerton, Wash.
Education: U. of Washington, B.A. 1963; U. of Washington, J.D. 1968.
Occupation: Congressional aide.
Family: Wife, Suzanne Callison; two children.
Religion: Lutheran.
Political Career: No previous office.

Capitol Office: 2429 Rayburn House Office Building 20515; 225-5916.
Office Staff: Office Manager, Pam Gell; Press Secretary, George Behan; Scheduler, Julie Wirkkala.
Committees: Appropriations.

Washington 6th — Puget Sound — Bremerton; Tacoma. The district vote for George Bush was 48% in 1988.

CQ Voting Studies

	1989	1990
Presidential	38%	28%
Party	91%	91%
Participation	96%	98%

Interest Groups

	1988	1989
ADA	85%	75%
ACU	9%	7%
AFL-CIO	86%	91%
CCUS	36%	40%

Elections

	1988	1990
General	68%	61%
Primary	69%	58%

John D. Dingell   (D-Mich.)
Of Trenton • Elected 1955

Born: July 8, 1926, Colorado Springs, Colo.
Education: Georgetown U., B.S. 1949; Georgetown U., LL.B. 1952.
Military Career: Army, 1944-46.
Occupation: Lawyer.
Family: Wife, Deborah Insley; four children.
Religion: Roman Catholic.
Political Career: Assistant Wayne County prosecutor, 1953-55.
Capitol Office: 2328 Rayburn House Office Building 20515; 225-4071.
Office Staff: Administrative Assistant, Eleanor G. Lewis; Communications Director, Dennis B. Fitzgibbons; Scheduling Assistant, Lorren Jewell.
Committees: Energy & Commerce (Chairman).

Michigan 16th — Southeast Wayne County; Monroe County. The district vote for George Bush was 54% in 1988.

CQ Voting Studies

	1989	1990
Presidential	35%	20%
Party	81%	87%
Participation	90%	93%

Interest Groups

	1988	1989
ADA	80%	75%
ACU	13%	8%
AFL-CIO	100%	82%
CCUS	29%	20%

Elections

	1988	1990
General	97%	67%
Primary	u/o	u/o

Julian C. Dixon (D-Calif.)

Of Culver City • Elected 1978

Born: August 8, 1934, Washington, D.C.
Education: California State U., Los Angeles, B.S. 1962; Southwestern U., LL.B. 1967.
Military Career: Army, 1957-60.
Occupation: Legislative aide; lawyer.
Family: Wife, Betty Lee; one child.
Religion: Episcopalian.
Political Career: Calif. Assembly, 1973-79.

Capitol Office: 2400 Rayburn House Office Building 20515; 225-7084.
Office Staff: Administrative Assistant/Press Secretary, Andrea Tracy Holmes; Personal Secretary, Deanne Clarke.
Committees: Appropriations; Standards of Official Conduct (Chairman).

California 28th — Southern Los Angeles; Culver City. The district vote for George Bush was 26% in 1988.

CQ Voting Studies

	1989	1990
Presidential	29%	20%
Party	87%	89%
Participation	88%	94%

Interest Groups

	1988	1989
ADA	85%	85%
ACU	0%	0%
AFL-CIO	100%	100%
CCUS	25%	40%

Elections

	1988	1990
General	76%	73%
Primary	u/o	u/o

CQ Voting Studies

	1989	1990
Presidential	33%	26%
Party	85%	82%
Participation	94%	93%

Interest Groups

	1988	1989
ADA	80%	75%
ACU	8%	12%
AFL-CIO	100%	92%
CCUS	23%	30%

Elections

	1988	1990
General	81%	u/o
Primary	86%	u/o

Brian Donnelly (D-Mass.)
Of Dorchester • Elected 1978

Born: March 2, 1946, Dorchester, Mass.
Education: Boston U., B.S. 1970.
Occupation: High school teacher and football coach.
Family: Wife, Virginia Norton; two children.
Religion: Roman Catholic.
Political Career: Mass. House, 1973-79; assistant majority leader, 1977-79.

Capitol Office: 2229 Rayburn House Office Building 20515; 225-3215.
Office Staff: Press Secretary, Gary Galanis; Executive Assistant, Kathi Raftery.
Committees: Ways & Means.

Massachusetts 11th — Part of Boston and South Shore Suburbs. The district vote for George Bush was 47% in 1988.

Calvin Dooley (D-Calif.)
Of Visalia • Elected 1990

Born: January 11, 1954, Visalia, Calif.
Education: U. of Calif., Davis, B.S. 1977;
Stanford U., M.A. 1987.
Occupation: Farmer.
Family: Wife, Linda Phillips; two children.
Religion: Protestant.
Political Career: No previous office.

Capitol Office: 1022 Rayburn House
Office Building 20515; 225-3341.
Office Staff: Administrative Assistant, Lisa
Quigley; Press Secretary, Tim Miller; Staff
Assistant, Jonathan Alexander.
Committees: Agriculture; Small Business.

California 17th — Southern San Joaquin
Valley. The district vote for George Bush
was 59% in 1988.

Elections

	1990
General	55%
Primary	59%

Elections

	1990
General	51%
Primary	u/o

John T. Doolittle (R-Calif.)
Of Rocklin • Elected 1990

Born: October 30, 1950, Glendale, Calif.
Education: U. of California, Santa Cruz, B.A. 1972; U. of the Pacific, J.D. 1978.
Occupation: Lawyer.
Family: Wife, Julia Harlow; one child.
Religion: Morman.
Political Career: Calif. Senate, 1981-91.

Capitol Office: 1223 Rayburn House Office Building 20515; 225-2511.
Office Staff: Administrative Assistant, David Lopez; Press Secretary, Eric Schultzky; Executive Assistant, Martha Franco.
Committees: Interior & Insular Affairs; Merchant Marine & Fisheries.

California 14th — Northeastern California — Part of San Joaquin County. The district vote for George Bush was 59% in 1988.

Byron L. Dorgan (D-N.D.)
Of Bismarck • Elected 1980

Born: May 14, 1942, Regent, N.D.
Education: U. of North Dakota, B.S. 1965;
U. of Denver, M.B.A. 1966.
Occupation: Public official.
Family: Wife, Kimberly Olson; three
children.
Religion: Lutheran.
Political Career: N.D. tax commissioner,
1969-80; Democratic nominee for U.S.
House, 1974.

Capitol Office: 203 Cannon House
Office Building 20515; 225-2611.
Office Staff: Administrative Assistant,
Susan Brophy; Press Secretary, Marc
Kimball; Executive Secretary, Mary Beth
Buchholz.
Committees: Ways & Means.

North Dakota — At Large. The district
vote for George Bush was 56% in 1988.

CQ Voting Studies

	1989	1990
Presidential	24%	17%
Party	83%	82%
Participation	96%	97%

Interest Groups

	1988	1989
ADA	75%	85%
ACU	17%	21%
AFL-CIO	93%	75%
CCUS	38%	30%

Elections

	1988	1990
General	71%	65%
Primary	u/o	93%

CQ Voting Studies

	1989	1990
Presidential	70%	68%
Party	81%	83%
Participation	91%	93%

Interest Groups

	1988	1989
ADA	0%	0%
ACU	100%	96%
AFL-CIO	7%	10%
CCUS	91%	100%

Elections

	1988	1990
General	60%	58%
Primary	u/o	u/o

Robert K. Dornan   (R-Calif.)
Of Garden Grove • Elected 1976

Born: April 3, 1933, New York, N.Y.
Education: Loyola U., Los Angeles, 1950-53.
Military Career: Air Force, 1953-58.
Occupation: Broadcast journalist and producer.
Family: Wife, Sallie Hansen; five children.
Religion: Roman Catholic.
Political Career: Candidate for mayor of Los Angeles, 1973; U.S. House, 1977-83; sought Republican nomination for U.S. Senate, 1982; reelected to House, 1984.

Capitol Office: 301 Cannon House Office Building 20515; 225-2965.
Office Staff: Administrative Assistant, Paul Morrell; Press Secretary, Paul Morrell; Office Manager, Maggie Fogarty.
Committees: Armed Services; Select Intelligence.

California 38th — Northwestern Orange County; Santa Ana; Garden Grove. The district vote for George Bush was 61% in 1988.

Thomas J. Downey (D-N.Y.)
Of Amityville • Elected 1974

Born: January 28, 1949, Ozone Park, N.Y.
Education: Cornell U., B.S. 1970; St. John's U., 1972-74; American U., J.D. 1978.
Occupation: Personnel manager.
Family: Wife, D. Chris Milanos; two children.
Religion: Methodist.
Political Career: Suffolk County Legislature, 1972-75.

Capitol Office: 2232 Rayburn House Office Building 20515; 225-3335.
Office Staff: Administrative Assistant, Kathleen Tynan McLaughlin; Press Secretary, Lawrence Spinelli; Personal Secretary, Jennifer Casey.
Committees: Ways & Means.

New York 2nd — Long Island — Western Suffolk County. The district vote for George Bush was 61% in 1988.

CQ Voting Studies

	1989	1990
Presidential	28%	19%
Party	96%	93%
Participation	98%	98%

Interest Groups

	1988	1989
ADA	100%	95%
ACU	0%	0%
AFL-CIO	86%	100%
CCUS	36%	10%

Elections

	1988	1990
General	62%	56%
Primary	u/o	u/o

CQ Voting Studies

	1989	1990
Presidential	76%	73%
Party	77%	94%
Participation	98%	99%

Interest Groups

	1988	1989
ADA	5%	0%
ACU	100%	96%
AFL-CIO	0%	0%
CCUS	92%	100%

Elections

	1988	1990
General	69%	64%
Primary	u/o	u/o

David Dreier (R-Calif.)
Of La Verne • Elected 1980

Born: July 5, 1952, Kansas City, Mo.
Education: Claremont McKenna College, B.A. 1975; Claremont Graduate School, M.A. 1976.
Occupation: Real estate developer.
Family: Single.
Religion: Christian Scientist.
Political Career: Republican nominee for U.S. House, 1978.

Capitol Office: 409 Cannon House Office Building 20515; 225-2305.
Office Staff: Staff Director/Press Secretary, Brad Smith; Personal Assistant, Carol Maltman.
Committees: Rules.

California 33rd — Eastern Los Angeles — Pomona; Whittier. The district vote for George Bush was 62% in 1988.

John J. "Jimmy" Duncan, Jr.
(R-Tenn.)
Of Knoxville • Elected 1988

Born: July 21, 1947, Lebanon, Tenn.
Education: U. of Tennessee, B.S. 1969;
George Washington U., J.D. 1973.
Military Career: Army National Guard,
1970-87.
Occupation: Lawyer; judge.
Family: Wife, Lynn Hawkins; four
children.
Religion: Presbyterian.
Political Career: Knox County criminal
court judge, 1980-88.

Capitol Office: 115 Cannon House
Office Building 20515; 225-5435.
Office Staff: Administrative Assistant,
Judy Whitbred; Press Secretary, Jim
Edwards; Appointments Secretary, Susan
Butler.
Committees: Banking, Finance & Urban
Affairs; Interior & Insular Affairs; Public
Works & Transportation.

Tennessee 2nd — East — Knoxville. The
district vote for George Bush was 64% in
1988.

CQ Voting Studies

	1989	1990
Presidential	64%	74%
Party	73%	87%
Participation	99%	100%

Interest Groups

	1989
ADA	20%
ACU	75%
AFL-CIO	33%
CCUS	90%

Elections

	1988	1990
General	56%	81%
Primary	87%	u/o

Richard J. Durbin (D-Ill.)
Of Springfield • Elected 1982

Born: November 21, 1944, East St. Louis, Ill.
Education: Georgetown U., B.S. 1966; Georgetown U., J.D. 1969.
Occupation: Lawyer; congressional and legislative aide.
Family: Wife, Loretta Schaefer; three children.
Religion: Roman Catholic.
Political Career: Democratic nominee for Ill. Senate, 1976; Democratic nominee for lieutenant governor, 1978.

Capitol Office: 129 Cannon House Office Building 20515; 225-5271.
Office Staff: Administrative Assistant, Ed Greelegs; Press Secretary, Melissa Batty; Personal Secretary, Kathy Brooks.
Committees: Appropriations; Budget.

Illinois 20th — Central — Springfield; Decatur; Quincy. The district vote for George Bush was 51% in 1988.

CQ Voting Studies

	1989	1990
Presidential	24%	16%
Party	95%	91%
Participation	99%	97%

Interest Groups

	1988	1989
ADA	90%	95%
ACU	16%	4%
AFL-CIO	100%	83%
CCUS	36%	30%

Elections

	1988	1990
General	69%	66%
Primary	u/o	u/o

Bernard J. Dwyer (D-N.J.)
Of Edison • Elected 1980

Born: January 24, 1921, Perth Amboy, N.J.
Education: Rutgers U..
Military Career: Navy, 1940-45.
Occupation: Insurance salesman and executive.
Family: Wife, Lilyan Sudzina; one child.
Religion: Roman Catholic.
Political Career: Edison Township Council, 1958-69; mayor of Edison, 1969-73; N.J. Senate, 1974-80; majority leader, 1980.

Capitol Office: 2428 Rayburn House Office Building 20515; 225-6301.
Office Staff: Administrative Assistant/Press Secretary, Lyle B. Dennis; Executive Assistant, Karen M. Kearns.
Committees: Appropriations; Budget.

New Jersey 6th — Central—New Brunswick, Perth Amboy. The district vote for George Bush was 53% in 1988.

CQ Voting Studies

	1989	1990
Presidential	34%	19%
Party	91%	87%
Participation	96%	93%

Interest Groups

	1988	1989
ADA	85%	80%
ACU	4%	0%
AFL-CIO	100%	92%
CCUS	31%	40%

Elections

	1988	1990
General	61%	51%
Primary	u/o	88%

CQ Voting Studies

	1989	1990
Presidential	29%	11%
Party	88%	87%
Participation	92%	92%

Interest Groups

	1988	1989
ADA	90%	90%
ACU	0%	0%
AFL-CIO	100%	83%
CCUS	23%	20%

Elections

	1988	1990
General	72%	67%
Primary	85%	73%

Mervyn M. Dymally (D-Calif.)
Of Compton • Elected 1980
Pronounced DIE mal ee

Born: May 12, 1926, Cedros, Trinidad.
Education: California State U., Los
Angeles, B.A. 1954; California State U.,
Sacramento, M.A. 1969; U.S.
International U., Ph.D. 1978.
Occupation: Special education teacher.
Family: Wife, Alice M. Gueno; two
children.
Religion: Episcopalian.
Political Career: Calif. Assembly, 1963-
67; Calif. Senate, 1967-75; lieutenant
governor, 1975-79; defeated for re-
election, 1978.

Capitol Office: 1717 Longworth House
Office Building 20515; 225-5425.
Office Staff: Administrative Assistant,
Vacant; Press Secretary, Marwan Burgan;
Special Assistant, Brenda S. Young.
Committees: District of Columbia;
Foreign Affairs; Post Office & Civil
Service.

California 31st — Southern Los Angeles
County — Compton; Carson. The district
vote for George Bush was 34% in 1988.

Joseph D. Early (D-Mass.)
Of Worcester • Elected 1974

Born: January 31, 1933, Worcester, Mass.
Education: College of the Holy Cross, B.S. 1955.
Military Career: Navy, 1955-57.
Occupation: Teacher and basketball coach.
Family: Wife, Marilyn Powers; eight children.
Religion: Roman Catholic.
Political Career: Mass. House, 1963-75.

Capitol Office: 2349 Rayburn House Office Building 20515; 225-6101.
Office Staff: Administrative Assistant, Fred Rhodes; Press Secretary, Mark Provost; Office Manager/Appointments Secretary, Diedre McMorris.
Committees: Appropriations.

Massachusetts 3rd — Central — Worcester. The district vote for George Bush was 50% in 1988.

CQ Voting Studies

	1989	1990
Presidential	23%	28%
Party	74%	78%
Participation	89%	90%

Interest Groups

	1988	1989
ADA	85%	80%
ACU	8%	20%
AFL-CIO	100%	73%
CCUS	36%	40%

Elections

	1988	1990
General	u/o	u/o
Primary	u/o	u/o

Dennis E. Eckart (D-Ohio)
Of Mentor • Elected 1980

Born: April 6, 1950, Cleveland, Ohio.
Education: Xavier U., B.S. 1971;
Cleveland State U., J.D. 1974.
Occupation: Lawyer.
Family: Wife, Sandra Pestotnik; one child.
Religion: Roman Catholic.
Political Career: Assistant prosecutor,
Lake County, 1974; Ohio House, 1975-81.

Capitol Office: 1111 Longworth House
Office Building 20515; 225-6331.
Office Staff: Administrative Assistant,
Greg Means; Office Manager/Executive
Secretary, Carol Simons.
Committees: Energy & Commerce; Small
Business.

Ohio 11th — Northeast — Cleveland
Suburbs. The district vote for George
Bush was 55% in 1988.

CQ Voting Studies

	1989	1990
Presidential	31%	20%
Party	87%	83%
Participation	99%	98%

Interest Groups

	1988	1989
ADA	90%	90%
ACU	8%	18%
AFL-CIO	100%	83%
CCUS	29%	40%

Elections

	1988	1990
General	61%	66%
Primary	u/o	u/o

Chet Edwards (D-Texas)
Of Waco • Elected 1990

Born: November 24, 1951, Corpus
Christi, Texas.
Education: Texas A&M U., B.A. 1974;
Harvard U., M.B.A. 1981.
Occupation: Radio station owner.
Family: Single.
Religion: Methodist.
Political Career: Sought Democratic
nomination for U.S. House, 1978; Texas
Senate, 1983-91.

Capitol Office: 425 Cannon House
Office Building 20515; 225-6105.
Office Staff: Administrative
Assistant/Press Secretary, Jay Neel;
Personal Secretary, Renatta Lynch.
Committees: Armed Services; Veterans'
Affairs.

Texas 11th — Central — Waco. The
district vote for George Bush was 58% in
1988.

Elections

	1990
General	53%
Primary	u/o

Don Edwards (D-Calif.)
Of San Jose • Elected 1962

Born: January 6, 1915, San Jose, Calif.
Education: Stanford U., A.B. 1936; Stanford U. Law School, 1936-38.
Military Career: Navy, 1942-45.
Occupation: Title company executive; lawyer; FBI agent.
Family: Wife, Edith Wilkie; five children.
Religion: Unitarian.
Political Career: No previous office.

Capitol Office: 2307 Rayburn House Office Building 20515; 225-3072.
Office Staff: Administrative Assistant/Press Secretary, Roberta Haeberle; Office Manager, Doris Barnes.
Committees: Judiciary; Veterans' Affairs.

California 10th — Southeast Bay Area — Downtown San Jose; Fremont. The district vote for George Bush was 44% in 1988.

CQ Voting Studies

	1989	1990
Presidential	27%	17%
Party	93%	92%
Participation	95%	96%

Interest Groups

	1988	1989
ADA	100%	100%
ACU	0%	0%
AFL-CIO	100%	100%
CCUS	23%	20%

Elections

	1988	1990
General	86%	63%
Primary	83%	u/o

Mickey Edwards (R-Okla.)
Of Oklahoma City • Elected 1976

Born: July 12, 1937, Cleveland, Ohio.
Education: U. of Oklahoma, B.S. 1958;
Oklahoma City U., J.D. 1969.
Occupation: Lawyer; journalist.
Family: Wife, Lisa Reagan; three children.
Religion: Episcopalian.
Political Career: Republican nominee for
U.S. House, 1974.

Capitol Office: 2330 Rayburn House
Office Building 20515; 225-2132.
Office Staff: Administrative Assistant,
Susan Cloud; Press Secretary, Craig G.
Veith; Executive Assistant/Scheduler,
Tracy Grant.
Committees: Appropriations.

Oklahoma 5th — North Central — Part
of Oklahoma City; Bartlesville. The
district vote for George Bush was 67% in
1988.

CQ Voting Studies

	1989	1990
Presidential	81%	69%
Party	72%	79%
Participation	91%	89%

Interest Groups

	1988	1989
ADA	10%	0%
ACU	92%	85%
AFL-CIO	36%	18%
CCUS	93%	100%

Elections

	1988	1990
General	72%	70%
Primary	83%	u/o

Bill Emerson (R-Mo.)
Of Cape Girardeau • Elected 1980

Born: January 1, 1938, St. Louis, Mo.
Education: Westminster College, B.A. 1959; U. of Baltimore, LL.B. 1964.
Military Career: Air Force Reserve, 1964-present.
Occupation: Government relations executive.
Family: Wife, Jo Ann Hermann; four children.
Religion: Presbyterian.
Political Career: No previous office.

Capitol Office: 438 Cannon House Office Building 20515; 225-4404.
Office Staff: Executive Assistant, Bill Coffield; Press Secretary, Marianna Rowe; Office Manager, Tricia Schade.
Committees: Agriculture; Public Works & Transportation.

Missouri 8th — Southest — Cape Giradeau. The district vote for George Bush was 55% in 1988.

CQ Voting Studies

	1989	1990
Presidential	78%	57%
Party	75%	65%
Participation	98%	97%

Interest Groups

	1988	1989
ADA	10%	10%
ACU	90%	93%
AFL-CIO	50%	17%
CCUS	83%	100%

Elections

	1988	1990
General	58%	57%
Primary	u/o	u/o

Eliot L. Engel (D-N.Y.)
Of the Bronx • Elected 1988

Born: February 18, 1947, New York, N.Y.
Education: Hunter-Lehman College, B.A.
1969; Lehman College, M.A. 1973; New
York Law School, J.D. 1987.
Occupation: Public official; teacher.
Family: Wife, Patricia Ennis; two children.
Religion: Jewish.
Political Career: N.Y. Assembly, 1977-88.

Capitol Office: 1213 Longworth House
Office Building 20515; 225-2464.
Office Staff: Communications Director,
Frank Pizzurro; Administrative Assistant,
John Calvelli; Office Manager, Pamela
Segal.
Committees: Foreign Affairs; Small
Business.

New York 19th — South Yonkers; East
and Central Bronx. The district vote for
George Bush was 45% in 1988.

CQ Voting Studies

	1989	1990
Presidential	30%	18%
Party	92%	83%
Participation	93%	86%

Interest Groups

	1989
ADA	95%
ACU	4%
AFL-CIO	100%
CCUS	33%

Elections

	1988	1990
General	56%	61%
Primary	48%	72%

CQ Voting Studies

	1989	1990
Presidential	64%	47%
Party	60%	60%
Participation	98%	99%

Interest Groups

	1988	1989
ADA	40%	25%
ACU	60%	68%
AFL-CIO	64%	33%
CCUS	71%	100%

Elections

	1988	1990
General	73%	80%
Primary	84%	u/o

Glenn English   (D-Okla.)
Of Cordell • Elected 1974

Born: November 30, 1940, Cordell, Okla.
Education: Southwestern State College, B.A. 1964.
Military Career: Army Reserve, 1965-71.
Occupation: Petroleum landman.
Family: Wife, Jan Pangle; two children.
Religion: Methodist.
Political Career: No previous office.

Capitol Office: 2206 Rayburn House Office Building 20515; 225-5565.
Office Staff: Special Assistant, Scott Ingham; Press Secretary, Greg Tucker; Legislative Assistant/Personal Secretary, Lee Elliott.
Committees: Agriculture; Government Operations.

Oklahoma 6th — West and Panhandle; Part of Oklahoma City. The district vote for George Bush was 58% in 1988.

Ben Erdreich (D-Ala.)
Of Birmingham • Elected 1982
Pronounced ER dritch

Born: December 9, 1938, Birmingham, Ala.
Education: Yale U., B.A. 1960; U. of Alabama, J.D. 1963.
Military Career: Army, 1963-65.
Occupation: Lawyer.
Family: Wife, Ellen Cooper; two children.
Religion: Jewish.
Political Career: Ala. House, 1971-75; Democratic nominee for U.S. House, 1972; Jefferson County Commission, 1975-83.

Capitol Office: 439 Cannon House Office Building 20515; 225-4921.
Office Staff: Administrative Assistant (Appointments), Judy Weinstein; Press Secretary, Debra Leak.
Committees: Banking, Finance & Urban Affairs; Government Operations.

Alabama 6th — Birmingham and Suburbs. The district vote for George Bush was 57% in 1988.

CQ Voting Studies

	1989	1990
Presidential	49%	37%
Party	71%	73%
Participation	99%	100%

Interest Groups

	1988	1989
ADA	50%	55%
ACU	60%	46%
AFL-CIO	79%	67%
CCUS	64%	50%

Elections

	1988	1990
General	66%	93%
Primary	u/o	u/o

Mike Espy (D-Miss.)
Of Yazoo City • Elected 1986

Born: November 30, 1953, Yazoo City, Miss.
Education: Howard U., B.A. 1975; Santa Clara U., J.D. 1978.
Occupation: Lawyer; businessman.
Family: Wife, Sheila Bell; two children.
Religion: Baptist.
Political Career: Miss. assistant secretary of state, 1980-84; assistant attorney general, 1984-85.

Capitol Office: 216 Cannon House Office Building 20515; 225-5876.
Office Staff: Administrative Assistant, Wardell Townsend; Press Secretary, Mary Dixon; Executive Assistant/Scheduler, Sharron Harris.
Committees: Agriculture; Budget.

Mississippi 2nd — North Central — Mississippi Delta. The district vote for George Bush was 48% in 1988.

CQ Voting Studies

	1989	1990
Presidential	35%	20%
Party	80%	82%
Participation	90%	89%

Interest Groups

	1988	1989
ADA	85%	80%
ACU	12%	16%
AFL-CIO	93%	92%
CCUS	25%	40%

Elections

	1988	1990
General	65%	84%
Primary	88%	u/o

Lane Evans (D-Ill.)
Of Rock Island • Elected 1982

Born: August 4, 1951, Rock Island, Ill.
Education: Augustana College (Ill.), B.A. 1974; Georgetown U., J.D. 1978.
Military Career: Marine Corps, 1969-71.
Occupation: Lawyer.
Family: Single.
Religion: Roman Catholic.
Political Career: No previous office.

Capitol Office: 1121 Longworth House Office Building 20515; 225-5905.
Office Staff: Administrative Assistant, Dennis J. King; Press Secretary, Steve Vetzner; Office Manager, Eda S. Robinson.
Committees: Armed Services; Veterans' Affairs.

Illinois 17th — West — Rock Island; Moline; Galesburg. The district vote for George Bush was 47% in 1988.

CQ Voting Studies

	1989	1990
Presidential	23%	16%
Party	97%	97%
Participation	99%	100%

Interest Groups

	1988	1989
ADA	100%	100%
ACU	0%	7%
AFL-CIO	100%	92%
CCUS	14%	40%

Elections

	1988	1990
General	65%	67%
Primary	u/o	u/o

CQ Voting Studies

	1989	1990
Presidential	40%	24%
Party	89%	88%
Participation	96%	96%

Interest Groups

	1988	1989
ADA	75%	60%
ACU	17%	4%
AFL-CIO	93%	92%
CCUS	36%	20%

Elections

	1988	1990
General	72%	62%
Primary	85%	u/o

Dante B. Fascell (D-Fla.)
Of Miami • *Elected 1954*
Pronounced DON tay fuh SELL

Born: March 9, 1917, Bridgehampton, N.Y.
Education: U. of Miami, J.D. 1938.
Military Career: Army, 1941-46.
Occupation: Lawyer.
Family: Wife, Jeanne-Marie Pelot; two children.
Religion: Protestant.
Political Career: Fla. House, 1951-54.

Capitol Office: 2354 Rayburn House Office Building 20515; 225-4506.
Office Staff: Administrative Assistant, Charles R. O' Regan; Press/Special Assistant, Barbara Burris; Appointment Secretary, Nina Hudson.
Committees: Foreign Affairs (Chairman).

Florida 19th — South — Coral Gables; Key West. The district vote for George Bush was 58% in 1988.

Glen Browder (D-Ala.)
Of Jacksonville • Elected 1989
Pronounced BROW der

Born: January 15, 1943, Sumter, S.C.
Education: Presbyterian College, B.A.
1965; Emory U., M.A. 1971; Emory U.,
Ph.D. 1971.
Occupation: Professor of political
science.
Family: Wife, Rebecca Moore; one child.
Religion: Methodist.
Political Career: Ala. House, 1983-86;
Ala. secretary of state, 1987-89.

Capitol Office: 1221 Longworth House
Office Building 20515; 225-3261.
Office Staff: Administrative Assistant,
Ray Minter; Press Secretary, Marti
Thomas; Personal Secretary, Debby
McBride.
Committees: Armed Services; Science,
Space & Technology.

Alabama 3rd — East — Annistan;
Auburn. The district vote for George
Bush was 60% in 1988.

CQ Voting Studies

	1989	1990
Presidential	54%	41%
Party	68%	74%
Participation	98%	99%

Interest Groups

	1988	1989
ADA		44%
ACU		58%
AFL-CIO		63%
CCUS		70%

Elections

	1989*	1990
General	65%	74%
Primary	63%	u/o

*Special election.

George E. Brown, Jr. (D-Calif.)
Of Riverside • Elected 1962

Born: March 6, 1920, Holtville, Calif.
Education: El Centro Junior College, 1938; U.C.L.A., B.A. 1946.
Military Career: Army, 1942-46.
Occupation: Management consultant; physicist.
Family: Widowed; four children.
Religion: Methodist.
Political Career: Monterey Park City Council, 1954-55; mayor of Monterey Park, 1955-58; Calif. Assembly, 1959-63; sought Democratic nomination for U.S. Senate, 1970; reelected to House, 1972.

Capitol Office: 2188 Rayburn House Office Building 20515; 225-6161.
Office Staff: Administrative Assistant, Pete Didisheim; Press Secretary, Maria Padian; Office Manager/Appointments Secretary, Ruth Hogue.
Committees: Agriculture; Science, Space & Technology (Chairman).

California 36th — San Bernadino; Riverside. The district vote for George Bush was 51% in 1988.

CQ Voting Studies

	1989	1990
Presidential	31%	19%
Party	87%	79%
Participation	91%	87%

Interest Groups

	1988	1989
ADA	80%	75%
ACU	5%	0%
AFL-CIO	100%	100%
CCUS	25%	40%

Elections

	1988	1990
General	54%	53%
Primary	82%	u/o

Terry L. Bruce (D-Ill.)
Of Olney • Elected 1984

Born: March 25, 1944, Olney, Ill.
Education: U. of Illinois, B.S. 1966; U. of Illinois, J.D. 1969.
Occupation: Lawyer; farmer.
Family: Wife, Charlotte Roberts; two children.
Religion: Methodist.
Political Career: Ill. Senate, 1971-85; Democratic nominee for U.S. House, 1978.

Capitol Office: 419 Cannon House Office Building 20515; 225-5001.
Office Staff: Co-Director, Joan Mooney; Co-Director, Michael Bushman; Press Secretary, Mike Casey; Staff Assistant, Denise Shotwell.
Committees: Energy & Commerce; Science, Space & Technology.

Illinois 19th — Southeast — Danville; Champaign-Urbana. The district vote for George Bush was 54% in 1988.

CQ Voting Studies

	1989	1990
Presidential	33%	20%
Party	86%	90%
Participation	99%	99%

Interest Groups

	1988	1989
ADA	75%	75%
ACU	24%	14%
AFL-CIO	100%	83%
CCUS	36%	30%

Elections

	1988	1990
General	64%	66%
Primary	u/o	u/o

CQ Voting Studies

	1989	1990
Presidential	24%	13%
Party	70%	89%
Participation	72%	98%

Interest Groups

	1988	1989
ADA	85%	75%
ACU	9%	12%
AFL-CIO	100%	91%
CCUS	27%	30%

Elections

	1988	1990
General	61%	60%
Primary	u/o	u/o

John Bryant (D-Texas)
Of Dallas • Elected 1982

Born: February 22, 1947, Lake Jackson, Texas.
Education: Southern Methodist U., B.A. 1969; Southern Methodist U., J.D. 1972.
Occupation: Lawyer.
Family: Wife, Janet Elizabeth Watts; three children.
Religion: Methodist.
Political Career: Texas House, 1974-83.

Capitol Office: 208 Cannon House Office Building 20515; 225-2231.
Office Staff: Administrative Assistant, Randy White; Press Secretary, Carlton Carl; Office Manager, Carol Jordan.
Committees: Budget; Energy & Commerce; Judiciary.

Texas 5th — Downtown Dallas; Eastern and Southern Suburbs. The district vote for George Bush was 50% in 1988.

Harris W. Fawell (R-Ill.)
Of Naperville • Elected 1984
Pronounced FAY well

Born: March 25, 1929, West Chicago, Ill.
Education: North Central College, 1947-49; Chicago-Kent College of Law, J.D. 1952.
Occupation: Lawyer.
Family: Wife, Ruth Johnson; three children.
Religion: Methodist.
Political Career: Ill. Senate, 1963-77; candidate for Ill. Supreme Court, 1976.

Capitol Office: 435 Cannon House Office Building 20515; 225-3515.
Office Staff: Chief of Staff/Press Secretary, Alan Mertz; Executive Assistant, Holly Spofford.
Committees: Education & Labor; Science, Space & Technology.

Illinois 13th — Southwest Chicago Suburbs — Downers Grove. The district vote for George Bush was 69% in 1988.

CQ Voting Studies

	1989	1990
Presidential	60%	70%
Party	73%	88%
Participation	98%	99%

Interest Groups

	1988	1989
ADA	40%	10%
ACU	64%	93%
AFL-CIO	14%	0%
CCUS	92%	100%

Elections

	1988	1990
General	70%	66%
Primary	77%	u/o

CQ Voting Studies

	1989	1990
Presidential	35%	19%
Party	95%	91%
Participation	99%	95%

Interest Groups

	1988	1989
ADA	85%	80%
ACU	0%	4%
AFL-CIO	100%	100%
CCUS	29%	20%

Elections

	1988	1990
General	u/o	55%
Primary	u/o	79%

Vic Fazio (D-Calif.)

Of West Sacramento • *Elected 1978*
Pronounced FAY zee o

Born: October 11, 1942, Winchester, Mass.
Education: Union College, B.A. 1965.
Occupation: Journalist.
Family: Wife, Judy Kern; four children.
Religion: Episcopalian.
Political Career: Calif. Assembly, 1975-79.

Capitol Office: 2113 Rayburn House Office Building 20515; 225-5716.
Office Staff: Chief of Staff, Sandra Stuart; Press Secretary, Laura Nichols; Executive Assistant, Vicki Baird.
Committees: Appropriations.

California 4th — Suburban Sacramento to Bay Area. The district vote for George Bush was 51% in 1988.

Edward F. Feighan (D-Ohio)
Of Lakewood • Elected 1982
Pronounced FEE an

Born: October 22, 1947, Lakewood, Ohio.
Education: Borromeo College of Ohio, 1965-66; Loyola University, New Orleans, B.A. 1969; Cleveland-Marshall College of Law, J.D. 1978.
Occupation: Lawyer.
Family: Wife, Nadine Hopwood; four children.
Religion: Roman Catholic.
Political Career: Ohio House, 1973-79; candidate for mayor of Cleveland, 1977; Cuyahoga County Commission, 1979-83.

Capitol Office: 1124 Longworth House Office Building 20515; 225-5731.
Office Staff: Administrative Assistant, Michael J. Rosenberg; Press Secretary, James T. Sweeney; Executive Assistant, George Cody.
Committees: Foreign Affairs; Judiciary.

Ohio 19th — Cleveland Suburbs. The district vote for George Bush was 55% in 1988.

CQ Voting Studies

	1989	1990
Presidential	31%	18%
Party	89%	86%
Participation	93%	90%

Interest Groups

	1988	1989
ADA	95%	90%
ACU	0%	4%
AFL-CIO	100%	100%
CCUS	38%	40%

Elections

	1988	1990
General	70%	65%
Primary	u/o	85%

Jack Fields (R-Texas)
Of Humble • Elected 1980

Born: February 3, 1952, Humble, Texas.
Education: Baylor U., B.A. 1974; Baylor U., J.D. 1977.
Occupation: Lawyer; cemetery executive.
Family: Wife, Lynn Hughes; one child, one stepchild.
Religion: Baptist.
Political Career: No previous office.

Capitol Office: 108 Cannon House Office Building 20515; 225-4901.
Office Staff: Administrative Assistant, Robert E.H. Ferguson; Press Secretary, Bryan H. Wirwicz; Personal Secretary, Judy Alvarez.
Committees: Energy & Commerce; Merchant Marine & Fisheries.

Texas 8th — Houston Suburbs; Eastern Harris County. The district vote for George Bush was 53% in 1988.

CQ Voting Studies

	1989	1990
Presidential	78%	79%
Party	88%	92%
Participation	96%	95%

Interest Groups

	1988	1989
ADA	0%	0%
ACU	100%	96%
AFL-CIO	0%	8%
CCUS	100%	100%

Elections

	1988	1990
General	u/o	u/o
Primary	u/o	u/o

Hamilton Fish, Jr. (R-N.Y.)
Of Millbrook • Elected 1968

Born: June 3, 1926, Washington, D.C.
Education: Harvard U., A.B. 1949; New York U., LL.B. 1957.
Military Career: Naval Reserve, 1944-46.
Occupation: Lawyer.
Family: Wife, Mary Ann Knauss; four children.
Religion: Episcopalian.
Political Career: Republican nominee for U.S. House, 1966.

Capitol Office: 2269 Rayburn House Office Building 20515; 225-5441.
Office Staff: Administrative Assistant, Nicholas Hayes; Press Secretary, Fred Stokeld; Appointments Secretary, Heather Whyte.
Committees: Judiciary (Ranking).

New York 21st — Hudson Valley — Poughkeepsie. The district vote for George Bush was 62% in 1988.

CQ Voting Studies

	1989	1990
Presidential	65%	42%
Party	37%	44%
Participation	92%	93%

Interest Groups

	1988	1989
ADA	60%	45%
ACU	32%	41%
AFL-CIO	86%	42%
CCUS	71%	70%

Elections

	1988	1990
General	75%	71%
Primary	u/o	u/o

Floyd H. Flake (D-N.Y.)
Of Queens • Elected 1986

Born: January 30, 1945, Los Angeles, Calif.
Education: Wilberforce U., B.A. 1967;
Payne Theological Seminary, 1968-70;
Northeastern U., 1974-75; St. John's U.,
1982-85.
Occupation: Minister.
Family: Wife, M. Elaine McCollins; four
children.
Religion: African Methodist Episcopal.
Political Career: No previous office.

Capitol Office: 1034 Longworth House
Office Building 20515; 225-3461.
Office Staff: Chief of Staff, Edwin Reed;
Appointments Secretary, Arlene Gibbs.
Committees: Banking, Finance & Urban
Affairs; Small Business.

New York 6th — Southern Queens —
Ozone Park; Jamaica. The district vote for
George Bush was 28% in 1988.

CQ Voting Studies

	1989	1990
Presidential	27%	14%
Party	85%	85%
Participation	89%	89%

Interest Groups

	1988	1989
ADA	95%	95%
ACU	0%	4%
AFL-CIO	100%	100%
CCUS	30%	30%

Elections

	1988	1990
General	86%	73%
Primary	u/o	u/o

Thomas M. Foglietta (D-Pa.)
Of Philadelphia • Elected 1980
Pronounced fo lee ET ah

Born: December 3, 1928, Philadelphia, Penn.
Education: St. Joseph's College, B.A. 1949; Temple U., J.D. 1952.
Occupation: Lawyer.
Family: Single.
Religion: Roman Catholic.
Political Career: Philadelphia City Council, 1955-75; Republican nominee for mayor of Philadelphia, 1975.

Capitol Office: 231 Cannon House Office Building 20515; 225-4731.
Office Staff: Administrative Assistant/Press Secretary, Anthony Green; Executive Assistant, Ann Wagner.
Committees: Armed Services; Foreign Affairs; Merchant Marine & Fisheries.

Pennsylvania 1st — South and Central Philadelphia. The district vote for George Bush was 35% in 1988.

CQ Voting Studies

	1989	1990
Presidential	28%	24%
Party	91%	92%
Participation	92%	97%

Interest Groups

	1988	1989
ADA	90%	95%
ACU	4%	0%
AFL-CIO	92%	100%
CCUS	42%	40%

Elections

	1988	1990
General	76%	79%
Primary	u/o	83%

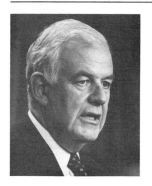

Thomas S. Foley (D-Wash.)
Of Spokane • Elected 1964

Born: March 6, 1929, Spokane, Wash.
Education: U. of Washington, B.A. 1951;
U. of Washington, LL.B. 1957.
Occupation: Lawyer.
Family: Wife, Heather Strachan.
Religion: Roman Catholic.
Political Career: No previous office.

Capitol Office: 1201 Longworth House
Office Building 20515; 225-2006.
Office Staff: Administrative Assistant,
Susan Moos; Press Secretary, Jeffrey R.
Biggs; Scheduler, Mary Beth Schultheis.
Committees: Speaker of the House.

Washington 5th — East — Spokane. The
district vote for George Bush was 51% in
1988.

CQ Voting Studies

	1989	1990
Presidential	27%	40%
Party	97%	100%
Participation	97%	100%

Interest Groups

	1988	1989
ADA	85%	n/a
ACU	4%	0%
AFL-CIO	86%	100%
CCUS	38%	n/a

Elections

	1988	1990
General	76%	69%
Primary	76%	98%

Harold E. Ford   (D-Tenn.)
Of Memphis • Elected 1974

Born: May 20, 1945, Memphis, Tenn.
Education: Tennessee State U., B.S. 1967;
John Gupton Mortuary, L.F.D. 1969; John
Gupton Mortuary, L.E.D. 1969; Howard
U., M.B.A. 1982.
Occupation: Mortician.
Family: Wife, Dorothy Bowles; three
children.
Religion: Baptist.
Political Career: Tenn. House, 1971-75.

Capitol Office: 2305 Rayburn House
Office Building 20515; 225-3265.
Office Staff: Administrative Assistant/Tax
Counsel, Vanessa Brooks; Office
Manager, Bernadette Connor.
Committees: Ways & Means.

Tennessee 9th — Memphis. The district
vote for George Bush was 34% in 1988.

CQ Voting Studies

	1989	1990
Presidential	21%	8%
Party	85%	62%
Participation	83%	62%

Interest Groups

	1988	1989
ADA	85%	80%
ACU	0%	0%
AFL-CIO	100%	100%
CCUS	36%	10%

Elections

	1988	1990
General	82%	65%
Primary	80%	69%

William D. Ford (D-Mich.)
Of Taylor • Elected 1964

Born: August 6, 1927, Detroit, Mich.
Education: Nebraska State Teachers College, 1946; Wayne State U., 1947-48; U. of Denver, B.S. 1949; U. of Denver, LL.B. 1951.
Military Career: Navy, 1944-46; Air Force Reserve, 1950-58.
Occupation: Lawyer.
Family: Wife, Mary; three children.
Religion: United Church of Christ.
Political Career: Taylor Township justice of the peace, 1955-57; Melvindale city attorney, 1957-59; Taylor Township attorney, 1957-64; Mich. Senate, 1963-65.

Capitol Office: 2371 Rayburn House Office Building 20515; 225-6261.
Office Staff: Administrative Assistant, David Geiss; Press Secretary, Mike Russell; Executive Assistant, Janice MacDonald.
Committees: Education & Labor (Chairman).

Michigan 15th — Southwestern Wayne County. The district vote for George Bush was 54% in 1988.

CQ Voting Studies

	1989	1990
Presidential	24%	12%
Party	90%	67%
Participation	94%	74%

Interest Groups

	1988	1989
ADA	100%	95%
ACU	0%	0%
AFL-CIO	100%	91%
CCUS	23%	40%

Elections

	1988	1990
General	64%	63%
Primary	u/o	u/o

Barney Frank (D-Mass.)
Of Newton • Elected 1980

Born: March 31, 1940, Bayonne, N.J.
Education: Harvard U., B.A. 1962;
Harvard U., J.D. 1977.
Occupation: Lawyer.
Family: Single.
Religion: Jewish.
Political Career: Mass. House, 1973-81.

Capitol Office: 2404 Rayburn House
Office Building 20515; 225-5931.
Office Staff: Administrative Assistant,
Douglas Cahn; Press Secretary, Douglas
Cahn; Office Manager/Personal
Secretary, Maria Giesta.
Committees: Banking, Finance & Urban
Affairs; Budget; Judiciary.

Massachusetts 4th — Boston Suburbs; Fall
River. The district vote for George Bush
was 42% in 1988.

CQ Voting Studies

	1989	1990
Presidential	27%	19%
Party	92%	90%
Participation	98%	95%

Interest Groups

	1988	1989
ADA	100%	95%
ACU	0%	7%
AFL-CIO	93%	92%
CCUS	21%	30%

Elections

	1988	1990
General	70%	66%
Primary	u/o	u/o

Gary Franks (R-Conn.)
Of Waterbury • Elected 1990

Born: February 9, 1953, Waterbury, Conn.
Education: Yale U., B.A. 1975.
Occupation: Real estate investor.
Family: Wife, Donna Williams; one stepchild.
Religion: Baptist.
Political Career: Waterbury alderman, 1986-90.

Capitol Office: 1609 Longworth House Office Building 20515; 225-3822.
Office Staff: Administrative Assistant, Pat Browne; Press Secretary, Chris Healy; Appointments Secretary, Stephanie Ward.
Committees: Armed Services; Small Business.

Connecticut 5th — West — Waterbury; Danbury. The district vote for George Bush was 58% in 1988.

Elections

	1990
General	52%
Primary	u/o

Martin Frost (D-Texas)
Of Dallas • Elected 1978

Born: January 1, 1942, Glendale, Calif.
Education: U. of Missouri, B.A. 1964; U. of Missouri, B.S. 1964; Georgetown U., J.D. 1970.
Military Career: Army Reserve, 1966-72.
Occupation: Lawyer.
Family: Wife, Valerie Hall; three children.
Religion: Jewish.
Political Career: Sought Democratic nomination for U.S. House, 1974.

Capitol Office: 2459 Rayburn House Office Building 20515; 225-3605.
Office Staff: Administrative Assistant, Matt Angle; Press Secretary, Robert Mansker; Personal Secretary/Scheduler, Delane McHone.
Committees: House Administration; Rules.

Texas 24th — South Dallas and Western Suburbs. The district vote for George Bush was 47% in 1988.

CQ Voting Studies

	1989	1990
Presidential	38%	22%
Party	86%	91%
Participation	94%	95%

Interest Groups

	1988	1989
ADA	70%	75%
ACU	9%	4%
AFL-CIO	92%	82%
CCUS	23%	40%

Elections

	1988	1990
General	93%	u/o
Primary	u/o	u/o

Elton Gallegly (R-Calif.)
Of Simi Valley • Elected 1986
Pronounced GAL uh glee

Born: March 7, 1944, Huntington Park, Calif.
Education: Los Angeles State College, 1962-63.
Occupation: Real estate broker.
Family: Wife, Janice Shrader; four children.
Religion: Protestant.
Political Career: Simi Valley City Council, 1979-80; mayor of Simi Valley, 1980-86.

Capitol Office: 107 Cannon House Office Building 20515; 225-5811.
Office Staff: Administrative Assistant, Lisa Boepple; Press Secretary, John Frith; Executive Assistant, Patricia Evans.
Committees: Foreign Affairs; Interior & Insular Affairs.

California 21st — Part of Ventura County; Western San Fernando Valley. The district vote for George Bush was 64% in 1988.

CQ Voting Studies

	1989	1990
Presidential	76%	70%
Party	90%	91%
Participation	98%	98%

Interest Groups

	1988	1989
ADA	15%	5%
ACU	96%	89%
AFL-CIO	21%	18%
CCUS	100%	100%

Elections

	1988	1990
General	69%	58%
Primary	82%	68%

Dean A. Gallo (R-N.J.)
Of Parsippanny • Elected 1984

Born: November 23, 1935, Hackensack, N.J.
Education: Boonton (N.J.) High School, graduated.
Occupation: Real estate broker.
Family: Divorced; two children.
Religion: Methodist.
Political Career: Parsippany-Troy Hills Township Council, 1968-70; Morris County Board of Chosen Freeholders, 1971-75; N.J. Assembly, 1976-84; minority leader, 1981-84.

Capitol Office: 1318 Longworth House Office Building 20515; 225-5034.
Office Staff: Chief of Staff, Tami McMinn; Press Secretary, Robert LeGrand; Office Manager, Lorraine Genovese.
Committees: Appropriations; Budget.

New Jersey 11th — North — Morris County. The district vote for George Bush was 65% in 1988.

CQ Voting Studies

	1989	1990
Presidential	64%	60%
Party	48%	65%
Participation	97%	96%

Interest Groups

	1988	1989
ADA	30%	25%
ACU	72%	61%
AFL-CIO	31%	25%
CCUS	79%	100%

Elections

	1988	1990
General	70%	65%
Primary	u/o	u/o

Joseph M. Gaydos (D-Pa.)
Of McKeesport • Elected 1968

Born: July 3, 1926, Braddock, Penn.
Education: Duquesne U., 1945-47; U. of Notre Dame, LL.B. 1951.
Military Career: Naval Reserve, 1944-46.
Occupation: Lawyer.
Family: Wife, Alice Gray; five children.
Religion: Roman Catholic.
Political Career: Pa. Senate, 1967-68.

Capitol Office: 2186 Rayburn House Office Building 20515; 225-4631.
Office Staff: Administrative Assistant, Barbara Pogue; Executive Assistant, Hedianne Grimes.
Committees: House Administration; Education & Labor.

Pennsylvania 20th — Pittsburgh Suburbs — McKeesport. The district vote for George Bush was 34% in 1988.

CQ Voting Studies

	1989	1990
Presidential	42%	32%
Party	73%	78%
Participation	93%	96%

Interest Groups

	1988	1989
ADA	65%	55%
ACU	24%	26%
AFL-CIO	100%	100%
CCUS	25%	40%

Elections

	1988	1990
General	98%	66%
Primary	u/o	66%

Sam Gejdenson (D-Conn.)
Of Bozrah • Elected 1980
Pronounced GAY den son

Born: May 20, 1948, Eschwege, Germany.
Education: Mitchell Junior College, A.S. 1968; U. of Connecticut, B.A. 1970.
Occupation: Dairy farmer.
Family: Wife, Karen Fleming; two children.
Religion: Jewish.
Political Career: Conn. House, 1975-79.

Capitol Office: 2416 Rayburn House Office Building 20515; 225-2076.
Office Staff: Administrative Assistant, Perry Pockros; Press Secretary, Maureen McGuire; Special Assistant, Jeanne Zulick.
Committees: House Administration; Foreign Affairs; Interior & Insular Affairs.

Connecticut 2nd — East — New London. The district vote for George Bush was 50% in 1988.

CQ Voting Studies

	1989	1990
Presidential	26%	19%
Party	96%	95%
Participation	98%	99%

Interest Groups

	1988	1989
ADA	95%	100%
ACU	0%	0%
AFL-CIO	92%	100%
CCUS	29%	30%

Elections

	1988	1990
General	64%	60%
Primary	u/o	u/o

CQ Voting Studies

	1989	1990
Presidential	69%	81%
Party	92%	92%
Participation	98%	99%

Interest Groups

	1988	1989
ADA	10%	15%
ACU	92%	96%
AFL-CIO	21%	0%
CCUS	93%	100%

Elections

	1988	1990
General	u/o	u/o
Primary	u/o	u/o

George W. Gekas (R-Pa.)
Of Harrisburg • Elected 1982

Born: April 14, 1930, Harrisburg, Penn.
Education: Dickinson College, B.A. 1952;
Dickinson School of Law, LL.B. 1958;
Dickinson School of Law, J.D. 1958.
Military Career: Army, 1953-55.
Occupation: Lawyer.
Family: Wife, Evangeline Charas.
Religion: Greek Orthodox.
Political Career: Pa. House, 1967-75; Pa.
Senate, 1977-83.

Capitol Office: 1519 Longworth House
Office Building 20515; 225-4315.
Office Staff: Administrative Assistant,
Allan Cagnoli; Press Secretary, Brian
Sansoni; Office Manager, Kelly Surrick.
Committees: Judiciary; Select
Intelligence.

Pennsylvania 17th — Central —
Harrisburg; Williamsport. The district
vote for George Bush was 63% in 1988.

Richard A. Gephardt (D-Mo.)
Of St. Louis • Elected 1976

Born: January 31, 1941, St. Louis, Mo.
Education: Northwestern U., B.S. 1962;
U. of Michigan, J.D. 1965.
Military Career: Air National Guard,
1965-71.
Occupation: Lawyer.
Family: Wife, Jane Ann Byrnes; three
children.
Religion: Baptist.
Political Career: St. Louis Board of
Aldermen, 1971-76; sought Democratic
nomination for president, 1988.

Capitol Office: 1432 Longworth House
Office Building 20515; 225-2671.
Office Staff: Administrative Assistant,
Andrea King; Press Secretary, Deborah
Johns; Office Manager, Barbara Davis.
Committees: Budget.

Missouri 3rd — South St. Louis; Southeast
St. Louis County and Jefferson County.
The district vote for George Bush was
53% in 1988.

CQ Voting Studies

	1989	1990
Presidential	33%	14%
Party	95%	89%
Participation	96%	90%

Interest Groups

	1988	1989
ADA	75%	90%
ACU	10%	4%
AFL-CIO	92%	100%
CCUS	20%	30%

Elections

	1988	1990
General	63%	57%
Primary	82%	80%

CQ Voting Studies

	1989	1990
Presidential	51%	44%
Party	74%	69%
Participation	97%	99%

Interest Groups

	1989
ADA	n/a
ACU	78%
AFL-CIO	60%
CCUS	83%

Elections

	1989*	1990
General	51%	71%
Primary	32%	u/o

*Special election.

Pete Geren (D-Texas)
Of Fort Worth • Elected 1989

Born: January 29, 1952, Fort Worth, Texas.
Education: Georgia Institute of Technology, 1970-73; U. of Texas, B.A. 1974; U. of Texas, J.D. 1978.
Occupation: Lawyer.
Family: Wife, Rebecca Ray; one child.
Religion: Baptist.
Political Career: Democratic nominee for U.S. House, 6th District, 1986.

Capitol Office: 1730 Longworth House Office Building 20515; 225-5071.
Office Staff: Administrative Assistant, A. Scott Sudduth; Press Secretary, Greta Creech; Executive Assistant, Dorothy C. Wing.
Committees: Public Works & Transportation; Science, Space & Technology; Veterans' Affairs.

Texas 12th — Fort Worth; Northwest Tarrant County. The district vote for George Bush was 53% in 1988.

Sam M. Gibbons (D-Fla.)
Of Tampa • Elected 1962

Born: January 20, 1920, Tampa, Fla.
Education: U. of Florida, 1938-41; U. of Florida, J.D. 1947.
Military Career: Army, 1941-45.
Occupation: Lawyer.
Family: Wife, Martha Hanley; three children.
Religion: Presbyterian.
Political Career: Fla. House, 1953-59; Fla. Senate, 1959-63.

Capitol Office: 2204 Rayburn House Office Building 20515; 225-3376.
Office Staff: Chief of Staff, Jan Stoorza; Legislative Director, Flora Sullivan.
Committees: Ways & Means.

Florida 7th — West — Tampa. The district vote for George Bush was 58% in 1988.

CQ Voting Studies

	1989	1990
Presidential	37%	32%
Party	78%	82%
Participation	92%	95%

Interest Groups

	1988	1989
ADA	60%	80%
ACU	35%	19%
AFL-CIO	71%	70%
CCUS	64%	40%

Elections

	1988	1990
General	u/o	68%
Primary	u/o	u/o

Wayne T. Gilchrest (R-Md.)
Of Kennedyville • Elected 1990

Born: April 15, 1946, Rahway, N.J.
Education: Wesley College, A.A. 1971;
Delaware State U., B.A. 1973; Loyola
College, Baltimore, 1990.
Military Career: Marine Corps, 1964-68.
Occupation: High school history and
government teacher.
Family: Wife, Barbara Rawley; three
children.
Religion: Methodist.
Political Career: Republican nominee for
U.S. House, 1988.

Capitol Office: 502 Cannon House
Office Building 20515; 225-5311.
Office Staff: Administrative Assistant,
Tony Caligiuri; Press Secretary, Jill
McCartney; Appointments Secretary,
Stacey Robert.
Committees: Merchant Marine &
Fisheries; Science, Space & Technology.

Maryland 1st — Eastern Shore; Southern
Maryland. The district vote for George
Bush was 63% in 1988.

Elections

	1990
General	57%
Primary	29%

Paul E. Gillmor (R-Ohio)
Of Port Clinton • Elected 1988

Born: February 1, 1939, Tiffin, Ohio.
Education: Ohio Wesleyan U., B.A. 1961;
U. of Michigan, J.D. 1964.
Military Career: Air Force, 1965-66.
Occupation: Lawyer.
Family: Wife, Karen Lako; two children.
Religion: Protestant.
Political Career: Ohio Senate, 1967-88;
minority leader, 1978-80; president,
1981-82; minority leader, 1983-84;
president, 1985-88; sought Republican
nomination for governor, 1986.

Capitol Office: 1203 Longworth House
Office Building 20515; 225-6405.
Office Staff: Administrative Assistant,
Mark Wellman; Press Secretary, Mark
Isakowitz; Executive Assistant, Karen
Parker.
Committees: House Administration;
Banking, Finance & Urban Affairs.

Ohio 5th — Northwest — Bowling
Green; Sandusky. The district vote for
George Bush was 61% in 1988.

CQ Voting Studies

	1989	1990
Presidential	77%	69%
Party	65%	66%
Participation	97%	97%

Interest Groups

	1988	1989
ADA		0%
ACU		93%
AFL-CIO		0%
CCUS		100%

Elections

	1988	1990
General	61%	73%
Primary	45%	u/o

Benjamin A. Gilman (R-N.Y.)
Of Middletown • Elected 1972

Born: December 6, 1922, Poughkeepsie, N.Y.
Education: U. of Pennsylvania, B.S. 1946; New York Law School, LL.B. 1950.
Military Career: Army, 1943-45.
Occupation: Lawyer.
Family: Wife, Rita Gail Kelhoffer; four children, two stepchildren.
Religion: Jewish.
Political Career: N.Y. Assembly, 1967-73.

Capitol Office: 2185 Rayburn House Office Building 20515; 225-3776.
Office Staff: Administrative Assistant, Nancy L. Colandrea; Press Secretary, Andrew Zarutskie; Appointments Secretary, Beverly Wiand Vitarelli.
Committees: Foreign Affairs; Post Office & Civil Service (Ranking).

New York 22nd — Lower Hudson Valley. The district vote for George Bush was 57% in 1988.

CQ Voting Studies

	1989	1990
Presidential	44%	33%
Party	29%	35%
Participation	99%	99%

Interest Groups

	1988	1989
ADA	55%	55%
ACU	42%	43%
AFL-CIO	93%	92%
CCUS	50%	60%

Elections

	1988	1990
General	71%	69%
Primary	u/o	u/o

Newt Gingrich (R-Ga.)
Of Jonesboro • Elected 1978

Born: June 17, 1943, Harrisburg, Penn.
Education: Emory U., B.A. 1965; Tulane
U., M.A. 1968; Tulane U., Ph.D. 1971.
Occupation: Professor of history.
Family: Wife, Marianne Ginther; two
children.
Religion: Baptist.
Political Career: Republican nominee for
U.S. House, 1974; Rebublican nominee
for U.S. House, 1976.

Capitol Office: 2438 Rayburn House
Office Building 20515; 225-4501.
Office Staff: Administrative Assistant,
Mary N. Brown; Press Secretary, Sheila
Ward; Executive Assistant, Karen
Cologne.
Committees: House Administration.

Georgia 6th — West Central — Atlanta
Suburbs. The district vote for George
Bush was 67% in 1988.

CQ Voting Studies

	1989	1990
Presidential	87%	66%
Party	71%	83%
Participation	95%	90%

Interest Groups

	1988	1989
ADA	5%	0%
ACU	100%	88%
AFL-CIO	15%	8%
CCUS	100%	100%

Elections

	1988	1990
General	59%	50%
Primary	u/o	u/o

Dan Glickman (D-Kan.)
Of Wichita • Elected 1976

Born: November 24, 1944, Wichita, Kan.
Education: U. of Michigan, B.A. 1966;
George Washington U., J.D. 1969.
Occupation: Lawyer.
Family: Wife, Rhoda Yura; two children.
Religion: Jewish.
Political Career: Wichita Board of
Education, 1973-76; president, 1975-76.

Capitol Office: 2311 Rayburn House
Office Building 20515; 225-6216.
Office Staff: Administrative Assistant,
Myrne Roe; Press Secretary, Jim
Petterson; Personal Secretary/Scheduler,
Carole Angle.
Committees: Agriculture; Judiciary;
Select Intelligence; Science, Space &
Technology.

Kansas 4th — Central — Wichita. The
district vote for George Bush was 55% in
1988.

CQ Voting Studies

	1989	1990
Presidential	37%	27%
Party	80%	81%
Participation	98%	97%

Interest Groups

	1988	1989
ADA	80%	80%
ACU	16%	18%
AFL-CIO	86%	67%
CCUS	43%	50%

Elections

	1988	1990
General	64%	71%
Primary	u/o	u/o

Henry B. Gonzalez (D-Texas)
Of San Antonio • Elected 1961

Born: May 3, 1916, San Antonio, Texas.
Education: San Antonio Junior College, graduated 1937; U. of Texas, Austin, 1937-39; St. Mary's U. of San Antonio, LL.B. 1943.
Occupation: Lawyer; public relations consultant; translator.
Family: Wife, Bertha Cuellar; eight children.
Religion: Roman Catholic.
Political Career: Bexar County chief probation officer, 1946-50; San Antonio Housing Authority deputy director, 1951-53; San Antonio City Council, 1953-56; San Antonio mayor pro tem, 1955-56; Texas Senate, 1957-61; sought Democratic nomination for governor, 1958; candidate for U.S. Senate, special election, 1961.

Capitol Office: 2413 Rayburn House Office Building 20515; 225-3236.
Office Staff: Administrative Assistant, Gail Beagle; Press Secretary, Gail Beagle; Appointments Secretary, Christine Ochoa.
Committees: Banking, Finance & Urban Affairs (Chairman).

Texas 20th — Central San Antonio. The district vote for George Bush was 32% in 1988.

CQ Voting Studies

	1989	1990
Presidential	38%	15%
Party	93%	93%
Participation	99%	99%

Interest Groups

	1988	1989
ADA	100%	80%
ACU	0%	0%
AFL-CIO	100%	92%
CCUS	15%	30%

Elections

	1988	1990
General	71%	u/o
Primary	u/o	u/o

CQ Voting Studies

	1989	1990
Presidential	65%	54%
Party	76%	71%
Participation	92%	93%

Interest Groups

	1988	1989
ADA	30%	25%
ACU	63%	68%
AFL-CIO	50%	17%
CCUS	93%	90%

Elections

	1988	1990
General	77%	u/o
Primary	u/o	88%

Bill Goodling (R-Pa.)
Of Jacobus • Elected 1974

Born: December 5, 1927, Loganville, Penn.
Education: U. of Maryland, B.S. 1953; Western Maryland College, M.Ed. 1956; Pennsylvania State U., 1960-62.
Military Career: Army, 1946-48.
Occupation: Public school superintendent.
Family: Wife, Hilda Wright; two children.
Religion: Methodist.
Political Career: Dallastown School Board president, 1964-67.

Capitol Office: 2263 Rayburn House Office Building 20515; 225-5836.
Office Staff: Administrative Assistant, Jay Eagen; Press Secretary, Karen Baker; Personal Secretary, Pat Khatami.
Committees: Education & Labor (Ranking); Foreign Affairs.

Pennsylvania 19th — South Central — York. The district vote for George Bush was 66% in 1988.

Bart Gordon (D-Tenn.)
Of Murfreesboro • Elected 1984

Born: January 24, 1949, Murfreesboro, Tenn.
Education: Middle Tennessee State U., B.S. 1971; U. of Tennessee, J.D. 1973.
Occupation: Lawyer.
Family: Single.
Religion: Methodist.
Political Career: Tenn. Democratic Party chairman, 1981-83.

Capitol Office: 103 Cannon House Office Building 20515; 225-4231.
Office Staff: Administrative Assistant, Jeff Whorley; Press Secretary, B.D. Steven Rogers; Scheduler, Leigh Ann Brown.
Committees: Rules.

Tennessee 6th — North Central — Murfreesboro. The district vote for George Bush was 60% in 1988.

CQ Voting Studies

	1989	1990
Presidential	35%	25%
Party	91%	93%
Participation	98%	98%

Interest Groups

	1988	1989
ADA	80%	75%
ACU	12%	11%
AFL-CIO	93%	92%
CCUS	36%	50%

Elections

	1988	1990
General	76%	67%
Primary	u/o	u/o

Porter J. Goss   (R-Fla.)
Of Sanibel • Elected 1988

Born: November 26, 1938, Waterbury, Conn.
Education: Yale U., B.A. 1960.
Military Career: Army, 1960-62.
Occupation: Small businessman; newspaper founder; CIA agent.
Family: Wife, Mariel Robinson; four children.
Religion: Presbyterian.
Political Career: Sanibel City Council, 1974-82; mayor of Sanibel, 1975-77; mayor of Sanibel, 1982; Lee County Commission, 1983-88; chairman, 1985-86.
Capitol Office: 224 Cannon House Office Building 20515; 225-2536.
Office Staff: Administrative Assistant, Mark Dyckman; Communications Director, Wendy Donath; Office Manager, Maggie Knutson.
Committees: Foreign Affairs; Merchant Marine & Fisheries.

Florida 13th — Southwest — Sarasota; Fort Myers. The district vote for George Bush was 68% in 1988.

CQ Voting Studies

	1989	1990
Presidential	69%	72%
Party	87%	88%
Participation	99%	99%

Interest Groups

	1989
ADA	5%
ACU	89%
AFL-CIO	25%
CCUS	100%

Elections

	1988	1990
General	71%	u/o
Primary	38%	u/o

Bill Gradison (R-Ohio)
Of Cincinnati • Elected 1974

Born: December 28, 1928, Cincinnati, Ohio.
Education: Yale U., B.A. 1948; Harvard U., M.B.A. 1951; Harvard U., D.C.S. 1954.
Occupation: Investment broker; federal official.
Family: Wife, Heather Jane Stirton; nine children.
Religion: Jewish.
Political Career: Cincinnati City Council, 1961-74; mayor of Cincinnati, 1971.

Capitol Office: 1125 Longworth House Office Building 20515; 225-3164.
Office Staff: Administrative Assistant, Margaret Totten.
Committees: Budget (Ranking); Ways & Means.

Ohio 2nd — Hamilton County — Eastern Cincinnati and Suburbs. The district vote for George Bush was 62% in 1988.

CQ Voting Studies

	1989	1990
Presidential	67%	76%
Party	51%	74%
Participation	96%	97%

Interest Groups

	1988	1989
ADA	35%	15%
ACU	62%	68%
AFL-CIO	21%	8%
CCUS	83%	80%

Elections

	1988	1990
General	72%	64%
Primary	u/o	u/o

CQ Voting Studies

	1989	1990
Presidential	74%	63%
Party	86%	81%
Participation	99%	99%

Interest Groups

	1988	1989
ADA	40%	25%
ACU	64%	64%
AFL-CIO	57%	8%
CCUS	86%	100%

Elections

	1988	1990
General	64%	72%
Primary	u/o	u/o

Fred Grandy (R-Iowa)
Of Sioux City • Elected 1986

Born: June 29, 1948, Sioux City, Iowa.
Education: Harvard U., B.A. 1970.
Occupation: Actor.
Family: Wife, Catherine Mann; three children.
Religion: Episcopalian.
Political Career: No previous office.

Capitol Office: 418 Cannon House Office Building 20515; 225-5476.
Office Staff: Chief of Staff, Craig Tufty; Press Secretary, Georgia Dunn; Office Manager/Scheduler, Nancy Sheppard.
Committees: Standards of Official Conduct; Ways & Means.

Iowa 6th — Northwest — Sioux City. The district vote for George Bush was 50% in 1988.

William H. Gray, III (D-Pa.)
Of Philadelphia • Elected 1978

Born: August 20, 1941, Baton Rouge, La.
Education: Franklin and Marshall College, B.A. 1963; Drew Theological Seminary, M.Div. 1966; Princeton Theological Seminary, Th.M. 1970.
Occupation: Clergyman.
Family: Wife, Andrea Dash; three children.
Religion: Baptist.
Political Career: Sought Democratic nomination for U.S. House, 1976.

Capitol Office: 2454 Rayburn House Office Building 20515; 225-4001.
Office Staff: Chief of Staff, Alan C. Bowser; Press Secretary, Michael Tucker; Office Manager, Wendy R. Lewis.
Committees: House Administration; Appropriations; District of Columbia.

Pennsylvania 2nd — North and West Philadelphia. The district vote for George Bush was 8% in 1988.

CQ Voting Studies

	1989	1990
Presidential	30%	16%
Party	88%	90%
Participation	91%	89%

Interest Groups

	1988	1989
ADA	95%	95%
ACU	0%	4%
AFL-CIO	100%	100%
CCUS	31%	30%

Elections

	1988	1990
General	94%	92%
Primary	u/o	u/o

CQ Voting Studies

	1989	1990
Presidential	57%	41%
Party	28%	37%
Participation	96%	98%

Interest Groups

	1988	1989
ADA	75%	50%
ACU	25%	39%
AFL-CIO	50%	20%
CCUS	64%	90%

Elections

	1988	1990
General	61%	59%
Primary	u/o	u/o

Bill Green (R-N.Y.)
Of Manhattan • Elected 1978

Born: October 16, 1929, New York, N.Y.
Education: Harvard U., B.A. 1950;
Harvard U., J.D. 1953.
Military Career: Army, 1953-55.
Occupation: State government lawyer;
federal housing official.
Family: Wife, Patricia Freiberg; two
children.
Religion: Jewish.
Political Career: N.Y. Assembly, 1965-68;
sought Republican nomination for U.S.
House, 1968.

Capitol Office: 2301 Rayburn House
Office Building 20515; 225-2436.
Office Staff: Administrative Assistant,
Sheila Greenwald; Press Secretary, Barrie
Joseph-Henken; Legislative
Assistant/Personal Secretary, Ann
Saurman.
Committees: Appropriations.

New York 15th — Manhattan — East
Side. The district vote for George Bush
was 33% in 1988.

Frank J. Guarini (D-N.J.)

Of Jersey City • Elected 1978
Pronounced gwar EE nee

Born: August 20, 1924, Jersey City, N.J.
Education: Dartmouth College, B.A.
1947; New York U., J.D. 1950; New York
U., LL.M. 1955.
Military Career: Navy, 1944-46.
Occupation: Lawyer.
Family: Single.
Religion: Roman Catholic.
Political Career: N.J. Senate, 1966-72;
sought Democratic nomination for U.S.
Senate, 1970.

Capitol Office: 2458 Rayburn House
Office Building 20515; 225-2765.
Office Staff: Chief of Staff, Fariborz S.
Fatemi; Press Secretary, Karin Walser;
Scheduler, Desiree Moses-El.
Committees: Budget; Ways & Means.

New Jersey 14th — North — Jersey City.
The district vote for George Bush was
44% in 1988.

CQ Voting Studies

	1989	1990
Presidential	34%	33%
Party	90%	78%
Participation	95%	94%

Interest Groups

	1988	1989
ADA	70%	85%
ACU	14%	11%
AFL-CIO	100%	92%
CCUS	46%	40%

Elections

	1988	1990
General	67%	66%
Primary	67%	91%

Steve Gunderson (R-Wis.)
Of Osseo • Elected 1980

Born: May 10, 1951, Eau Claire, Wis.
Education: U. of Wisconsin, B.A. 1973; Brown School of Broadcasting, 1974.
Occupation: Public official.
Family: Single.
Religion: Lutheran.
Political Career: Wis. House, 1975-79.

Capitol Office: 2235 Rayburn House Office Building 20515; 225-5506.
Office Staff: Administrative Assistant, Kris Deininger; Press Secretary, Jennifer Koberstein; Executive Administrator, Callista Bisek.
Committees: Agriculture; Education & Labor.

Wisconsin 3rd — West — Eau Claire; La Crosse. The district vote for George Bush was 47% in 1988.

CQ Voting Studies

	1989	1990
Presidential	77%	60%
Party	66%	67%
Participation	99%	98%

Interest Groups

	1988	1989
ADA	45%	20%
ACU	54%	81%
AFL-CIO	79%	17%
CCUS	71%	100%

Elections

	1988	1990
General	68%	61%
Primary	u/o	u/o

Ralph M. Hall (D-Texas)
Of Rockwall • Elected 1980

Born: May 3, 1923, Rockwall County, Texas.

Education: Texas Christian U., 1943; U. of Texas, 1946-47; Southern Methodist U., LL.B. 1951.

Military Career: Navy, 1942-45.

Occupation: Lawyer; businessman.

Family: Wife, Mary Ellen Murphy; three children.

Religion: Methodist.

Political Career: Rockwall County judge, 1950-62; Texas Senate, 1963-73; sought Democratic nomination for lieutenant governor, 1972.

Capitol Office: 2236 Rayburn House Office Building 20515; 225-6673.

Office Staff: Administrative Assistant/Office Manager, James D. Cole; Press Secretary, Rebecca Hebert.

Committees: Energy & Commerce; Science, Space & Technology.

Texas 4th — Northeast — Tyler; Longview. The district vote for George Bush was 61% in 1988.

CQ Voting Studies

	1989	1990
Presidential	69%	51%
Party	39%	39%
Participation	97%	81%

Interest Groups

	1988	1989
ADA	15%	5%
ACU	92%	89%
AFL-CIO	43%	8%
CCUS	86%	80%

Elections

	1988	1990
General	66%	u/o
Primary	u/o	u/o

Tony P. Hall (D-Ohio)
Of Dayton • Elected 1978

Born: January 16, 1942, Dayton, Ohio.
Education: Denison U., A.B. 1964.
Occupation: Real estate salesman.
Family: Wife, Janet Dick; two children.
Religion: Christian.
Political Career: Ohio House, 1969-73; Ohio Senate, 1973-79; Democratic nominee for Ohio secretary of state, 1974.

Capitol Office: 2162 Rayburn House Office Building 20515; 225-6465.
Office Staff: Administrative Assistant, George Lowrey; Communications Director/Press, Michael Gessel; Office Manager/Personal Secretary, Bonnie Ruestow.
Committees: Hunger (Chairman); Rules.

Ohio 3rd — Southwest — Dayton. The district vote for George Bush was 54% in 1988.

CQ Voting Studies

	1989	1990
Presidential	31%	22%
Party	77%	78%
Participation	91%	90%

Interest Groups

	1988	1989
ADA	75%	80%
ACU	17%	7%
AFL-CIO	93%	83%
CCUS	23%	56%

Elections

	1988	1990
General	77%	u/o
Primary	u/o	u/o

Lee H. Hamilton (D-Ind.)

Of Nashville • Elected 1964

Born: April 20, 1931, Daytona Beach, Fla.
Education: DePauw U., B.A. 1952;
Goethe U., Frankfurt, West Germany,
1952-53; Indiana U., J.D. 1956.
Occupation: Lawyer.
Family: Wife, Nancy Nelson; three
children.
Religion: Methodist.
Political Career: No previous office.

Capitol Office: 2187 Rayburn House
Office Building 20515; 225-5315.
Office Staff: Executive Assistant,
Jonathan Friedman; Press Assistant, Chris
Mehl; Office Manager, Nora Coulter.
Committees: Foreign Affairs.

Indiana 9th — Southeast —
Bloomington; New Albany. The district
vote for George Bush was 58% in 1988.

CQ Voting Studies

	1989	1990
Presidential	42%	27%
Party	77%	78%
Participation	99%	99%

Interest Groups

	1988	1989
ADA	85%	60%
ACU	8%	21%
AFL-CIO	100%	67%
CCUS	36%	60%

Elections

	1988	1990
General	71%	69%
Primary	u/o	92%

John Paul Hammerschmidt
(R-Ark.)
Of Harrison • Elected 1966

Born: May 4, 1922, Harrison, Ark.
Education: The Citadel, 1938-39; U. of
Arkansas, 1940-41; Oklahoma State U.,
1945-46.
Military Career: Army, 1942-45; Ark.
Army Reserve, 1945-60; D.C. Army
Reserve, 1977-81.
Occupation: Lumber company
executive.
Family: Wife, Virginia Sharp; one child.
Religion: Presbyterian.
Political Career: Ark. Republican Party
chairman, 1964-66.

Capitol Office: 2110 Rayburn House
Office Building 20515; 225-4301.
Office Staff: Administrative Assistant,
Raymond T. Reid; Scheduler, Janet
Martin.
Committees: Public Works &
Transportation (Ranking); Veterans'
Affairs.

Arkansas 3rd — Northwest — Ozark
Plateau; Fort Smith. The district vote for
George Bush was 66% in 1988.

CQ Voting Studies

	1989	1990
Presidential	81%	59%
Party	73%	72%
Participation	96%	95%

Interest Groups

	1988	1989
ADA	10%	5%
ACU	96%	85%
AFL-CIO	29%	8%
CCUS	86%	90%

Elections

	1988	1990
General	75%	71%
Primary	u/o	u/o

Mel Hancock (R-Mo.)

Of Springfield • Elected 1988

Born: September 14, 1929, Cape Fair, Mo.
Education: Southwest Missouri State U., B.S. 1951.
Military Career: Air Force, 1951-53; Air Force Reserve, 1953-65.
Occupation: Businessman.
Family: Wife, Alma "Sug" McDaniel; three children.
Religion: Church of Christ.
Political Career: Sought Republican nomination for U.S. Senate, 1982; Republican nominee for lieutenant governor, 1984.

Capitol Office: 318 Cannon House Office Building 20515; 225-6536.
Office Staff: Administrative Assistant, Gerry Henson; Press Secretary, Sam Coring; Staff Assistant, Shannon Scruggs.
Committees: Banking, Finance & Urban Affairs; Public Works & Transportation; Small Business.

Missouri 7th — Southwest — Springfield; Joplin. The district vote for George Bush was 61% in 1988.

CQ Voting Studies

	1989	1990
Presidential	78%	80%
Party	98%	98%
Participation	99%	99%

Interest Groups

	1989
ADA	0%
ACU	96%
AFL-CIO	8%
CCUS	90%

Elections

	1988	1990
General	53%	52%
Primary	39%	86%

James V. Hansen (R-Utah)
Of Farmington • Elected 1980

Born: August 14, 1932, Salt Lake City, Utah.
Education: U. of Utah, B.S. 1960.
Military Career: Navy, 1952-54.
Occupation: Insurance executive; land developer.
Family: Wife, Ann Burgoyne; five children.
Religion: Mormon.
Political Career: Farmington City Council, 1968-70; Utah House, 1973-81; Speaker, 1979-81.

Capitol Office: 2421 Rayburn House Office Building 20515; 225-0453.
Office Staff: Administrative Assistant, Nancee Blockinger; Press Secretary, Rick Guldan.
Committees: Armed Services; Interior & Insular Affairs.

Utah 1st — Ogden and Rural Utah. The district vote for George Bush was 72% in 1988.

CQ Voting Studies

	1989	1990
Presidential	80%	83%
Party	89%	85%
Participation	95%	96%

Interest Groups

	1988	1989
ADA	0%	0%
ACU	100%	100%
AFL-CIO	0%	8%
CCUS	100%	100%

Elections

	1988	1990
General	60%	52%
Primary	u/o	u/o

Claude Harris (D-Ala.)
Of Tuscaloosa • Elected 1986

Born: June 29, 1940, Bessemer, Ala.
Education: U. of Alabama, B.S. 1962; U. of Alabama, LL.B. 1965.
Military Career: Army National Guard, 1967-present.
Occupation: Judge; lawyer.
Family: Wife, Barbara Cork; two children.
Religion: Baptist.
Political Career: Alabama circuit judge, 6th Circuit, 1977-85.

Capitol Office: 1009 Longworth House Office Building 20515; 225-2665.
Office Staff: Administrative Assistant/Press Secretary, Walter E. Braswell; Office Manager, Sandy Webster.
Committees: Energy & Commerce; Veterans' Affairs.

Alabama 7th — West Central — Tuscaloosa; Bessemer. The district vote for George Bush was 59% in 1988.

CQ Voting Studies

	1989	1990
Presidential	52%	39%
Party	71%	73%
Participation	99%	98%

Interest Groups

	1988	1989
ADA	40%	55%
ACU	68%	50%
AFL-CIO	79%	58%
CCUS	64%	60%

Elections

	1988	1990
General	68%	71%
Primary	94%	u/o

CQ Voting Studies

	1989	1990
Presidential	76%	67%
Party	90%	91%
Participation	98%	97%

Interest Groups

	1988	1989
ADA	10%	10%
ACU	92%	85%
AFL-CIO	21%	17%
CCUS	86%	100%

Elections

	1988	1990
General	74%	67%
Primary	u/o	u/o

Dennis Hastert (R-Ill.)
Of Yorkville • Elected 1986

Born: January 2, 1942, Aurora, Ill.
Education: Wheaton College, A.B. 1964; Northern Illinois U., M.S. 1967.
Occupation: Teacher; restaurateur.
Family: Wife, Jean Kahl; two children.
Religion: Protestant.
Political Career: Ill. House, 1981-87.

Capitol Office: 515 Cannon House Office Building 20515; 225-2976.
Office Staff: Chief of Staff, Scott B. Palmer; Press Secretary, Eron Shosteck; Office Manager, Samuel Lancaster.
Committees: Energy & Commerce; Government Operations.

Illinois 14th — North Central — De Kalb; Elgin. The district vote for George Bush was 64% in 1988.

Charles Hatcher (D-Ga.)
Of Newton • Elected 1980

Born: July 1, 1939, Doerun, Ga.
Education: Georgia Southern U., B.S. 1965; U. of Georgia, J.D. 1969.
Military Career: Air Force, 1958-62.
Occupation: Lawyer; teacher.
Family: Wife, Ellen Wilson; three children.
Religion: Episcopalian.
Political Career: Ga. House, 1973-81.

Capitol Office: 2434 Rayburn House Office Building 20515; 225-3631.
Office Staff: Administrative Assistant/Press Secretary, Krysta Harden; Personal Assistant, Harriet James.
Committees: Agriculture; Small Business.

Georgia 2nd — Southwest — Albany; Valdosta. The district vote for George Bush was 58% in 1988.

CQ Voting Studies

	1989	1990
Presidential	49%	37%
Party	70%	76%
Participation	91%	93%

Interest Groups

	1988	1989
ADA	50%	35%
ACU	43%	31%
AFL-CIO	62%	55%
CCUS	64%	80%

Elections

	1988	1990
General	62%	73%
Primary	67%	u/o

Charles A. Hayes (D-Ill.)
Of Chicago • Elected 1983

Born: February 17, 1918, Cairo, Ill.
Education: High school graduate.
Occupation: Labor official; packinghouse worker.
Family: Wife, Edna J. Miller; two children, two stepchildren.
Religion: Baptist.
Political Career: No previous office.

Capitol Office: 1131 Longworth House Office Building 20515; 225-4372.
Office Staff: Administrative Assistant, Harriet C. Pritchett; Press Secretary, Bruce Taylor; Office Manager/Personal Secretary, Norma Collins.
Committees: Education & Labor; Post Office & Civil Service.

Illinois 1st — Chicago — South Side. The district vote for George Bush was 4% in 1988.

CQ Voting Studies

	1989	1990
Presidential	27%	13%
Party	98%	95%
Participation	99%	97%

Interest Groups

	1988	1989
ADA	95%	100%
ACU	0%	0%
AFL-CIO	100%	100%
CCUS	14%	30%

Elections

	1988	1990
General	96%	94%
Primary	87%	93%

Jimmy Hayes (D-La.)
Of Lafayette • Elected 1986

Born: December 21, 1946, Lafayette, La.
Education: U. of Southwestern Louisiana, B.S. 1967; Tulane U., J.D. 1970.
Military Career: Louisiana Air National Guard, 1968-74.
Occupation: Lawyer; real estate developer.
Family: Wife, Leslie Owen; three children.
Religion: Methodist.
Political Career: No previous office.

Capitol Office: 503 Cannon House Office Building 20515; 225-2031.
Office Staff: Chief of Staff, Rhod Shaw; Press Secretary, Sally Freeman; Executive Secretary, Lynn Hargroder.
Committees: Public Works & Transportation; Science, Space & Technology.

Louisiana 7th — Southwest — Lake Charles; Lafayette. The district vote for George Bush was 49% in 1988.

CQ Voting Studies

	1989	1990
Presidential	59%	38%
Party	64%	63%
Participation	95%	88%

Interest Groups

	1988	1989
ADA	55%	30%
ACU	52%	56%
AFL-CIO	92%	67%
CCUS	62%	60%

Elections

	1988	1990
General	u/o	u/o
Primary	u/o	58%

CQ Voting Studies

	1989	1990
Presidential	65%	71%
Party	89%	90%
Participation	97%	98%

Interest Groups

	1988	1989
ADA	5%	5%
ACU	100%	93%
AFL-CIO	7%	17%
CCUS	100%	100%

Elections

	1988	1990
General	75%	66%
Primary	u/o	u/o

Joel Hefley (R-Colo.)
Of Colorado Springs • Elected 1986

Born: April 18, 1935, Ardmore, Okla.
Education: Oklahoma Baptist U., B.A.
1957; Oklahoma State U., M.S. 1962.
Occupation: Community planner.
Family: Wife, Lynn Christian; three
children.
Religion: Presbyterian.
Political Career: Colo. House, 1977-79;
Colo. Senate, 1979-87.

Capitol Office: 222 Cannon House
Office Building 20515; 225-4422.
Office Staff: Administrative Assistant,
William C. Scott; Press Secretary, Lauren
Simmons; Executive Assistant, Kim Cook.
Committees: Armed Services; Interior &
Insular Affairs; Small Business.

Colorado 5th — South Central —
Colorado Springs. The district vote for
George Bush was 67% in 1988.

W.G. Bill Hefner (D-N.C.)
Of Concord • Elected 1974

Born: April 11, 1930, Elora, Tenn.
Education: High school graduate.
Occupation: Broadcasting executive.
Family: Wife, Nancy Hill; two children.
Religion: Baptist.
Political Career: No previous office.

Capitol Office: 2161 Rayburn House
Office Building 20515; 225-3715.
Office Staff: Administrative Assistant, Bill
McEwen; Press Secretary, Sandra Latta;
Executive Assistant, Maddie Preston.
Committees: Appropriations.

North Carolina 8th — South Central —
Kannapolis; Salisbury. The district vote
for George Bush was 62% in 1988.

CQ Voting Studies

	1989	1990
Presidential	41%	33%
Party	75%	79%
Participation	95%	98%

Interest Groups

	1988	1989
ADA	65%	65%
ACU	25%	26%
AFL-CIO	92%	75%
CCUS	50%	50%

Elections

	1988	1990
General	51%	55%
Primary	u/o	81%

Paul B. Henry (R-Mich.)
Of Grand Rapids • Elected 1984

Born: July 9, 1942, Chicago, Ill.
Education: Wheaton College, B.A. 1963;
Duke U., M.A. 1968; Duke U., Ph.D. 1970.
Occupation: Professor of political
science.
Family: Wife, Karen Anne Borthistle;
three children.
Religion: Christian Reformed.
Political Career: Mich. House, 1979-83;
Mich. Senate, 1983-85.

Capitol Office: 215 Cannon House
Office Building 20515; 225-3831.
Office Staff: Administrative Assistant,
Mary Lobisco; Press Secretary, Stephen
Ward.
Committees: Education & Labor;
Science, Space & Technology.

Michigan 5th — West Central — Grand
Rapids. The district vote for George Bush
was 64% in 1988.

CQ Voting Studies

	1989	1990
Presidential	66%	58%
Party	69%	75%
Participation	98%	97%

Interest Groups

	1988	1989
ADA	50%	30%
ACU	52%	68%
AFL-CIO	57%	8%
CCUS	93%	90%

Elections

	1988	1990
General	73%	75%
Primary	u/o	u/o

Wally Herger (R-Calif.)
Of Rio Oso • Elected 1986

Born: May 20, 1945, Sutter County, Calif.
Education: American River Community College, A.A. 1967; California State U., 1968-69.
Occupation: Rancher; gas company president.
Family: Wife, Pamela Sargent; eight children.
Religion: Mormon.
Political Career: Calif. Assembly, 1981-87.

Capitol Office: 1108 Longworth House Office Building 20515; 225-3076.
Office Staff: Administrative Assistant, John P. Magill; Press Secretary, Roger Mahan; Appointments Secretary, Pamela Mattox.
Committees: Agriculture; Merchant Marine & Fisheries.

California 2nd — North Central — Chico; Redding. The district vote for George Bush was 58% in 1988.

CQ Voting Studies

	1989	1990
Presidential	76%	69%
Party	91%	94%
Participation	99%	98%

Interest Groups

	1988	1989
ADA	0%	10%
ACU	92%	100%
AFL-CIO	29%	25%
CCUS	93%	100%

Elections

	1988	1990
General	59%	64%
Primary	u/o	u/o

CQ Voting Studies

	1989	1990
Presidential	28%	18%
Party	86%	93%
Participation	93%	99%

Interest Groups

	1988	1989
ADA	95%	90%
ACU	4%	12%
AFL-CIO	100%	100%
CCUS	21%	30%

Elections

	1988	1990
General	63%	66%
Primary	u/o	u/o

Dennis M. Hertel (D-Mich.)
Of Harper Woods • Elected 1980

Born: December 7, 1948, Detroit, Mich.
Education: Eastern Michigan U., B.A. 1971; Wayne State U., J.D. 1974.
Occupation: Lawyer.
Family: Wife, Cynthia S. Grosscup; four children.
Religion: Roman Catholic.
Political Career: Candidate for Detroit City Council, 1973; Mich. House, 1975-81.

Capitol Office: 2442 Rayburn House Office Building 20515; 225-6276.
Office Staff: Administrative Assistant/Press Secretary, E. Raymond O'Malley; Congressional Aide/Scheduler, Greg Hawkins.
Committees: Armed Services; Merchant Marine & Fisheries.

Michigan 14th — Detroit Suburbs — Warren. The district vote for George Bush was 56% in 1988.

Peter Hoagland (D-Neb.)
Of Omaha • Elected 1988

Born: November 17, 1941, Omaha, Neb.
Education: Stanford U., A.B. 1963; Yale U., LL.B. 1968.
Military Career: Army, 1963-65.
Occupation: Lawyer.
Family: Wife, Barbara Erickson; four children.
Religion: Episcopalian.
Political Career: Neb. Legislature, 1979-87.

Capitol Office: 1710 Longworth House Office Building 20515; 225-4155.
Office Staff: Administrative Assistant, Jim Crouse; Executive Assistant, Susan Carey.
Committees: Banking, Finance & Urban Affairs; Interior & Insular Affairs; Judiciary.

Nebraska 2nd — East — Omaha. The district vote for George Bush was 58% in 1988.

CQ Voting Studies

	1989	1990
Presidential	35%	27%
Party	86%	84%
Participation	99%	99%

Interest Groups

	1989
ADA	70%
ACU	25%
AFL-CIO	92%
CCUS	40%

Elections

	1988	1990
General	50%	58%
Primary	51%	87%

David L. Hobson (R-Ohio)
Of Springfield • Elected 1990

Born: October 17, 1936, Cincinnati, Ohio.
Education: Ohio Wesleyan U., B.A. 1958; Ohio State College of Law, J.D. 1963.
Occupation: Financial corporation executive.
Family: Wife, Carolyn Alexander; three children.
Religion: Methodist.
Political Career: Ohio Senate, 1983-91.

Capitol Office: 1338 Longworth House Office Building 20515; 225-4324.
Office Staff: Administrative Assistant, Mary Beth Corozza; Press Secretary, Terri Farell; Executive Assistant, Ginny Gano.
Committees: Government Operations; Public Works & Transportation.

Ohio 7th — West Central — Springfield; Marion. The district vote for George Bush was 64% in 1988.

Elections

	1990
General	62%
Primary	79%

George J. Hochbrueckner

(D-N.Y.)

Of Coram • Elected 1986

Pronounced HOCK brewk ner

Born: September 20, 1938, Queens, N.Y.
Education: State U. of New York, 1959-
60; Hofstra U., 1960-61; Pierce College,
1961-62; U. of California, Northridge,
1962-63.
Military Career: Navy, 1956-59.
Occupation: Aerospace engineer.
Family: Wife, Carol Ann Joan Seifert; four
children.
Religion: Roman Catholic.
Political Career: N.Y. Assembly, 1975-85;
Democratic nominee for U.S. House,
1984.

Capitol Office: 124 Cannon House
Office Building 20515; 225-3826.
Office Staff: Administrative Assistant,
Tom Downs; Press Secretary, Mary Ann
Webber; Executive Assistant, Jeanie
Dunn.
Committees: Armed Services; Merchant
Marine & Fisheries.

New York 1st — Long Island — Eastern
Suffolk County. The district vote for
George Bush was 60% in 1988.

CQ Voting Studies

	1989	1990
Presidential	33%	23%
Party	92%	94%
Participation	97%	99%

Interest Groups

	1988	1989
ADA	80%	85%
ACU	12%	7%
AFL-CIO	93%	100%
CCUS	36%	30%

Elections

	1988	1990
General	51%	56%
Primary	u/o	u/o

Clyde C. Holloway (R-La.)
Of Forest Hill • Elected 1986

Born: November 28, 1943, Lecompte, La.
Education: National School of Aeronautics, Kansas City, Mo., 1966.
Occupation: Nursery owner.
Family: Wife, Cathy Kohlhepp; four children.
Religion: Baptist.
Political Career: Sought Republican nomination for U.S. House, 1980; sought Republican nomination for U.S. House, 1985.

Capitol Office: 1206 Longworth House Office Building 20515; 225-4926.
Office Staff: Administrative Assistant, Julie King; Press Secretary, Steve LeBlanc; Executive Assistant, Dorothy Boger.
Committees: Energy & Commerce.

Louisiana 8th — Central — Alexandria. The district vote for George Bush was 45% in 1988.

CQ Voting Studies

	1989	1990
Presidential	66%	67%
Party	88%	84%
Participation	96%	93%

Interest Groups

	1988	1989
ADA	0%	15%
ACU	96%	93%
AFL-CIO	36%	33%
CCUS	92%	90%

Elections

	1988	1990
General	57%	u/o
Primary	44%	56%

Larry J. Hopkins (R-Ky.)
Of Lexington • Elected 1978

Born: October 25, 1933, Detroit, Mich.
Education: Murray State U., 1952-54.
Military Career: Marine Corps, 1954-56.
Occupation: Stockbroker.
Family: Wife, Carolyn Pennebaker; three children.
Religion: Methodist.
Political Career: Republican nominee for Fayette County Commission, 1970; Ky. House, 1972-78; Ky. Senate, 1978-79.

Capitol Office: 2437 Rayburn House Office Building 20515; 225-4706.
Office Staff: Administrative Assistant, Larry VanHoose; Press Secretary, Stephanie Collins; Legislative Assistant/Systems Operator, Joy Rangel.
Committees: Agriculture; Armed Services.

Kentucky 6th — North Central — Lexington; Frankfort. The district vote for George Bush was 57% in 1988.

CQ Voting Studies

	1989	1990
Presidential	72%	66%
Party	87%	90%
Participation	99%	98%

Interest Groups

	1988	1989
ADA	20%	20%
ACU	76%	82%
AFL-CIO	36%	17%
CCUS	93%	100%

Elections

	1988	1990
General	74%	u/o
Primary	u/o	u/o

Joan Kelly Horn (D-Mo.)
Of St. Louis • Elected 1990

Born: October 18, 1936, St. Louis, Mo.
Education: U. of Missouri, St. Louis, B.A.
1973; U. of Missouri, St. Louis, M.A. 1975.
Occupation: Political research and
consulting firm president.
Family: Husband, E. Terrence Jones; six
children.
Religion: Roman Catholic.
Political Career: Mo. Women's Political
Caucus, 1982-91; St. Louis County
Democratic Central Committee, 1987-91;
Mo. Democratic State Committee, 1988-
91.

Elections

	1990
General	50%
Primary	66%

Capitol Office: 1008 Longworth House
Office Building 20515; 225-2561.
Office Staff: Administrative Assistant,
Bruce Singleton.
Committees: Public Works &
Transportation; Science, Space &
Technology.

Missouri 2nd — Western St. Louis
County. The district vote for George
Bush was 61% in 1988.

Frank Horton (R-N.Y.)
Of Penfield • Elected 1962

Born: December 12, 1919, Cuero, Texas.
Education: Louisiana State U., B.A. 1941;
Cornell U., LL.B. 1947.
Military Career: Army, 1941-45.
Occupation: Lawyer.
Family: Wife, Nancy Richmond; two
children, two stepchildren.
Religion: Presbyterian.
Political Career: Rochester City Council,
1955-61.

Capitol Office: 2108 Rayburn House
Office Building 20515; 225-4916.
Office Staff: Administrative
Assistant/Chief of Staff, Ruby G. Moy;
Executive Assistant, Robert Schillinger.
Committees: Government Operations
(Ranking); Post Office & Civil Service.

New York 29th — West — Part of
Rochester. The district vote for George
Bush was 53% in 1988.

CQ Voting Studies

	1989	1990
Presidential	50%	32%
Party	25%	27%
Participation	93%	95%

Interest Groups

	1988	1989
ADA	65%	70%
ACU	22%	29%
AFL-CIO	92%	92%
CCUS	50%	56%

Elections

	1988	1990
General	69%	63%
Primary	u/o	u/o

CQ Voting Studies

	1989	1990
Presidential	65%	57%
Party	45%	58%
Participation	92%	94%

Interest Groups

	1988	1989
ADA	45%	20%
ACU	56%	65%
AFL-CIO	57%	10%
CCUS	100%	90%

Elections

	1988	1990
General	96%	70%
Primary	u/o	u/o

Amo Houghton (R-N.Y.)

Of Corning • Elected 1986
Pronounced Ay mo HO tun

Born: August 7, 1926, Corning, N.Y.
Education: Harvard U., B.A. 1950;
Harvard U., M.B.A. 1952.
Military Career: Marine Corps, 1945-46.
Occupation: Glassworks company
executive.
Family: Wife, Priscilla Dewey; four
children.
Religion: Episcopalian.
Political Career: No previous office.

Capitol Office: 1217 Longworth House
Office Building 20515; 225-3161.
Office Staff: Administrative Assistant,
Tom Lederer; Press Secretary, Mike
Hyland; Scheduler, Jackie Dreher.
Committees: Budget; Foreign Affairs.

New York 34th — Southern Tier —
Jamestown; Elmira. The district vote for
George Bush was 60% in 1988.

Steny H. Hoyer (D-Md.)
Of Berkshire • Elected 1981

Born: June 14, 1939, New York, N.Y.
Education: U. of Maryland, B.S. 1963;
Georgetown U., J.D. 1966.
Occupation: Lawyer.
Family: Wife, Judith Pickett; three
children.
Religion: Baptist.
Political Career: Md. Senate, 1967-79;
president, 1975-79; sought Democratic
nomination for lieutenant governor,
1978.

Capitol Office: 1214 Longworth House
Office Building 20515; 225-4131.
Office Staff: Chief of Staff, Sam
Wynkoop; Press Secretary, Charles Seigel;
Personal Secretary, Kathleen May.
Committees: House Administration;
Appropriations.

Maryland 5th — Northern Prince
George's County. The district vote for
George Bush was 40% in 1988.

CQ Voting Studies

	1989	1990
Presidential	35%	19%
Party	93%	96%
Participation	97%	98%

Interest Groups

	1988	1989
ADA	95%	80%
ACU	0%	0%
AFL-CIO	100%	100%
CCUS	21%	20%

Elections

	1988	1990
General	79%	81%
Primary	u/o	79%

CQ Voting Studies

	1989	1990
Presidential	49%	42%
Party	64%	59%
Participation	98%	99%

Interest Groups

	1988	1989
ADA	50%	50%
ACU	54%	58%
AFL-CIO	86%	64%
CCUS	50%	89%

Elections

	1988	1990
General	95%	87%
Primary	73%	u/o

Carroll Hubbard, Jr. (D-Ky.)
Of Mayfield • Elected 1974

Born: July 7, 1937, Murray, Ky.
Education: Georgetown College, B.S. 1959; U. of Louisville, J.D. 1962.
Military Career: Ky. Air National Guard, 1962-67; Ky. Army National Guard, 1968-70.
Occupation: Lawyer.
Family: Wife, Carol Brown; two children, three stepchildren.
Religion: Baptist.
Political Career: Ky. Senate, 1968-75; sought Democratic nomination for governor, 1979.

Capitol Office: 2267 Rayburn House Office Building 20515; 225-3115.
Office Staff: Administrative Assistant (Appointments), Lorraine Grant; Press Secretary, Joey Lucas.
Committees: Banking, Finance & Urban Affairs; Merchant Marine & Fisheries.

Kentucky 1st — West — Paducah. The district vote for George Bush was 51% in 1988.

Jerry Huckaby (D-La.)
Of Ringgold • Elected 1976

Born: July 19, 1941, Hodge, La.
Education: Louisiana State U., B.S. 1963; Georgia State U., M.B.A. 1968.
Occupation: Farmer; engineer; manager.
Family: Wife, Suzanna Woodard; two children.
Religion: Methodist.
Political Career: No previous office.

Capitol Office: 2182 Rayburn House Office Building 20515; 225-2376.
Office Staff: Administrative Assistant, Lou Gehrig Burnett; Press Secretary, Sophia Blanks; Executive Secretary, Hanna Curzon.
Committees: Agriculture; Budget.

Louisiana 5th — North — Monroe. The district vote for George Bush was 62% in 1988.

CQ Voting Studies

	1989	1990
Presidential	74%	50%
Party	50%	54%
Participation	93%	94%

Interest Groups

	1988	1989
ADA	40%	15%
ACU	65%	62%
AFL-CIO	57%	27%
CCUS	77%	100%

Elections

	1988	1990
General	u/o	u/o
Primary	71%	74%

William J. Hughes (D-N.J.)
Of Ocean City • Elected 1974

Born: October 17, 1932, Salem, N.J.
Education: Rutgers U., A.B. 1955; Rutgers U., J.D. 1958.
Occupation: Lawyer.
Family: Wife, Nancy L. Gibson; four children.
Religion: Episcopalian.
Political Career: Assistant prosecutor, Cape May County, 1960-70; Democratic nominee for U.S. House, 1970; Ocean City solicitor, 1970-74.

Capitol Office: 341 Cannon House Office Building 20515; 225-6572.
Office Staff: Administrative Assistant/Press Assistant, Mark Brown; Personal Secretary, Mary Minutes.
Committees: Judiciary; Merchant Marine & Fisheries.

New Jersey 2nd — South — Atlantic City; Vineland. The district vote for George Bush was 59% in 1988.

CQ Voting Studies

	1989	1990
Presidential	30%	26%
Party	84%	79%
Participation	98%	98%

Interest Groups

	1988	1989
ADA	70%	70%
ACU	16%	14%
AFL-CIO	100%	75%
CCUS	43%	50%

Elections

	1988	1990
General	66%	88%
Primary	u/o	u/o

Duncan Hunter (R-Calif.)
Of Coronado • Elected 1980

Born: May 31, 1948, Riverside, Calif.
Education: U. of Montana, 1966-67; U. of California, Santa Barbara, 1967-68; Western State U., B.S.L. 1976; Western State U., J.D. 1976.
Military Career: Army, 1969-71.
Occupation: Lawyer.
Family: Wife, Lynne Layh; two children.
Religion: Baptist.
Political Career: No previous office.

Capitol Office: 133 Cannon House Office Building 20515; 225-5672.
Office Staff: Administrative Assistant/Press Secretary, John Palafoutas; Office Manager/Personal Secretary, Melinda Patterson.
Committees: Armed Services.

California 45th — Imperial Valley; Part of San Diego. The district vote for George Bush was 66% in 1988.

CQ Voting Studies

	1989	1990
Presidential	76%	69%
Party	85%	84%
Participation	92%	95%

Interest Groups

	1988	1989
ADA	0%	10%
ACU	100%	96%
AFL-CIO	15%	18%
CCUS	77%	100%

Elections

	1988	1990
General	74%	73%
Primary	u/o	u/o

Earl Hutto (D-Fla.)
Of Panama City • Elected 1978

Born: May 12, 1926, Midland City, Ala.
Education: Troy State U., B.S. 1949; Northwestern U., 1951.
Military Career: Navy, 1944-46.
Occupation: Advertising and broadcasting executive; high school English teacher; sportscaster.
Family: Wife, Nancy Myers; two children.
Religion: Baptist.
Political Career: Fla. House, 1973-79.

Capitol Office: 2435 Rayburn House Office Building 20515; 225-4136.
Office Staff: Administrative Assistant, Gary P. Pulliam; Press Secretary, Brian C. Keeter; Executive Secretary, Cathie H. McCarley.
Committees: Armed Services; Merchant Marine & Fisheries.

Florida 1st — Northwest — Pensacola; Panama City. The district vote for George Bush was 73% in 1988.

CQ Voting Studies

	1989	1990
Presidential	70%	54%
Party	54%	51%
Participation	96%	96%

Interest Groups

	1988	1989
ADA	20%	10%
ACU	76%	85%
AFL-CIO	57%	45%
CCUS	69%	100%

Elections

	1988	1990
General	67%	52%
Primary	72%	73%

Henry J. Hyde (R-Ill.)

Of Densenville • Elected 1974

Born: April 18, 1924, Chicago, Ill.
Education: Georgetown U., 1942-43;
Duke U., 1943-44; Georgetown U., B.S.
1947; Loyola U., J.D. 1949.
Military Career: Navy, 1942-46; Naval
Reserve, 1949-68.
Occupation: Lawyer.
Family: Wife, Jeanne Simpson; four
children.
Religion: Roman Catholic.
Political Career: Republican nominee for
U.S. House, 1962; Ill. House, 1967-75;
majority leader, 1971-72.

Capitol Office: 2262 Rayburn House
Office Building 20515; 225-4561.
Office Staff: Chief of Staff, Judy
Wolverton; Press Secretary, Sam
Stratman; Personal Secretary, Ann Kelly.
Committees: Foreign Affairs; Judiciary.

Illinois 6th — Far West Chicago Suburbs
— Wheaton. The district vote for George
Bush was 69% in 1988.

CQ Voting Studies

	1989	1990
Presidential	66%	68%
Party	58%	78%
Participation	72%	96%

Interest Groups

	1988	1989
ADA	15%	5%
ACU	92%	95%
AFL-CIO	14%	10%
CCUS	100%	89%

Elections

	1988	1990
General	74%	67%
Primary	u/o	u/o

James M. Inhofe (R-Okla.)
Of Tulsa • Elected 1986
Pronounced IN hoff

Born: November 11, 1934, Des Moines, Iowa.
Education: U. of Tulsa, B.A. 1959.
Military Career: Army, 1954-56.
Occupation: Real estate developer; insurance company executive.
Family: Wife, Kay Kirkpatrick; four children.
Religion: Presbyterian.
Political Career: Okla. House, 1967-69; Okla. Senate, 1969-77; Republican nominee for governor, 1974; Republican nominee for U.S. House, 1976; Tulsa mayor, 1978-84; sought re-election as mayor, 1984.

Capitol Office: 408 Cannon House Office Building 20515; 225-2211.
Office Staff: Chief of Staff, V. Bruce Thompson; Press Secretary, Danny Finnerty; Executive Assistant, Dorothy Brown.
Committees: Merchant Marine & Fisheries; Public Works & Transportation.

Oklahoma 1st — Tulsa; Parts of Osage, Creek and Washington Counties. The district vote for George Bush was 61% in 1988.

CQ Voting Studies

	1989	1990
Presidential	72%	69%
Party	93%	92%
Participation	97%	98%

Interest Groups

	1988	1989
ADA	10%	5%
ACU	92%	96%
AFL-CIO	38%	17%
CCUS	92%	100%

Elections

	1988	1990
General	53%	56%
Primary	u/o	u/o

Andy Ireland (R-Fla.)
Of Winter Haven • Elected 1976

Born: August 23, 1930, Cincinnati, Ohio.
Education: Yale U., B.S. 1952; Columbia
U. School of Business, 1953-54; Louisiana
State U. School of Banking, 1959.
Occupation: Banker.
Family: Wife, Nancy Haydock; four
children.
Religion: Episcopalian.
Political Career: Winter Haven City
Commission, 1966-68; Democratic
nominee for Fla. Senate, 1972.

Capitol Office: 2466 Rayburn House
Office Building 20515; 225-5015.
Office Staff: Administrative Assistant,
Katharine Calhoun Wood; Press
Secretary, Jeanne Morin; Executive
Assistant, Kristen Martty.
Committees: Armed Services; Small
Business.

Florida 10th — Central — Lakeland;
Winter Haven; Bradenton. The district
vote for George Bush was 66% in 1988.

CQ Voting Studies

	1989	1990
Presidential	65%	75%
Party	82%	83%
Participation	90%	90%

Interest Groups

	1988	1989
ADA	5%	10%
ACU	100%	88%
AFL-CIO	14%	8%
CCUS	100%	100%

Elections

	1988	1990
General	73%	u/o
Primary	u/o	u/o

CQ Voting Studies

	1989	1990
Presidential	27%	23%
Party	48%	55%
Participation	94%	97%

Interest Groups

	1988	1989
ADA	95%	85%
ACU	12%	33%
AFL-CIO	100%	83%
CCUS	42%	50%

Elections

	1988	1990
General	61%	66%
Primary	92%	90%

Andy Jacobs, Jr. (D-Ind.)
Of Indianapolis • Elected 1964

Born: February 24, 1932, Indianapolis, Ind.
Education: Catholic U., 1949; Indiana U., B.S. 1955; Indiana U., LL.B. 1958.
Military Career: Marine Corps, 1950-52.
Occupation: Lawyer; police officer.
Family: Wife, Kimberly Hood.
Religion: Roman Catholic.
Political Career: Ind. House, 1959-61; Democratic nominee for Ind. Senate, 1960; Democratic nominee for U.S. House, 1962; defeated for reelection to U.S. House, 1972; reelected, 1974.

Capitol Office: 2313 Rayburn House Office Building 20515; 225-4011.
Office Staff: Administrative Assistant, David Wildes; Appointments Secretary, Deborah McGinn.
Committees: Ways & Means.

Indiana 10th — Indianapolis. The district vote for George Bush was 48% in 1988.

Craig T. James (R-Fla.)
Of DeLand • Elected 1988

Born: May 5, 1941, Augusta, Ga.
Education: Stetson U., B.S. 1963; Stetson U., J.D. 1967.
Military Career: Army National Guard, 1963-65; Army Reserve, 1965-69.
Occupation: Lawyer.
Family: Wife, Katherine Folks.
Religion: Baptist.
Political Career: No previous office.

Capitol Office: 1408 Longworth House Office Building 20515; 225-4035.
Office Staff: Chief of Staff, Brian Flood; Communications Director, Barbara Atkinson; Scheduler, Kim Snyder.
Committees: Judiciary; Veterans' Affairs.

Florida 4th — Northeast — Daytona Beach. The district vote for George Bush was 63% in 1988.

CQ Voting Studies

	1989	1990
Presidential	69%	58%
Party	87%	83%
Participation	99%	99%

Interest Groups

	1988	1989
ADA		0%
ACU		89%
AFL-CIO		8%
CCUS		100%

Elections

	1988	1990
General	50%	56%
Primary	50%	u/o

William J. Jefferson (D-La.)
Of New Orleans • Elected 1990

Born: March 14, 1947, Lake Providence, La.

Education: Southern U., B.A. 1969; Harvard U., J.D. 1972.

Occupation: Lawyer.

Family: Wife, Andrea Green; five children.

Religion: Baptist.

Political Career: La. Senate, 1981-91; candidate for mayor of New Orleans, 1982; candidate for mayor of New Orleans, 1986.

Capitol Office: 506 Cannon House Office Building 20515; 225-6636.

Office Staff: Administrative Assistant, Weldon Rougeau; Press Secretary, Jean LaPlace.

Committees: Education & Labor; Merchant Marine & Fisheries.

Louisiana 2nd — Jefferson Parish — New Orleans. The district vote for George Bush was 31% in 1988.

Elections

	1990
General	53%
Primary	24%

Ed Jenkins (D-Ga.)
Of Jasper • Elected 1976

Born: January 4, 1933, Young Harris, Ga.
Education: Young Harris College, A.A.
1951; Emory U., 1957-59; U. of Georgia,
LL.B. 1959.
Military Career: Coast Guard, 1952-55.
Occupation: Lawyer.
Family: Wife, Jo Thomasson; two
children.
Religion: Baptist.
Political Career: No previous office.

Capitol Office: 2427 Rayburn House
Office Building 20515; 225-5211.
Office Staff: Administrative Assistant,
Sammy Smith; Press Secretary, Jackie
Sosby; Executive Secretary, Lisa M. Perez.
Committees: Ways & Means.

Georgia 9th — Northeast — Gainesville.
The district vote for George Bush was
71% in 1988.

CQ Voting Studies

	1989	1990
Presidential	47%	44%
Party	63%	62%
Participation	90%	92%

Interest Groups

	1988	1989
ADA	45%	35%
ACU	54%	50%
AFL-CIO	64%	58%
CCUS	71%	60%

Elections

	1988	1990
General	63%	56%
Primary	u/o	u/o

Nancy L. Johnson (R-Conn.)
Of New Britain • Elected 1982

Born: January 5, 1935, Chicago, Ill.
Education: U. of Chicago, 1951; U. of Chicago, 1953; Radcliffe College, B.A. 1957; U. of London, 1957-58.
Occupation: Civic leader.
Family: Husband, Theodore Johnson; three children.
Religion: Unitarian.
Political Career: Republican candidate for New Britain Common Council, 1975; Conn. Senate, 1977-83.

Capitol Office: 227 Cannon House Office Building 20515; 225-4476.
Office Staff: Administrative Assistant, Eric Thompson; Press Secretary, Erin Sweeny; Office Manager/Executive Assistant, Jean Levicki.
Committees: Ways & Means.

Connecticut 6th — Northwest — New Britain. The district vote for George Bush was 53% in 1988.

CQ Voting Studies

	1989	1990
Presidential	60%	52%
Party	43%	54%
Participation	96%	98%

Interest Groups

	1988	1989
ADA	50%	30%
ACU	56%	50%
AFL-CIO	71%	33%
CCUS	69%	80%

Elections

	1988	1990
General	66%	74%
Primary	u/o	u/o

Tim Johnson (D-S.D.)
Of Vermillion • Elected 1986

Born: December 28, 1946, Canton, S.D.
Education: U. of South Dakota, B.A. 1969;
U. of South Dakota, M.A. 1970; Michigan
State U., 1970-71; U. of South Dakota, J.D.
1975.
Occupation: Lawyer.
Family: Wife, Barbara Brooks; three
children.
Religion: Lutheran.
Political Career: S.D. House, 1979-83;
S.D. Senate, 1983-87.

Capitol Office: 428 Cannon House
Office Building 20515; 225-2801.
Office Staff: Administrative Assistant,
Drey Samuelson; Press Secretary, John
Devereaux; Office Manager, Kelly Weiss.
Committees: Agriculture; Interior &
Insular Affairs.

South Dakota — At Large. The district
vote for George Bush was 53% in 1988.

CQ Voting Studies

	1989	1990
Presidential	34%	25%
Party	83%	82%
Participation	99%	99%

Interest Groups

	1988	1989
ADA	70%	85%
ACU	28%	21%
AFL-CIO	93%	83%
CCUS	36%	40%

Elections

	1988	1990
General	72%	68%
Primary	u/o	u/o

Harry A. Johnston (D-Fla.)
Of West Palm Beach • Elected 1988

Born: December 2, 1931, West Palm Beach, Fla.
Education: Virginia Military Institute, B.A. 1953; U. of Florida, LL.B. 1958.
Military Career: Army, 1953-55.
Occupation: Lawyer.
Family: Wife, Mary Otley; two children.
Religion: Presbyterian.
Political Career: Fla. Senate, 1975-87; president, 1985-87; sought Democratic nomination for governor, 1986.

Capitol Office: 1028 Longworth House Office Building 20515; 225-3001.
Office Staff: Chief of Staff, Suzanne M. Stoll; Press Secretary, Brian Geiger; Executive Assistant, Lisa White.
Committees: Foreign Affairs; Interior & Insular Affairs.

Florida 14th — Southeast — Parts of Palm Beach and West Palm Beach. The district vote for George Bush was 53% in 1988.

CQ Voting Studies

	1989	1990
Presidential	34%	23%
Party	88%	81%
Participation	97%	91%

Interest Groups

	1989
ADA	70%
ACU	7%
AFL-CIO	83%
CCUS	50%

Elections

	1988	1990
General	55%	66%
Primary	59%	u/o

Ben Jones (D-Ga.)
Of Covington • Elected 1988

Born: August 30, 1941, Tarboro, N.C.
Education: U. of North Carolina, 1961-65.
Occupation: Actor.
Family: Wife, Vivian Walker; two children.
Religion: Baptist.
Political Career: Democratic nominee for U.S. House, 1986.

Capitol Office: 514 Cannon House Office Building 20515; 225-4272.
Office Staff: Administrative Assistant, Wendy Herzog; Press Secretary, Peter Ruzicka; Office Manager/Scheduler, Maggie Pollock.
Committees: Public Works & Transportation; Veterans' Affairs.

Georgia 4th — Atlanta Suburbs — De Kalb County. The district vote for George Bush was 59% in 1988.

CQ Voting Studies

	1989	1990
Presidential	38%	34%
Party	86%	84%
Participation	97%	98%

Interest Groups

	1989
ADA	70%
ACU	14%
AFL-CIO	67%
CCUS	60%

Elections

	1988	1990
General	60%	53%
Primary	62%	u/o

Walter B. Jones (D-N.C.)
Of Farmville • Elected 1966

Born: August 19, 1913, Fayetteville, N.C.
Education: North Carolina State U., B.A. 1934.
Occupation: Office supply company owner.
Family: Wife, Elizabeth Fisher; two children.
Religion: Baptist.
Political Career: Farmville commissioner, 1948; Mayor of Farmville, 1948-52; N.C. House, 1955-59; sought Democratic nomination for U.S. House, 1960; N.C. Senate, 1965-66.

Capitol Office: 241 Cannon House Office Building 20515; 225-3101.
Office Staff: Administrative Assistant, Floyd Lupton; Press Secretary, Nancy Fish; Appointments Secretary, Gloria Curry.
Committees: Agriculture; Merchant Marine & Fisheries (Chairman).

North Carolina 1st — Northeast — Greenville; Kinston. The district vote for George Bush was 54% in 1988.

CQ Voting Studies

	1989	1990
Presidential	36%	28%
Party	78%	80%
Participation	91%	94%

Interest Groups

	1988	1989
ADA	80%	70%
ACU	13%	26%
AFL-CIO	75%	75%
CCUS	46%	60%

Elections

	1988	1990
General	65%	65%
Primary	u/o	u/o

Jim Jontz (D-Ind.)

Of Monticello • Elected 1986

Born: December 18, 1951, Indianapolis, Ind.
Education: Indiana U., B.S. 1973.
Occupation: Public official.
Family: Single.
Religion: Methodist.
Political Career: Ind. House, 1975-85; Ind. Senate, 1985-87.

Capitol Office: 1317 Longworth House Office Building 20515; 225-5037.
Office Staff: Administrative Assistant, Christopher Klose; Press Secretary, Scott Campbell; Appointments Secretary, Bruce Ehrle.
Committees: Agriculture; Interior & Insular Affairs.

Indiana 5th — North — Kokomo. The district vote for George Bush was 65% in 1988.

CQ Voting Studies

	1989	1990
Presidential	22%	14%
Party	94%	90%
Participation	100%	99%

Interest Groups

	1988	1989
ADA	95%	100%
ACU	4%	4%
AFL-CIO	100%	83%
CCUS	21%	20%

Elections

	1988	1990
General	56%	53%
Primary	92%	u/o

Paul E. Kanjorski (D-Pa.)
Of Nanticoke • Elected 1984

Born: April 2, 1937, Nanticoke, Penn.
Education: Temple U., 1957-62;
Dickinson School of Law, 1962-65.
Military Career: Army, 1960-61.
Occupation: Lawyer.
Family: Wife, Nancy Hickerson; one
child.
Religion: Roman Catholic.
Political Career: Sought Democratic
nomination for U.S. House, special
election, 1980; sought Democratic
nomination for U.S. House, 1980.

Capitol Office: 424 Cannon House
Office Building 20515; 225-6511.
Office Staff: Chief of Staff, W. Robert
Hall; Press Secretary, Eva Malecki;
Executive Assistant, Karen Feather.
Committees: Banking, Finance & Urban
Affairs; Post Office & Civil Service.

Pennsylvania 11th — Northeast —
Wilkes-Barre. The district vote for
George Bush was 52% in 1988.

CQ Voting Studies

	1989	1990
Presidential	36%	25%
Party	85%	87%
Participation	99%	99%

Interest Groups

	1988	1989
ADA	70%	80%
ACU	20%	14%
AFL-CIO	100%	92%
CCUS	36%	40%

Elections

	1988	1990
General	u/o	u/o
Primary	u/o	u/o

Marcy Kaptur (D-Ohio)
Of Toledo • Elected 1982

Born: June 17, 1946, Toledo, Ohio.
Education: U. of Wisconsin, B.A. 1968; U. of Michigan, M.U.P. 1974; Massachusetts Institute of Technology, 1981.
Occupation: Urban planner; White House staff member.
Family: Single.
Religion: Roman Catholic.
Political Career: Democratic County Central Committee secretary, 1970-74; Assistant Director for Urban Affairs, White House Domestic Policy Staff, 1977-79.

Capitol Office: 1228 Longworth House Office Building 20515; 225-4146.
Office Staff: Administrative Assistant, Ted Mastroianni; Press Secretary, Rochelle Stratton; Office Manager, Norma Olsen.
Committees: Appropriations.

Ohio 9th — Northwest — Toledo. The district vote for George Bush was 46% in 1988.

CQ Voting Studies

	1989	1990
Presidential	33%	23%
Party	86%	86%
Participation	95%	95%

Interest Groups

	1988	1989
ADA	75%	75%
ACU	13%	11%
AFL-CIO	100%	82%
CCUS	43%	44%

Elections

	1988	1990
General	81%	78%
Primary	u/o	u/o

John R. Kasich (R-Ohio)
Of Westerville • Elected 1982
Pronounced KAY sick

Born: May 13, 1952, McKees Rocks, Penn.
Education: Ohio State U., B.A. 1974.
Occupation: Legislative aide.
Family: Divorced.
Religion: Roman Catholic.
Political Career: Ohio Senate, 1979-83.

Capitol Office: 1133 Longworth House Office Building 20515; 225-5355.
Office Staff: Chief of Staff, Don Thibaut; Press Secretary, Bruce Cuthbertson; Executive Assistant, Mimi McCarthy.
Committees: Armed Services; Budget.

Ohio 12th — Northeast Columbus and Suburbs. The district vote for George Bush was 61% in 1988.

CQ Voting Studies

	1989	1990
Presidential	70%	69%
Party	68%	78%
Participation	99%	97%

Interest Groups

	1988	1989
ADA	15%	20%
ACU	92%	100%
AFL-CIO	29%	9%
CCUS	93%	90%

Elections

	1988	1990
General	79%	72%
Primary	u/o	u/o

Joseph P. Kennedy II
(D-Mass.)
Of Boston • Elected 1986

Born: September 24, 1952, Boston, Mass.
Education: U. of Massachusetts, B.A. 1976.
Occupation: Energy company executive.
Family: Divorced; two children.
Religion: Roman Catholic.
Political Career: No previous office.

Capitol Office: 1208 Longworth House Office Building 20515; 225-5111.
Office Staff: Administrative Assistant, William Cunningham; Press Assistant, Maureen Toal; Personal Secretary/Scheduler, Beth Kelly.
Committees: Banking, Finance & Urban Affairs; Veterans' Affairs.

Massachusetts 8th — Boston and Suburbs — Cambridge. The district vote for George Bush was 33% in 1988.

CQ Voting Studies

	1989	1990
Presidential	23%	21%
Party	95%	90%
Participation	98%	94%

Interest Groups

	1988	1989
ADA	95%	95%
ACU	4%	4%
AFL-CIO	100%	100%
CCUS	21%	40%

Elections

	1988	1990
General	80%	72%
Primary	u/o	u/o

CQ Voting Studies

	1989	1990
Presidential	28%	22%
Party	93%	92%
Participation	97%	99%

Interest Groups

	1988	1989
ADA	90%	95%
ACU	8%	7%
AFL-CIO	100%	92%
CCUS	36%	30%

Elections

	1988	1990
General	77%	71%
Primary	u/o	u/o

Barbara B. Kennelly (D-Conn.)
Of Hartford • *Elected 1982*
Pronounced ka NEL ly

Born: July 10, 1936, Hartford, Conn.
Education: Trinity College, Washington, B.A. 1958; Trinity College, Hartford, M.A. 1973.
Occupation: Public official.
Family: Husband, James J. Kennelly; four children.
Religion: Roman Catholic.
Political Career: Hartford Court of Common Council, 1975-79; Conn. secretary of state, 1979-82.

Capitol Office: 204 Cannon House Office Building 20515; 225-2265.
Office Staff: Administrative Assistant, Michael Prucker; Press Secretary, Ranit Schmelzer; Personal Secretary, Emma Lee Harrell.
Committees: Select Intelligence; Ways & Means.

Connecticut 1st — Central — Hartford. The district vote for George Bush was 44% in 1988.

Dale E. Kildee (D-Mich.)
Of Flint • Elected 1976

Born: September 16, 1929, Flint, Mich.
Education: Sacred Heart Seminary, B.A.
1952; U. of Detroit, 1954; U. of Peshawar,
Pakistan, 1958-59; U. of Michigan, M.A.
1961.
Occupation: Teacher.
Family: Wife, Gayle Heyn; three children.
Religion: Roman Catholic.
Political Career: Mich. House, 1965-74;
Mich. Senate, 1975-77.

Capitol Office: 2239 Rayburn House
Office Building 20515; 225-3611.
Office Staff: Administrative Assistant,
Christopher Mansour; Press Secretary,
Christopher R. Ludwig; Personal
Secretary/Business Manager, Dolores
Nouhan.
Committees: Budget; Education & Labor.

Michigan 7th — East Central — Flint. The
district vote for George Bush was 44% in
1988.

CQ Voting Studies

	1989	1990
Presidential	35%	19%
Party	94%	95%
Participation	100%	100%

Interest Groups

	1988	1989
ADA	95%	95%
ACU	4%	11%
AFL-CIO	100%	100%
CCUS	14%	20%

Elections

	1988	1990
General	76%	68%
Primary	u/o	u/o

Gerald D. Kleczka (D-Wis.)
Of Milwaukee • Elected 1984
Pronounced KLETCH ka

Born: November 26, 1943, Milwaukee, Wis.
Education: U. of Wisconsin, 1961-62; U. of Wisconsin, 1967; U. of Wisconsin, 1970.
Military Career: Wis. Air National Guard, 1963-69.
Occupation: Accountant.
Family: Wife, Bonnie L. Scott.
Religion: Roman Catholic.
Political Career: Wis. Assembly, 1969-73; Wis. Senate, 1975-84.

CQ Voting Studies

	1989	1990
Presidential	28%	21%
Party	88%	91%
Participation	93%	96%

Capitol Office: 226 Cannon House Office Building 20515; 225-4572.
Office Staff: Administrative Assistant, Brian Doherty; Press Secretary, Pamela S. Moen; Office Manager, Joyce L. Freeland.
Committees: House Administration; Banking, Finance & Urban Affairs; Government Operations.

Interest Groups

	1988	1989
ADA	95%	95%
ACU	4%	0%
AFL-CIO	93%	83%
CCUS	36%	40%

Wisconsin 4th — Southern Milwaukee and Suburbs — Waukesha. The district vote for George Bush was 44% in 1988.

Elections

	1988	1990
General	u/o	69%
Primary	u/o	81%

Scott L. Klug (R-Wis.)
Of Madison • Elected 1990
Pronounced KLOOG

Born: January 16, 1953, Milwaukee, Wis.
Education: Lawrence U., B.S. 1975;
Northwestern U., M.S.J. 1976; U. of
Wisconsin, Madison, M.B.A. 1990.
Occupation: Business development firm
vice president.
Family: Wife, Tess Summers; two
children.
Religion: Roman Catholic.
Political Career: No previous office.

Capitol Office: 1224 Longworth House
Office Building 20515; 225-2906.
Office Staff: Administrative Assistant,
Brandon Scholz; Press Secretary, Jackie
Dailey; Scheduler, Terri Peacock.
Committees: Education & Labor;
Government Operations.

Wisconsin 2nd — South — Madison. The
district vote for George Bush was 44% in
1988.

Elections

	1990
General	53%
Primary	u/o

Jim Kolbe (R-Ariz.)
Of Tucson • Elected 1984
Pronounced COLE bee

Born: June 28, 1942, Evanston, Ill.
Education: Northwestern U., B.A. 1965;
Stanford U., M.B.A. 1967.
Military Career: Navy, 1967-69.
Occupation: Real estate consultant.
Family: Wife, Sarah Dinham.
Religion: Methodist.
Political Career: Ariz. Senate, 1977-83;
Republican nominee for U.S. House,
1982.

Capitol Office: 410 Cannon House
Office Building 20515; 225-2542.
Office Staff: Administrative Assistant,
Rowdy Yeates; Press Secretary, Pilar
Keagy; Office Manager/Personal
Assistant, Jill Haddad.
Committees: Appropriations.

Arizona 5th — Southeast. The district
vote for George Bush was 55% in 1988.

CQ Voting Studies

	1989	1990
Presidential	69%	64%
Party	81%	82%
Participation	98%	97%

Interest Groups

	1988	1989
ADA	20%	15%
ACU	80%	85%
AFL-CIO	14%	0%
CCUS	93%	100%

Elections

	1988	1990
General	68%	65%
Primary	78%	u/o

Joe Kolter (D-Pa.)
Of New Brighton • Elected 1982

Born: September 3, 1926, McDonald, Ohio.
Education: Geneva College, B.S., B.A. 1950.
Military Career: Air Force, 1945-46.
Occupation: Accountant.
Family: Wife, Dorothy Gray; four children.
Religion: Roman Catholic.
Political Career: New Brighton City Council, 1962-66; Pa. House, 1968-83; sought Democratic nomination for U.S. House, 1974.

Capitol Office: 212 Cannon House Office Building 20515; 225-2565.
Office Staff: Office Coordinator, Mike Short; Press Secretary, Mike Short; Appointments Secretary, Charlotte Beltz.
Committees: House Administration; Public Works & Transportation.

Pennsylvania 4th — West — New Castle. The district vote for George Bush was 45% in 1988.

CQ Voting Studies

	1989	1990
Presidential	45%	24%
Party	73%	83%
Participation	91%	94%

Interest Groups

	1988	1989
ADA	60%	65%
ACU	22%	28%
AFL-CIO	100%	100%
CCUS	17%	40%

Elections

	1988	1990
General	70%	56%
Primary	u/o	83%

Mike Kopetski (D-Ore.)
Of Keizer • Elected 1990

Born: October 27, 1949, Pendleton, Ore.
Education: American U., B.A. 1971; Lewis and Clark College, J.D. 1978.
Occupation: Advertising executive.
Family: Wife, Linda Zuckerman; one child.
Religion: Not specified.
Political Career: Sought Democratic nomination for U.S. House, 1982; Oregon House, 1985-89; Democratic nominee for U.S. House, 1988.

Capitol Office: 1520 Longworth House Office Building 20515; 225-5711.
Office Staff: Administrative Assistant, Phil Rotondi; Press Secretary, Maureen Driscoll; Appointments Secretary, Penny Gross.
Committees: Agriculture; Judiciary; Science, Space & Technology.

Oregon 5th — Willamette Valley — Salem; Corvallis. The district vote for George Bush was 50% in 1988.

Elections

	1990
General	55%
Primary	u/o

Peter H. Kostmayer (D-Pa.)
Of New Hope • Elected 1976

Born: September 27, 1946, New York, N.Y.
Education: Columbia U., B.A. 1971.
Occupation: Public relations consultant.
Family: Wife, Pamela Jones Rosenberg; two stepchildren.
Religion: Episcopalian.
Political Career: Defeated for reelection, 1980; reelected, 1982.

Capitol Office: 2436 Rayburn House Office Building 20515; 225-4276.
Office Staff: Administrative Assistant, Janet Lynch; Press Secretary, John W.P. Seager; Executive Assistant, Sallie Bell.
Committees: Energy & Commerce; Foreign Affairs; Interior & Insular Affairs.

Pennsylvania 8th — Northern Philadelphia Suburbs; Bucks County. The district vote for George Bush was 60% in 1988.

CQ Voting Studies

	1989	1990
Presidential	26%	20%
Party	94%	89%
Participation	98%	97%

Interest Groups

	1988	1989
ADA	85%	90%
ACU	4%	7%
AFL-CIO	100%	92%
CCUS	31%	50%

Elections

	1988	1990
General	57%	57%
Primary	90%	u/o

CQ Voting Studies

	1989	1990
Presidential	80%	79%
Party	96%	94%
Participation	99%	98%

Interest Groups

	1988	1989
ADA	0%	0%
ACU	100%	96%
AFL-CIO	8%	8%
CCUS	93%	100%

Elections

	1988	1990
General	87%	61%
Primary	u/o	u/o

Jon Kyl (R-Ariz.)
Of Phoenix • Elected 1986

Born: April 25, 1942, Oakland, Neb.
Education: U. of Arizona, B.A. 1964; U. of Arizona, LL.B. 1966.
Occupation: Lawyer.
Family: Wife, Caryll Collins; two children.
Religion: Presbyterian.
Political Career: No previous office.

Capitol Office: 336 Cannon House Office Building 20515; 225-3361.
Office Staff: Administrative Assistant, Patti Alderson; Communications Director, Bill Waters; Executive Assistant, Sherry Jackson.
Committees: Armed Services; Government Operations.

Arizona 4th — Northeast — Northern Phoenix; Scottsdale. The district vote for George Bush was 65% in 1988.

John J. LaFalce (D-N.Y.)
Of Tonawanda • Elected 1974

Born: October 6, 1939, Buffalo, N.Y.
Education: Canisius College, B.S. 1961;
Villanova U., J.D. 1964.
Military Career: Army, 1965-67.
Occupation: Lawyer.
Family: Wife, Patricia Fisher; one child.
Religion: Roman Catholic.
Political Career: N.Y. Senate, 1971-73;
N.Y. Assembly, 1973-75.

Capitol Office: 2367 Rayburn House
Office Building 20515; 225-3231.
Office Staff: Administrative Assistant,
Robert Walker; Communications
Director, Gary Luczak.
Committees: Banking, Finance & Urban
Affairs; Small Business (Chairman).

New York 32nd — West — Niagara Falls;
Part of Rochester. The district vote for
George Bush was 48% in 1988.

CQ Voting Studies

	1989	1990
Presidential	34%	30%
Party	81%	80%
Participation	95%	94%

Interest Groups

	1988	1989
ADA	80%	90%
ACU	8%	12%
AFL-CIO	93%	83%
CCUS	38%	50%

Elections

	1988	1990
General	73%	55%
Primary	u/o	u/o

CQ Voting Studies

	1989	1990
Presidential	73%	70%
Party	87%	89%
Participation	100%	99%

Interest Groups

	1988	1989
ADA	35%	0%
ACU	80%	93%
AFL-CIO	36%	8%
CCUS	93%	100%

Elections

	1988	1990
General	50%	55%
Primary	u/o	89%

Robert J. Lagomarsino
(R-Calif.)
Of Ventura • Elected 1974
Pronounced LAH go mar SEE no

Born: September 4, 1926, Ventura, Calif.
Education: U. of California, Santa Barbara, B.A. 1950; Santa Clara U., LL.B. 1953.
Military Career: Navy, 1944-46.
Occupation: Lawyer.
Family: Wife, Norma Smith; three children.
Religion: Roman Catholic.
Political Career: Mayor of Ojai, 1958-61; Calif. Senate, 1961-74.

Capitol Office: 2332 Rayburn House Office Building 20515; 225-3601.
Office Staff: Chief of Staff, Susan Gerrick; Press Secretary, John Doherty; Scheduler, Joanna Varautsos.
Committees: Foreign Affairs; Interior & Insular Affairs.

California 19th — South Central Coast — Santa Barbara. The district vote for George Bush was 54% in 1988.

H. Martin Lancaster (D-N C.)
Of Goldsboro • Elected 1986

Born: March 24, 1943, Goldsboro, N.C.
Education: U. of North Carolina, A.B. 1965; U. of North Carolina, J.D. 1967.
Military Career: Navy, 1967-70; Naval Reserve, 1970-present.
Occupation: Lawyer.
Family: Wife, Alice Matheny; two children.
Religion: Presbyterian.
Political Career: N.C. House, 1979-87.

Capitol Office: 1417 Longworth House Office Building 20515; 225-3415.
Office Staff: Administrative Assistant, Charles R. Rawls; Communications Director, Marshall Skip Smith; Executive Assistant/Scheduler, Polly Lamberth.
Committees: Armed Services; Small Business.

North Carolina 3rd — Southeast Central — Goldsboro. The district vote for George Bush was 58% in 1988.

CQ Voting Studies

	1989	1990
Presidential	45%	38%
Party	73%	76%
Participation	96%	99%

Interest Groups

	1988	1989
ADA	60%	40%
ACU	40%	30%
AFL-CIO	71%	42%
CCUS	64%	80%

Elections

	1988	1990
General	u/o	59%
Primary	u/o	u/o

Tom Lantos (D-Calif.)
Of San Mateo • Elected 1980

Born: February 1, 1928, Budapest, Hungary.
Education: U. of Washington, B.A. 1949; U. of Washington, M.A. 1950; U. of California, Ph.D. 1953.
Occupation: Professor of economics.
Family: Wife, Annette Tillemann; two children.
Religion: Jewish.
Political Career: Millbrae Board of Education, 1958-66.

Capitol Office: 1526 Longworth House Office Building 20515; 225-3531.
Office Staff: Administrative Assistant/Press Secretary, Robert King; Executive Secretary, Helena Anderson.
Committees: Finance & Urban Affairs; Foreign Affairs; Government Operations.

California 11th — Most of San Mateo County. The district vote for George Bush was 40% in 1988.

CQ Voting Studies

	1989	1990
Presidential	31%	26%
Party	90%	89%
Participation	92%	96%

Interest Groups

	1988	1989
ADA	85%	80%
ACU	8%	0%
AFL-CIO	100%	100%
CCUS	31%	40%

Elections

	1988	1990
General	71%	66%
Primary	u/o	u/o

Larry LaRocco (D-Idaho)
Of Boise • Elected 1990
Pronounced la ROCK oh

Born: August 25, 1946, Van Nuys, Calif.
Education: U. of Portland, B.A. 1967;
Stanford U., Institute of TV and Radio,
1967; Johns Hopkins School of Advanced
International Studies, 1968-69; Boston U.,
M.S. 1969.
Military Career: Army, 1969-72.
Occupation: Stockbroker.
Family: Wife, Chris Bideganeta; two
children.
Religion: Roman Catholic.
Political Career: Democratic nominee
for U.S. House, 1982; Democratic
nominee for Idaho Senate, 1986.

Capitol Office: 1117 Longworth House
Office Building 20515; 225-6611.
Office Staff: Chief of Staff, Garry
Wenske; Press Secretary/Field
Representative, Tom Knappenberger;
Appointments Secretary, Cherie Slayton.
Committees: Banking, Finance & Urban
Affairs; Interior & Insular Affairs.

Idaho 1st — North and West — Lewiston;
Boise. The district vote for George Bush
was 59% in 1988.

Elections

	1990
General	53%
Primary	43%

CQ Voting Studies

	1989	1990
Presidential	63%	47%
Party	59%	58%
Participation	94%	93%

Interest Groups

	1989
ADA	20%
ACU	56%
AFL-CIO	44%
CCUS	67%

Elections

	1988	1990
General	53%	54%
Primary	72%	u/o

Greg Laughlin (D-Texas)

Of West Columbia • Elected 1988

Pronounced LAWF lin

Born: January 21, 1942, Bay City, Texas.
Education: Texas A&M U., B.A. 1964; U. of Texas, LL.B. 1967.
Military Career: Army, 1968-70; Army Reserve, 1964-67; Army Reserve, 1970-present.
Occupation: Lawyer.
Family: Wife, Ginger Jones; two children.
Religion: Methodist.
Political Career: Democratic nominee for U.S. House, 1986.

Capitol Office: 218 Cannon House Office Building 20515; 225-2831.
Office Staff: Administrative Assistant, Jim Greenwood; Press Secretary, Clara C. Pizana; Appointments Secretary, Kristin Kessler.
Committees: Merchant Marine & Fisheries; Public Works & Transportation.

Texas 14th — Southeast; Gulf Coast. The district vote for George Bush was 57% in 1988.

Jim Leach (R Iowa)
Of Davenport • Elected 1976

Born: October 15, 1942, Davenport, Iowa.

Education: Princeton U., B.A. 1964; Johns Hopkins U., M.A. 1966; London School of Economics, 1966-68.

Occupation: Propane gas company executive; foreign service officer; congressional aide.

Family: Wife, Elisabeth Ann "Deba" Foxley; two children.

Religion: Episcopalian.

Political Career: Republican nominee for U.S. House, 1974.

Capitol Office: 1514 Longworth House Office Building 20515; 225-6576.

Office Staff: Administrative Assistant, Bill Tate; Press Secretary, Joe Pinder; Legislative Assistant, Janet Ruth.

Committees: Banking, Finance & Urban Affairs; Foreign Affairs.

Iowa 1st — Southeast — Davenport. The district vote for George Bush was 44% in 1988.

CQ Voting Studies

	1989	1990
Presidential	45%	38%
Party	59%	62%
Participation	94%	98%

Interest Groups

	1988	1989
ADA	75%	65%
ACU	32%	46%
AFL-CIO	79%	25%
CCUS	64%	67%

Elections

	1988	1990
General	61%	u/o
Primary	u/o	u/o

CQ Voting Studies

	1989	1990
Presidential	29%	19%
Party	92%	89%
Participation	94%	93%

Interest Groups

	1988	1989
ADA	85%	90%
ACU	9%	0%
AFL-CIO	100%	100%
CCUS	25%	40%

Elections

	1988	1990
General	70%	u/o
Primary	u/o	u/o

Richard H. Lehman (D-Calif.)
Of Fresno • Elected 1982
Pronounced LEE mun

Born: July 20, 1948, Sanger, Calif.
Education: Fresno City College, A.A.
1968; California State U., Fresno, 1969;
California State U., Santa Cruz, B.A. 1970.
Military Career: Army National Guard,
1970-76.
Occupation: Legislative aide.
Family: Wife, Patricia Ann Kandarian.
Religion: Lutheran.
Political Career: Calif. Assembly, 1977-
83.

Capitol Office: 1319 Longworth House
Office Building 20515; 225-4540.
Office Staff: Administrative Assistant,
Scott Nishioki; Press Secretary, Allen
Clark; Executive Assistant, Jill
Cunningham.
Committees: Energy & Commerce;
Interior & Insular Affairs.

California 18th — Central Valley; Fresno.
The district vote for George Bush was
46% in 1988.

William Lehman   (D-Fla.)
Of Biscayne Park • Elected 1972
Pronounced LAY mun

Born: October 5, 1913, Selma, Ala.
Education: U. of Alabama, B.S. 1934.
Occupation: Automobile dealer; high school English teacher.
Family: Wife, Joan Feibelman; two children.
Religion: Jewish.
Political Career: Dade County School Board, 1966-72; chairman, 1971-72.

Capitol Office: 2347 Rayburn House Office Building 20515; 225-4211.
Office Staff: Executive Assistant, Carolyn Cornish; Press Assistant, John Schelble; Personal Secretary, Karen Rosen.
Committees: Appropriations.

Florida 17th — Southeast — North Miami; Part of Hialeah. The district vote for George Bush was 40% in 1988.

CQ Voting Studies

	1989	1990
Presidential	24%	19%
Party	95%	94%
Participation	95%	97%

Interest Groups

	1988	1989
ADA	100%	95%
ACU	8%	0%
AFL-CIO	93%	100%
CCUS	36%	20%

Elections

	1988	1990
General	u/o	78%
Primary	u/o	u/o

Norman F. Lent (R-N.Y.)

Of East Rockaway • Elected 1970

Born: March 23, 1931, Oceanside, N.Y.
Education: Hofstra U., B.A. 1952; Cornell U., J.D. 1957.
Military Career: Navy, 1952-54.
Occupation: Lawyer.
Family: Wife, Barbara Morris; three children.
Religion: Methodist.
Political Career: N.Y. Senate, 1963-71.

Capitol Office: 2408 Rayburn House Office Building 20515; 225-7896.
Office Staff: Administrative Assistant, Michael Scrivner; Press Assistant, Jon Hymes; Personal Secretary, Carolyn Radcliff.
Committees: Energy & Commerce (Ranking); Merchant Marine & Fisheries.

New York 4th — Long Island — Southeastern Nassau County. The district vote for George Bush was 58% in 1988.

CQ Voting Studies

	1989	1990
Presidential	76%	67%
Party	56%	60%
Participation	93%	92%

Interest Groups

	1988	1989
ADA	25%	10%
ACU	68%	70%
AFL-CIO	62%	33%
CCUS	69%	90%

Elections

	1988	1990
General	70%	61%
Primary	u/o	u/o

Sander M. Levin (D-Mich.)
Of Southfield • Elected 1902

Born: September 6, 1931, Detroit, Mich.
Education: U. of Chicago, B.A. 1952;
Columbia U., M.A. 1954; Harvard U., LL.B.
1957.
Occupation: Lawyer.
Family: Wife, Victoria Schlafer; four
children.
Religion: Jewish.
Political Career: Mich. Senate, 1965-71;
Democratic nominee for governor, 1970;
Democratic nominee for governor, 1974.

Capitol Office: 323 Cannon House
Office Building 20515; 225-4961.
Office Staff: Administrative Assistant,
Kitty Higgins; Press Secretary, Cynthia
Mann; Office Manager/Personal
Secretary, Marilyn Lagios.
Committees: Ways & Means.

**Michigan 17th — Northwest Detroit;
Southeast Oakland County. The district
vote for George Bush was 46% in 1988.

CQ Voting Studies

	1989	1990
Presidential	31%	19%
Party	98%	97%
Participation	100%	99%

Interest Groups

	1988	1989
ADA	100%	95%
ACU	0%	0%
AFL-CIO	100%	100%
CCUS	31%	20%

Elections

	1988	1990
General	70%	68%
Primary	u/o	u/o

Mel Levine (D-Calif.)
Of Pacific Palisades • *Elected 1982*
Pronounced la VINE

Born: June 7, 1943, Los Angeles, Calif.
Education: U. of California, A.B. 1964;
Princeton U., M.P.A. 1966; Harvard U.,
J.D. 1969.
Occupation: Lawyer.
Family: Wife, Jan Greenberg; three
children.
Religion: Jewish.
Political Career: Calif. Assembly, 1977-
83.

Capitol Office: 2443 Rayburn House
Office Building 20515; 225-6451.
Office Staff: Administrative Assistant, Bill
Andresen; Press Secretary, Jon Cowan;
Personal Secretary/Office Manager,
Anne Johnson.
Committees: Foreign Affairs; Interior &
Insular Affairs; Judiciary.

California 27th — Pacific Coast — Santa
Monica. The district vote for George
Bush was 44% in 1988.

CQ Voting Studies

	1989	1990
Presidential	31%	19%
Party	96%	93%
Participation	96%	95%

Interest Groups

	1988	1989
ADA	95%	90%
ACU	4%	0%
AFL-CIO	86%	100%
CCUS	36%	40%

Elections

	1988	1990
General	68%	58%
Primary	88%	u/o

Jerry Lewis (R-Calif.)
Of Redlands • Elected 1978

Born: October 21, 1934, Seattle, Wash.
Education: U.C.L.A., B.A. 1956.
Occupation: Insurance executive.
Family: Wife, Arlene Willis; four children, three stepchildren.
Religion: Presbyterian.
Political Career: San Bernardino School Board, 1965-68; Calif. Assembly, 1969-79; Republican nominee for Calif. Senate, 1973.

Capitol Office: 2312 Rayburn House Office Building 20515; 225-5861.
Office Staff: Administrative Assistant, Arlene Willis; Press Secretary, David LesStrang; Executive Assistant, Deborah McPherson.
Committees: Appropriations.

California 35th — San Bernardino County. The district vote for George Bush was 65% in 1988.

CQ Voting Studies

	1989	1990
Presidential	78%	65%
Party	80%	70%
Participation	97%	88%

Interest Groups

	1988	1989
ADA	5%	10%
ACU	90%	79%
AFL-CIO	22%	25%
CCUS	67%	78%

Elections

	1988	1990
General	70%	61%
Primary	u/o	79%

John Lewis (D-Ga.)
Of Atlanta • Elected 1986

Born: February 21, 1940, Troy, Ala.
Education: American Baptist Theological Seminary, B.A. 1961; Fisk U., B.A. 1963.
Occupation: Civil rights activist.
Family: Wife, Lillian Miles; one child.
Religion: Baptist.
Political Career: Special-election candidate for U.S. House, 1977; Atlanta City Council, 1982-86.

Capitol Office: 329 Cannon House Office Building 20515; 225-3801.
Office Staff: Administrative Assistant/Chief of Staff, Linda Earley Chastang; Press Secretary, Ronald Roach; Office Manager/Scheduler, Anne Tunlinson.
Committees: Interior & Insular Affairs; Public Works & Transportation.

Georgia 5th — Atlanta. The district vote for George Bush was 31% in 1988.

CQ Voting Studies

	1989	1990
Presidential	28%	16%
Party	98%	95%
Participation	99%	100%

Interest Groups

	1988	1989
ADA	100%	100%
ACU	0%	4%
AFL-CIO	100%	100%
CCUS	17%	40%

Elections

	1988	1990
General	78%	76%
Primary	u/o	u/o

Tom Lewis (R-Fla.)
Of North Palm Beach • Elected 1982

Born: October 26, 1924, Philadelphia, Penn.
Education: Palm Beach Junior College, 1956-57; U. of Florida, 1957-58.
Military Career: Air Force, 1943-54.
Occupation: Real estate broker; aircraft testing specialist.
Family: Wife, Marian Vastine; three children.
Religion: Methodist.
Political Career: Mayor and councilman, North Palm Beach, 1964-71; Fla. House, 1973-81; minority leader, 1979-81; Fla. Senate, 1981-83.

Capitol Office: 1216 Longworth House Office Building 20515; 225-5792.
Office Staff: Administrative Assistant, Karen Hogan; Press Secretary, Ken McKinnon; Executive Assistant, Kathleen E. Mee.
Committees: Agriculture; Science, Space & Technology.

Florida 12th — South Central — Parts of Palm Beach; West Palm Beach. The district vote for George Bush was 64% in 1988.

CQ Voting Studies

	1989	1990
Presidential	72%	68%
Party	93%	86%
Participation	99%	95%

Interest Groups

	1988	1989
ADA	5%	5%
ACU	100%	93%
AFL-CIO	14%	17%
CCUS	93%	100%

Elections

	1988	1990
General	u/o	u/o
Primary	u/o	75%

CQ Voting Studies

	1989	1990
Presidential	72%	68%
Party	91%	90%
Participation	97%	97%

Interest Groups

	1988	1989
ADA	10%	5%
ACU	90%	79%
AFL-CIO	15%	0%
CCUS	85%	90%

Elections

	1988	1990
General	64%	68%
Primary	u/o	u/o

Jim Ross Lightfoot (R-Iowa)
Of Shenandoah • Elected 1984

Born: September 27, 1938, Sioux City, Iowa.

Education: U. of Iowa; U. of Tulsa.

Military Career: Army, 1955-56; Army Reserve, 1956-63.

Occupation: Radio broadcaster; store owner; police officer; flight instructor and charter pilot; farmer.

Family: Wife, Nancy Harrison; four children.

Religion: Roman Catholic.

Political Career: Corsicana, Texas, City Commission, 1974-76.

Capitol Office: 1222 Longworth House Office Building 20515; 225-3806.

Office Staff: Chief of Staff, Mark Anderson; Communications Director, Chris Galen; Appointments Secretary, Kathy Nelson.

Committees: Interior & Insular Affairs; Public Works & Transportation.

Iowa 5th — Southwest — Council Bluffs; Fort Dodge. The district vote for George Bush was 47% in 1988.

William O. Lipinski (D-Ill.)
Of Chicago • Elected 1982

Born: December 22, 1937, Chicago, Ill.
Education: Loras College, 1957-58.
Military Career: Army Reserve, 1961-67.
Occupation: Parks supervisor.
Family: Wife, Rose Marie Lipinski; two children.
Religion: Roman Catholic.
Political Career: Chicago city alderman, 1975-83.

Capitol Office: 1501 Longworth House Office Building 20515; 225-5701.
Office Staff: Administrative Assistant, H. Keith Lesnick; Executive Assistant, Natalie Hidalgo.
Committees: Merchant Marine & Fisheries; Public Works & Transportation.

Illinois 5th — South Central Chicago and Suburbs. The district vote for George Bush was 52% in 1988.

CQ Voting Studies

	1989	1990
Presidential	36%	41%
Party	70%	76%
Participation	83%	95%

Interest Groups

	1988	1989
ADA	55%	40%
ACU	35%	26%
AFL-CIO	100%	91%
CCUS	45%	44%

Elections

	1988	1990
General	61%	66%
Primary	u/o	u/o

CQ Voting Studies

	1989	1990
Presidential	79%	75%
Party	68%	71%
Participation	97%	96%

Interest Groups

	1988	1989
ADA	5%	5%
ACU	100%	93%
AFL-CIO	8%	17%
CCUS	100%	90%

Elections

	1988	1990
General	u/o	u/o
Primary	78%	84%

Robert L. Livingston (R-La.)
Of Metairie • Elected 1977

Born: April 30, 1943, Colorado Springs, Colo.
Education: Tulane U., B.A. 1967; Tulane U., J.D. 1968.
Military Career: Navy, 1961-63; Naval Reserve, 1963-67.
Occupation: Lawyer.
Family: Wife, Bonnie Robichaux; four children.
Religion: Episcopalian.
Political Career: Republican nominee for U.S. House, 1976; sought Republican nomination for governor, 1987.

Capitol Office: 2368 Rayburn House Office Building 20515; 225-3015.
Office Staff: Administrative Assistant, J. Allen Martin; Press Secretary, Peter Arnold; Executive Secretary, Jane Graham.
Committees: Appropriations.

Louisiana 1st — Southeast — Jefferson Parish. The district vote for George Bush was 70% in 1988.

Marilyn Lloyd (D-Tenn.)
Of Chattanooga • Elected 1974

Born: January 3, 1929, Fort Smith, Ark.
Education: Shorter College, 1959-63.
Occupation: Radio station owner and manager.
Family: Divorced; four children.
Religion: Church of Christ.
Political Career: No previous office.

Capitol Office: 2266 Rayburn House Office Building 20515; 225-3271.
Office Staff: Administrative Assistant, Sue Sloan Carlton; Press Secretary, Courtney Goodman; Office Manager/Scheduler, Claudia Collins.
Committees: Armed Services; Science, Space & Technology.

Tennessee 3rd — Southeast — Chattanooga; Oak Ridge. The district vote for George Bush was 62% in 1988.

CQ Voting Studies

	1989	1990
Presidential	56%	43%
Party	61%	71%
Participation	95%	97%

Interest Groups

	1988	1989
ADA	50%	35%
ACU	54%	52%
AFL-CIO	100%	73%
CCUS	46%	78%

Elections

	1988	1990
General	57%	53%
Primary	89%	86%

Jill Long (D-Ind.)
Of Larwill • Elected 1989

Born: July 15, 1952, Warsaw, Ind.
Education: Valparaiso U., B.S. 1974; Indiana U., M.B.A. 1978; Indiana U., Ph.D. 1984.
Occupation: Professor.
Family: Single.
Religion: Methodist.
Political Career: Valparaiso City Council, 1983-86; Democratic nominee for U.S. Senate, 1986; Democratic nominee for U.S. House, 1988.

Capitol Office: 1513 Longworth House Office Building 20515; 225-4436.
Office Staff: Administrative Assistant, Inga Smulkstys; Press Secretary, Mary Meagher; Scheduler, Jennifer Boehm.
Committees: Agriculture; Veterans' Affairs.

Indiana 4th — Northeast — Fort Wayne. The district vote for George Bush was 66% in 1988.

CQ Voting Studies

	1989	1990
Presidential	33%	29%
Party	89%	78%
Participation	99%	99%

Interest Groups

	1989
ADA	68%
ACU	25%
AFL-CIO	80%
CCUS	50%

Elections

	1989*	1990
General	51%	61%
Primary		94%

*Special election.

Bill Lowery (R-Calif.)
Of San Diego • Elected 1980

Born: May 2, 1947, San Diego, Calif.
Education: San Diego State U., 1965-69.
Occupation: Public relations executive.
Family: Wife, Kathleen Ellen Brown;
three children.
Religion: Roman Catholic.
Political Career: San Diego City Council,
1977-80; deputy mayor of San Diego,
1979-80.

Capitol Office: 2433 Rayburn House
Office Building 20515; 225-3201.
Office Staff: Administrative Assistant,
Benjamin A. Haddad; Press Secretary,
Tina Kreisher; Office Manager, Regina
Jaedicke.
Committees: Appropriations.

California 41st — North San Diego and
Suburbs. The district vote for George
Bush was 58% in 1988.

CQ Voting Studies

	1989	1990
Presidential	74%	67%
Party	71%	68%
Participation	93%	89%

Interest Groups

	1988	1989
ADA	15%	5%
ACU	92%	85%
AFL-CIO	14%	25%
CCUS	100%	90%

Elections

	1988	1990
General	66%	49%
Primary	89%	u/o

CQ Voting Studies

	1989	1990
Presidential	28%	14%
Party	94%	94%
Participation	96%	97%

Interest Groups

	1989
ADA	95%
ACU	7%
AFL-CIO	100%
CCUS	40%

Elections

	1988	1990
General	50%	63%
Primary	44%	u/o

Nita M. Lowey (D-N.Y.)
Of Harrison • Elected 1988
Pronounced LOW e

Born: July 5, 1937, The Bronx, N.Y.
Education: Mount Holyoke College, B.A.
1959.
Occupation: Public official.
Family: Husband, Stephen Lowey; three
children.
Religion: Jewish.
Political Career: N.Y. assistant secretary
of state, 1985-87.

Capitol Office: 1313 Longworth House
Office Building 20515; 225-6506.
Office Staff: Administrative
Assistant/Press Secretary, Scott Fleming;
Executive Assistant, Suzanne Tracy.
Committees: Education & Labor;
Merchant Marine & Fisheries.

New York 20th — Central and Southern
Westchester County. The district vote for
George Bush was 52% in 1988.

Charles Luken (D-Ohio)
Of Cincinnati • Elected 1990

Born: July 18, 1951, Cincinnati, Ohio.
Education: U. of Notre Dame, B.A. 1973;
U. of Cincinnati, J.D. 1976.
Occupation: Lawyer.
Family: Wife, Marcia Spaeth; three
children.
Religion: Roman Catholic.
Political Career: Cincinnati City Council,
1981-90; mayor of Cincinnati, 1985-90.

Capitol Office: 1632 Longworth House
Office Building 20515; 225-2216.
Office Staff: Administrative
Assistant/Press Secretary, Hannah
Margetich; Appointments, Cathy
Mangino.
Committees: Banking, Finance & Urban
Affairs; Government Operations.

Ohio 1st — Hamilton County — Western
Cincinatti and Suburbs. The district vote
for George Bush was 63% in 1988.

Elections

	1990
General	51%
Primary	u/o

Ronald K. Machtley (R-R.I.)
Of Portsmouth • Elected 1988
Pronounced MAKE lee

Born: July 13, 1948, Johnstown, Penn.
Education: U.S. Naval Academy, B.S.
1970; Suffolk U., J.D. 1978.
Military Career: Navy, 1970-75; Naval
Reserve, 1975-present.
Occupation: Lawyer.
Family: Wife, Kati Croft; two children.
Religion: Presbyterian.
Political Career: No previous office.

Capitol Office: 123 Cannon House
Office Building 20515; 225-4911.
Office Staff: Administrative Assistant,
Tim Meyer; Press Secretary, Donna J.
DePetro; Appointments Secretary,
Michelle McGlone.
Committees: Armed Services;
Government Operations; Small Business.

Rhode Island 1st — East — Part of
Providence; Pawtucket. The district vote
for George Bush was 42% in 1988.

CQ Voting Studies

	1989	1990
Presidential	49%	38%
Party	60%	50%
Participation	98%	98%

Interest Groups

	1989
ADA	55%
ACU	46%
AFL-CIO	50%
CCUS	70%

Elections

	1988	1990
General	56%	55%
Primary	u/o	u/o

Edward Madigan (R-Ill.)*
Of Lincoln • Elected 1972

Born: January 13, 1936, Lincoln, Ill.
Education: Lincoln College, A.A. 1956.
Occupation: Automobile leasing executive.
Family: Wife, Evelyn M. George; three children.
Religion: Roman Catholic.
Political Career: Ill. House, 1967-73.

Capitol Office: 2109 Rayburn House Office Building 20515; 225-2371.
Office Staff: Administrative Assistant, Diane Liesman; Press Secretary, Christine Kirby; Executive Assistants, Jackie Parke.
Committees: Agriculture (Ranking); Energy & Commerce.

Illinois 15th — Central — Bloomington; Kankakee. The district vote for George Bush was 63% in 1988.

* On Friday, January 25, 1991, President Bush appointed Rep. Madigan to be U.S. Secretary of Agriculture. The Senate had not confirmed the nomination as of January 29.

CQ Voting Studies

	1989	1990
Presidential	77%	69%
Party	81%	73%
Participation	95%	93%

Interest Groups

	1988	1989
ADA	15%	15%
ACU	77%	78%
AFL-CIO	27%	8%
CCUS	85%	100%

Elections

	1988	1990
General	72%	u/o
Primary	u/o	u/o

Thomas J. Manton (D-N.Y.)
Of Queens • Elected 1984

Born: November 3, 1932, New York, N.Y.
Education: St. John's U., B.B.A. 1958; St. John's U., LL.B. 1962.
Military Career: Marine Corps, 1951-53.
Occupation: Lawyer.
Family: Wife, Diane Mason Schley; four children.
Religion: Roman Catholic.
Political Career: N.Y. City Council, 1970-84; sought Democratic nomination for U.S. House, 1972; sought Democratic nomination for U.S. House, 1978.

Capitol Office: 331 Cannon House Office Building 20515; 225-3965.
Office Staff: Administrative Assistant/Press Secretary, David Springer; Office Manager, Lorraine Schrier.
Committees: House Administration; Energy & Commerce; Merchant Marine & Fisheries.

New York 9th — Western Queens — Astoria; Jackson Heights. The district vote for George Bush was 48% in 1988.

CQ Voting Studies

	1989	1990
Presidential	38%	26%
Party	82%	89%
Participation	91%	94%

Interest Groups

	1988	1989
ADA	60%	70%
ACU	18%	4%
AFL-CIO	100%	100%
CCUS	23%	40%

Elections

	1988	1990
General	u/o	64%
Primary	u/o	u/o

Matthew G. Martinez
(D-Calif.)
Of Monterey Park • Elected 1982

Born: February 14, 1929, Walsenburg, Colo.
Education: Los Angeles Trade-Technical College, 1959.
Military Career: Marine Corps, 1947-50.
Occupation: Upholstery company owner.
Family: Wife, Elvira Yoruba; five children.
Religion: Roman Catholic.
Political Career: Monterey Park City Council, 1974-80; mayor of Monterey Park, 1974-75; Calif. Assembly, 1981-82.

Capitol Office: 240 Cannon House Office Building 20515; 225-5464.
Office Staff: Administrative Assistant/Press Secretary, Maxine Grant; Scheduler, Tammy Tambourine.
Committees: Education & Labor; Government Operations.

California 30th — San Gabriel Valley — El Monte; Alhambra. The district vote for George Bush was 46% in 1988.

tudies

1989	1990
34%	18%
86%	81%
93%	87%

ps

1988	1989
90%	75%
0%	11%
100%	91%
23%	50%

1988	1990
60%	58%
74%	u/o

Edward J. Markey **(D-Mass.)**
Of Malden • Elected 1976

Born: July 11, 1946, Malden, Mass.
Education: Boston College, B.A. 1968; Boston College, J.D. 1972.
Military Career: Army Reserve, 1968-73.
Occupation: Lawyer.
Family: Wife, Susan Blumenthal.
Religion: Roman Catholic.
Political Career: Mass. House, 1973-77.

Capitol Office: 2133 Rayburn House Office Building 20515; 225-2836.
Office Staff: Administrative Assistant, David Moulton; Press Secretary, Michael J. Connolly; Executive Assistant, Nancy Morrissey.
Committees: Energy & Commerce; Interior & Insular Affairs.

Massachusetts 7th — Northern Suburbs — Medford; Malden. The district vote for George Bush was 45% in 1988.

CQ Voting Studies

	1989	1990
Presidential	28%	15%
Party	94%	92%
Participation	96%	95%

Interest Groups

	1988	1989
ADA	96%	100%
ACU	0%	0%
AFL-CIO	100%	100%
CCUS	0%	40%

Elections

	1988	1990
General	u/o	u/o
Primary	u/o	u/o

Ron Marlenee (R-Mont.)
Of Scobey • Elected 1976
Pronounced MAR la nay

Born: August 8, 1935, Scobey, Mont.
Education: U. of Montana, 1953; U. of Montana, 1960; Montana State U., 1960.
Occupation: Rancher.
Family: Wife, Cynthia Tiemann; three children.
Religion: Lutheran.
Political Career: No previous office.

Capitol Office: 2465 Rayburn House Office Building 20515; 225-1555.
Office Staff: Administrative Assistant, Tom Hannah; Press Secretary, Dan Dubray; Scheduler, Leslie Lucas.
Committees: Agriculture; Interior & Insular Affairs.

Montana 2nd — East. The district vote for George Bush was 54% in 1988.

CQ Voting Studies

	1989	1990
Presidential	70%	69%
Party	86%	83%
Participation	88%	93%

Interest Groups

	1988	1989
ADA	0%	0%
ACU	96%	96%
AFL-CIO	7%	0%
CCUS	86%	100%

Elections

	1988	1990
General	56%	63%
Primary	u/o	u/o

David O'B. Martin (R-N.Y.)
Of Canton • Elected 1980

Born: April 26, 1944, St. Lawrence County, N.Y.
Education: U. of Notre Dame, B.B.A. 1966; Albany Law School, J.D. 1973.
Military Career: Marine Corps, 1966-70.
Occupation: Lawyer.
Family: Wife, DeeAnn Hedlund; three children.
Religion: Roman Catholic.
Political Career: St. Lawrence County Legislature, 1974-77; N.Y. Assembly, 1977-81.

Capitol Office: 442 Cannon House Office Building 20515; 225-4611.
Office Staff: Administrative Assistant/Press Secretary, Cary R. Brick; Administrative Secretary, Donna Bell.
Committees: Armed Services; Select Intelligence.

New York 26th — North — Plattsburgh; Watertown. The district vote for George Bush was 55% in 1988.

CQ Voting S

Presidential
Party
Participation

Interest Grou

ADA
ACU
AFL-CIO
CCUS

Elections

General
Primary

Robert T. Matsui (D-Calif.)
Of Sacramento • Elected 1978

Born: September 17, 1941, Sacramento, Calif.
Education: U. of California, A.B. 1963; U. of California, J.D. 1966.
Occupation: Lawyer.
Family: Wife, Doris Okada; one child.
Religion: Methodist.
Political Career: Sacramento City Council, 1971-78.

Capitol Office: 2353 Rayburn House Office Building 20515; 225-7163.
Office Staff: Administrative Assistant, Neil Dhillon; Press Secretary, Tom Keanex; Executive Assistant, Shirley Queja.
Committees: Budget; Ways & Means.

California 3rd — Most of Sacramento; Eastern Suburbs. The district vote for George Bush was 50% in 1988.

CQ Voting Studies

	1989	1990
Presidential	33%	21%
Party	94%	89%
Participation	97%	95%

Interest Groups

	1988	1989
ADA	90%	95%
ACU	4%	4%
AFL-CIO	86%	92%
CCUS	36%	10%

Elections

	1988	1990
General	71%	60%
Primary	u/o	86%

CQ Voting Studies

	1989	1990
Presidential	37%	23%
Party	86%	88%
Participation	94%	94%

Interest Groups

	1988	1989
ADA	90%	85%
ACU	8%	11%
AFL-CIO	100%	100%
CCUS	23%	40%

Elections

	1988	1990
General	70%	65%
Primary	u/o	u/o

Nicholas Mavroules (D-Mass.)
Of Peabody • Elected 1978

Born: November 1, 1929, Peabody, Mass.
Education: Peabody High School, 1947.
Occupation: Personnel supervisor.
Family: Wife, Mary Silva; three children.
Religion: Greek Orthodox.
Political Career: Candidate for Peabody City Council, 1955; Peabody City Council, 1958-61; candidate for mayor of Peabody, 1961; Peabody City Council, 1964-65; mayor of Peabody, 1968-79.

Capitol Office: 2432 Rayburn House Office Building 20515; 225-8020.
Office Staff: Administrative Assistant, Grace Pearson Waters; Press Secretary, Margaret Sullivan; Executive Assistant/Scheduler, Kim Mack.
Committees: Armed Services; Select Intelligence; Small Business.

Massachusetts 6th — North Shore — Lynn; Peabody. The district vote for George Bush was 48% in 1988.

Romano L. Mazzoli (D-Ky.)
Of Louisville • Elected 1970

Born: November 2, 1932, Louisville, Ky.
Education: Notre Dame U., B.S. 1954; U. of Louisville, J.D. 1960.
Military Career: Army, 1954-56.
Occupation: Lawyer; professor of law.
Family: Wife, Helen Dillon; two children.
Religion: Roman Catholic.
Political Career: Ky. Senate, 1968-70; sought Democratic nomination for mayor of Louisville, 1969.

Capitol Office: 2246 Rayburn House Office Building 20515; 225-5401.
Office Staff: D.C. Staff Director, Jane Kirby; Communications Assistant, Dennis Ambach; Personal Secretary, Renee Benjamin.
Committees: Judiciary; Small Business.

Kentucky 3rd — Louisville and Suburbs. The district vote for George Bush was 47% in 1988.

CQ Voting Studies

	1989	1990
Presidential	50%	31%
Party	80%	87%
Participation	99%	99%

Interest Groups

	1988	1989
ADA	75%	40%
ACU	21%	32%
AFL-CIO	77%	25%
CCUS	54%	80%

Elections

	1988	1990
General	70%	61%
Primary	61%	45%

Al McCandless (R-Calif.)
Of La Quinta • Elected 1982

Born: July 23, 1927, Brawley, Calif.
Education: U.C.L.A., B.A. 1951.
Military Career: Marine Corps, 1945-46; Marine Corps, 1950-52.
Occupation: Automobile dealer.
Family: Wife, Gail Walmsley Glass; five children.
Religion: Protestant.
Political Career: Riverside County Supervisor, 1970-82; candidate for Calif. Assembly, 1975.

Capitol Office: 2422 Rayburn House Office Building 20515; 225-5330.
Office Staff: Administrative Assistant/Press Secretary, Signy Ellerton; Appointments Secretary, Pat Rinaldi.
Committees: Banking, Finance & Urban Affairs; Government Operations.

California 37th — Riverside County. The district vote for George Bush was 61% in 1988.

CQ Voting Studies

	1989	1990
Presidential	77%	71%
Party	86%	92%
Participation	92%	99%

Interest Groups

	1988	1989
ADA	10%	0%
ACU	95%	88%
AFL-CIO	0%	0%
CCUS	92%	100%

Elections

	1988	1990
General	64%	50%
Primary	83%	74%

Frank McCloskey (D-Ind.)
Of Bloomington • Elected 1982

Born: June 12, 1939, Philadelphia, Penn.
Education: Indiana U., A.B. 1968; Indiana U., J.D. 1971.
Military Career: Air Force, 1957-61.
Occupation: Lawyer; journalist.
Family: Wife, Roberta Ann Barker; two children.
Religion: Roman Catholic.
Political Career: Democratic nominee for Ind. House, 1970; mayor of Bloomington, 1972-83.

Capitol Office: 127 Cannon House Office Building 20515; 225-4636.
Office Staff: Chief of Staff, Merrill Spiegel; Press Secretary, Ron Critchlow; Receptionist, Carol Davis.
Committees: Armed Services; Foreign Affairs; Post Office & Civil Service.

Indiana 8th — Southwest — Evansville. The district vote for George Bush was 57% in 1988.

CQ Voting Studies

	1989	1990
Presidential	31%	20%
Party	89%	93%
Participation	97%	98%

Interest Groups

	1988	1989
ADA	75%	85%
ACU	16%	7%
AFL-CIO	100%	92%
CCUS	21%	30%

Elections

	1988	1990
General	62%	55%
Primary	89%	89%

CQ Voting Studies

	1989	1990
Presidential	72%	74%
Party	76%	83%
Participation	95%	96%

Interest Groups

	1988	1989
ADA	0%	0%
ACU	100%	96%
AFL-CIO	17%	9%
CCUS	75%	100%

Elections

	1988	1990
General	u/o	60%
Primary	u/o	u/o

Bill McCollum (R-Fla.)
Of Altamonte Springs • Elected 1980

Born: July 12, 1944, Brooksville, Fla.
Education: U. of Florida, B.A. 1965; U. of Florida, J.D. 1968.
Military Career: Navy, 1969-72; Naval Reserve, 1972-present.
Occupation: Lawyer.
Family: Wife, Ingrid Seebohm; three children.
Religion: Episcopalian.
Political Career: Seminole County Republican Executive Committee chairman, 1976-80.

Capitol Office: 2453 Rayburn House Office Building 20515; 225-2176.
Office Staff: Chief of Staff, Vaughn S. Forrest; Press Secretary, Melissa Burns; Office Manager/Personal Secretary, Mary Reed.
Committees: Banking, Finance & Urban Affairs; Judiciary.

Florida 5th — North Central — Orlando and Northern Suburbs. The district vote for George Bush was 69% in 1988.

Jim McCrery (R-La.)
Of Shreveport • Elected 1988

Born: September 18, 1949, Shreveport, La.
Education: Louisiana Tech U., B.A. 1971; Louisiana State U., J.D. 1975.
Occupation: Lawyer; congressional aide; corporate government affairs executive.
Family: Single.
Religion: Methodist.
Political Career: Candidate for Leesville City Council, 1978.

Capitol Office: 429 Cannon House Office Building 20515; 225-2777.
Office Staff: Administrative Assistant, Grace Wiegers; Press Secretary, Leslie Corkern; Office Manager/Personal Secretary, Christine Negley.
Committees: Armed Services; Budget.

Louisiana 4th — Northwest — Shreveport. The district vote for George Bush was 59% in 1988.

CQ Voting Studies

	1989	1990
Presidential	85%	68%
Party	71%	62%
Participation	93%	87%

Interest Groups

	1988	1989
ADA	12%	0%
ACU	94%	86%
AFL-CIO	20%	8%
CCUS	100%	90%

Elections

	1988	1990
General	u/o	u/o
Primary	69%	55%

CQ Voting Studies

	1989	1990
Presidential	55%	44%
Party	69%	73%
Participation	93%	97%

Interest Groups

	1988	1989
ADA	60%	35%
ACU	30%	40%
AFL-CIO	71%	50%
CCUS	64%	89%

Elections

	1988	1990
General	u/o	74%
Primary	83%	u/o

Dave McCurdy (D-Okla.)
Of Norman • Elected 1980

Born: March 30, 1950, Canadian, Texas.
Education: U. of Oklahoma, B.A. 1972; U. of Oklahoma, J.D. 1975; U. of Edinburgh, Scotland, 1977-78.
Military Career: Air Force Reserve, 1969-72; Air Force Reserve, 1985-present.
Occupation: Lawyer.
Family: Wife, Pamela Plumb; three children.
Religion: Lutheran.
Political Career: Okla. assistant attorney general, 1975-77.

Capitol Office: 2344 Rayburn House Office Building 20515; 225-6165.
Office Staff: Administrative Assistant, Steve Patterson; Press Secretary, Cynthia Cain; Scheduler, Carrie Friar.
Committees: Armed Services; Select Intelligence; Science, Space & Technology.

Oklahoma 4th — Southwest — Part of Oklahoma City. The district vote for George Bush was 58% in 1988.

Joseph M. McDade (R-Pa.)
Of Scranton • Elected 1962

Born: September 29, 1931, Scranton, Penn.
Education: U. of Notre Dame, B.A. 1953; U. of Pennsylvania, LL.B. 1956.
Occupation: Lawyer.
Family: Wife, Sarah Scripture; five children.
Religion: Roman Catholic.
Political Career: No previous office.

Capitol Office: 2370 Rayburn House Office Building 20515; 225-3731.
Office Staff: Administrative Assistant, Deborah Weatherly; Press Secretary, John O'Donnell; Appointments Secretary, Carol Berg.
Committees: Appropriations; Small Business (Ranking).

Pennsylvania 10th — Northeast — Scranton. The district vote for George Bush was 58% in 1988.

CQ Voting Studies

	1989	1990
Presidential	66%	47%
Party	47%	43%
Participation	90%	84%

Interest Groups

	1988	1989
ADA	40%	35%
ACU	54%	46%
AFL-CIO	86%	67%
CCUS	50%	80%

Elections

	1988	1990
General	73%	u/o
Primary	u/o	u/o

CQ Voting Studies

	1989	1990
Presidential	29%	20%
Party	94%	92%
Participation	96%	99%

Interest Groups

	1989
ADA	95%
ACU	4%
AFL-CIO	100%
CCUS	20%

Elections

	1988	1990
General	76%	72%
Primary	38%	73%

Jim McDermott (D-Wash.)
Of Seattle • Elected 1988

Born: December 28, 1936, Chicago, Ill.
Education: Wheaton College, B.S. 1958;
U. of Illinois, M.D. 1963.
Military Career: Navy Medical Corps,
1968-70.
Occupation: Psychiatrist.
Family: Divorced; two children.
Religion: Episcopalian.
Political Career: Wash. House, 1971-72;
sought Democratic nomination for
governor, 1972; Wash. Senate, 1975-87;
Democratic nominee for governor, 1980;
sought Democratic nomination for
governor, 1984.

Capitol Office: 1707 Longworth House
Office Building 20515; 225-3106.
Office Staff: Administrative Assistant,
Charles M. Williams; Press Secretary,
Jenny Holladay; Executive Assistant,
Wilda Chisolm.
Committees: District of Columbia; Ways
& Means.

Washington 7th — Seattle and Suburbs.
The district vote for George Bush was
31% in 1988.

Bob McEwen (R-Ohio)

Of Hillsboro • Elected 1980

Pronounced ma KEW in

Born: January 12, 1950, Hillsboro, Ohio.
Education: U. of Miami (Fla.), B.B.A. 1972;
Ohio State U., 1973-74.
Occupation: Real estate developer.
Family: Wife, Elizabeth Boebinger; four
children.
Religion: Protestant.
Political Career: Ohio House, 1975-81.

Capitol Office: 2431 Rayburn House
Office Building 20515; 225-5705.
Office Staff: Administrative Assistant,
Phil Bond; Press Secretary, Lisa Wright;
Personal Secretary, Lisa Greener.
Committees: Rules.

Ohio 6th — South Central —
Portsmouth; Chillicothe. The district vote
for George Bush was 64% in 1988.

CQ Voting Studies

	1989	1990
Presidential	72%	69%
Party	67%	77%
Participation	94%	94%

Interest Groups

	1988	1989
ADA	5%	5%
ACU	96%	93%
AFL-CIO	14%	17%
CCUS	100%	100%

Elections

	1988	1990
General	74%	71%
Primary	u/o	u/o

Raymond J. McGrath (R-N.Y.)
Of Valley Stream • Elected 1980

Born: March 27, 1942, Valley Stream, N.Y.
Education: State U. of New York, Brockport, B.S. 1963; New York U., M.A. 1968.
Occupation: Physical education teacher.
Family: Wife, Sheryl Peterson; two children.
Religion: Roman Catholic.
Political Career: N.Y. Assembly, 1977-81.

Capitol Office: 205 Cannon House Office Building 20515; 225-5516.
Office Staff: Administrative Assistant, Arthur DeCelle; Press Secretary, Daniel Zielinski; Personal Secretary, Gretchen Gipson.
Committees: Ways & Means.

New York 5th — Long Island — Southwestern Nassau County. The district vote for George Bush was 56% in 1988.

CQ Voting Studies

	1989	1990
Presidential	60%	49%
Party	59%	56%
Participation	95%	94%

Interest Groups

	1988	1989
ADA	25%	30%
ACU	55%	59%
AFL-CIO	83%	50%
CCUS	82%	70%

Elections

	1988	1990
General	65%	55%
Primary	u/o	u/o

Matthew F. McHugh (D-N.Y.)
Of Ithaca • Elected 1974

Born: December 6, 1938, Philadelphia, Penn.
Education: Mount St. Mary's College, B.S. 1960; Villanova U., J.D. 1963.
Occupation: Lawyer.
Family: Wife, Eileen Alanna Higgins; three children.
Religion: Roman Catholic.
Political Career: Tompkins County district attorney, 1969-72.

Capitol Office: 2335 Rayburn House Office Building 20515; 225-6335.
Office Staff: Administrative Assistant, Thomas Parkhurst; Press Secretary, Gabe Kajeckas; Personal Secretary, June Elmore.
Committees: Appropriations.

New York 28th — Southern Tier — Binghamton; Ithaca. The district vote for George Bush was 52% in 1988.

CQ Voting Studies

	1989	1990
Presidential	35%	23%
Party	92%	92%
Participation	98%	99%

Interest Groups

	1988	1989
ADA	95%	85%
ACU	4%	0%
AFL-CIO	92%	92%
CCUS	46%	30%

Elections

	1988	1990
General	93%	65%
Primary	u/o	u/o

Alex McMillan (R-N.C.)
Of Charlotte • Elected 1984

Born: May 9, 1932, Charlotte, N.C.
Education: U. of North Carolina, B.A.
1954; U. of Virginia, M.B.A. 1958.
Military Career: Army, 1954-56.
Occupation: Food store executive.
Family: Wife, Caroline Houston; two
children.
Religion: Presbyterian.
Political Career: Mecklenburg County
Commission, 1972-74.

Capitol Office: 401 Cannon House
Office Building 20515; 225-1976.
Office Staff: Chief of Staff, Frank Hill;
Executive Assistant/Office Manager, Pat
Hinshaw.
Committees: Budget; Energy &
Commerce.

North Carolina 9th — West Central —
Charlotte. The district vote for George
Bush was 61% in 1988.

CQ Voting Studies

	1989	1990
Presidential	80%	66%
Party	78%	79%
Participation	98%	98%

Interest Groups

	1988	1989
ADA	15%	0%
ACU	88%	74%
AFL-CIO	21%	8%
CCUS	100%	100%

Elections

	1988	1990
General	66%	62%
Primary	u/o	u/o

Tom McMillen (D-Md.)

Of Crofton • Elected 1986

Born: May 26, 1952, Elmira, N.Y.
Education: U. of Maryland, B.S. 1974; Oxford U., M.A. 1978.
Occupation: Professional basketball player; communications equipment distributor.
Family: Single.
Religion: Roman Catholic.
Political Career: No previous office.

Capitol Office: 420 Cannon House Office Building 20515; 225-8090.
Office Staff: Administrative Assistant, Jerry Grant; Press Secretary, Brad Fitch; Executive Assistant/Scheduler, Amy Hickox.
Committees: Energy & Commerce; Science, Space & Technology.

Maryland 4th — Anne Arundel, Southern Prince George's Counties. The district vote for George Bush was 57% in 1988.

CQ Voting Studies

	1989	1990
Presidential	45%	27%
Party	86%	92%
Participation	100%	100%

Interest Groups

	1988	1989
ADA	75%	60%
ACU	12%	29%
AFL-CIO	100%	92%
CCUS	36%	40%

Elections

	1988	1990
General	68%	59%
Primary	87%	83%

CQ Voting Studies

	1989	1990
Presidential	42%	27%
Party	83%	92%
Participation	98%	99%

Interest Groups

	1989
ADA	75%
ACU	25%
AFL-CIO	100%
CCUS	40%

Elections

	1988	1990
General	62%	64%
Primary	u/o	u/o

Michael R. McNulty (D-N.Y.)
Of Green Island • Elected 1988

Born: September 16, 1947, Troy, N.Y.
Education: College of the Holy Cross, A.B. 1969.
Occupation: Public official.
Family: Wife, Nancy Ann Lazzaro; four children.
Religion: Roman Catholic.
Political Career: Green Island supervisor, 1970-77; Democratic nominee for N.Y. Assembly, 1976; Green Island mayor, 1977-83; N.Y. Assembly, 1983-89.

Capitol Office: 414 Cannon House Office Building 20515; 225-5076.
Office Staff: Chief of Staff, Lana Helfrich; Press Secretary, Charles Segal.
Committees: Armed Services; Post Office & Civil Service.

New York 23rd — Hudson and Mohawk Valleys — Albany, Schenectady. The district vote for George Bush was 43% in 1988.

Jan Meyers (R-Kan.)
Of Overland Park • Elected 1984

Born: July 20, 1928, Lincoln, Neb.
Education: William Woods College,
A.F.A. 1948; U. of Nebraska, B.A. 1951.
Occupation: Homemaker; community
volunteer.
Family: Husband, Louis "Dutch" Meyers;
two children.
Religion: Methodist.
Political Career: Overland Park City
Council, 1967-72; council president,
1970-72; Kan. Senate, 1973-85; sought
Republican nomination for U.S. Senate,
1978.

Capitol Office: 1230 Longworth House
Office Building 20515; 225-2865.
Office Staff: Administrative Assistant,
Brian Gaston; Personal Secretary, Alice
Mayer.
Committees: Foreign Affairs; Small
Business.

Kansas 3rd — East — Kansas City. The
district vote for George Bush was 54% in
1988.

CQ Voting Studies

	1989	1990
Presidential	69%	65%
Party	53%	70%
Participation	98%	99%

Interest Groups

	1988	1989
ADA	35%	15%
ACU	58%	64%
AFL-CIO	23%	17%
CCUS	85%	100%

Elections

	1988	1990
General	74%	60%
Primary	85%	u/o

Kweisi Mfume (D-Md.)
Of Baltimore • Elected 1986
Pronounced kwy E say mm FU may

Born: October 24, 1948, Baltimore, Md.
Education: Morgan State U., B.S. 1976;
Johns Hopkins U., M.A. 1984.
Occupation: Assistant professor of
political science and communications;
radio station program director; talk show
host.
Family: Divorced; five children.
Religion: Baptist.
Political Career: Baltimore City Council,
1979-87.

Capitol Office: 217 Cannon House
Office Building 20515; 225-4741.
Office Staff: Administrative Assistant,
Tammy Hawley; Communications
Director, David Brown; Appointments
Secretary, Nancy McCormick.
Committees: Banking, Finance & Urban
Affairs; Small Business.

Maryland 7th — Baltimore — West and
Central. The district vote for George
Bush was 17% in 1988.

CQ Voting Studies

	1989	1990
Presidential	31%	15%
Party	86%	86%
Participation	95%	96%

Interest Groups

	1988	1989
ADA	95%	90%
ACU	4%	8%
AFL-CIO	100%	100%
CCUS	21%	30%

Elections

	1988	1990
General	u/o	85%
Primary	u/o	89%

Robert H. Michel (R-Ill.)
Of Peoria • Elected 1956

Born: March 2, 1923, Peoria, Ill.
Education: Bradley U., B.S. 1948.
Military Career: Army, 1942-46.
Occupation: Congressional aide.
Family: Wife, Corinne Woodruff; four children.
Religion: Apostolic Christian.
Political Career: No previous office.

Capitol Office: 2112 Rayburn House Office Building 20515; 225-6201.
Office Staff: Administrative Assistant (Appointments), Sharon Yard; Press Secretary, Missi Tessier; Executive Assistant, Sue Bell.
Committees: House Minority Leader.

Illinois 18th — Central — Peoria. The district vote for George Bush was 55% in 1988.

CQ Voting Studies

	1989	1990
Presidential	88%	75%
Party	75%	78%
Participation	94%	92%

Interest Groups

	1988	1989
ADA	10%	10%
ACU	92%	84%
AFL-CIO	31%	18%
CCUS	85%	89%

Elections

	1988	1990
General	55%	98%
Primary	86%	u/o

CQ Voting Studies

	1989	1990
Presidential	76%	68%
Party	85%	87%
Participation	98%	98%

Interest Groups

	1988	1989
ADA	15%	0%
ACU	92%	100%
AFL-CIO	43%	17%
CCUS	93%	100%

Elections

	1988	1990
General	72%	63%
Primary	84%	u/o

Clarence E. Miller (R-Ohio)
Of Lancaster • Elected 1966

Born: November 1, 1917, Lancaster, Ohio.

Education: Lancaster H.S., graduated 1935.

Occupation: Electrical engineer.

Family: Widowed; two children.

Religion: Methodist.

Political Career: Lancaster City Council, 1957-63; mayor of Lancaster, 1963-65.

Capitol Office: 2308 Rayburn House Office Building 20515; 225-5131.

Office Staff: Administrative Assistant/Press Secretary, Bob Reintsema; Office Manager, Linda Roderick.

Committees: Appropriations.

Ohio 10th — Southeast — Lancaster; Zanesville. The district vote for George Bush was 61% in 1988.

George Miller (D-Calif.)
Of Martinez • Elected 1974

Born: May 17, 1945, Richmond, Calif.
Education: San Francisco State College, B.A. 1968; U. of California, Davis, J.D. 1972.
Occupation: Lawyer; legislative aide.
Family: Wife, Cynthia Caccavo; two children.
Religion: Roman Catholic.
Political Career: Democratic nominee for Calif. Senate, 1969.

Capitol Office: 2228 Rayburn House Office Building 20515; 225-2095.
Office Staff: Administrative Assistant, John Lawrence; Press Secretary, Daniel Weiss; Personal Secretary, Sylvia Arthur.
Committees: Education & Labor; Interior & Insular Affairs.

California 7th — Most of Contra Costa County; Richmond. The district vote for George Bush was 46% in 1988.

CQ Voting Studies

	1989	1990
Presidential	22%	16%
Party	89%	89%
Participation	95%	95%

Interest Groups

	1988	1989
ADA	95%	100%
ACU	4%	0%
AFL-CIO	93%	91%
CCUS	31%	20%

Elections

	1988	1990
General	68%	61%
Primary	u/o	u/o

John Miller (R-Wash.)
Of Seattle • Elected 1984

Born: May 23, 1938, New York, N.Y.
Education: Bucknell U., B.A. 1959; Yale U., M.A. 1964; Yale U., LL.B. 1964.
Military Career: Army, 1960-61; Army Reserve, 1961-69.
Occupation: Lawyer.
Family: Wife, June Marion Makar; one child.
Rellgion: Jewish.
Political Career: Seattle City Council, 1972-80; president, 1978-80; candidate for Seattle mayor, 1977; independent candidate for Wash. attorney general, 1980.

Capitol Office: 322 Cannon House Office Building 20515; 225-6311.
Office Staff: Chief of Staff, Bruce Agnew; Communications Director, Abby Daniell; Executive Assistant, JoAnn Schneider.
Committees: Budget; Foreign Affairs.

Washington 1st — Northern Seattle and Suburbs. The district vote for George Bush was 49% in 1988.

CQ Voting Studies

	1989	1990
Presidential	59%	55%
Party	46%	68%
Participation	98%	95%

Interest Groups

	1988	1989
ADA	60%	35%
ACU	38%	68%
AFL-CIO	64%	25%
CCUS	79%	100%

Elections

	1988	1990
General	55%	52%
Primary	51%	52%

Norman Y. Mineta (D-Calif.)
Of San Jose • Elected 1974

Born: November 12, 1931, San Jose, Calif.
Education: U. of California, B.S. 1953.
Military Career: Army, 1953-56.
Occupation: Insurance executive.
Family: Divorced; two children.
Religion: Methodist.
Political Career: San Jose City Council, 1967-71; mayor of San Jose, 1971-74.

Capitol Office: 2350 Rayburn House Office Building 20515; 225-2631.
Office Staff: Washington Staff Director, Tim Newell; Press Secretary, Eric K. Federing; Executive Assistant/Office Manager, Diane Evans.
Committees: Public Works & Transportation; Science, Space & Technology.

California 13th — Santa Clara County — San Jose; Santa Clara. The district vote for George Bush was 49% in 1988.

CQ Voting Studies

	1989	1990
Presidential	29%	16%
Party	93%	92%
Participation	93%	96%

Interest Groups

	1988	1989
ADA	95%	95%
ACU	4%	11%
AFL-CIO	93%	91%
CCUS	31%	50%

Elections

	1988	1990
General	67%	58%
Primary	u/o	u/o

CQ Voting Studies

	1990
Presidential	22%
Party	81%
Participation	88%

Elections

	1990*	1990
General	35%	68%
Primary		39%

*Special election.

Patsy T. Mink (D-Hawaii)
Of Honolulu • Elected 1990

Born: December 6, 1927, Paia, Maui, Hawaii.
Education: U. of Hawaii, B.A. 1948; U. of Chicago, J.D. 1951.
Occupation: Lawyer.
Family: Husband, John Francis Mink; one child.
Religion: Protestant.
Political Career: Hawaii Territorial House, 1956-58; Hawaii Territorial Senate, 1958-59; Hawaii Senate, 1962-64; U.S. House, 1965-77; sought Democratic nomination for president, 1972; Democratic nominee for U.S. Senate, 1976; Honolulu City Council, 1983-87; Democratic nominee for governor, 1986; mayor of Honolulu, 1988.

Capitol Office: 2135 Rayburn House Office Building 20515; 225-4906.
Office Staff: Communications Director, Dan Merriman; Office Manager, Helen E. Lewis.
Committees: Education & Labor; Government Operations.

Hawaii 2nd — Honululu Suburbs; Outer Islands. The district vote for George Bush was 44% in 1988.

Joe Moakley (D-Mass.)
Of Boston • Elected 1972

Born: April 27, 1927, Boston, Mass.
Education: U. of Miami; Suffolk U., J.D.
1956.
Military Career: Navy, 1943-46.
Occupation: Lawyer.
Family: Wife, Evelyn Duffy.
Religion: Roman Catholic.
Political Career: Mass. House, 1953-65;
Mass. Senate, 1965-69; sought
Democratic nomination for U.S. House,
1970; Boston City Council, 1971-73.

Capitol Office: 221 Cannon House
Office Building 20515; 225-8273.
Office Staff: Administrative Assistant,
John Weinfurter; Press Assistant, Jim
McGovern; Appointments Secretary,
Deborah Spriggs.
Committees: Rules (Chairman).

**Massachusetts 9th — Boston; Southern
Suburbs.** The district vote for George
Bush was 45% in 1988.

CQ Voting Studies

	1989	1990
Presidential	31%	24%
Party	89%	95%
Participation	95%	99%

Interest Groups

	1988	1989
ADA	90%	95%
ACU	8%	4%
AFL-CIO	100%	100%
CCUS	21%	44%

Elections

	1988	1990
General	u/o	70%
Primary	u/o	u/o

CQ Voting Studies

	1990
Presidential	56%
Party	70%
Participation	98%

Elections

	1990*	1990
General	58%	60%
Primary		u/o

*Special election.

Susan Molinari   (R-N.Y.)
Of Staten Island • Elected 1990

Born: March 27, 1958, Staten Island, N.Y.
Education: State University of New York, Albany, B.A. 1980; State University of New York, Albany, M.A. 1981.
Occupation: Political aide.
Family: Separated.
Religion: Roman Catholic.
Political Career: N.Y. City Council, 1985-90.

Capitol Office: 315 Cannon House Office Building 20515; 225-3371.
Office Staff: Administrative Asistant/Press Secretary, Dan Leonard; Executive Assistant, Peggy Maughlin.
Committees: Education & Labor; Public Works & Transportation.

New York 14th — Staten Island; Southwest Brooklyn. The district vote for George Bush was 56% in 1988.

Alan B. Mollohan (D-W.Va.)
Of Fairmont • Elected 1982

Born: May 14, 1943, Fairmont, W.Va.
Education: College of William and Mary,
A.B. 1966; West Virginia U., J.D. 1970.
Military Career: Army Reserve, 1970-82.
Occupation: Lawyer.
Family: Wife, Barbara Whiting; five
children.
Religion: Baptist.
Political Career: No previous office.

Capitol Office: 229 Cannon House
Office Building 20515; 225-4172.
Office Staff: Administrative Assistant,
Mary McGovern; Press Secretary, Ron
Hudok; Personal Secretary, Jane Bobbitt.
Committees: Appropriations.

West Virginia 1st — Northern Panhandle
— Wheeling. The district vote for
George Bush was 49% in 1988.

CQ Voting Studies

	1989	1990
Presidential	55%	31%
Party	74%	84%
Participation	98%	93%

Interest Groups

	1988	1989
ADA	50%	55%
ACU	48%	36%
AFL-CIO	100%	92%
CCUS	23%	40%

Elections

	1988	1990
General	75%	67%
Primary	u/o	u/o

G.V. ''Sonny'' Montgomery
(D-Miss.)
Of Meridian • Elected 1966

Born: August 5, 1920, Meridian, Miss.
Education: Mississippi State U., B.S. 1943.
Military Career: Army, 1943-46; Army National Guard, 1946-80; active duty, 1951-52.
Occupation: Insurance executive.
Family: Single.
Religion: Episcopalian.
Political Career: Miss. Senate, 1956-66.

Capitol Office: 2184 Rayburn House Office Building 20515; 225-5031.
Office Staff: Administrative Assistant, Andre Clemandot; Press Secretary, Kyle Steward; Personal Secretary, Louise Medlin.
Committees: Armed Services; Veterans' Affairs (Chairman).

Mississippi 3rd — South Central — Meridian. The district vote for George Bush was 65% in 1988.

CQ Voting Studies

	1989	1990
Presidential	78%	56%
Party	57%	60%
Participation	99%	97%

Interest Groups

	1988	1989
ADA	25%	10%
ACU	71%	59%
AFL-CIO	57%	25%
CCUS	71%	90%

Elections

	1988	1990
General	89%	u/o
Primary	u/o	u/o

Jim Moody (D-Wis.)
Of Milwaukee • Elected 1982

Born: September 2, 1935, Richlands, Va.
Education: Haverford College, B.A. 1957;
Harvard U., M.P.A. 1967; U. of California,
Ph.D. 1973.
Occupation: Economist.
Family: Divorced.
Religion: Protestant.
Political Career: Wis. House, 1977-79;
Wis. Senate, 1979-83.

Capitol Office: 1019 Longworth House
Office Building 20515; 225-3571.
Office Staff: Administrative
Assistant/Press Secretary, Marcus Kunian;
Executive Assistant/Office Manager,
Natalie C. Greene.
Committees: Ways & Means.

Wisconsin 5th — Northern Milwaukee
and Suburbs — Wauwatosa. The district
vote for George Bush was 36% in 1988.

CQ Voting Studies

	1989	1990
Presidential	27%	17%
Party	87%	79%
Participation	96%	91%

Interest Groups

	1988	1989
ADA	80%	95%
ACU	5%	11%
AFL-CIO	100%	75%
CCUS	23%	40%

Elections

	1988	1990
General	64%	68%
Primary	59%	79%

Carlos J. Moorhead (R-Calif.)
Of Glendale • Elected 1972

Born: May 6, 1922, Long Beach, Calif.
Education: U.C.L.A., B.A. 1943; U. of Southern California, J.D. 1949.
Military Career: Army, 1942-45; Army Reserve, 1945-82.
Occupation: Lawyer.
Family: Wife, Valery Joan Tyler; five children.
Religion: Presbyterian.
Political Career: Calif. Assembly, 1967-73.

Capitol Office: 2346 Rayburn House Office Building 20515; 225-4176.
Office Staff: Administrative Assistant, Alice Andersen; Press Assistant, Dave Joergenson.
Committees: Energy & Commerce; Judiciary.

California 22nd — Glendale; Part of Burbank; Part of Pasadena. The district vote for George Bush was 64% in 1988.

CQ Voting Studies

	1989	1990
Presidential	72%	74%
Party	88%	93%
Participation	96%	99%

Interest Groups

	1988	1989
ADA	10%	0%
ACU	96%	93%
AFL-CIO	7%	0%
CCUS	100%	100%

Elections

	1988	1990
General	70%	60%
Primary	87%	u/o

James P. Moran, Jr. (D-Va.)
Of Alexandria • Elected 1990

Born: May 16, 1945, Buffalo, N.Y.
Education: College of the Holy Cross,
B.A. 1967; City University of N.Y.,
Graduate School of Finance, 1967-68; U.
of Pittsburgh, M.A. 1970; U. of Southern
California, 1980.
Occupation: Investment banker.
Family: Wife, Mary Howard; four
children.
Religion: Roman Catholic.
Political Career: Alexandria City Council,
1979-84; vice mayor, 1982-84; mayor of
Alexandria, 1985-91.

Capitol Office: 523 Cannon House
Office Building 20515; 225-4376.
Office Staff: Administrative Assistant,
Mame Reiley; Press Secretary, Cathy Lash;
Executive Secretary, Mary Miller.
Committees: Banking, Finance & Urban
Affairs; Post Office & Civil Service.

Virginia 8th — D.C. Suburbs —
Alexandria; Southern Fairfax County. The
district vote for George Bush was 60% in
1988.

Elections

	1990
General	52%
Primary	u/o

Constance A. Morella (R-Md.)
Of Bethesda • Elected 1986

Born: February 12, 1931, Somerville, Mass.
Education: Boston U., B.A. 1954; American U., M.A. 1967.
Occupation: Professor.
Family: Husband, Anthony C. Morella; nine children.
Religion: Roman Catholic.
Political Career: Md. House, 1979-87; sought Republican nomination for U.S. House, 1980.

Capitol Office: 1024 Longworth House Office Building 20515; 225-5341.
Office Staff: Administrative Assistant, David A. Nathan; Executive Assistant, Patricia Donnelly.
Committees: Post Office & Civil Service; Science, Space & Technology.

Maryland 8th — Montgomery County. The district vote for George Bush was 46% in 1988.

CQ Voting Studies

	1989	1990
Presidential	41%	26%
Party	18%	32%
Participation	96%	96%

Interest Groups

	1988	1989
ADA	90%	80%
ACU	8%	21%
AFL-CIO	79%	67%
CCUS	46%	80%

Elections

	1988	1990
General	63%	74%
Primary	u/o	87%

Sid Morrison (R-Wash.)
Of Zillah • Elected 1980

Born: May 13, 1933, Yakima, Wash.
Education: Yakima Valley College, 1951; Washington State U., B.S. 1954.
Military Career: Army, 1954-56.
Occupation: Fruit grower; nurseryman.
Family: Wife, Marcella Britton; four children.
Religion: Methodist.
Political Career: Wash. House, 1967-75; Wash. Senate, 1975-81.

Capitol Office: 1434 Longworth House Office Building 20515; 225-5816.
Office Staff: Chief of Staff, Gretchen White; News Secretary, Rick Olson; Office Manager/Personal Secretary, Koni Gleason.
Committees: Agriculture; Science, Space & Technology.

Washington 4th — Central — Yakima; Tri-Cities. The district vote for George Bush was 58% in 1988.

CQ Voting Studies

	1989	1990
Presidential	67%	51%
Party	51%	49%
Participation	99%	95%

Interest Groups

	1988	1989
ADA	55%	20%
ACU	64%	68%
AFL-CIO	36%	17%
CCUS	93%	100%

Elections

	1988	1990
General	75%	71%
Primary	73%	77%

Robert J. Mrazek (D-N.Y.)
Of Centerport • Elected 1982
Pronounced ma RAH zik

Born: November 6, 1945, Newport, R.I.
Education: Cornell U., B.A. 1967.
Military Career: Navy, 1967-68.
Occupation: Small businessman; congressional aide.
Family: Wife, Catherine Susan Gurick; two children.
Religion: Methodist.
Political Career: Sought Democratic nomination for U.S. House, 1972; Suffolk County Legislature, 1976-83; Democratic nominee for N.Y. Senate, 1978.

Capitol Office: 306 Cannon House Office Building 20515; 225-5956.
Office Staff: Administrative Assistant, Thomas V. Barry; Press Secretary, Tad Boggs; Office Manager, Deborah Brenchick.
Committees: Appropriations.

New York 3rd — Long Island — Parts of Nassau and Suffolk Counties. The district vote for George Bush was 59% in 1988.

CQ Voting Studies

	1989	1990
Presidential	31%	16%
Party	91%	92%
Participation	94%	93%

Interest Groups

	1988	1989
ADA	95%	80%
ACU	4%	8%
AFL-CIO	79%	82%
CCUS	31%	40%

Elections

	1988	1990
General	57%	53%
Primary	u/o	u/o

Austin J. Murphy   (D-Pa.)
Of Monongahela • Elected 1976

Born: June 17, 1927, Speers, Penn.
Education: Duquesne U., B.A. 1949; U. of Pittsburgh, LL.B. 1952; U. of Pittsburgh, J.D. 1972.
Military Career: Marine Corps, 1944-46; Marine Corps Reserve, 1948-50.
Occupation: Lawyer.
Family: Wife, Eileen Ramona McNamara; six children.
Religion: Roman Catholic.
Political Career: Washington County assistant district attorney, 1953-59; Pa. House, 1959-71; Pa. Senate, 1971-77.

Capitol Office: 2210 Rayburn House Office Building 20515; 225-4665.
Office Staff: Administrative Assistant, Frederick P. McLuckie; Press Secretary, John Casey; Executive Assistant, Marissa Creager.
Committees: Education & Labor; Foreign Affairs; Interior & Insular Affairs.

Pennsylvania 22nd — Southwest — Washington. The district vote for George Bush was 35% in 1988.

CQ Voting Studies

	1989	1990
Presidential	34%	29%
Party	49%	61%
Participation	93%	94%

Interest Groups

	1988	1989
ADA	60%	75%
ACU	24%	30%
AFL-CIO	100%	92%
CCUS	33%	50%

Elections

	1988	1990
General	72%	63%
Primary	73%	70%

John P. Murtha (D-Pa.)
Of Johnstown • Elected 1974

Born: June 17, 1932, New Martinsville, W.Va.
Education: U. of Pittsburgh, B.A. 1962; Indiana U., Pa.
Military Career: Marine Corps, 1952-55; Marine Corps, 1966-67.
Occupation: Car wash operator.
Family: Wife, Joyce Bell; three children.
Religion: Roman Catholic.
Political Career: Pa. House, 1969-74.

Capitol Office: 2423 Rayburn House Office Building 20515; 225-2065.
Office Staff: Executive Assistant, William Allen; Communications Director, Brad Clemenson; Schedule Coordinator, Winifred Frederick.
Committees: Appropriations.

Pennsylvania 12th — Southwest — Johnstown. The district vote for George Bush was 47% in 1988.

CQ Voting Studies

	1989	1990
Presidential	51%	33%
Party	77%	85%
Participation	95%	97%

Interest Groups

	1988	1989
ADA	55%	45%
ACU	46%	27%
AFL-CIO	100%	100%
CCUS	29%	30%

Elections

	1988	1990
General	u/o	62%
Primary	u/o	51%

John T. Myers   (R-Ind.)
Of Covington • Elected 1966

Born: February 8, 1927, Covington, Ind.
Education: Indiana State U., B.S. 1951.
Military Career: Army, 1945-46.
Occupation: Banker; farmer.
Family: Wife, Carol Carruthers; two children.
Religion: Episcopalian.
Political Career: No previous office.

Capitol Office: 2372 Rayburn House Office Building 20515; 225-5805.
Office Staff: Administrative Assistant, Ron Hardman; Press Secretary, Doug Wasitis; Appointments Secretary, Sallie Davis.
Committees: Appropriations; Post Office & Civil Service.

Indiana 7th — West Central — Terre Haute; Lafayette. The district vote for George Bush was 63% in 1988.

CQ Voting Studies

	1989	1990
Presidential	73%	69%
Party	56%	65%
Participation	97%	98%

Interest Groups

	1988	1989
ADA	15%	20%
ACU	83%	74%
AFL-CIO	15%	25%
CCUS	92%	100%

Elections

	1988	1990
General	62%	58%
Primary	u/o	u/o

CQ Voting Studies

	1989	1990
Presidential	41%	20%
Party	88%	88%
Participation	96%	96%

Interest Groups

	1988	1989
ADA	80%	80%
ACU	8%	7%
AFL-CIO	100%	92%
CCUS	36%	40%

Elections

	1988	1990
General	63%	u/o
Primary	92%	u/o

Dave Nagle (D-Iowa)
Of Cedar Falls • Elected 1986

Born: April 15, 1943, Grinnell, Iowa.
Education: U. of Northern Iowa, 1961-65;
U. of Iowa, LL.B. 1968.
Occupation: Lawyer.
Family: Wife, Diane Lewis; one child.
Religion: Roman Catholic.
Political Career: Black Hawk County
Democratic chairman, 1978-82; Iowa
Democratic chairman, 1982-85.

Capitol Office: 214 Cannon House
Office Building 20515; 225-3301.
Office Staff: Administrative Assistant,
Riley Grimes; Press Secretary, Barry Piatt;
Legislative Assistant/Scheduler, Steve
Ward.
Committees: Agriculture; Science, Space
& Technology.

Iowa 3rd — North Central — Waterloo;
Iowa City. The district vote for George
Bush was 43% in 1988.

William H. Natcher (D-Ky.)
Of Bowling Green • Elected 1953

Born: September 11, 1909, Bowling Green, Ky.
Education: Western Kentucky U., B.A. 1930; Ohio State U., LL.B. 1933.
Military Career: Navy, 1942-45.
Occupation: Lawyer.
Family: Widowed; two children.
Religion: Baptist.
Political Career: Federal conciliation commissioner of western Kentucky, 1936-37; Warren County attorney, 1937-49; commonwealth attorney, 8th judicial district, 1951-53.

Capitol Office: 2333 Rayburn House Office Building 20515; 225-3501.
Office Staff: Associate Staff, Diane Rihely.
Committees: Appropriations.

Kentucky 2nd — West Central — Owensboro. The district vote for George Bush was 58% in 1988.

CQ Voting Studies

	1989	1990
Presidential	49%	29%
Party	83%	86%
Participation	100%	100%

Interest Groups

	1988	1989
ADA	75%	65%
ACU	16%	25%
AFL-CIO	100%	83%
CCUS	21%	50%

Elections

	1988	1990
General	61%	66%
Primary	76%	u/o

Richard E. Neal (D-Mass.)
Of Springfield • Elected 1988

Born: February 14, 1949, Worcester, Mass.
Education: American International College, B.A. 1972; U. of Hartford, M.P.A. 1976.
Occupation: Public official.
Family: Wife, Maureen Conway; four children.
Religion: Roman Catholic.
Political Career: Springfield City Council, 1978-84; mayor of Springfield, 1984-89.

Capitol Office: 437 Cannon House Office Building 20515; 225-5601.
Office Staff: Administrative Assistant, Morgan Broman; Press Assistant, William Tranghese; Executive Assistant, Ann Brozek.
Committees: Banking, Finance & Urban Affairs; Small Business.

Massachusetts 2nd — West-Central — Springfield. The district vote for George Bush was 47% in 1988.

CQ Voting Studies

	1989	1990
Presidential	30%	19%
Party	88%	85%
Participation	94%	93%

Interest Groups

	1989
ADA	85%
ACU	11%
AFL-CIO	100%
CCUS	30%

Elections

	1988	1990
General	80%	u/o
Primary	u/o	64%

Stephen L. Neal (D-N.C.)
Of Winston-Salem • Elected 1974

Born: November 7, 1934, Winston-Salem, N.C.
Education: U. of California, Santa Barbara, 1954-56; U. of Hawaii, A.B. 1962.
Occupation: Publisher; mortgage banker.
Family: Wife, Rachel Landis Miller; two children.
Religion: Presbyterian.
Political Career: No previous office.

Capitol Office: 2463 Rayburn House Office Building 20515; 225-2071.
Office Staff: Administrative Assistant, Robert Wrigley; Press Assistant, Bill Connelly; Executive Assistant, June Hunnicutt.
Committees: Banking, Finance & Urban Affairs; Government Operations.

North Carolina 5th — Northwest — Winston-Salem. The district vote for George Bush was 60% in 1988.

CQ Voting Studies

	1989	1990
Presidential	29%	36%
Party	74%	66%
Participation	89%	94%

Interest Groups

	1988	1989
ADA	70%	65%
ACU	21%	19%
AFL-CIO	92%	67%
CCUS	50%	60%

Elections

	1988	1990
General	53%	59%
Primary	u/o	u/o

Dick Nichols (R-Kan.)
Of McPherson • Elected 1990

Born: April 29, 1926, Fort Scott, Kan.
Education: Kansas State U., B.S. 1951.
Military Career: U.S. Navy, 1944-46.
Occupation: Banker.
Family: Wife, Constance Weinbrenner; three children.
Religion: Methodist.
Political Career: No previous office.

Capitol Office: 1605 Longworth House Office Building 20515; 225-3911.
Office Staff: Administrative Assistant, Carolyn Jackson; Press Secretary, Jamie Fall; Appointments, Bonnie Matlas.
Committees: Public Works & Transportation; Veterans' Affairs.

Kansas 5th — Southeast — Emporia; Pittsburg. The district vote for George Bush was 56% in 1988.

Elections

	1990
General	59%
Primary	29%

Henry J. Nowak (D-N.Y.)
Of Buffalo • Elected 1974

Born: February 21, 1935, Buffalo, N.Y.
Education: Canisius College, B.A. 1957;
U. of Buffalo, J.D. 1961.
Military Career: Army, 1957-62.
Occupation: Lawyer.
Family: Wife, Rose Santa Lucia; two
children.
Religion: Roman Catholic.
Political Career: Erie County
comptroller, 1966-74.

Capitol Office: 2240 Rayburn House
Office Building 20515; 225-3306.
Office Staff: Administrative
Assistant/Press Secretary, Ronald J.
Maselka; Executive Assistant, E. Plummer
Godby.
Committees: Public Works &
Transportation; Science, Space &
Technology.

New York 33rd — West — Buffalo. The
district vote for George Bush was 33% in
1988.

CQ Voting Studies

	1989	1990
Presidential	37%	17%
Party	85%	90%
Participation	97%	97%

Interest Groups

	1988	1989
ADA	90%	80%
ACU	12%	15%
AFL-CIO	100%	83%
CCUS	36%	40%

Elections

	1988	1990
General	u/o	78%
Primary	91%	86%

Jim Nussle (R-Iowa)
Of Manchester • Elected 1990

Born: June 27, 1960, Des Moines, Iowa.
Education: Luther College, B.A. 1983;
Drake U., J.D. 1985.
Occupation: Lawyer.
Family: Wife, Leslie Harbison; one child.
Religion: Lutheran.
Political Career: Delaware County
attorney, 1986-90.

Capitol Office: 507 Cannon House
Office Building 20515; 225-2911.
Office Staff: Administrative Assistant,
Steve Greiner; Press Secretary, Anne
Sessions; Appointments Secretary, Diana
Taliga.
Committees: Agriculture; Banking,
Finance & Urban Affairs.

Iowa 2nd — Northeast — Cedar Rapids.
The district vote for George Bush was
43% in 1988.

Elections

	1990
General	50%
Primary	40%

Mary Rose Oakar (D-Ohio)
Of Cleveland • Elected 1976

Born: March 5, 1940, Cleveland, Ohio.
Education: Ursuline College, B.A. 1962;
John Carroll U., M.A. 1966.
Occupation: High school English and
speech teacher.
Family: Single.
Religion: Roman Catholic.
Political Career: Cleveland City Council,
1973-77.

Capitol Office: 2231 Rayburn House
Office Building 20515; 225-5871.
Office Staff: Administrative Assistant,
Thomas A. Albert; Press Secretary, Jim
Belles; Office Manager, Eileen Walley
Fayyad.
Committees: House Administration;
Banking, Finance & Urban Affairs; Post
Office & Civil Service.

Ohio 20th — Cleveland — Central, West
Suburbs. The district vote for George
Bush was 42% in 1988.

CQ Voting Studies

	1989	1990
Presidential	33%	17%
Party	91%	87%
Participation	94%	92%

Interest Groups

	1988	1989
ADA	90%	90%
ACU	8%	0%
AFL-CIO	100%	92%
CCUS	17%	40%

Elections

	1988	1990
General	83%	73%
Primary	77%	80%

CQ Voting Studies

	1989	1990
Presidential	35%	17%
Party	88%	92%
Participation	97%	98%

Interest Groups

	1988	1989
ADA	90%	95%
ACU	12%	4%
AFL-CIO	100%	83%
CCUS	21%	30%

Elections

	1988	1990
General	75%	71%
Primary	u/o	u/o

James L. Oberstar (D-Minn.)
Of Chisholm • Elected 1974

Born: September 10, 1934, Chisholm, Minn.
Education: College of St Thomas, B.A. 1956; College of Europe, Bruges, Belgium, M.A. 1957.
Occupation: Language teacher; congressional aide.
Family: Wife, Jo Garlick; four children.
Religion: Roman Catholic.
Political Career: Sought Democratic nomination for U.S. Senate, 1984.

Capitol Office: 2209 Rayburn House Office Building 20515; 225-6211.
Office Staff: Deputy Administrative Assistant, William G. Richard; Press Secretary, Jim Berard; Appointments Secretary, Halle Czechowski.
Committees: Budget; Public Works & Transportation.

Minnesota 8th — Northeast — Duluth. The district vote for George Bush was 39% in 1988.

David R. Obey (D-Wis.)
Of Wausau • Elected 1969

Born: October 3, 1938, Okmulgee, Okla.
Education: U. of Wisconsin, B.S. 1960; U. of Wisconsin, M.A. 1962.
Occupation: Real estate broker.
Family: Wife, Joan Lepinski; two children.
Religion: Roman Catholic.
Political Career: Wis. Assembly, 1963-69.

Capitol Office: 2462 Rayburn House Office Building 20515; 225-3365.
Office Staff: Staff Director, Joseph R. Crapa; Press Secretary, Lyle Stitt; Personal Secretary, Carly Burns.
Committees: Appropriations.

Wisconsin 7th — Northwest — Wausau; Superior. The district vote for George Bush was 45% in 1988.

CQ Voting Studies

	1989	1990
Presidential	31%	15%
Party	88%	92%
Participation	97%	97%

Interest Groups

	1988	1989
ADA	90%	95%
ACU	4%	0%
AFL-CIO	100%	83%
CCUS	9%	20%

Elections

	1988	1990
General	62%	62%
Primary	u/o	u/o

Jim Olin (D-Va.)
Of Roanoke • Elected 1982

Born: February 28, 1920, Chicago, Ill.
Education: Deep Springs College (Calif.), 1941; Cornell U., B.E.E. 1943.
Military Career: Army, 1943-46.
Occupation: Retired electronics executive.
Family: Wife, Phyllis Avery; five children.
Religion: Unitarian.
Political Career: Rotterdam (N.Y.) town supervisor, Schenectady County supervisor, 1953-55.

Capitol Office: 1314 Longworth House Office Building 20515; 225-5431.
Office Staff: Administrative Assistant, William Black; Press Secretary, Catherine Miller; Office Manager/Personal Secretary, Patricia Grondin.
Committees: Agriculture; Small Business.

Virginia 6th — West — Roanoke; Lynchburg. The district vote for George Bush was 61% in 1988.

CQ Voting Studies

	1989	1990
Presidential	36%	35%
Party	84%	76%
Participation	98%	98%

Interest Groups

	1988	1989
ADA	70%	65%
ACU	28%	14%
AFL-CIO	71%	67%
CCUS	64%	50%

Elections

	1988	1990
General	64%	83%
Primary	u/o	u/o

Solomon P. Ortiz (D-Texas)
Of Corpus Christi • Elected 1982

Born: June 3, 1937, Robstown, Texas.
Education: Del Mar College, 1966-67.
Military Career: Army, 1960-62.
Occupation: Law enforcement official.
Family: Divorced; two children.
Religion: Methodist.
Political Career: Nueces County constable, 1965-68; commissioner, 1969-76; sheriff, 1977-82.

Capitol Office: 1524 Longworth House Office Building 20515; 225-7742.
Office Staff: Administrative Assistant, Florencio Rendon; Press Secretary, Cathy Travis; Executive Assistant/Scheduler, Vicki Hoffpauir.
Committees: Armed Services; Merchant Marine & Fisheries.

Texas 27th — Gulf Coast — Corpus Christi; Brownsville. The district vote for George Bush was 45% in 1988.

CQ Voting Studies

	1989	1990
Presidential	50%	30%
Party	77%	86%
Participation	97%	98%

Interest Groups

	1988	1989
ADA	55%	60%
ACU	26%	29%
AFL-CIO	100%	73%
CCUS	29%	50%

Elections

	1988	1990
General	u/o	u/o
Primary	u/o	u/o

Bill Orton (D-Utah)
Of Provo • Elected 1990

Born: September 22, 1949, North Ogden, Utah.
Education: Brigham Young U., B.S. 1973; Brigham Young U., J.D. 1979.
Occupation: Lawyer.
Family: Single.
Religion: Mormon.
Political Career: No previous office.

Capitol Office: 1723 Longworth House Office Building 20515; 225-7751.
Office Staff: Administrative Assistant, Billie Jay Larson.
Committees: Banking, Finance & Urban Affairs; Foreign Affairs; Small Business.

Utah 3rd — Provo and Rural Utah. The district vote for George Bush was 69% in 1988.

Elections

	1990
General	58%
Primary	u/o

Major R. Owens (D-N.Y.)
Of Brooklyn • Elected 1982

Born: June 28, 1936, Memphis, Tenn.
Education: Morehouse College, B.A.
1956; Atlanta U., M.S. 1957.
Occupation: Librarian.
Family: Divorced; three children.
Religion: Baptist.
Political Career: N.Y. Senate, 1975-83.

Capitol Office: 114 Cannon House
Office Building 20515; 225-6231.
Office Staff: Administrative Assistant,
Jacqueline Ellis; Press Secretary, Margaret
Summers; Executive Assistant, Deborah
Aledo-Simpson.
Committees: Education & Labor;
Government Operations.

New York 12th — Central Brooklyn —
Crown Heights. The district vote for
George Bush was 12% in 1988.

CQ Voting Studies

	1989	1990
Presidential	21%	12%
Party	91%	86%
Participation	90%	88%

Interest Groups

	1988	1989
ADA	95%	100%
ACU	0%	4%
AFL-CIO	100%	100%
CCUS	15%	20%

Elections

	1988	1990
General	93%	95%
Primary	u/o	u/o

Wayne Owens (D-Utah)
Of Salt Lake City • Elected 1986

Born: May 2, 1937, Panguitch, Utah.
Education: U. of Utah, 1958-61; U. of Utah, J.D. 1964.
Occupation: Lawyer.
Family: Wife, Marlene Wessel; five children.
Religion: Mormon.
Political Career: U.S. House, 1973-75; Democratic nominee for U.S. Senate, 1974; Democratic nominee for governor, 1984.

Capitol Office: 1728 Longworth House Office Building 20515; 225-3011.
Office Staff: Administrative Assistant, Scott Kearin; Press Secretary, Art Kingdom; Scheduler, Dianne Tremblay.
Committees: Foreign Affairs; Interior & Insular Affairs.

Utah 2nd — Salt Lake City. The district vote for George Bush was 58% in 1988.

CQ Voting Studies

	1989	1990
Presidential	27%	21%
Party	86%	84%
Participation	90%	96%

Interest Groups

	1988	1989
ADA	75%	70%
ACU	16%	11%
AFL-CIO	93%	73%
CCUS	36%	30%

Elections

	1988	1990
General	57%	58%
Primary	u/o	u/o

Michael G. Oxley (R-Ohio)
Of Findlay • Elected 1981

Born: February 11, 1944, Findlay, Ohio.
Education: Miami U. (Ohio), B.A. 1966; Ohio State U., J.D. 1969.
Occupation: FBI agent; lawyer.
Family: Wife, Patricia Pluguez; one child.
Religion: Lutheran.
Political Career: Ohio House, 1973-81.

Capitol Office: 2448 Rayburn House Office Building 20515; 225-2676.
Office Staff: Administrative Assistant, Jim Conzelman; Press Secretary, Peggy Peterson; Office Manager/Personal Secretary, Debi Deimling.
Committees: Energy & Commerce.

Ohio 4th — West Central — Lima; Findlay. The district vote for George Bush was 68% in 1988.

CQ Voting Studies

	1989	1990
Presidential	80%	73%
Party	86%	82%
Participation	98%	97%

Interest Groups

	1988	1989
ADA	20%	5%
ACU	88%	93%
AFL-CIO	14%	8%
CCUS	100%	100%

Elections

	1988	1990
General	u/o	62%
Primary	u/o	u/o

Ron Packard (R-Calif.)
Of Oceanside • Elected 1982

Born: January 19, 1931, Meridian, Idaho.
Education: Brigham Young U., 1948-50; Portland State U., 1952-53; U. of Oregon, D.M.D. 1957.
Military Career: Navy, 1957-59.
Occupation: Dentist.
Family: Wife, Roma Jean Sorenson; seven children.
Religion: Mormon.
Political Career: Carlsbad School Board, 1960-72; Carlsbad City Council, 1976-78; mayor of Carlsbad, 1978-82.

Capitol Office: 434 Cannon House Office Building 20515; 225-3906.
Office Staff: Chief of Staff/Press Secretary, David C. Coggin; Office Manager/Personal Secretary, Susie Davis.
Committees: Public Works & Transportation; Science, Space & Technology.

California 43rd — Northern San Diego County; Southern Orange County. The district vote for George Bush was 68% in 1988.

CQ Voting Studies

	1989	1990
Presidential	81%	71%
Party	69%	82%
Participation	96%	96%

Interest Groups

	1988	1989
ADA	5%	0%
ACU	100%	93%
AFL-CIO	15%	9%
CCUS	92%	100%

Elections

	1988	1990
General	72%	68%
Primary	u/o	u/o

Frank Pallone, Jr. (D-N.J.)
Of Long Branch • Elected 1988
Pronounced pa LONE

Born: October 30, 1951, Long Branch,
N.J.
Education: Middlebury College, B.A.
1973; Tufts U., M.A. 1974; Rutgers U., J.D.
1978.
Occupation: Lawyer.
Family: Single.
Religion: Roman Catholic.
Political Career: Long Branch City
Council, 1982-88; N.J. Senate, 1984-88.

Capitol Office: 213 Cannon House
Office Building 20515; 225-4671.
Office Staff: Administrative Assistant,
Seth Maiman; Press Secretary, Ted Loud;
Scheduler/Receptionist, Lori Denno.
Committees: Merchant Marine &
Fisheries; Public Works & Transportation.

New Jersey 3rd — Central Coast —
Asbury Park; Long Branch. The district
vote for George Bush was 62% in 1988.

CQ Voting Studies

	1989	1990
Presidential	34%	29%
Party	82%	79%
Participation	98%	99%

Interest Groups

	1989
ADA	75%
ACU	25%
AFL-CIO	92%
CCUS	40%

Elections

	1988	1990
General	52%	49%
Primary	u/o	80%

CQ Voting Studies

	1989	1990
Presidential	31%	20%
Party	91%	89%
Participation	98%	97%

Interest Groups

	1988	1989
ADA	90%	95%
ACU	4%	7%
AFL-CIO	93%	91%
CCUS	33%	30%

Elections

	1988	1990
General	79%	74%
Primary	95%	93%

Leon E. Panetta (D-Calif.)
Of Carmel Valley • Elected 1976

Born: June 28, 1938, Monterey, Calif.
Education: Santa Clara U., B.A. 1960; Santa Clara U., J.D. 1963.
Military Career: Army, 1963-65.
Occupation: Lawyer.
Family: Wife, Sylvia Marie Varni; three children.
Religion: Roman Catholic.
Political Career: No previous office.

Capitol Office: 339 Cannon House Office Building 20515; 225-2861.
Office Staff: Administrative Assistant (Appointments), J. Diane Marino; Press Secretary, Barry Toiv; Office Manager, Marilyn Forrester.
Committees: House Administration; Agriculture; Budget (Chairman).

California 16th — Central Coast — Salinas; Monterey. The district vote for George Bush was 44% in 1988.

Mike Parker (D-Miss.)
Of Brookhaven • Elected 1988

Born: October 31, 1949, Laurel, Miss.
Education: William Carey College, B.A. 1970.
Occupation: Funeral director.
Family: Wife, Rosemary Prather; three children.
Religion: Presbyterian.
Political Career: No previous office.

Capitol Office: 1504 Longworth House Office Building 20515; 225-5865.
Office Staff: Administrative Assistant, Arthur D. Rhodes; Communications Director, Stan Flint; Executive Assistant, Pat Holland.
Committees: Budget; Public Works & Transportation.

Mississippi 4th — Southwest — Jackson. The district vote for George Bush was 56% in 1988.

CQ Voting Studies

	1989	1990
Presidential	71%	56%
Party	47%	52%
Participation	92%	98%

Interest Groups

	1988	1989
ADA		20%
ACU		68%
AFL-CIO		27%
CCUS		100%

Elections

	1988	1990
General	55%	81%
Primary	25%	u/o

Liz J. Patterson (D-S.C.)
Of Spartanburg • Elected 1986

Born: November 18, 1939, Columbia, S.C.
Education: Columbia College, B.A. 1961; U. of South Carolina, 1962.
Occupation: Legislative aide; Peace Corps officer; Head Start official.
Family: Husband, Dwight Fleming Patterson Jr.; three children.
Religion: Methodist.
Political Career: Spartanburg County Council, 1975-76; S.C. Senate, 1979-87.

Capitol Office: 1641 Longworth House Office Building 20515; 225-6030.
Office Staff: Administrative Assistant, Rita Hayes; Press Secretary, Chuck Carr; Executive Assistant, Miriam Wilson.
Committees: Banking, Finance & Urban Affairs; Veterans' Affairs.

South Carolina 4th — Northwest — Greensville; Spartanburg. The district vote for George Bush was 67% in 1988.

CQ Voting Studies

	1989	1990
Presidential	55%	37%
Party	64%	66%
Participation	99%	99%

Interest Groups

	1988	1989
ADA	45%	40%
ACU	48%	68%
AFL-CIO	71%	42%
CCUS	57%	90%

Elections

	1988	1990
General	52%	61%
Primary	u/o	u/o

Bill Paxon (R-N.Y.)
Of Amherst • Elected 1988

Born: April 29, 1954, Buffalo, N.Y.
Education: Canisius College, B.A. 1977.
Occupation: Public official.
Family: Single.
Religion: Roman Catholic.
Political Career: Erie County Legislature, 1978-83; N.Y. Assembly, 1983-89.

Capitol Office: 1314 Longworth House Office Building 20515; 225-5265.
Office Staff: Administrative Assistant, Maria Cino; Press Secretary, Mike Zabel; Executive Assistant/Scheduler, Ginger Miller.
Committees: Banking, Finance & Urban Affairs; Veterans' Affairs.

New York 31st — West — Buffalo Suburbs; Canandaigua. The district vote for George Bush was 56% in 1988.

CQ Voting Studies

	1989	1990
Presidential	73%	69%
Party	89%	93%
Participation	98%	97%

Interest Groups

	1989
ADA	0%
ACU	93%
AFL-CIO	8%
CCUS	100%

Elections

	1988	1990
General	53%	57%
Primary	u/o	u/o

CQ Voting Studies

	1989	1990
Presidential	24%	16%
Party	86%	92%
Participation	89%	95%

Interest Groups

	1989
ADA	90%
ACU	4%
AFL-CIO	100%
CCUS	30%

Elections

	1988	1990
General	77%	81%
Primary	73%	u/o

Donald M. Payne (D-N.J.)
Of Newark • Elected 1988

Born: July 16, 1934, Newark, N.J.
Education: Seton Hall U., B.A. 1957.
Occupation: Community development executive.
Family: Widowed; two children.
Religion: Baptist.
Political Career: Essex County Board of Chosen Freeholders, 1972-78; sought Democratic nomination for Essex County executive, 1978; sought Democratic nomination for U.S. House, 1980; Newark Municipal Council, 1982-88; sought Democratic nomination for U.S. House, 1986.

Capitol Office: 417 Cannon House Office Building 20515; 225-3436.
Office Staff: Administrative Assistant, Maxine James; Press Secretary, Kerry B. McKenney; Executive Assistant, Donna Crews.
Committees: Education & Labor; Foreign Affairs; Government Operations.

New Jersey 10th — Newark. The district vote for George Bush was 21% in 1988.

Lewis F. Payne, Jr. (D-Va.)
Of Wintergreen • Elected 1988

Born: July 9, 1945, Amherst, Va.
Education: Virginia Military Institute, B.S. 1967; U. of Virginia, M.B.A. 1973.
Military Career: Army, 1968-70.
Occupation: Developer; businessman.
Family: Wife, Susan King; four children.
Religion: Presbyterian.
Political Career: No previous office.

Capitol Office: 1118 Longworth House Office Building 20515; 225-4711.
Office Staff: Administrative Assistant, Jim Johnson; Press Secretary, Terry C. Hoye; Personal Secretary, Leigh Emick.
Committees: Budget; Public Works & Transportation; Veterans' Affairs.

Virginia 5th — South — Danville. The district vote for George Bush was 62% in 1988.

CQ Voting Studies

	1989	1990
Presidential	56%	42%
Party	69%	75%
Participation	97%	99%

Interest Groups

	1988	1989
ADA	n/a	35%
ACU	50%	50%
AFL-CIO	83%	36%
CCUS	56%	90%

Elections

	1988	1990
General	54%	u/o
Primary	u/o	u/o

CQ Voting Studies

	1989	1990
Presidential	30%	30%
Party	86%	87%
Participation	97%	98%

Interest Groups

	1988	1989
ADA	90%	90%
ACU	8%	0%
AFL-CIO	86%	91%
CCUS	50%	10%

Elections

	1988	1990
General	70%	60%
Primary	83%	u/o

Don J. Pease (D-Ohio)
Of Oberlin • Elected 1976

Born: September 26, 1931, Toledo, Ohio.
Education: Ohio U., B.S. 1953; Ohio U., M.S. 1955; U. of Durham, England, 1954-55.
Military Career: Army, 1955-57.
Occupation: Newspaper editor.
Family: Wife, Jeanne Wendt; one child.
Religion: Methodist.
Political Career: Oberlin City Council, 1962-64; Ohio Senate, 1965-67; sought Democratic nomination for Ohio Senate, 1966; Ohio House, 1969-75; Ohio Senate, 1975-77.

Capitol Office: 2410 Rayburn House Office Building 20515; 225-3401.
Office Staff: Chief of Staff, Bill Goold; Press Secretary, Peg O'Laughlin; Executive Secretary, Adrienne Harchik.
Committees: Budget; Ways & Means.

Ohio 13th — North — Lorian. The district vote for George Bush was 54% in 1988.

Edward J. Markey (D-Mass.)
Of Malden • Elected 1976

Born: July 11, 1946, Malden, Mass.
Education: Boston College, B.A. 1968;
Boston College, J.D. 1972.
Military Career: Army Reserve, 1968-73.
Occupation: Lawyer.
Family: Wife, Susan Blumenthal.
Religion: Roman Catholic.
Political Career: Mass. House, 1973-77.

Capitol Office: 2133 Rayburn House
Office Building 20515; 225-2836.
Office Staff: Administrative Assistant,
David Moulton; Press Secretary, Michael
J. Connolly; Executive Assistant, Nancy
Morrissey.
Committees: Energy & Commerce;
Interior & Insular Affairs.

Massachusetts 7th — Northern Suburbs
— Medford; Malden. The district vote
for George Bush was 45% in 1988.

CQ Voting Studies

	1989	1990
Presidential	28%	15%
Party	94%	92%
Participation	96%	95%

Interest Groups

	1988	1989
ADA	96%	100%
ACU	0%	0%
AFL-CIO	100%	100%
CCUS	0%	40%

Elections

	1988	1990
General	u/o	u/o
Primary	u/o	u/o

CQ Voting Studies

	1989	1990
Presidential	70%	69%
Party	86%	83%
Participation	88%	93%

Interest Groups

	1988	1989
ADA	0%	0%
ACU	96%	96%
AFL-CIO	7%	0%
CCUS	86%	100%

Elections

	1988	1990
General	56%	63%
Primary	u/o	u/o

Ron Marlenee (R-Mont.)
Of Scobey • Elected 1976
Pronounced MAR la nay

Born: August 8, 1935, Scobey, Mont.
Education: U. of Montana, 1953; U. of Montana, 1960; Montana State U., 1960.
Occupation: Rancher.
Family: Wife, Cynthia Tiemann; three children.
Religion: Lutheran.
Political Career: No previous office.

Capitol Office: 2465 Rayburn House Office Building 20515; 225-1555.
Office Staff: Administrative Assistant, Tom Hannah; Press Secretary, Dan Dubray; Scheduler, Leslie Lucas.
Committees: Agriculture; Interior & Insular Affairs.

Montana 2nd — East. The district vote for George Bush was 54% in 1988.

David O'B. Martin (R-N.Y.)

Of Canton • Elected 1980

Born: April 26, 1944, St. Lawrence County, N.Y.
Education: U. of Notre Dame, B.B.A. 1966; Albany Law School, J.D. 1973.
Military Career: Marine Corps, 1966-70.
Occupation: Lawyer.
Family: Wife, DeeAnn Hedlund; three children.
Religion: Roman Catholic.
Political Career: St. Lawrence County Legislature, 1974-77; N.Y. Assembly, 1977-81.

Capitol Office: 442 Cannon House Office Building 20515; 225-4611.
Office Staff: Administrative Assistant/Press Secretary, Cary R. Brick; Administrative Secretary, Donna Bell.
Committees: Armed Services; Select Intelligence.

New York 26th — North — Plattsburgh; Watertown. The district vote for George Bush was 55% in 1988.

CQ Voting Studies

	1989	1990
Presidential	71%	60%
Party	70%	72%
Participation	94%	95%

Interest Groups

	1988	1989
ADA	25%	5%
ACU	68%	81%
AFL-CIO	64%	17%
CCUS	79%	89%

Elections

	1988	1990
General	75%	u/o
Primary	u/o	u/o

Matthew G. Martinez
(D-Calif.)
Of Monterey Park • Elected 1982

Born: February 14, 1929, Walsenburg, Colo.
Education: Los Angeles Trade-Technical College, 1959.
Military Career: Marine Corps, 1947-50.
Occupation: Upholstery company owner.
Family: Wife, Elvira Yoruba; five children.
Religion: Roman Catholic.
Political Career: Monterey Park City Council, 1974-80; mayor of Monterey Park, 1974-75; Calif. Assembly, 1981-82.

Capitol Office: 240 Cannon House Office Building 20515; 225-5464.
Office Staff: Administrative Assistant/Press Secretary, Maxine Grant; Scheduler, Tammy Tambourine.
Committees: Education & Labor; Government Operations.

California 30th — San Gabriel Valley — El Monte; Alhambra. The district vote for George Bush was 46% in 1988.

CQ Voting Studies

	1989	1990
Presidential	34%	18%
Party	86%	81%
Participation	93%	87%

Interest Groups

	1988	1989
ADA	90%	75%
ACU	0%	11%
AFL-CIO	100%	91%
CCUS	23%	50%

Elections

	1988	1990
General	60%	58%
Primary	74%	u/o

Nancy Pelosi (D-Calif.)
Of San Francisco • Elected 1987
Pronounced pel LO see

Born: March 26, 1940, Baltimore, Md.
Education: Trinity College, A.B. 1962.
Occupation: Public relations consultant.
Family: Husband, Paul Pelosi; five children.
Religion: Roman Catholic.
Political Career: No previous office.

Capitol Office: 1005 Longworth House Office Building 20515; 225-4965.
Office Staff: Administrative Assistant, Judith Lemons; Press Secretary, Craig Middleton; Personal Assistant, Sheri Hamamoto.
Committees: Appropriations.

California 5th — Most of San Francisco. The district vote for George Bush was 28% in 1988.

CQ Voting Studies

	1989	1990
Presidential		
Party	26%	15%
Participation	93%	92%
Participation	96%	96%

Interest Groups

	1988	1989
ADA	100%	95%
ACU	0%	0%
AFL-CIO	93%	100%
CCUS	21%	20%

Elections

	1988	1990
General	76%	77%
Primary	u/o	u/o

Timothy J. Penny (D-Minn.)
Of New Richland • Elected 1982

Born: November 19, 1951, Albert Lea, Minn.
Education: Winona State U., B.A. 1974; U. of Minnesota, 1975.
Military Career: Naval Reserve, 1987-present.
Occupation: Sales representative.
Family: Wife, Barbara Christianson; four children.
Religion: Lutheran.
Political Career: Minn. Senate, 1977-83.

Capitol Office: 436 Cannon House Office Building 20515; 225-2472.
Office Staff: Administrative Assistant, Steve Kingsley; Press Secretary, Jeff Custer; Executive Assistant, Christopher Hoven.
Committees: Agriculture; Veterans' Affairs.

Minnesota 1st — Southeast — Rochester; Mankato. The district vote for George Bush was 51% in 1988.

CQ Voting Studies

	1989	1990
Presidential	57%	34%
Party	67%	66%
Participation	100%	99%

Interest Groups

	1988	1989
ADA	60%	55%
ACU	36%	46%
AFL-CIO	71%	50%
CCUS	64%	80%

Elections

	1988	1990
General	70%	78%
Primary	u/o	u/o

Carl C. Perkins (D-Ky.)
Of Hindman • Elected 1984

Born: August 6, 1954, Washington, D.C.
Education: Davidson College, B.A. 1976;
U. of Louisville, J.D. 1979.
Occupation: Lawyer.
Family: Wife, Janet Neville; two children.
Religion: Baptist.
Political Career: Ky. House, 1982-84.

Capitol Office: 1004 Longworth House
Office Building 20515; 225-4935.
Office Staff: Administrative Assistant,
David M. Whalin; Press Secretary,
Richard Lewis; Office Manager, Charlotte
Reiley Welch.
Committees: Education & Labor;
Science, Space & Technology.

Kentucky 7th — East — Ashland. The
district vote for George Bush was 44% in
1988.

CQ Voting Studies

	1989	1990
Presidential		
Party	37%	24%
Participation	88%	88%
	99%	100%

Interest Groups

	1988	1989
ADA	85%	85%
ACU	12%	21%
AFL-CIO	100%	83%
CCUS	14%	40%

Elections

	1988	1990
General	59%	51%
Primary	u/o	68%

Collin C. Peterson (D-Minn.)
Of Detroit Lakes • Elected 1990

Born: June 29, 1944, Fargo, N.D.
Education: Moorhead State U., B.A. 1966.
Military Career: Army National Guard, 1963-69.
Occupation: Accountant.
Family: Divorced; three children.
Religion: Lutheran.
Political Career: Minn. Senate, 1976-86; sought Democratic nomination for U.S. House, 1982; Democratic nominee for U.S. House, 1984; Democratic nominee for U.S. House, 1986; sought Democratic nomination for U.S. House, 1988.

Capitol Office: 1725 Longworth House Office Building 20515; 225-2165.
Office Staff: Chief of Staff/Press Secretary, James A. DeChaine; Scheduler, Emily Baker.
Committees: Agriculture; Government Operations.

Minnesota 7th — Northwest — St. Cloud; Moorhead. The district vote for George Bush was 51% in 1988.

Elections

	1990
General	54%
Primary	u/o

Pete Peterson (D-Fla.)
Of Marianna • Elected 1990

Born: June 26, 1935, Omaha, Neb.
Education: U. of Tampa, B.S. 1976; U. of Michigan, 1977.
Occupation: Educational administrator.
Family: Wife, Carlotta Ann Neal; three children.
Religion: Roman Catholic.
Political Career: No previous office.

Capitol Office: 1415 Longworth House Office Building 20515; 225-5235.
Office Staff: Administrative Assistant, Suzanne Farmer; Scheduler, Kathleen Semmel.
Committees: Public Works & Transportation; Veterans' Affairs.

Florida 2nd — North — Tallahassee. The district vote for George Bush was 59% in 1988.

Elections

	1990
General	57%
Primary	60%

CQ Voting Studies

	1989	1990
Presidential	66%	69%
Party	67%	78%
Participation	100%	97%

Interest Groups

	1988	1989
ADA	35%	20%
ACU	75%	75%
AFL-CIO	50%	17%
CCUS	79%	90%

Elections

	1988	1990
General	74%	u/o
Primary	u/o	u/o

Tom Petri (R-Wis.)
Of Fond du Lac • Elected 1979
Pronounced PEE tree

Born: May 28, 1940, Marinette, Wis.
Education: Harvard U., B.A. 1962; Harvard U., J.D. 1965.
Occupation: Lawyer.
Family: Wife, Anne Neal; one child.
Religion: Lutheran.
Political Career: Wis. Senate, 1973-79; Republican nominee for U.S. Senate, 1974.

Capitol Office: 2245 Rayburn House Office Building 20515; 225-2476.
Office Staff: Administrative Assistant, Joe Flader; Press Secretary, Niel Wright; Executive Assistant, Derek Huseboe.
Committees: Education & Labor; Public Works & Transportation; Standards of Official Conduct.

Wisconsin 6th — Central — Oshkosh; Fond du Lac; Manitowoc. The district vote for George Bush was 53% in 1988.

Owen B. Pickett (D-Va.)
Of Virginia Beach • Elected 1986

Born: August 31, 1930, Richmond, Va.
Education: Virginia Polytechnic Institute and State U., B.S. 1952; U. of Richmond, LL.B. 1955.
Occupation: Lawyer; accountant.
Family: Wife, Sybil Catherine Kelly; three children.
Religion: Baptist.
Political Career: Va. House, 1973-87; withdrew from campaign for Democratic nomination for U.S. Senate, 1982.

Capitol Office: 1204 Longworth House Office Building 20515; 225-4215.
Office Staff: Administrative Assistant, Patrick Baskette; Press Secretary, Paul J. Reagan; Office Manager/Scheduler, Donna T. Wooten.
Committees: Armed Services; Merchant Marine & Fisheries; Veterans' Affairs.

Virginia 2nd — Norfolk; Virginia Beach. The district vote for George Bush was 60% in 1988.

CQ Voting Studies

	1989	1990
Presidential	52%	47%
Party	72%	72%
Participation	97%	99%

Interest Groups

	1988	1989
ADA	50%	45%
ACU	40%	37%
AFL-CIO	86%	42%
CCUS	50%	80%

Elections

	1988	1990
General	61%	75%
Primary	u/o	u/o

CQ Voting Studies

	1989	1990
Presidential	47%	33%
Party	82%	81%
Participation	97%	97%

Interest Groups

	1988	1989
ADA	80%	50%
ACU	16%	33%
AFL-CIO	100%	67%
CCUS	38%	30%

Elections

	1988	1990
General	93%	65%
Primary	u/o	89%

J.J. Pickle (D-Texas)
Of Austin • Elected 1963

Born: October 11, 1913, Roscoe, Texas.
Education: U. of Texas, B.A. 1938.
Military Career: Navy, 1942-45.
Occupation: Public relations and advertising executive.
Family: Wife, Beryl Bolton McCarroll; three children.
Religion: Methodist.
Political Career: No previous office.

Capitol Office: 242 Cannon House Office Building 20515; 225-4865.
Office Staff: Administrative Assistant, Barbara Pate; Press Assistant, Dave Mason; Executive Secretary, Molly Mitchell.
Committees: Ways & Means.

Texas 10th — Central — Austin. The district vote for George Bush was 46% in 1988.

John Porter (R-Ill.)
Of Wilmette • Elected 1980

Born: June 1, 1935, Evanston, Ill.
Education: Massachusetts Institute of Technology, 1953-54; Northwestern U., B.S., B.A. 1957; U. of Michigan, J.D. 1961.
Military Career: Army Reserve, 1958-64.
Occupation: Lawyer.
Family: Wife, Kathryn Cameron; five children.
Religion: Presbyterian.
Political Career: Ill. House, 1973-79; Republican nominee for U.S. House, 1978; Republican nominee for Cook County circuit court judge, 1970.

Capitol Office: 1026 Longworth House Office Building 20515; 225-4835.
Office Staff: Administrative Assistant, Robert Bradner; Press Secretary, David Kohn; Appointments Secretary, Lynn Collison.
Committees: Appropriations.

Illinois 10th — North and Northwest Suburbs — Waukegan. The district vote for George Bush was 62% in 1988.

CQ Voting Studies

	1989	1990
Presidential	65%	65%
Party	54%	69%
Participation	93%	97%

Interest Groups

	1988	1989
ADA	30%	30%
ACU	68%	63%
AFL-CIO	15%	8%
CCUS	100%	100%

Elections

	1988	1990
General	72%	68%
Primary	u/o	u/o

Glenn Poshard (D-Ill.)
Of Carterville • Elected 1988
Pronounced pa SHARD

Born: October 30, 1945, Herald, Ill.
Education: Southern Illinois U., B.S. 1970; Southern Illinois U., M.S. 1974; Southern Illinois U., Ph.D. 1984.
Military Career: Army, 1962-65.
Occupation: Educator.
Family: Wife, Jo Roetzel; two children.
Religion: Baptist.
Political Career: Sought nomination for Ill. Senate, 1982; Ill. Senate, 1984-89.

Capitol Office: 314 Cannon House Office Building 20515; 225-5201.
Office Staff: Administrative Assistant, ElizaBeth Pierce; Press Secretary, David Stricklin; Scheduler, Nola Cowsert.
Committees: Public Works & Transportation; Small Business.

Illinois 22nd — South — Carbondale. The district vote for George Bush was 48% in 1988.

CQ Voting Studies

	1989	1990
Presidential	35%	23%
Party	79%	85%
Participation	99%	99%

Interest Groups

	1989
ADA	80%
ACU	21%
AFL-CIO	92%
CCUS	40%

Elections

	1988	1990
General	65%	84%
Primary	u/o	u/o

David Price (D-N.C.)
Of Chapel Hill • Elected 1986

Born: August 17, 1940, Johnson City, Tenn.
Education: Mars Hill College, 1958-59; U. of North Carolina, B.A. 1961; Yale U., B.D. 1964; Yale U., Ph.D. 1969.
Occupation: Professor of political science and public policy.
Family: Wife, Lisa Kanwit; two children.
Religion: American Baptist.
Political Career: N.C. Democratic Party chairman, 1983-84.

Capitol Office: 1406 Longworth House Office Building 20515; 225-1784.
Office Staff: Administrative Assistant, Gene Conti; Press Secretary, Rachel Perry; Staff Assistant, Sally Maddison.
Committees: Appropriations.

North Carolina 4th — Central — Raleigh; Chapel Hill. The district vote for George Bush was 55% in 1988.

CQ Voting Studies

	1989	1990
Presidential	34%	24%
Party	90%	92%
Participation	98%	99%

Interest Groups

	1988	1989
ADA	75%	75%
ACU	24%	14%
AFL-CIO	93%	83%
CCUS	62%	60%

Elections

	1988	1990
General	58%	58%
Primary	u/o	91%

CQ Voting Studies

	1989	1990
Presidential	60%	53%
Party	52%	57%
Participation	94%	89%

Interest Groups

	1988	1989
ADA	45%	30%
ACU	46%	57%
AFL-CIO	62%	8%
CCUS	79%	100%

Elections

	1988	1990
General	55%	64%
Primary	u/o	u/o

Carl D. Pursell (R-Mich.)
Of Plymouth • Elected 1976

Born: December 19, 1932, Imlay City, Mich.

Education: Eastern Michigan U., B.A. 1956; Eastern Michigan U., M.A. 1961.

Military Career: Army, 1957-59; Army Reserve, 1959-65.

Occupation: High school teacher; real estate salesman, owner of office supply business.

Family: Wife, Peggy Jean Brown; three children.

Religion: Protestant.

Political Career: Sought Republican nomination for Mich. Senate, 1966; Wayne County Commission, 1969-70; Mich. Senate, 1971-77.

Capitol Office: 1414 Longworth House Office Building 20515; 225-4401.

Office Staff: Administrtative Assistant, William R. McBride; Press Secretary, Gary Cates; Appointments Secretary, Diane Williams.

Committees: Appropriations.

Michigan 2nd — Southeast — Ann Arbor; Jackson. The district vote for George Bush was 56% in 1988.

James H. Quillen (R-Tenn.)
Of Kingsport • Elected 1962

Born: January 11, 1916, near Gate City,
Va.
Education: Dobyns-Bennett High School,
1934.
Military Career: Navy, 1942-46.
Occupation: Newspaper publisher; real
estate and insurance salesman; banker.
Family: Wife, Cecile Cox.
Religion: Methodist.
Political Career: Tenn. House, 1955-63.

Capitol Office: 102 Cannon House
Office Building 20515; 225-6356.
Office Staff: Administrative Assistant,
Frances Light Currie; Press Secretary, Paul
Mays; Personal Secretary, Dolores
Kefalas.
Committees: Rules.

Tennessee 1st — Northeast — Tri-cities.
The district vote for George Bush was
68% in 1988.

CQ Voting Studies

	1989	1990
Presidential	71%	65%
Party	60%	60%
Participation	91%	92%

Interest Groups

	1988	1989
ADA	15%	15%
ACU	91%	85%
AFL-CIO	36%	25%
CCUS	100%	100%

Elections

	1988	1990
General	80%	u/o
Primary	u/o	u/o

CQ Voting Studies

	1989	1990
Presidential	40%	14%
Party	80%	79%
Participation	95%	95%

Interest Groups

	1988	1989
ADA	70%	85%
ACU	22%	19%
AFL-CIO	100%	91%
CCUS	29%	40%

Elections

	1988	1990
General	61%	52%
Primary	73%	57%

Nick J. Rahall, II (D-W.Va.)
Of Beckley • *Elected 1976*

Born: May 20, 1949, Beckley, W.Va.
Education: Duke U., A.B. 1971; George Washington U., 1972.
Occupation: Broadcasting executive; travel agent; congressional aide.
Family: Divorced; three children.
Religion: Presbyterian.
Political Career: No previous office.

Capitol Office: 2104 Rayburn House Office Building 20515; 225-3452.
Office Staff: Administrative Assistant, Kent Keyser; Press Secretary, Stephen Spina; Executive Secretary, Vicki Bandy.
Committees: Interior & Insular Affairs; Public Works & Transportation.

West Virginia 4th — South and West — Huntington; Beckley. The district vote for George Bush was 42% in 1988.

Jim Ramstad (R-Minn.)
Of Minnetonka • Elected 1990

Born: May 6, 1946, Jamestown, N.D.
Education: U. of Minnesota, B.A. 1968;
George Washington U., J.D. 1973.
Military Career: Army Reserve, 1968-74.
Occupation: Lawyer; legislative aide.
Family: Single.
Religion: Protestant.
Political Career: Minn. Senate, 1981-91.

Capitol Office: 504 Cannon House
Office Building 20515; 225-2871.
Office Staff: Administrative Assistant,
Maybeth Christensen; Communications
Director, Lance Olson; Scheduler,
Patricia Rooney.
Committees: Judiciary; Small Business.

Minnesota 3rd — Southern and Western
Twin Cities Suburbs. The district vote for
George Bush was 54% in 1988.

Elections

	1990
General	66%
Primary	79%

CQ Voting Studies

	1989	1990
Presidential	27%	13%
Party	86%	85%
Participation	89%	89%

Interest Groups

	1988	1989
ADA	85%	85%
ACU	0%	0%
AFL-CIO	100%	100%
CCUS	31%	11%

Elections

	1988	1990
General	97%	97%
Primary	u/o	u/o

Charles B. Rangel (D-N.Y.)
Of Manhattan • Elected 1970

Born: June 11, 1930, New York, N.Y.
Education: New York U., B.S. 1957; St. John's U., LL.B. 1960.
Military Career: Army, 1948-52.
Occupation: Lawyer.
Family: Wife, Alma Carter; two children.
Religion: Roman Catholic.
Political Career: N.Y. Assembly, 1967-71; sought Democratic nomination for N.Y. City Council president, 1969.

Capitol Office: 2252 Rayburn House Office Building 20515; 225-4365.
Office Staff: Administrative Assistant, Annette Samuels; Executive Assistant/Office Manager, Patricia Bradley.
Committees: Narcotics Abuse & Control (Chairman); Ways & Means.

New York 16th — Manhattan — Harlem. The district vote for George Bush was 13% in 1988.

Arthur Ravenel, Jr. (R-S.C.)
Of Mount Pleasant • Elected 1986
Pronounced RAV nel

Born: March 29, 1927, St. Andrews Parish, S.C.
Education: College of Charleston, B.A. 1950.
Military Career: Marine Corps, 1945-46.
Occupation: Businessman.
Family: Wife, Jean Rickenbaker; six children, four stepchildren.
Religion: French Huguenot.
Political Career: S.C. House, 1953-59; S.C. Senate, 1981-87.

Capitol Office: 508 Cannon House Office Building 20515; 225-3176.
Office Staff: Administrative Assistant (Appointments), Jeanne Moore; Press Secretary, Sharon Chellis.
Committees: Armed Services; Merchant Marine & Fisheries.

South Carolina 1st — South — Charleston. The district vote for George Bush was 61% in 1988.

CQ Voting Studies

	1989	1990
Presidential	64%	54%
Party	50%	59%
Participation	93%	98%

Interest Groups

	1988	1989
ADA	25%	25%
ACU	76%	70%
AFL-CIO	64%	25%
CCUS	86%	100%

Elections

	1988	1990
General	64%	65%
Primary	u/o	90%

Richard Ray (D-Ga.)
Of Perry • Elected 1982

Born: February 2, 1927, Fort Valley, Ga.
Education: Crawford County High School.
Military Career: Navy, 1944-45.
Occupation: Exterminator; Senate aide.
Family: Wife, Barbara Elizabeth Giles; three children.
Religion: Methodist.
Political Career: Perry City Council, 1962-64; mayor of Perry, 1964-70.

Capitol Office: 225 Cannon House Office Building 20515; 225-5901.
Office Staff: Administrative Assistant/Office Manager, Laura Redding; Press Secretary, Jimmy Hendricks; Executive Assistant, Audrey Balkcom.
Committees: Armed Services; Small Business.

Georgia 3rd — West Central — Columbus. The district vote for George Bush was 57% in 1988.

CQ Voting Studies

	1989	1990
Presidential	69%	53%
Party	48%	56%
Participation	96%	94%

Interest Groups

	1988	1989
ADA	20%	15%
ACU	53%	65%
AFL-CIO	56%	9%
CCUS	56%	100%

Elections

	1988	1990
General	u/o	63%
Primary	u/o	u/o

John F. Reed (D-R.I.)
Of Cranston • Elected 1990

Born: November 12, 1949, Providence, R.I.
Education: U.S. Military Academy, West Point, B.S. 1971; Harvard U., M.P.P. 1973; Harvard U., J.D. 1982.
Military Career: Army, 1967-69.
Occupation: Lawyer.
Family: Single.
Religion: Roman Catholic.
Political Career: R.I. Senate, 1985-91.

Capitol Office: 1229 Longworth House Office Building 20515; 225-2735.
Office Staff: Administrative Assistant, J. B. Poersch; Office Manager, Mary Kay Dawson.
Committees: Education & Labor; Judiciary; Merchant Marine & Fisheries.

Rhode Island 2nd — West — Western Providence; Warwick. The district vote for George Bush was 46% in 1988.

Elections

	1990
General	59%
Primary	49%

CQ Voting Studies

	1989	1990
Presidential	70%	56%
Party	60%	75%
Participation	99%	98%

Interest Groups

	1988	1989
ADA	30%	20%
ACU	76%	54%
AFL-CIO	64%	25%
CCUS	93%	100%

Elections

	1988	1990
General	79%	59%
Primary	u/o	u/o

Ralph Regula (R-Ohio)
Of Navarre • Elected 1972
Pronounced REG you la

Born: December 3, 1924, Beach City, Ohio.
Education: Mount Union College, B.A. 1948; William McKinley School of Law, LL.B. 1952.
Military Career: Navy, 1944-46.
Occupation: Lawyer.
Family: Wife, Mary Rogusky; three children.
Religion: Episcopalian.
Political Career: Ohio House, 1965-67; Ohio Senate, 1967-73.

Capitol Office: 2207 Rayburn House Office Building 20515; 225-3876.
Office Staff: Press Secretary, Julie Lawson; Executive Secretary/Scheduler, Sylvia Snyder.
Committees: Appropriations.

Ohio 16th — Northeast — Canton. The district vote for George Bush was 57% in 1988.

John J. Rhodes III (R-Ariz.)

Of Mesa • Elected 1986

Born: September 8, 1943, Mesa, Ariz.
Education: Yale U., B.A. 1965; U. of
Arizona, J.D. 1968.
Military Career: Army, 1968-70.
Occupation: Lawyer.
Family: Wife, Ann Chase; four children.
Religion: Protestant.
Political Career: Mesa School Board,
1972-76; Republican district chairman,
1973-75; vice president, Central Arizona
Water Conservation District, 1983-87.

Capitol Office: 326 Cannon House
Office Building 20515; 225-2635.
Office Staff: Administrative Assistant,
Jack Seum; Press Secretary, Doug Cole;
Executive Assistant, Marcia Summers.
Committees: Interior & Insular Affairs;
Science, Space & Technology.

Arizona 1st — Eastern Phoenix; Tempe;
Mesa. The district vote for George Bush
was 65% in 1988.

CQ Voting Studies

	1989	1990
Presidential	86%	77%
Party	88%	90%
Participation	99%	99%

Interest Groups

	1988	1989
ADA	10%	10%
ACU	96%	82%
AFL-CIO	7%	8%
CCUS	100%	100%

Elections

	1988	1990
General	72%	u/o
Primary	u/o	62%

Bill Richardson (D-N.M.)
Of Santa Fe • Elected 1982

Born: November 15, 1947, Pasadena, Calif.
Education: Tufts U., B.A. 1970; Tufts U., M.A. 1971.
Occupation: Business consultant.
Family: Wife, Barbara Flavin.
Religion: Roman Catholic.
Political Career: Executive director, New Mexico Democratic Party, 1978-80; Democratic nominee for U.S. House, 1980.

Capitol Office: 332 Cannon House Office Building 20515; 225-6190.
Office Staff: Administrative Assistant, Pablo Collins; Press Secretary, Stu Nagurka; Executive Assistant, Isabelle Watkins.
Committees: Energy & Commerce; Interior & Insular Affairs; Select Intelligence.

New Mexico 3rd — North and West — Farmington; Santa Fe. The district vote for George Bush was 44% in 1988.

CQ Voting Studies

	1989	1990
Presidential	37%	29%
Party	86%	84%
Participation	96%	97%

Interest Groups

	1988	1989
ADA	75%	70%
ACU	21%	21%
AFL-CIO	93%	92%
CCUS	42%	44%

Elections

	1988	1990
General	73%	74%
Primary	u/o	u/o

Tom Ridge (R-Pa.)
Of Erie • Elected 1982

Born: August 26, 1945, Munhall, Penn.
Education: Harvard U., B.A. 1967;
Dickinson School of Law, J.D. 1972.
Military Career: Army, 1968-70.
Occupation: Lawyer.
Family: Wife, Michele Moore; two
children.
Religion: Roman Catholic.
Political Career: Assistant district
attorney, 1980-82.

Capitol Office: 1714 Longworth House
Office Building 20515; 225-5406.
Office Staff: Administrative Assistant,
Mark Holman; Press Secretary, Mark
Campbell; Office Manager/Personal
Secretary, Leslie Fitting.
Committees: Banking, Finance & Urban
Affairs; Post Office & Civil Service;
Veterans' Affairs.

Pennsylvania 21st — Northwest — Erie.
The district vote for George Bush was
49% in 1988.

CQ Voting Studies

	1989	1990
Presidential	56%	49%
Party	69%	68%
Participation	95%	95%

Interest Groups

	1988	1989
ADA	50%	45%
ACU	36%	57%
AFL-CIO	86%	67%
CCUS	71%	80%

Elections

	1988	1990
General	79%	u/o
Primary	u/o	u/o

Frank Riggs (R-Calif.)
Of Windsor • Elected 1990

Born: September 5, 1950, Louisville, Ky.
Education: Golden Gate U., B.A. 1980.
Military Career: Army, 1972-75.
Occupation: Real estate developer.
Family: Wife, Cathy Anne Maillard; three children.
Religion: Episcopalian.
Political Career: Windsor School Board, 1984-88.

Capitol Office: 1517 Longworth House Office Building 20515; 225-3311.
Office Staff: Administrative Assistant, Steve Appel; Press Secretary, Jeff Fedorchak; Appointments Secretary, Shelley Tantau.
Committees: Banking, Finance & Urban Affairs; Public Works & Transportation.

California 1st — Northern Coast — Santa Rosa; Eureka. The district vote for George Bush was 43% in 1988.

Elections

	1990
General	43%
Primary	77%

Matthew J. Rinaldo (R-N.J.)
Of Union • Elected 1972

Born: September 1, 1931, Elizabeth, N.J.
Education: Rutgers U., B.S. 1953; Seton Hall U., M.B.A. 1959; New York U., D.P.A. 1979.
Occupation: Management consultant; lecturer.
Family: Single.
Religion: Roman Catholic.
Political Career: Union County Board of Freeholders, 1963-64; N.J. Senate, 1968-72.

Capitol Office: 2469 Rayburn House Office Building 20515; 225-5361.
Office Staff: Administrative Assistant/Press Secretary, John Arnold; Office Manager, Betty Blackshaw.
Committees: Energy & Commerce.

New Jersey 7th — North and Central — Elizabeth. The district vote for George Bush was 59% in 1988.

CQ Voting Studies

	1989	1990
Presidential	55%	47%
Party	39%	46%
Participation	98%	98%

Interest Groups

	1988	1989
ADA	45%	45%
ACU	54%	56%
AFL-CIO	100%	83%
CCUS	36%	60%

Elections

	1988	1990
General	75%	75%
Primary	u/o	u/o

CQ Voting Studies

	1989	1990
Presidential	69%	66%
Party	70%	73%
Participation	96%	96%

Interest Groups

	1988	1989
ADA	10%	10%
ACU	84%	100%
AFL-CIO	62%	17%
CCUS	77%	100%

Elections

	1988	1990
General	57%	60%
Primary	u/o	u/o

Don Ritter (R-Pa.)
Of Coopersburg • Elected 1978

Born: October 21, 1940, New York, N.Y.
Education: Lehigh U., B.S. 1961; Massachusetts Institute of Technology, M.S. 1963; Massachusetts Institute of Technology, Sc.D. 1966.
Occupation: Engineering consultant; professor.
Family: Wife, Edith Duerksen; two children.
Religion: Unitarian.
Political Career: No previous office.

Capitol Office: 2202 Rayburn House Office Building 20515; 225-6411.
Office Staff: Administrative Assistant, Patty Sheetz; Press Secretary, Ann Freeh; Appointments Secretary, Darryl Schumaker.
Committees: Energy & Commerce; Science, Space & Technology.

Pennsylvania 15th — East — Allentown; Bethlehem. The district vote for George Bush was 55% in 1988.

Pat Roberts (R-Kan.)
Of Dodge City • Elected 1980

Born: April 20, 1936, Topeka, Kan.
Education: Kansas State U., B.A. 1958.
Military Career: Marine Corps, 1958-62.
Occupation: Journalist; congressional aide.
Family: Wife, Franki Fann; three children.
Religion: Methodist.
Political Career: No previous office.

Capitol Office: 1110 Longworth House Office Building 20515; 225-2715.
Office Staff: Administrative Assistant, Leroy Towns; Press Secretary, Sarah Coleman; Personal Secretary, Merry Tobin.
Committees: House Administration; Agriculture.

Kansas 1st — West — Salina; Dodge City. The district vote for George Bush was 60% in 1988.

CQ Voting Studies

	1989	1990
Presidential	79%	71%
Party	86%	87%
Participation	98%	98%

Interest Groups

	1988	1989
ADA	10%	5%
ACU	79%	79%
AFL-CIO	25%	0%
CCUS	100%	100%

Elections

	1988	1990
General	u/o	63%
Primary	u/o	u/o

CQ Voting Studies

	1989	1990
Presidential	35%	27%
Party	77%	86%
Participation	87%	96%

Interest Groups

	1988	1989
ADA	70%	65%
ACU	13%	25%
AFL-CIO	100%	83%
CCUS	21%	44%

Elections

	1988	1990
General	u/o	77%
Primary	u/o	80%

Robert A. Roe (D-N.J.)
Of West Wayne • Elected 1969

Born: February 28, 1924, Lyndhurst, N.J.
Education: Oregon State U.; Washington State U..
Military Career: Army, 1943-46.
Occupation: Construction company owner; engineer.
Family: Single.
Religion: Roman Catholic.
Political Career: Wayne Township Committee, 1955-56; mayor of Wayne Township, 1956-61; Passaic County freeholder, 1959-63; sought Democratic nomination for governor, 1977; sought Democratic nomination for governor, 1981.

Capitol Office: 2243 Rayburn House Office Building 20515; 225-5751.
Office Staff: Administrative Assistant, Angela Milazzo; Press Secretary, Bob Maitlin; Appointments Secretary, Sandra J. Ferguson.
Committees: Public Works & Transportation (Chairman).

New Jersey 8th — North — Paterson. The district vote for George Bush was 56% in 1988.

Tim Roemer (D-Ind.)
Of South Bend • Elected 1990

Born: October 30, 1956, South Bend, Ind.
Education: U. of California, San Diego, B.A. 1979; Notre Dame U., M.A. 1982; Notre Dame U., Ph.D. 1986.
Occupation: Congressional aide.
Family: Wife, Sally Johnston.
Religion: Roman Catholic.
Political Career: No previous office.

Capitol Office: 415 Cannon House Office Building 20515; 225-3915.
Office Staff: Administrative Assistant, Bernie Toon; Press Secretary, Kimberly Smithton; Executive Assistant, Jane Armstrong.
Committees: Education & Labor; Science, Space & Technology.

Indiana 3rd — North Central — South Bend. The district vote for George Bush was 59% in 1988.

Elections

	1990
General	51%
Primary	64%

CQ Voting Studies

	1989	1990
Presidential	80%	69%
Party	83%	85%
Participation	99%	99%

Interest Groups

	1988	1989
ADA	5%	10%
ACU	96%	71%
AFL-CIO	21%	25%
CCUS	100%	80%

Elections

	1988	1990
General	u/o	u/o
Primary	u/o	u/o

Harold Rogers (R-Ky.)
Of Somerset • Elected 1980

Born: December 31, 1937, Barrier, Ky.
Education: Western Kentucky U., 1956-57; U. of Kentucky, B.A. 1962; U. of Kentucky, LL.B. 1964.
Military Career: Army National Guard, 1956-64.
Occupation: Lawyer.
Family: Wife, Shirley McDowell; three children.
Religion: Baptist.
Political Career: Commonwealth attorney, Pulaski and Rockcastle counties, 1969-79; Republican nominee for lieutenant governor, 1979.

Capitol Office: 343 Cannon House Office Building 20515; 225-4601.
Office Staff: Administrative Assistant, Marty Driesler; Press Secretary, Frank Purcell; Office Manager/Appointments Secretary, Kimberly Tremble.
Committees: Appropriations; Budget.

Kentucky 5th — Southeast — Middlesboro. The district vote for George Bush was 67% in 1988.

Dana Rohrabacher (R-Calif.)

Of Palos Verdes Estates • Elected 1988
Pronounced ROAR ah bach er

Born: June 21, 1947, Coronado, Calif.
Education: Los Angeles Harbor College,
1965-67; California State U., Long Beach,
B.A. 1969; U. of Southern California, M.A.
1971.
Occupation: White House speechwriter;
journalist.
Family: Single.
Religion: Baptist.
Political Career: No previous office.

Capitol Office: 1039 Longworth House
Office Building 20515; 225-2415.
Office Staff: Chief of Staff, Gary L.
Curran; Press Secretary, Larry Hart;
Personal Assistant, Steve Johnson.
Committees: District of Columbia;
Science, Space & Technology.

California 42nd — Coastal Los Angeles
and Orange Counties. The district vote
for George Bush was 65% in 1988.

CQ Voting Studies

	1989	1990
Presidential	70%	74%
Party	82%	90%
Participation	98%	99%

Interest Groups

	1988	1989
ADA		10%
ACU		96%
AFL-CIO		9%
CCUS		90%

Elections

	1988	1990
General	64%	59%
Primary	35%	u/o

CQ Voting Studies

	1989	1990
Presidential	66%	50%
Party	74%	70%
Participation	99%	97%

Interest Groups

	1989
ADA	n/a
ACU	100%
AFL-CIO	40%
CCUS	100%

Elections

	1989*	1990
General	53%	60%
Primary		u/o

*Special election.

Ileana Ros-Lehtinen (R-Fla.)
Of Miami • Elected 1989
Pronounced ill EE ahn ah Ross LAY tin un

Born: July 15, 1952, Havana, Cuba.
Education: Miami-Dade Community College, A.A. 1972; Florida International U., B.A. 1975; Florida International U., M.S. 1986.
Occupation: Teacher; private school administrator.
Family: Husband, Dexter Lehtinen; two children.
Religion: Roman Catholic.
Political Career: Fla. House, 1982-86; Fla. Senate, 1986-89.

Capitol Office: 416 Cannon House Office Building 20515; 225-3931.
Office Staff: Administrative Assistant, Russell L. Roberts; Press Secretary, Rafael Bejar; PersonalSecretary/Scheduler, Betty Nunez.
Committees: Foreign Affairs; Government Operations.

Florida 18th — Southeast — Miami and Miami Beach. The district vote for George Bush was 58% in 1988.

Charlie Rose (D-N.C.)
Of Fayetteville • Elected 1972

Born: August 10, 1939, Fayetteville, N.C.
Education: Davidson College, B.A. 1961;
U. of North Carolina, LL.B. 1964.
Occupation: Lawyer.
Family: Wife, Joan Teague; three
children.
Religion: Presbyterian.
Political Career: Chief district court
prosecutor, 12th Judicial District, 1967-
71; sought Democratic nomination for
U.S. House, 1970.

Capitol Office: 2230 Rayburn House
Office Building 20515; 225-2731.
Office Staff: Administrative Assistant, A.
Turner-Scott; Personal Assistant, Robin
Sterling.
Committees: House Administration
(Chairman); Agriculture.

North Carolina 7th — Southeast —
Fayetteville; Wilmington. The district
vote for George Bush was 51% in 1988.

CQ Voting Studies

	1989	1990
Presidential	36%	19%
Party	85%	88%
Participation	94%	95%

Interest Groups

	1988	1989
ADA	60%	80%
ACU	11%	15%
AFL-CIO	100%	83%
CCUS	25%	50%

Elections

	1988	1990
General	67%	66%
Primary	u/o	u/o

Dan Rostenkowski (D-Ill.)
Of Chicago • Elected 1958

Born: January 2, 1928, Chicago, Ill.
Education: Loyola U., 1948-51.
Military Career: Army, 1946-48.
Occupation: Insurance executive.
Family: Wife, LaVerne Pirkins; four children.
Religion: Roman Catholic.
Political Career: Ill. House, 1953-55; Ill. Senate, 1955-59.

Capitol Office: 2111 Rayburn House Office Building 20515; 225-4061.
Office Staff: Administrative Assistant (Appointments), Virginia Fletcher; Press Secretary, Jim Jaffe.
Committees: Ways & Means (Chairman).

Illinois 8th — Chicago — North and Northwest Sides. The district vote for George Bush was 41% in 1988.

CQ Voting Studies

	1989	1990
Presidential	36%	33%
Party	85%	76%
Participation	93%	89%

Interest Groups

	1988	1989
ADA	65%	70%
ACU	19%	19%
AFL-CIO	85%	100%
CCUS	50%	10%

Elections

	1988	1990
General	75%	79%
Primary	u/o	u/o

Toby Roth (R-Wis.)
Of Appleton • Elected 1978

Born: October 10, 1938, Strasburg, N.D.
Education: Marquette U., B.A. 1961.
Military Career: Army Reserve, 1962-69.
Occupation: Real estate broker.
Family: Wife, Barbara Fischer; three children.
Religion: Roman Catholic.
Political Career: Wis. Assembly, 1973-79.

Capitol Office: 2352 Rayburn House Office Building 20515; 225-5665.
Office Staff: Administrative Assistant, George Ann Way; Press Assistant, John Hines; Personal Assistant, Susan Grimes.
Committees: Banking, Finance & Urban Affairs; Foreign Affairs.

Wisconsin 8th — Northeast — Green Bay; Appleton. The district vote for George Bush was 53% in 1988.

CQ Voting Studies

	1989	1990
Presidential	72%	63%
Party	81%	77%
Participation	95%	98%

Interest Groups

	1988	1989
ADA	10%	10%
ACU	83%	86%
AFL-CIO	36%	9%
CCUS	92%	100%

Elections

	1988	1990
General	70%	54%
Primary	u/o	79%

CQ Voting Studies

	1989	1990
Presidential	53%	45%
Party	60%	58%
Participation	96%	90%

Interest Groups

	1988	1989
ADA	40%	30%
ACU	50%	57%
AFL-CIO	79%	33%
CCUS	69%	90%

Elections

	1988	1990
General	76%	76%
Primary	u/o	u/o

Marge Roukema (R-N.J.)
Of Ridgewood • Elected 1980
Pronounced ROCK ah ma

Born: September 19, 1929, West Orange, N.J.
Education: Montclair State College, B.A. 1951; Montclair State College, 1951-53; Rutgers U., 1975.
Occupation: High school government and history teacher.
Family: Husband, Richard Roukema; two children.
Religion: Protestant.
Political Career: Ridgewood Board of Education, 1970-73; Republican nominee for U.S. House, 1978.

Capitol Office: 2244 Rayburn House Office Building 20515; 225-4465.
Office Staff: Administrative Assistant, Steve Wilson; Press Secretary, Jeffrey DeKorte; Legislative Aide, Kim Parish.
Committees: Banking, Finance & Urban Affairs; Education & Labor.

New Jersey 5th — North and West — Ridgewood. The district vote for George Bush was 66% in 1988.

J. Roy Rowland (D-Ga.)
Of Dublin • Elected 1982

Born: February 3, 1926, Wrightsville, Ga.
Education: Emory at Oxford U., 1943;
South Georgia College, 1946-47; U. of
Georgia, 1947-48; Medical College of
Georgia, M.D. 1952.
Military Career: Army, 1944-46.
Occupation: Physician.
Family: Wife, Luella Price; three children.
Religion: Methodist.
Political Career: Ga. House, 1977-83.

Capitol Office: 423 Cannon House
Office Building 20515; 225-6531.
Office Staff: Administrative
Assistant/Press Assistant, Selby McCash;
Office Manager/Executive Secretary,
Barbara Schlein.
Committees: Energy & Commerce;
Veterans' Affairs.

Georgia 8th — South Central — Macon;
Waycross. The district vote for George
Bush was 54% in 1988.

CQ Voting Studies

	1989	1990
Presidential	52%	42%
Party	73%	73%
Participation	98%	96%

Interest Groups

	1988	1989
ADA	55%	30%
ACU	46%	54%
AFL-CIO	57%	42%
CCUS	69%	90%

Elections

	1988	1990
General	u/o	69%
Primary	86%	u/o

Edward R. Roybal (D-Calif.)
Of Pasadena • Elected 1962

Born: February 10, 1916, Albuquerque, N.M.
Education: U.C.L.A., 1935; Southwestern U., 1952.
Military Career: Army, 1944-45.
Occupation: Public health educator; social worker.
Family: Wife, Lucille Beserra; three children.
Religion: Roman Catholic.
Political Career: Los Angeles City Council, 1949-62; sought Democratic nomination for lieutenant governor, 1954.

Capitol Office: 2211 Rayburn House Office Building 20515; 225-6235.
Office Staff: Administrative Assistant, Jorge Lambrinos; Press Assistant, Austin Hogan; Executive Assistant/Office Manager, Christinia Mendoza.
Committees: Aging (Chairman); Appropriations.

California 25th — Central and East Los Angeles. The district vote for George Bush was 32% in 1988.

CQ Voting Studies

	1989	1990
Presidential	24%	16%
Party	90%	92%
Participation	90%	97%

Interest Groups

	1988	1989
ADA	95%	95%
ACU	0%	0%
AFL-CIO	100%	100%
CCUS	23%	33%

Elections

	1988	1990
General	85%	70%
Primary	u/o	u/o

Marty Russo (D-Ill.)
Of South Holland • Elected 1974

Born: January 23, 1944, Chicago, Ill.
Education: DePaul U., B.A. 1965; DePaul U., J.D. 1967.
Occupation: Lawyer.
Family: Wife, Karen Jorgenson; two children.
Religion: Roman Catholic.
Political Career: Assistant Cook County state's attorney, 1971-73.

Capitol Office: 2233 Rayburn House Office Building 20515; 225-5736.
Office Staff: Administrative Assistant, Rosanne Marini; Press Secretary, Mike Kelleher; Personal Assistant/Scheduler, Jennifer Alcorn.
Committees: House Administration; Ways & Means.

Illinois 3rd — Southwest Chicago and Suburbs. The district vote for George Bush was 59% in 1988.

CQ Voting Studies

	1989	1990
Presidential	27%	29%
Party	78%	82%
Participation	94%	97%

Interest Groups

	1988	1989
ADA	80%	80%
ACU	28%	11%
AFL-CIO	93%	83%
CCUS	46%	30%

Elections

	1988	1990
General	62%	71%
Primary	91%	u/o

CQ Voting Studies

	1989	1990
Presidential	30%	19%
Party	97%	95%
Participation	99%	99%

Interest Groups

	1988	1989
ADA	100%	95%
ACU	0%	0%
AFL-CIO	100%	92%
CCUS	21%	20%

Elections

	1988	1990
General	72%	73%
Primary	92%	u/o

Martin Olav Sabo (D-Minn.)
Of Minneapolis • Elected 1978

Born: February 28, 1938, Crosby, N.D.
Education: Augsburg College, B.A. 1959; U. of Minnesota, 1960.
Occupation: Public official.
Family: Wife, Sylvia Ann Lee; two children.
Religion: Lutheran.
Political Career: Minn. House, 1961-79; minority leader, 1969-73; Speaker, 1973-79.

Capitol Office: 2201 Rayburn House Office Building 20515; 225-4755.
Office Staff: Administrative Assistant, Eileen Baumgartner; Press Assistant, Colin McGinnis; Appointments Secretary, Bonnie Gottwald.
Committees: Appropriations; Budget.

Minnesota 5th — Minneapolis and Suburbs. The district vote for George Bush was 33% in 1988.

Bernard Sanders (I-Vt.)
Of Burlington • Elected 1990

Born: September 8, 1941, Brooklyn, N.Y.
Education: U. of Chicago, B.A. 1964.
Occupation: College professor; freelance writer.
Family: Wife, Jane O'Meara Driscoll; one child.
Religion: Jewish.
Political Career: Independent candidate for U.S. Senate, 1972; independent candidate for governor, 1972; independent candidate for U.S. Senate, 1974; independent candidate for governor, 1976; mayor of Burlington, 1981-89; independent candidate for governor, 1986; independent candidate for U.S. House, 1988.

Elections

	1990
General	56%

Capitol Office: 509 Cannon House Office Building 20515; 225-4115.
Office Staff: Administrative Assistant/Press Secretary, Doug Boucher; Scheduler, Ruthan Wirman.
Committees: Banking, Finance & Urban Affairs; Government Operations.
Vermont — At Large. The district vote for George Bush was 51% in 1988.

CQ Voting Studies

	1989	1990
Presidential	21%	32%
Party	86%	77%
Participation	97%	96%

Interest Groups

	1989
ADA	90%
ACU	14%
AFL-CIO	92%
CCUS	50%

Elections

	1988	1990
General	50%	59%
Primary	78%	u/o

George E. Sangmeister (D-Ill.)
Of Mokena • Elected 1988
Pronounced SANG my stir

Born: February 16, 1931, Joliet, Ill.
Education: Elmhurst College, B.A. 1957; John Marshall Law School, J.D. 1960.
Military Career: Army, 1951-53.
Occupation: Lawyer.
Family: Wife, Doris M. Hinspeter; two children.
Religion: Lutheran.
Political Career: Ill. House, 1973-76; Ill. Senate, 1976-87; sought Democratic nomination for lieutenant governor, 1986.

Capitol Office: 1032 Longworth House Office Building 20515; 225-3635.
Office Staff: Administrative Assistant, Emma Bechler; Office Manager/Personal Secretary, Mary Kay Dawson.
Committees: Judiciary; Public Works & Transportation; Veterans' Affairs.

Illinois 4th — Southern Chicago Suburbs; Joliet; Aurora. The district vote for George Bush was 56% in 1988.

Rick Santorum (R-Pa.)
Of Mount Lebanon • Elected 1990
Pronounced san TORE um

Born: May 10, 1958, Winchester, Va.
Education: Pennsylvania State U., B.A.
1980; U. of Pittsburgh, M.B.A. 1981;
Dickinson School of Law, J.D. 1986.
Occupation: Lawyer; legislative aide.
Family: Wife, Karen Garver.
Religion: Roman Catholic.
Political Career: No previous office.

Capitol Office: 1708 Longworth House
Office Building 20515; 225-2135.
Office Staff: Administrative Assistant,
Mark Rodgurs; Press Secretary, Mike
Mihalke; Executive Assistant, Mary Ellen
Obitko.
Committees: Budget; Veterans' Affairs.

Pennsylvania 18th — Pittsburgh Suburbs.
The district vote for George Bush was
53% in 1988.

Elections

	1990
General	51%
Primary	u/o

CQ Voting Studies

	1989	1990
Presidential	60%	48%
Party	60%	58%
Participation	99%	96%

Interest Groups

	1989
ADA	40%
ACU	64%
AFL-CIO	42%
CCUS	80%

Elections

	1988	1990
General	52%	56%
Primary	55%	u/o

Bill Sarpalius (D-Texas)
Of Amarillo • Elected 1988
Pronounced sar POLL us

Born: January 10, 1948, Los Angeles, Calif.
Education: Clarendon Junior College, A.S. 1970; Texas Tech U., B.A. 1972; West Texas State U., M.A. 1978.
Occupation: Agriculture consultant; public school teacher.
Family: Divorced; one child.
Religion: Methodist.
Political Career: Texas Senate, 1981-89.

Capitol Office: 126 Cannon House Office Building 20515; 225-3706.
Office Staff: Administrative Assistant, Phil Duncan; Press Secretary, Joel Brandenberger; Executive Assistant, Tricia Wilson.
Committees: Agriculture; Small Business.

Texas 13th — The Panhandle — Amarillo; Wichita Falls. The district vote for George Bush was 64% in 1988.

Gus Savage (D-Ill.)
Of Chicago • Elected 1980

Born: October 30, 1925, Detroit, Mich.
Education: Roosevelt U., B.A. 1951;
graduate work in political science, 1952;
Chicago-Kent College of Law, 1952-53.
Military Career: Army, 1943-46.
Occupation: Newspaper publisher.
Family: Widowed; two children.
Religion: Baptist.
Political Career: Sought Democratic
nomination for U.S. House, 1968; sought
Democratic nomination for U.S. House,
1970.

Capitol Office: 2419 Rayburn House
Office Building 20515; 225-0773.
Office Staff: Chief of Staff, Louanner
Peters; Press Secretary, Donnovan
Dunkley; Executive Assistant/Scheduler,
Stanley Boucree.
Committees: Public Works &
Transportation; Small Business.

Illinois 2nd — South Side Chicago;
Harvey. The district vote for George Bush
was 15% in 1988.

CQ Voting Studies

	1989	1990
Presidential	23%	19%
Party	88%	79%
Participation	91%	89%

Interest Groups

	1988	1989
ADA	100%	100%
ACU	0%	0%
AFL-CIO	100%	91%
CCUS	23%	22%

Elections

	1988	1990
General	83%	78%
Primary	52%	51%

Tom Sawyer (D-Ohio)
Of Akron • Elected 1986

Born: August 15, 1945, Akron, Ohio.
Education: U. of Akron, B.A. 1968; U. of Akron, M.A. 1970.
Occupation: Teacher.
Family: Wife, Joyce Handler; one child.
Religion: Presbyterian.
Political Career: Ohio House, 1977-84; Akron mayor, 1984-87.

Capitol Office: 1518 Longworth House Office Building 20515; 225-5231.
Office Staff: Administrative Assistant, Robert Jones; Executive Assistant, Jane Armstrong.
Committees: Education & Labor; Foreign Affairs; Post Office & Civil Service.

Ohio 14th — Northeast — Akron. The district vote for George Bush was 47% in 1988.

CQ Voting Studies

	1989	1990
Presidential	33%	21%
Party	97%	92%
Participation	99%	99%

Interest Groups

	1988	1989
ADA	95%	95%
ACU	4%	0%
AFL-CIO	93%	100%
CCUS	36%	40%

Elections

	1988	1990
General	75%	60%
Primary	u/o	73%

H. James Saxton (R-N.J.)
Of Mount Holly • Elected 1984

Born: January 22, 1943, Nicholson, Penn.
Education: East Stroudsburg (Pa.) State U.,
B.A. 1965; Temple U., 1967-68.
Occupation: Real estate broker;
elementary school teacher.
Family: Separated; two children.
Religion: Methodist.
Political Career: N.J. Assembly, 1976-82;
N.J. Senate, 1982-84.

Capitol Office: 324 Cannon House
Office Building 20515; 225-4765.
Office Staff: Administrative Assistant,
Ralph Shrom; Press Secretary, Ralph
Morano; Office Manager/Appointments
Secretary, Susan Dotteweich.
Committees: Armed Services; Merchant
Marine & Fisheries.

New Jersey 13th — South and Central.
The district vote for George Bush was
61% in 1988.

CQ Voting Studies

	1989	1990
Presidential	65%	57%
Party	50%	68%
Participation	98%	98%

Interest Groups

	1988	1989
ADA	30%	20%
ACU	72%	64%
AFL-CIO	50%	42%
CCUS	79%	100%

Elections

	1988	1990
General	69%	58%
Primary	u/o	93%

Dan Schaefer (R-Colo.)
Of Lakewood • Elected 1983

Born: January 25, 1936, Guttenberg, Iowa.
Education: Niagara U., B.A. 1961; Potsdam State U. (N.Y.), 1961-64.
Military Career: Marine Corps, 1955-57.
Occupation: Public relations consultant.
Family: Wife, Mary Lenney; four children.
Religion: Roman Catholic.
Political Career: Colo. House, 1977-79; Colo. Senate, 1979-83; president pro tempore, 1981-83.

Capitol Office: 1007 Longworth House Office Building 20515; 225-7882.
Office Staff: Administrative Assistant/Press Secretary, Holly Propst; Appointments Secretary, Helen Morrell.
Committees: Energy & Commerce.

Colorado 6th — Denver Suburbs — Aurora; Lakewood. The district vote for George Bush was 56% in 1988.

CQ Voting Studies

	1989	1990
Presidential	69%	64%
Party	84%	88%
Participation	96%	98%

Interest Groups

	1988	1989
ADA	15%	5%
ACU	83%	89%
AFL-CIO	50%	25%
CCUS	71%	90%

Elections

	1988	1990
General	63%	65%
Primary	u/o	u/o

James H. Scheuer (D-N.Y.)
Of Queens • Elected 1964
Pronounced SHOY yur

Born: February 6, 1920, New York, N.Y.
Education: Swarthmore College, A.B.
1942; Harvard U., M.A. 1943; Columbia
U., LL.B. 1948.
Military Career: Army, 1943-45.
Occupation: Lawyer.
Family: Wife, Emily Malino; four
children.
Religion: Jewish.
Political Career: Sought Democratic
nomination for mayor of N.Y. City, 1969;
defeated for renomination for U.S.
House, 1972; reelected, 1974.

Capitol Office: 2221 Rayburn House
Office Building 20515; 225-5471.
Office Staff: Administrative Assistant,
Karen Johnson; Press Secretary, John St.
Croix; Executive Assistant, Marilyn Storm.
Committees: Energy & Commerce;
Science, Space & Technology.

New York 8th — Northern Queens;
Eastern Bronx; Western Nassau County.
The district vote for George Bush was
41% in 1988.

CQ Voting Studies

	1989	1990
Presidential	30%	16%
Party	89%	93%
Participation	93%	96%

Interest Groups

	1988	1989
ADA	85%	85%
ACU	5%	0%
AFL-CIO	86%	100%
CCUS	46%	44%

Elections

	1988	1990
General	u/o	72%
Primary	u/o	u/o

CQ Voting Studies

	1989	1990
Presidential	69%	55%
Party	63%	56%
Participation	99%	98%

Interest Groups

	1989
ADA	15%
ACU	86%
AFL-CIO	25%
CCUS	90%

Elections

	1988	1990
General	51%	70%
Primary	41%	u/o

Steven H. Schiff (R-N.M.)
Of Albuquerque • Elected 1988

Born: March 18, 1947, Chicago, Ill.
Education: U. of Illinois, Chicago Circle, B.A. 1968; U. of New Mexico, J.D. 1972.
Military Career: N.M. Air National Guard, 1969-present.
Occupation: Lawyer.
Family: Wife, Marcia Lewis; two children.
Religion: Jewish.
Political Career: Assistant district attorney, 1972-77; candidate for district judge, 1978; assistant Albuquerque city attorney, 1979-81; Bernalillo County district attorney, 1981-89.

Capitol Office: 1427 Longworth House Office Building 20515; 225-6316.
Office Staff: Administrative Assistant, Judy Butler; Communications Director, Mike Cook; Scheduler, Ken Scott.
Committees: Government Operations; Judiciary; Science, Space & Technology.

New Mexico 1st — Central — Albuquerque. The district vote for George Bush was 54% in 1988.

Patricia Schroeder (D-Colo.)
Of Denver • Elected 1972
Pronounced SHRO dur

Born: July 30, 1940, Portland, Ore.
Education: U. of Minnesota, B.A. 1961;
Harvard U., J.D. 1964.
Occupation: Lawyer; Law instructor.
Family: Husband, James Schroeder; two
children.
Religion: United Church of Christ.
Political Career: No previous office.

Capitol Office: 2208 Rayburn House
Office Building 20515; 225-4431.
Office Staff: Administrative Assistant,
Dan Buck; Press Secretary, Andrea Camp;
Appointments Secretary, B. M. Ramlow.
Committees: Armed Services; Judiciary;
Post Office & Civil Service.

Colorado 1st — Denver. The district vote
for George Bush was 36% in 1988.

CQ Voting Studies

	1989	1990
Presidential	19%	18%
Party	67%	72%
Participation	97%	98%

Interest Groups

	1988	1989
ADA	95%	100%
ACU	0%	11%
AFL-CIO	100%	92%
CCUS	31%	40%

Elections

	1988	1990
General	70%	64%
Primary	u/o	u/o

Dick Schulze (R-Pa.)
Of Berwyn • Elected 1974
Pronounced SHOOLS

Born: August 7, 1929, Philadelphia, Penn.
Education: U. of Houston, 1949-50;
Villanova U., 1952; Temple U., 1968.
Military Career: Army, 1951-53.
Occupation: Household appliance
dealer.
Family: Widowed; four children.
Religion: Presbyterian.
Political Career: Tredyffrin Township
Republican Committee, 1960-67; Chester
County Registrar of Wills and Clerk of
Orphans Court, 1967-69; Pa. House,
1969-75.

Capitol Office: 2369 Rayburn House
Office Building 20515; 225-5761.
Office Staff: Administrative
Assistant/Press Secretary, Robert V. L.
Hartwell; Office Manager/Scheduler,
Camille Conway.
Committees: Interior & Insular Affairs;
Ways & Means.

Pennsylvania 5th — Western Philadelphia
Suburbs — Chester. The district vote for
George Bush was 65% in 1988.

CQ Voting Studies

	1989	1990
Presidential	69%	61%
Party	64%	67%
Participation	96%	90%

Interest Groups

	1988	1989
ADA	30%	20%
ACU	76%	71%
AFL-CIO	46%	25%
CCUS	92%	90%

Elections

	1988	1990
General	78%	57%
Primary	u/o	u/o

Charles E. Schumer (D-N.Y.)
Of Brooklyn • Elected 1980

Born: November 23, 1950, Brooklyn, N.Y.
Education: Harvard U., B.A. 1971; Harvard U., J.D. 1974.
Occupation: Lawyer.
Family: Wife, Iris Weinshall; two children.
Religion: Jewish.
Political Career: N.Y. Assembly, 1975-81.

Capitol Office: 2412 Rayburn House Office Building 20515; 225-6616.
Office Staff: Chief of Staff, Carol Kellerman; Press Secretary, Eric Hauser; Office Manager, Sarah Callahan.
Committees: Banking, Finance & Urban Affairs; Interior & Insular Affairs; Judiciary.

New York 10th — Central and Southern Brooklyn — Flatbush. The district vote for George Bush was 42% in 1988.

CQ Voting Studies

	1989	1990
Presidential	26%	19%
Party	91%	89%
Participation	93%	96%

Interest Groups

	1988	1989
ADA	100%	95%
ACU	4%	0%
AFL-CIO	86%	100%
CCUS	36%	30%

Elections

	1988	1990
General	78%	80%
Primary	u/o	u/o

F. James Sensenbrenner, Jr.
(R-Wis.)
Of Menomonee Falls • Elected 1978

Born: June 14, 1943, Chicago, Ill.
Education: Stanford U., A.B. 1965; U. of Wisconsin, J.D. 1968.
Occupation: Lawyer.
Family: Wife, Cheryl Warren; two children.
Religion: Episcopalian.
Political Career: Wis. Assembly, 1969-75; Wis. Senate, 1975-79.

Capitol Office: 2444 Rayburn House Office Building 20515; 225-5105.
Office Staff: Administrative Assistant, Todd Schultz; Office Manager, Arlene Davis.
Committees: Judiciary; Science, Space & Technology.

Wisconsin 9th — Milwaukee Suburbs; Sheboygan. The district vote for George Bush was 60% in 1988.

CQ Voting Studies

	1989	1990
Presidential	66%	75%
Party	88%	93%
Participation	98%	99%

Interest Groups

	1988	1989
ADA	15%	20%
ACU	88%	71%
AFL-CIO	21%	0%
CCUS	100%	89%

Elections

	1988	1990
General	75%	u/o
Primary	u/o	u/o

Jose E. Serrano (D-N.Y.)
Of The Bronx • Elected 1990
Pronounced ho ZAY sa RAH no

Born: October 24, 1943, Mayaguez, Puerto Rico.
Education: Dodge Vocational High School, graduated 1961.
Military Career: Army, 1964-66.
Occupation: Public official.
Family: Wife, Mary Staucet; three children, two stepchildren.
Religion: Roman Catholic.
Political Career: N.Y. Assembly, 1975-90; sought Democratic nomination for Bronx borough president, 1985.

Capitol Office: 1107 Longworth House Office Building 20515; 225-4361.
Office Staff: Administrative Assistant, Roger Strickland; Press Secretary, Bill Alexander; Scheduler/Executive Secretary, Jenifer Martin.
Committees: Education & Labor; Small Business.

New York 18th — South Bronx. The district vote for George Bush was 12% in 1988.

CQ Voting Studies

	1990
Presidential	17%
Party	93%
Participation	94%

Elections

	1990*	1990
General	93%	93%
Primary		89%

*Special election.

Philip R. Sharp (D-Ind.)
Of Muncie • Elected 1974

Born: July 15, 1942, Baltimore, Md.
Education: Georgetown U., B.S. 1964;
Oxford U., 1966; Georgetown U., Ph.D.
1974.
Occupation: Professor of political
science.
Family: Wife, Marilyn Augburn; two
children.
Religion: Methodist.
Political Career: Democratic nominee
for U.S. House, 1970; Democratic
nominee for U.S. House, 1972.

Capitol Office: 2217 Rayburn House
Office Building 20515; 225-3021.
Office Staff: Administrative Assistant,
Ron Gyure; Press Secretary, Robert
McCarson; Executive Assistant, Jackie
Paullin.
Committees: Energy & Commerce;
Interior & Insular Affairs.

Indiana 2nd — East Central — Muncie;
Richmond. The district vote for George
Bush was 62% in 1988.

CQ Voting Studies

	1989	1990
Presidential	28%	20%
Party	76%	79%
Participation	94%	95%

Interest Groups

	1988	1989
ADA	75%	80%
ACU	20%	20%
AFL-CIO	100%	83%
CCUS	50%	33%

Elections

	1988	1990
General	53%	59%
Primary	u/o	u/o

E. Clay Shaw, Jr. (R-Fla.)
Of Fort Lauderdale • Elected 1980

Born: April 19, 1939, Miami, Fla.
Education: Stetson U., B.A. 1961; U. of
Alabama, M.B.A. 1963; Stetson U., J.D.
1966.
Occupation: Nurseryman; lawyer.
Family: Wife, Emilie Costar; four
children.
Religion: Roman Catholic.
Political Career: Fort Lauderdale assistant
city attorney, 1968; chief city prosecutor,
1968-69; associate municipal judge, 1969-
71; city commissioner, 1971-73; vice
mayor, 1973-75; mayor of Fort
Lauderdale, 1975-81.

Capitol Office: 2338 Rayburn House
Office Building 20515; 225-3026.
Office Staff: Administrative Assistant, Lee
Johnson; Press Secretary, Nancy Roman;
Office Manager/Personal Secretary,
Mary Kay McClure.
Committees: Ways & Means.

Florida 15th — Southeast — Fort
Lauderdale. The district vote for George
Bush was 53% in 1988.

CQ Voting Studies

	1989	1990
Presidential	77%	75%
Party	65%	75%
Participation	97%	96%

Interest Groups

	1988	1989
ADA	5%	5%
ACU	96%	89%
AFL-CIO	21%	17%
CCUS	92%	90%

Elections

	1988	1990
General	66%	98%
Primary	u/o	u/o

Christopher Shays (R-Conn.)
Of Stamford • Elected 1987

Born: October 18, 1945, Stamford, Conn.
Education: Principia College, B.A. 1968;
New York U., M.B.A. 1974; New York U.,
M.P.A. 1978.
Occupation: Real estate broker.
Family: Wife, Betsi de Raismes; one child.
Religion: Christian Scientist.
Political Career: Conn. House, 1975-87;
Republican candidate for mayor of
Stamford, 1983.

Capitol Office: 1531 Longworth House
Office Building 20515; 225-5541.
Office Staff: Administrative Assistant,
Paul Audley; Press Secretary, Mary Darby;
Executive Assistant, Teryn Weintz.
Committees: Budget; Government
Operations.

Connecticut 4th — Southwest —
Stamford; Bridgeport. The district vote
for George Bush was 57% in 1988.

CQ Voting Studies

	1989	1990
Presidential	36%	34%
Party	54%	60%
Participation	100%	100%

Interest Groups

	1988	1989
ADA	90%	85%
ACU	24%	29%
AFL-CIO	64%	67%
CCUS	57%	70%

Elections

	1988	1990
General	72%	77%
Primary	u/o	u/o

Bud Shuster (R-Pa.)

Of Everett • Elected 1972

Born: January 23, 1932, Glassport, Penn.
Education: U. of Pittsburgh, B.S. 1954;
Duquesne U., M.B.A. 1960; American U.,
Ph.D. 1967.
Military Career: Army, 1954-56.
Occupation: Computer industry
executive.
Family: Wife, Patricia Rommel; five
children.
Religion: United Church of Christ.
Political Career: No previous office.

Capitol Office: 2268 Rayburn House
Office Building 20515; 225-2431.
Office Staff: Chief of Staff, Ann Eppard;
Press Assistant, Karen Schecter;
Appointments Secretary, Sheri Monier.
Committees: Public Works &
Transportation; Select Intelligence.

Pennsylvania 9th — South Central —
Altoona. The district vote for George
Bush was 61% in 1988.

CQ Voting Studies

	1989	1990
Presidential	76%	63%
Party	74%	78%
Participation	99%	96%

Interest Groups

	1988	1989
ADA	5%	10%
ACU	100%	89%
AFL-CIO	14%	17%
CCUS	100%	100%

Elections

	1988	1990
General	u/o	u/o
Primary	u/o	u/o

CQ Voting Studies

	1989	1990
Presidential	30%	15%
Party	72%	79%
Participation	99%	97%

Interest Groups

	1988	1989
ADA	90%	100%
ACU	12%	4%
AFL-CIO	100%	92%
CCUS	36%	40%

Elections

	1988	1990
General	65%	64%
Primary	u/o	u/o

Gerry Sikorski (D-Minn.)
Of Stillwater • Elected 1982

Born: April 26, 1948, Breckenridge, Minn.
Education: U. of Minnesota, B.A. 1970; U. of Minnesota, J.D. 1973.
Military Career: Naval Reserve, 1984-present.
Occupation: Lawyer.
Family: Wife, Susan Erkel; one child.
Religion: Roman Catholic.
Political Career: Minn. Senate, 1977-83; Democratic nominee for U.S. House, 1978.

Capitol Office: 403 Cannon House Office Building 20515; 225-2271.
Office Staff: Special Assistant, Dennis McGrann; Press Secretary, Laurie de Freese; Office Manager/Executive Assistant, Carin Moran Otero.
Committees: Energy & Commerce; Post Office & Civil Service.

Minnesota 6th — Northern and Eastern Twin Cities Suburbs. The district vote for George Bush was 48% in 1988.

Norman Sisisky (D-Va.)

Of Petersburg • Elected 1982

Born: June 9, 1927, Baltimore, Md.
Education: Virginia Commonwealth U., B.S. 1949.
Military Career: Navy, 1945-46.
Occupation: Beer and soft drink distributor.
Family: Wife, Rhoda Brown; four children.
Religion: Jewish.
Political Career: Va. House, 1974-82.

Capitol Office: 426 Cannon House Office Building 20515; 225-6365.
Office Staff: Administrative Assistant, Jan Faircloth; Communications Director, Greg Gibbs; Office Manager/Personal Secretary, Tiffanee Johnson.
Committees: Armed Services; Small Business.

Virginia 4th — Southeast — Chesapeake; Portsmouth. The district vote for George Bush was 55% in 1988.

CQ Voting Studies

	1989	1990
Presidential	51%	43%
Party	73%	77%
Participation	98%	99%

Interest Groups

	1988	1989
ADA	55%	55%
ACU	40%	21%
AFL-CIO	86%	67%
CCUS	50%	60%

Elections

	1988	1990
General	u/o	78%
Primary	u/o	u/o

CQ Voting Studies

	1989	1990
Presidential	35%	21%
Party	94%	93%
Participation	99%	99%

Interest Groups

	1988	1989
ADA	95%	85%
ACU	16%	7%
AFL-CIO	86%	83%
CCUS	57%	30%

Elections

	1988	1990
General	63%	61%
Primary	u/o	u/o

David E. Skaggs (D-Colo.)
Of Boulder • Elected 1986

Born: February 22, 1943, Cincinnati, Ohio.
Education: Wesleyan U., B.A. 1964; Yale U., LL.B. 1967.
Military Career: Marine Corps, 1968-71; Marine Corps Reserve, 1971-77.
Occupation: Lawyer; congressional aide.
Family: Wife, Laura Locher; one child, two stepchildren.
Religion: Congregationalist.
Political Career: Colo. House, 1981-87; minority leader, 1983-85.

Capitol Office: 1507 Longworth House Office Building 20515; 225-2161.
Office Staff: Chief of Staff, Stephen Saunders; Press Secretary, Nancy Hughes; Executive Assistant/Scheduler, Joyce Edelson.
Committees: Appropriations.

Colorado 2nd — Northern Denver Suburbs; Boulder. The district vote for George Bush was 48% in 1988.

Joe Skeen (R-N.M.)
Of Picacho • Elected 1980

Born: June 30, 1927, Roswell, N.M.
Education: Texas A&M U., B.S. 1950.
Military Career: Navy, 1945-46; Air Force Reserve, 1949-52.
Occupation: Sheep rancher; soil and water engineer; flying service operator.
Family: Wife, Mary Jones; two children.
Religion: Roman Catholic.
Political Career: N.M. Senate, 1961-71; minority leader, 1965-71; N.M. Republican Party chairman, 1962-65; Republican nominee for lieutenant governor, 1970; Republican nominee for governor, 1974 and 1978.

Capitol Office: 2447 Rayburn House Office Building 20515; 225-2365.
Office Staff: Chief of Staff, Suzanne Eisold; Press Secretary, Sherry Kiesling; Office Manager/Executive Assistant, Lin Rhode.
Committees: Appropriations.

New Mexico 2nd — South and East — Las Cruces; Roswell. The district vote for George Bush was 58% in 1988.

CQ Voting Studies

	1989	1990
Presidential	86%	68%
Party	70%	63%
Participation	99%	99%

Interest Groups

	1988	1989
ADA	5%	0%
ACU	100%	96%
AFL-CIO	29%	0%
CCUS	93%	90%

Elections

	1988	1990
General	u/o	u/o
Primary	u/o	u/o

CQ Voting Studies

	1989	1990
Presidential	59%	50%
Party	62%	68%
Participation	95%	96%

Interest Groups

	1988	1989
ADA	40%	35%
ACU	58%	56%
AFL-CIO	83%	58%
CCUS	62%	70%

Elections

	1988	1990
General	72%	62%
Primary	u/o	u/o

Ike Skelton (D-Mo.)
Of Lexington • Elected 1976

Born: December 20, 1931, Lexington, Mo.
Education: Wentworth Military Academy, 1949-51; U. of Edinburgh, Scotland, 1953; U. of Missouri, B.A. 1953; U. of Missouri, LL.B. 1956.
Occupation: Lawyer.
Family: Wife, Susan Anding; three children.
Religion: Christian Church.
Political Career: Lafayette County Democratic Committee chairman, 1962-66; Mo. Senate, 1971-77.

Capitol Office: 2134 Rayburn House Office Building 20515; 225-2876.
Office Staff: Administrative Assistant, Jack Pollard; Press Secretary, Anne Raugh; Office Manager/Appointments Secretary, Catharine Miller.
Committees: Armed Services; Small Business.

Missouri 4th — West — Kansas City Suburbs; Jefferson City. The district vote for George Bush was 59% in 1988.

Jim Slattery (D-Kan.)
Of Topeka • Elected 1982

Born: August 4, 1948, Good Intent, Kan.
Education: Netherlands School of International Economics and Business, 1969-70; Washburn U., B.S. 1970; Washburn U., J.D. 1974.
Military Career: Army National Guard, 1970-75.
Occupation: Realtor.
Family: Wife, Linda Smith; two children.
Religion: Roman Catholic.
Political Career: Kan. House, 1973-79.

Capitol Office: 1512 Longworth House Office Building 20515; 225-6601.
Office Staff: Press Secretary, Ken Rivlin; Executive Assistant, Rebecca S. Banta-Kuhn.
Committees: Banking, Finance & Urban Affairs; Energy & Commerce; Veterans' Affairs.

Kansas 2nd — Topeka; Lawrence. The district vote for George Bush was 53% in 1988.

CQ Voting Studies

	1989	1990
Presidential	45%	32%
Party	74%	73%
Participation	98%	96%

Interest Groups

	1988	1989
ADA	55%	55%
ACU	33%	21%
AFL-CIO	85%	75%
CCUS	38%	60%

Elections

	1988	1990
General	73%	63%
Primary	u/o	86%

D. French Slaughter, Jr.

(R-Va.)
Of Culpeper • Elected 1984

Born: May 20, 1925, Culpeper, Va.
Education: Virginia Military Institute, 1942-43; U. of Virginia, B.A. 1949; U. of Virginia, LL.B. 1953.
Military Career: U.S. Army, 1943-47.
Occupation: Lawyer.
Family: Widowed; two children.
Religion: Episcopalian.
Political Career: Va. House, 1958-78; Democratic nominee for lieutenant governor, 1972.

Capitol Office: 1404 Longworth House Office Building 20515; 225-6561.
Office Staff: Chief of Staff, Richard D. Holcomb; Press Secretary, L. Carter Cornick; Staff Assistant/Scheduler, Jennifer Harned.
Committees: Judiciary; Science, Space & Technology; Small Business.

Virginia 7th — North — Charlottesville; Winchester. The district vote for George Bush was 66% in 1988.

CQ Voting Studies

	1989	1990
Presidential	77%	68%
Party	93%	87%
Participation	99%	99%

Interest Groups

	1988	1989
ADA	10%	0%
ACU	92%	96%
AFL-CIO	14%	0%
CCUS	93%	100%

Elections

	1988	1990
General	u/o	58%
Primary	u/o	u/o

Louise M. Slaughter (D-N.Y.)
Of Fairport • Elected 1986

Born: August 14, 1929, Harlan County, Ky.

Education: U. of Kentucky, B.S. 1951; U. of Kentucky, M.S. 1953.

Occupation: Market researcher.

Family: Husband, Robert Slaughter; three children.

Religion: Episcopalian.

Political Career: Monroe County legislator, 1975-79; N.Y. Assembly, 1983-87.

Capitol Office: 1424 Longworth House Office Building 20515; 225-3615.

Office Staff: Administrative Assistant, Elaine Ryan; Press Secretary, Michael Kiernan; Executive Assistant, Elizabeth Ripton.

Committees: Budget; Rules.

New York 30th — West — Part of Rochester; Batavia. The district vote for George Bush was 54% in 1988.

CQ Voting Studies

	1989	1990
Presidential	27%	16%
Party	93%	94%
Participation	97%	99%

Interest Groups

	1988	1989
ADA	85%	95%
ACU	8%	4%
AFL-CIO	100%	100%
CCUS	43%	40%

Elections

	1988	1990
General	57%	59%
Primary	u/o	u/o

Bob Smith (R-Ore.)
Of Burns • Elected 1982

Born: June 16, 1931, Portland, Ore.
Education: Willamette U., B.A. 1953.
Occupation: Cattle rancher.
Family: Wife, Kaye Tomlinson; three children.
Religion: Presbyterian.
Political Career: Ore. House, 1961-73; Speaker, 1969-73; Ore. Senate, 1973-82; minority leader, 1977-82.

Capitol Office: 118 Cannon House Office Building 20515; 225-6730.
Office Staff: Chief of Staff, Paul Unger; Press Secretary, David Redmond; Office Manager/Personal Secretary, Roberta J. Clark.
Committees: Agriculture; Interior & Insular Affairs.

Oregon 2nd — East and Southwest — Bend; Medford. The district vote for George Bush was 54% in 1988.

CQ Voting Studies

	1989	1990
Presidential	79%	66%
Party	89%	91%
Participation	98%	99%

Interest Groups

	1988	1989
ADA	5%	10%
ACU	92%	79%
AFL-CIO	21%	17%
CCUS	86%	100%

Elections

	1988	1990
General	63%	68%
Primary	u/o	88%

Christopher H. Smith (R-N.J.)
Of Hamilton Square • Elected 1980

Born: March 4, 1953, Rahway, N.J.
Education: Trenton State College, B.A. 1975.
Occupation: Sporting goods wholesaler.
Family: Wife, Marie Hahn; four children.
Religion: Roman Catholic.
Political Career: Republican nominee for U.S. House, 1978.

Capitol Office: 2440 Rayburn House Office Building 20515; 225-3765.
Office Staff: Administrative Assistant, Martin Dannenfelser; Press Secretary, Mary McDermott; Office Manager, Martha Wlajnitz.
Committees: Foreign Affairs; Veterans' Affairs.

New Jersey 4th — Central — Trenton. The district vote for George Bush was 56% in 1988.

CQ Voting Studies

	1989	1990
Presidential	55%	43%
Party	36%	44%
Participation	98%	98%

Interest Groups

	1988	1989
ADA	60%	45%
ACU	48%	43%
AFL-CIO	100%	75%
CCUS	43%	70%

Elections

	1988	1990
General	66%	63%
Primary	u/o	u/o

Lamar Smith (R-Texas)
Of San Antonio • Elected 1986

Born: November 19, 1947, San Antonio, Texas.
Education: Yale U., B.A. 1969; Southern Methodist U., J.D. 1975.
Occupation: Lawyer; rancher.
Family: Widowed; two children.
Religion: Christian Scientist.
Political Career: Bexar County Republican Party chairman, 1978-81; Texas House, 1981-82; Bexar County commissioner, 1983-85.

Capitol Office: 422 Cannon House Office Building 20515; 225-4236.
Office Staff: Administrative Assistant, John Lampmann; Press Secretary, Juli Branson; Office Manager/Appointments Secretary, Lucy Harwood Weber.
Committees: Judiciary; Science, Space & Technology.

Texas 21st — San Antonio Suburbs; San Angelo; Midland. The district vote for George Bush was 71% in 1988.

CQ Voting Studies

	1989	1990
Presidential	80%	68%
Party	85%	82%
Participation	94%	95%

Interest Groups

	1988	1989
ADA	5%	0%
ACU	100%	93%
AFL-CIO	23%	0%
CCUS	92%	100%

Elections

	1988	1990
General	93%	75%
Primary	u/o	u/o

Lawrence J. Smith (D-Fla.)
Of Hollywood • Elected 1982

Born: April 25, 1941, Brooklyn, N.Y.
Education: New York U., 1958-61;
Brooklyn Law School, LL.B. 1964;
Brooklyn Law School, J.D. 1967.
Occupation: Lawyer.
Family: Wife, Sheila Cohen; two children.
Religion: Jewish.
Political Career: Fla. House, 1979-83.

Capitol Office: 113 Cannon House
Office Building 20515; 225-7931.
Office Staff: Administrative Assistant,
Marc Pearl; Press Secretary, Paul Bledsoe;
Office Manager/Scheduler, Miamah
Braddox.
Committees: Appropriations.

Florida 16th — Southeast — Hollywood;
Part of Dade County. The district vote for
George Bush was 55% in 1988.

CQ Voting Studies

	1989	1990
Presidential	34%	18%
Party	89%	87%
Participation	93%	90%

Interest Groups

	1988	1989
ADA	85%	90%
ACU	17%	0%
AFL-CIO	100%	100%
CCUS	23%	20%

Elections

	1988	1990
General	69%	u/o
Primary	u/o	u/o

CQ Voting Studies

	1989	1990
Presidential	31%	27%
Party	82%	88%
Participation	90%	98%

Interest Groups

	1988	1989
ADA	80%	70%
ACU	16%	11%
AFL-CIO	86%	75%
CCUS	46%	40%

Elections

	1988	1990
General	72%	u/o
Primary	90%	u/o

Neal Smith (D-Iowa)
Of Altoona • Elected 1958

Born: March 23, 1920, Hedrick, Iowa.
Education: U. of Missouri, 1945-46;
Syracuse U., 1946-47; Drake U., LL.B.
1950.
Military Career: Army Air Corps, 1942-45.
Occupation: Lawyer; farmer.
Family: Wife, Beatrix Havens; two
children.
Religion: Methodist.
Political Career: Sought Democratic
nomination for U.S. House, 1956.

Capitol Office: 2373 Rayburn House
Office Building 20515; 225-4426.
Office Staff: Administrative Assistant,
Tom Dawson; Press Secretary, Park
Rinard; Office Manager, Nancy Simplicio.
Committees: Appropriations; Small
Business.

Iowa 4th — Central — Des Moines;
Ames. The district vote for George Bush
was 41% in 1988.

Olympia J. Snowe (R-Maine)
Of Auburn • Elected 1978

Born: February 21, 1947, Augusta, Maine.
Education: U. of Maine, B.A. 1969.
Occupation: Concrete company executive; public official.
Family: Husband, John R. McKernan Jr..
Religion: Greek Orthodox.
Political Career: Maine House, 1973-77; Maine Senate, 1977-79.

Capitol Office: 2464 Rayburn House Office Building 20515; 225-6306.
Office Staff: Administrative Assistant, Kirk Walder; Press Secretary, Don Nathan; Executive Assistant, Carol Gardner.
Committees: Foreign Affairs.

Maine 2nd — North — Lewiston; Auburn; Bangor. The district vote for George Bush was 55% in 1988.

CQ Voting Studies

	1989	1990
Presidential	51%	48%
Party	47%	57%
Participation	99%	99%

Interest Groups

	1988	1989
ADA	60%	35%
ACU	40%	54%
AFL-CIO	86%	25%
CCUS	50%	90%

Elections

	1988	1990
General	66%	51%
Primary	u/o	u/o

Stephen J. Solarz (D-N.Y.)
Of Brooklyn • Elected 1974

Born: September 12, 1940, New York, N.Y.
Education: Brandeis U., A.B. 1962; Columbia U., M.A. 1967.
Occupation: Public official.
Family: Wife, Nina Koldin; two children.
Religion: Jewish.
Political Career: N.Y. Assembly, 1969-75; sought Democratic nomination for Brooklyn borough president, 1973.

Capitol Office: 1536 Longworth House Office Building 20515; 225-2361.
Office Staff: Administrative Assistant, Jeremy Rabinovitz; Press Secretary, Robert Hathaway; Personal Secretary, Carol Ditta.
Committees: Foreign Affairs; Merchant Marine & Fisheries; Select Intelligence.

New York 13th — Western and Southern Brooklyn — Bensonhurst; Brooklyn Heights. The district vote for George Bush was 45% in 1988.

CQ Voting Studies

	1989	1990
Presidential	37%	22%
Party	92%	89%
Participation	97%	95%

Interest Groups

	1988	1989
ADA	95%	85%
ACU	4%	0%
AFL-CIO	93%	92%
CCUS	33%	40%

Elections

	1988	1990
General	75%	80%
Primary	u/o	u/o

Gerald B.H. Solomon (R-N.Y.)
Of Glens Falls • Elected 1978

Born: August 14, 1930, Okeechobee, Fla.
Education: Siena College, 1949-50; St. Lawrence U., 1952-53.
Military Career: Marine Corps, 1951-52.
Occupation: Insurance salesman.
Family: Wife, Freda Parker; five children.
Religion: Presbyterian.
Political Career: Warren County Legislature, 1968-72; N.Y. Assembly, 1973-79.

Capitol Office: 2265 Rayburn House Office Building 20515; 225-5614.
Office Staff: Administrative Assistant, Geoffrey Gleason; Press Secretary/Executive Assistant, Dan Amon; Personal Secretary, Dorothy Cook.
Committees: Rules (Ranking).

New York 24th — Upper Hudson Valley — Sarasota Springs. The district vote for George Bush was 59% in 1988.

CQ Voting Studies

	1989	1990
Presidential	67%	67%
Party	86%	84%
Participation	99%	97%

Interest Groups

	1988	1989
ADA	15%	15%
ACU	88%	79%
AFL-CIO	57%	33%
CCUS	86%	80%

Elections

	1988	1990
General	72%	68%
Primary	u/o	u/o

Floyd D. Spence (R-S.C.)
Of Lexington • Elected 1970

Born: April 9, 1928, Columbia, S.C.
Education: U. of South Carolina, A.B. 1952; U. of South Carolina, J.D. 1956.
Military Career: Navy, 1952-54.
Occupation: Lawyer.
Family: Wife, Deborah Williams; four children.
Religion: Lutheran.
Political Career: S.C. House, 1957-63; Republican nominee for U.S. House, 1962; S.C. Senate, 1967-71; minority leader, 1967-71.

Capitol Office: 2405 Rayburn House Office Building 20515; 225-2452.
Office Staff: Administrative Assistant/Press Secretary, Ken Black; Executive Assistant, Caroline Bryson.
Committees: Armed Services; Veterans' Affairs.

South Carolina 2nd — Central — Columbia. The district vote for George Bush was 59% in 1988.

CQ Voting Studies

	1989	1990
Presidential	72%	62%
Party	69%	75%
Participation	98%	98%

Interest Groups

	1988	1989
ADA	10%	10%
ACU	85%	93%
AFL-CIO	50%	25%
CCUS	71%	100%

Elections

	1988	1990
General	53%	89%
Primary	u/o	u/o

John M. Spratt, Jr. (D-S.C.)
Of York • Elected 1982

Born: November 1, 1942, Charlotte, N.C.
Education: Davidson College, A.B. 1964;
Oxford U., M.A. 1966; Yale U., LL.B. 1969.
Military Career: Army, 1969-71.
Occupation: Lawyer; insurance agency
owner.
Family: Wife, Jane Stacy; three children.
Religion: Presbyterian.
Political Career: No previous office.

Capitol Office: 1533 Longworth House
Office Building 20515; 225-5501.
Office Staff: Administrative Assistant,
Ellen Buchanan; Press Secretary, Charles
H. Fant; Executive Assistant, Marilee
Sanders.
Committees: Armed Services; Budget.

South Carolina 5th — North Central —
Rock Hill. The district vote for George
Bush was 60% in 1988.

CQ Voting Studies

	1989	1990
Presidential	49%	29%
Party	83%	86%
Participation	98%	98%

Interest Groups

	1988	1989
ADA	55%	65%
ACU	29%	29%
AFL-CIO	79%	67%
CCUS	57%	80%

Elections

	1988	1990
General	70%	u/o
Primary	u/o	u/o

Harley O. Staggers, Jr.
(D-W.Va.)
Of Keyser • Elected 1982

Born: February 22, 1951, Washington, D.C.
Education: Harvard U., B.A. 1974; West Virginia U., J.D. 1977.
Occupation: Lawyer.
Family: Wife, Leslie Sergy
Religion: Roman Catholic.
Political Career: Sought Democratic nomination for U.S. House, 1980; W.Va. Senate, 1981-83.

Capitol Office: 1323 Longworth House Office Building 20515; 225-4331.
Office Staff: Administrative Assistant, James R. Rhodes; Press Secretary, James L. Watkins; Staff Assistant, Karl Britton.
Committees: Agriculture; Judiciary; Veterans' Affairs.

West Virginia 2nd — East — Morgantown; Eastern Panhandle. The district vote for George Bush was 52% in 1988.

CQ Voting Studies

	1989	1990
Presidential	40%	17%
Party	84%	88%
Participation	97%	98%

Interest Groups

	1988	1989
ADA	80%	80%
ACU	12%	18%
AFL-CIO	100%	83%
CCUS	21%	40%

Elections

	1988	1990
General	u/o	55%
Primary	u/o	u/o

Richard Stallings (D-Idaho)
Of Rexburg • Elected 1984

Born: October 7, 1940, Ogden, Utah.
Education: Weber State College, B.S.
1965; Utah State U., M.A. 1968.
Occupation: Professor of history.
Family: Wife, Ranae Garner; three
children.
Religion: Mormon.
Political Career: Democratic nominee
for Idaho House, 1974; Democratic
nominee for Idaho House, 1978;
Democratic nominee for U.S House,
1982.

Capitol Office: 1122 Longworth House
Office Building 20515; 225-5531.
Committees: Agriculture; Science, Space
& Technology.

Idaho 2nd — East — Pocatello; Idaho
Falls. The district vote for George Bush
was 65% in 1988.

CQ Voting Studies

	1989	1990
Presidential	45%	42%
Party	69%	67%
Participation	97%	97%

Interest Groups

	1988	1989
ADA	55%	45%
ACU	48%	41%
AFL-CIO	71%	45%
CCUS	71%	70%

Elections

	1988	1990
General	63%	64%
Primary	u/o	u/o

CQ Voting Studies

	1989	1990
Presidential	24%	16%
Party	90%	88%
Participation	93%	94%

Interest Groups

	1988	1989
ADA	90%	95%
ACU	0%	0%
AFL-CIO	85%	100%
CCUS	42%	20%

Elections

	1988	1990
General	73%	58%
Primary	u/o	u/o

Pete Stark (D-Calif.)
Of Oakland • Elected 1972

Born: November 11, 1931, Milwaukee, Wis.

Education: Massachusetts Institute of Technology, B.S. 1953; U. of California, M.B.A. 1960.

Military Career: Air Force, 1955-57.

Occupation: Banker.

Family: Wife, Carolyn Wente; four children.

Religion: Unitarian.

Political Career: Sought Democratic nomination for Calif. Senate, 1970.

Capitol Office: 239 Cannon House Office Building 20515; 225-5065.

Office Staff: Administrative Assistant, Bill Vaughan; Press Secretary, Perry Plumart; Personal Assistant, Ella Mumphard.

Committees: District of Columbia; Ways & Means.

California 9th — Suburban Alameda County — Hayward. The district vote for George Bush was 42% in 1988.

Cliff Stearns (R-Fla.)
Of Ocala • Elected 1988

Born: April 16, 1941, Washington, D.C.
Education: George Washington U., B.S.
1963.
Military Career: Air Force, 1963-67.
Occupation: Motel company executive.
Family: Wife, Joan Moore; three
children.
Religion: Presbyterian.
Political Career: No previous office.

Capitol Office: 1123 Longworth House
Office Building 20515; 225-5744.
Office Staff: Administrative Assistant,
John Davis; Press Secretary, David
Gilliland; Executive Assistant, Barbara
Reynolds.
Committees: Banking, Finance & Urban
Affairs; Veterans' Affairs.

Florida 6th — North Central —
Gainesville; Ocala. The district vote for
George Bush was 50% in 1988.

CQ Voting Studies

	1989	1990
Presidential	78%	71%
Party	85%	89%
Participation	99%	99%

Interest Groups

	1989
ADA	0%
ACU	93%
AFL-CIO	0%
CCUS	100%

Elections

	1988	1990
General	53%	59%
Primary	32%	78%

Charles W. Stenholm (D-Texas)
Of Stamford • Elected 1978

Born: October 26, 1938, Stamford, Texas.
Education: Tarleton State Junior College, 1957-59; Texas Tech U., B.S. 1961; Texas Tech U., M.S. 1962.
Occupation: Cotton grower.
Family: Wife, Cynthia Ann Watson; three children.
Religion: Lutheran.
Political Career: No previous office.

Capitol Office: 1226 Longworth House Office Building 20515; 225-6605.
Office Staff: Administrative Assistant (Appointments), Lois Auer; Press Assistant, Denise Crenwelge.
Committees: Agriculture; Budget.

Texas 17th — West Central — Abilene. The district vote for George Bush was 58% in 1988.

CQ Voting Studies

	1989	1990
Presidential	71%	56%
Party	54%	52%
Participation	98%	99%

Interest Groups

	1988	1989
ADA	20%	25%
ACU	78%	61%
AFL-CIO	46%	17%
CCUS	77%	80%

Elections

	1988	1990
General	u/o	u/o
Primary	u/o	u/o

Louis Stokes (D-Ohio)
Of Warrensville Heights • Elected 1968

Born: February 23, 1925, Cleveland, Ohio.
Education: Western Reserve U., 1946-48; Cleveland-Marshall College of Law, J.D. 1953.
Military Career: Army, 1943-46.
Occupation: Lawyer.
Family: Wife, Jeannette Francis; four children.
Religion: African Methodist Episcopal.
Political Career: No previous office.

Capitol Office: 2365 Rayburn House Office Building 20515; 225-7032.
Office Staff: Press Secretary, Joyce Larkin; Office Manager, Joanne White.
Committees: Appropriations.

Ohio 21st — Cleveland — East; Cleveland Heights. The district vote for George Bush was 19% in 1988.

CQ Voting Studies

	1989	1990
Presidential	28%	14%
Party	90%	88%
Participation	93%	95%

Interest Groups

	1988	1989
ADA	70%	95%
ACU	0%	0%
AFL-CIO	100%	91%
CCUS	25%	33%

Elections

	1988	1990
General	86%	80%
Primary	u/o	u/o

Gerry E. Studds (D-Mass.)
Of Cohasset • Elected 1972

Born: May 12, 1937, Mineola, N.Y.
Education: Yale U., B.A. 1959; Yale U., M.A.T. 1961.
Occupation: High school teacher.
Family: Single.
Religion: Episcopalian.
Political Career: Democratic nominee for U.S. House, 1970.

Capitol Office: 237 Cannon House Office Building 20515; 225-3111.
Office Staff: Administrative Assistant/Press Secretary, Steven Schwadron; Executive Assistant, Kate Dyer.
Committees: Energy & Commerce; Foreign Affairs; Merchant Marine & Fisheries.

Massachusetts 10th — South Shore; Southeast; Cape Cod. The district vote for George Bush was 48% in 1988.

CQ Voting Studies

	1989	1990
Presidential	27%	18%
Party	97%	95%
Participation	99%	99%

Interest Groups

	1988	1989
ADA	100%	100%
ACU	0%	0%
AFL-CIO	100%	100%
CCUS	21%	40%

Elections

	1988	1990
General	67%	53%
Primary	u/o	u/o

Bob Stump (R-Ariz.)
Of Tolleson • Elected 1976

Born: April 4, 1927, Phoenix, Ariz.
Education: Arizona State U., B.S. 1951.
Military Career: Navy, 1943-46.
Occupation: Cotton farmer.
Family: Divorced; three children.
Religion: Seventh-day Adventist.
Political Career: Ariz. House, 1959-67;
Ariz. Senate, 1967-77; Senate president,
1975-77.

Capitol Office: 211 Cannon House
Office Building 20515; 225-4576.
Office Staff: Administrative
Assistant/Press Secretary, Lisa Jackson;
Appointments Secretary, Dolores Dunn.
Committees: Armed Services; Veterans'
Affairs (Ranking).

Arizona 3rd — North and West —
Glendale; Flagstaff; Part of Phoenix. The
district vote for George Bush was 64% in
1988.

CQ Voting Studies

	1989	1990
Presidential	72%	73%
Party	96%	79%
Participation	98%	82%

Interest Groups

	1988	1989
ADA	0%	0%
ACU	100%	96%
AFL-CIO	0%	0%
CCUS	85%	100%

Elections

	1988	1990
General	69%	57%
Primary	u/o	u/o

Don Sundquist (R-Tenn.)
Of Memphis • Elected 1982

Born: March 15, 1936, Moline, Ill.
Education: Augustana College (Ill.), B.A. 1957.
Military Career: Navy, 1957-59.
Occupation: Owner of printing, advertising and marketing firm.
Family: Wife, Martha Swanson; three children.
Religion: Lutheran.
Political Career: No previous office.

Capitol Office: 230 Cannon House Office Building 20515; 225-2811.
Office Staff: Administrative Assistant, Thomas J. McNamara; Press Secretary, Ralph Perrey; Executive Assistant, P.K. Rehbein.
Committees: Ways & Means.

Tennessee 7th — West Central — Clarksville; Part of Shelby County. The district vote for George Bush was 67% in 1988.

CQ Voting Studies

	1989	1990
Presidential	80%	74%
Party	86%	90%
Participation	95%	98%

Interest Groups

	1988	1989
ADA	10%	5%
ACU	96%	78%
AFL-CIO	17%	17%
CCUS	100%	90%

Elections

	1988	1990
General	80%	62%
Primary	u/o	u/o

Dick Swett (D-N.H.)
Of Bow • Elected 1990

Born: May 1, 1957, Bryn Mawr, Penn.
Education: Yale U., B.A. 1979.
Occupation: Architect.
Family: Wife, Katrina Lantos; five children.
Religion: Mormon.
Political Career: No previous office.

Capitol Office: 128 Cannon House Office Building 20515; 225-5206.
Office Staff: Administrative Assistant, Kay A. King; Scheduler, Eve Grossman.
Committees: Public Works & Transportation; Science, Space & Technology.

New Hampshire 2nd — West — Concord; Nashua. The district vote for George Bush was 61% in 1988.

Elections

	1990
General	53%
Primary	u/o

CQ Voting Studies

	1989	1990
Presidential	31%	19%
Party	93%	92%
Participation	96%	97%

Interest Groups

	1988	1989
ADA	90%	85%
ACU	0%	0%
AFL-CIO	85%	92%
CCUS	36%	40%

Elections

	1988	1990
General	u/o	51%
Primary	u/o	61%

Al Swift (D-Wash.)
Of Bellingham • Elected 1978

Born: September 12, 1935, Tacoma, Wash.
Education: Whitman College, 1953-55; Central Washington College, B.A. 1957.
Occupation: Broadcaster.
Family: Wife, Paula Jean Jackson.
Religion: Unitarian.
Political Career: No previous office.

Capitol Office: 1502 Longworth House Office Building 20515; 225-2605.
Office Staff: Administrative Assistant, Janet Thiessen; Press Secretary, Shawn Hanson; Personal Secretary, Mickey Hornbacher.
Committees: House Administration; Energy & Commerce.

Washington 2nd — Northwest — Everett; Part of Olympic Peninsula. The district vote for George Bush was 50% in 1988.

Mike Synar (D-Okla.)
Of Muskogee • Elected 1978

Born: October 17, 1950, Vinita, Okla.
Education: U. of Oklahoma, B.B.A. 1972; Northwestern U., M.S. 1973; U. of Oklahoma, LL.B. 1977; U. of Edinburgh, Scotland, 1974.
Occupation: Rancher; real estate broker; lawyer.
Family: Single.
Religion: Episcopalian.
Political Career: No previous office.

Capitol Office: 2441 Rayburn House Office Building 20515; 225-2701.
Office Staff: Administrative Assistant, Debbie Wesslund; Press Secretary, Sarah Silver; Office Manager, Sally LoVoi.
Committees: Energy & Commerce; Government Operations; Judiciary.

Oklahoma 2nd — Northeast — Tulsa; Muskogee. The district vote for George Bush was 53% in 1988.

CQ Voting Studies

	1989	1990
Presidential	28%	17%
Party	92%	93%
Participation	98%	97%

Interest Groups

	1988	1989
ADA	100%	85%
ACU	0%	4%
AFL-CIO	86%	67%
CCUS	38%	40%

Elections

	1988	1990
General	65%	61%
Primary	70%	56%

Robin Tallon (D-S.C.)
Of Florence • Elected 1982

Born: August 8, 1946, Hemingway, S.C.
Education: U. of South Carolina, 1964-65.
Occupation: Clothing store owner.
Family: Wife, Amelia Louise Johns; three children.
Religion: Methodist.
Political Career: S.C. House, 1981-83.

Capitol Office: 432 Cannon House Office Building 20515; 225-3315.
Office Staff: Administrative Assistant, Marva Smalls; Press Secretary, Reba Hull Campbell; Office Manager, Pamela Stevenson.
Committees: Agriculture; Merchant Marine & Fisheries.

South Carolina 6th — East — Florence. The district vote for George Bush was 56% in 1988.

CQ Voting Studies

	1989	1990
Presidential	56%	43%
Party	61%	67%
Participation	97%	98%

Interest Groups

	1988	1989
ADA	40%	50%
ACU	60%	46%
AFL-CIO	79%	58%
CCUS	62%	80%

Elections

	1988	1990
General	76%	u/o
Primary	89%	u/o

John Tanner (D-Tenn.)
Of Union City • Elected 1988

Born: September 22, 1944, Halls, Tenn.
Education: U. of Tennessee, B.S. 1966; U. of Tennessee, J.D. 1968.
Military Career: Navy, 1968-72; Tenn. Army National Guard, 1974-present.
Occupation: Lawyer; businessman.
Family: Wife, Betty Ann Portis; two children.
Religion: Disciples of Christ.
Political Career: Tenn. House, 1977-89.

Capitol Office: 512 Cannon House Office Building 20515; 225-4714.
Office Staff: Administrative Assistant/Press Secretary, Kelly M. Sharbel; Executive Assistant, Kathy Becker.
Committees: Armed Services; Science, Space & Technology.

Tennessee 8th — West — Jackson; Part of Shelby County. The district vote for George Bush was 56% in 1988.

CQ Voting Studies

	1989	1990
Presidential	47%	31%
Party	75%	73%
Participation	96%	95%

Interest Groups

	1989
ADA	40%
ACU	44%
AFL-CIO	67%
CCUS	70%

Elections

	1988	1990
General	62%	u/o
Primary	66%	u/o

W.J. "Billy" Tauzin (D-La.)
Of Thibodaux • Elected 1980
Pronounced TOE zan

Born: June 14, 1943, Chackbay, La.
Education: Nicholls State U., B.A. 1964;
Louisiana State U., J.D. 1967.
Occupation: Lawyer.
Family: Wife, Gayle Clement; five
children.
Religion: Roman Catholic.
Political Career: La. House, 1971-79;
sought Democratic nomination for
governor, 1987.

Capitol Office: 2342 Rayburn House
Office Building 20515; 225-4031.
Office Staff: Office Administrator,
Raychel Andrus; Press Secretary, Chris
Robichaux; Appointments Secretary,
Cecile Bergeron.
Committees: Energy & Commerce;
Merchant Marine & Fisheries.

Louisiana 3rd — South Central —
Houma; New Iberia. The district vote for
George Bush was 55% in 1988.

CQ Voting Studies

	1989	1990
Presidential	69%	46%
Party	48%	56%
Participation	96%	96%

Interest Groups

	1988	1989
ADA	45%	20%
ACU	64%	74%
AFL-CIO	86%	25%
CCUS	62%	80%

Elections

	1988	1990
General	u/o	u/o
Primary	89%	88%

Charles H. Taylor (R-N.C.)
Of Brevard • Elected 1990

Born: January 23, 1941, Brevard, N.C..
Education: Wake Forest U., B.A. 1963;
Wake Forest U., J.D. 1966.
Occupation: Tree farmer; banker.
Family: Wife, Elizabeth Owen; three
children.
Religion: Baptist.
Political Career: N.C. House, 1967-71;
N.C. Senate, 1973-75; Republican
nominee for U.S. House, 1988.

Capitol Office: 516 Cannon House
Office Building 20515; 225-6401.
Office Staff: Administrative Assistant,
Roger France; Press Secretary, Doug
Bassett.
Committees: Interior & Insular Affairs;
Public Works & Transportation.

North Carolina 11th — West —
Asheville. The district vote for George
Bush was 59% in 1988.

Elections

	1990
General	51%
Primary	56%

CQ Voting Studies

	1989	1990
Presidential	68%	49%
Party	67%	57%
Participation	100%	100%

Interest Groups

	1988	1989
ADA		n/a
ACU		100%
AFL-CIO		100%
CCUS		n/a

Elections

	1989*	1990
General	65%	81%
Primary	42%	u/o

*Special election.

Gene Taylor (D-Miss.)
Of Bay St. Louis • Elected 1989

Born: September 17, 1953, New Orleans, La.
Education: Tulane U., B.A. 1976; U. of Southern Mississippi, Gulf Park, 1978-80.
Military Career: Coast Guard, 1971-84.
Occupation: Sales representative.
Family: Wife, Margaret Gordon; three children.
Religion: Roman Catholic.
Political Career: Bay St. Louis City Council, 1981-83; Miss. Senate, 1983-89; Democratic nominee for U.S. House, 1988.

Capitol Office: 1429 Longworth House Office Building 20515; 225-5772.
Office Staff: Administrative Assistant, Wayne Weidie; Press Secretary, Sharon Souther; Personal Secretary, Stephanie Seymour.
Committees: Armed Services; Merchant Marine & Fisheries.

Mississippi 5th — Southeast — Gulf Coast; Hattiesburg. The district vote for George Bush was 69% in 1988.

Bill Thomas (R-Calif.)
Of Bakersfield • Elected 1978

Born: December 6, 1941, Wallace, Idaho.
Education: San Francisco State U., B.A. 1963; San Francisco State U., M.A. 1965.
Occupation: Professor of political science.
Family: Wife, Sharon Lynn Hamilton; two children.
Religion: Baptist.
Political Career: Calif. Assembly, 1975-79.

Capitol Office: 2402 Rayburn House Office Building 20515; 225-2915.
Office Staff: Administrative Assistant, Cathy Abernathy; Press Secretary, Jeff Nelligan; Scheduler, Cynthia Dooling.
Committees: House Administration (Ranking); Budget; Ways & Means.

California 20th — Bakersfield; San Luis Obispo. The district vote for George Bush was 65% in 1988.

CQ Voting Studies

	1989	1990
Presidential	72%	54%
Party	81%	74%
Participation	96%	87%

Interest Groups

	1988	1989
ADA	25%	15%
ACU	78%	78%
AFL-CIO	43%	8%
CCUS	100%	90%

Elections

	1988	1990
General	71%	60%
Primary	u/o	73%

CQ Voting Studies

	1989	1990
Presidential	72%	70%
Party	85%	86%
Participation	97%	97%

Interest Groups

	1989
ADA	5%
ACU	88%
AFL-CIO	0%
CCUS	89%

Elections

	1989*	1990
General	52%	55%
Primary		u/o

*Special election.

Craig Thomas (R-Wyo.)
Of Casper • Elected 1989

Born: February 17, 1933, Cody, Wyo.
Education: U. of Wyoming, B.A. 1955; LaSalle U., LL.B. 1963.
Military Career: Marine Corps, 1955-59.
Occupation: Businessman.
Family: Wife, Susan Roberts; four children.
Religion: Methodist.
Political Career: Sought Republican nomination for state treasurer, 1978; sought Republican nomination for state treasurer, 1982; Wyo. House, 1985-89.

Capitol Office: 1721 Longworth House Office Building 20515; 225-2311.
Office Staff: Administrative Assistant, Gale Eisenhauer; Press Secretary, Liz Brimmer; Executive Assistant, Mary Paxson.
Committees: Government Operations; Interior & Insular Affairs.

Wyoming — At Large. The district vote for George Bush was 61% in 1988.

Lindsay Thomas (D-Ga.)
Of Statesboro • Elected 1982

Born: November 20, 1943, Patterson, Ga.
Education: U. of Georgia, B.A. 1965.
Military Career: Ga. Air National Guard, 1966-72.
Occupation: Farmer; investment banker.
Family: Wife, Melinda Ann Fry; three children.
Religion: Methodist.
Political Career: No previous office.

Capitol Office: 240 Cannon House Office Building 20515; 225-5831.
Office Staff: Administrative Assistant, Robert H. Hurt; Press Secretary, Kathy Rafferty; Executive Assistant, Patrick R. Hanes.
Committees: Appropriations.

Georgia 1st — Southeast — Savannah; Brunswick. The district vote for George Bush was 60% in 1988.

CQ Voting Studies

	1989	1990
Presidential	58%	43%
Party	65%	76%
Participation	99%	98%

Interest Groups

	1988	1989
ADA	50%	25%
ACU	48%	54%
AFL-CIO	64%	33%
CCUS	64%	80%

Elections

	1988	1990
General	67%	71%
Primary	u/o	u/o

Elections

	1990
General	60%
Primary	u/o

Ray Thornton (D-Ark.)
Of Little Rock • Elected 1990

Born: July 26, 1928, Conway, Ark.
Education: Yale U., B.A. 1950; U. of Arkansas, J.D. 1956.
Military Career: Navy, 1951-54.
Occupation: Lawyer.
Family: Wife, Betty Jo Mann; three children.
Religion: Church of Christ.
Political Career: Ark. attorney general, 1971-73; U.S. House, 1973-79; sought Democratic nomination for U.S. Senate, 1978.

Capitol Office: 1705 Longworth House Office Building 20515; 225-2506.
Office Staff: Administrative Assistant, Ed Fry; Press Secretary, Julie Speed; Scheduler/Office Manager, Lauren Gaddy.
Committees: Government Operations; Science, Space & Technology.

Arkansas 2nd — Central — Little Rock. The district vote for George Bush was 56% in 1988.

Esteban E. Torres (D-Calif.)
Of West Covina • Elected 1982

Born: January 27, 1930, Miami, Ariz.
Education: East Los Angeles Community College, 1959-63; California State U., Los Angeles, 1963-64; U. of Maryland, 1965; American U., 1966.
Military Career: Army, 1949-53.
Occupation: International trade executive; autoworker; labor official.
Family: Wife, Arcy Sanchez; five children.
Religion: Roman Catholic.
Political Career: Sought Democratic nomination for U.S. House, 1974.

Capitol Office: 1740 Longworth House Office Building 20515; 225-5256.
Office Staff: Administrative Assistant, Robert Alcock; Press Secretary, Angelina Ornelas; Personal Secretary, Mary Ann Bloodworth.
Committees: Banking, Finance & Urban Affairs; Small Business.

California 34th — Los Angeles Suburbs — Norwalk. The district vote for George Bush was 49% in 1988.

CQ Voting Studies

	1989	1990
Presidential	29%	17%
Party	90%	94%
Participation	92%	97%

Interest Groups

	1988	1989
ADA	90%	95%
ACU	0%	0%
AFL-CIO	100%	100%
CCUS	23%	40%

Elections

	1988	1990
General	63%	61%
Primary	u/o	u/o

Robert G. Torricelli (D-N.J.)
Of Englewood • Elected 1982
Pronounced tor ah SELL ee

Born: August 26, 1951, Paterson, N.J.
Education: Rutgers U., A.B. 1974; Rutgers U., J.D. 1977; Harvard U., M.P.A. 1980.
Occupation: Lawyer.
Family: Wife, Susan Holloway.
Religion: Methodist.
Political Career: No previous office.

Capitol Office: 317 Cannon House Office Building 20515; 225-5061.
Office Staff: Administrative Assistant, Lewis Warshauer; Press Secretary, Rick Frost; Personal Assistant, Marcy Jennings.
Committees: Foreign Affairs; Science, Space & Technology.

New Jersey 9th — North — Fort Lee; Hackensack. The district vote for George Bush was 54% in 1988.

CQ Voting Studies

	1989	1990
Presidential	34%	20%
Party	86%	83%
Participation	89%	89%

Interest Groups

	1988	1989
ADA	85%	75%
ACU	4%	0%
AFL-CIO	100%	100%
CCUS	25%	30%

Elections

	1988	1990
General	67%	57%
Primary	u/o	96%

Edolphus Towns (D-N.Y.)
Of Brooklyn • Elected 1982

Born: July 21, 1934, Chadbourn, N.C.
Education: North Carolina A&T U., B.S.
1956; Adelphi U., M.S.W. 1973.
Military Career: Army, 1956-58.
Occupation: Professor; hospital
administrator.
Family: Wife, Gwendolyn Forbes; two
children.
Religion: Independent Baptist.
Political Career: Deputy Brooklyn
borough president (appointed), 1976-82.

Capitol Office: 1726 Longworth House
Office Building 20515; 225-5936.
Office Staff: Administrative
Assistant/Press Secretary, Brenda Pillors;
Personal Secretary, Kimi Washington.
Committees: Energy & Commerce;
Government Operations.

New York 11th — Northern Brooklyn —
Bedford-Stuyvesant. The district vote for
George Bush was 18% in 1988.

CQ Voting Studies

	1989	1990
Presidential	19%	11%
Party	83%	88%
Participation	87%	91%

Interest Groups

	1988	1989
ADA	90%	90%
ACU	0%	0%
AFL-CIO	100%	100%
CCUS	33%	33%

Elections

	1988	1990
General	89%	93%
Primary	76%	u/o

James A. Traficant, Jr. (D-Ohio)
Of Poland • Elected 1984

Born: May 8, 1941, Youngstown, Ohio.
Education: U. of Pittsburgh, B.S. 1963;
Youngstown State U., M.S. 1973;
Youngstown State U., M.S. 1976.
Occupation: County drug program
director; sheriff.
Family: Wife, Patricia Choppa; two
children.
Religion: Roman Catholic.
Political Career: Mahoning County
sheriff, 1981-85.

Capitol Office: 312 Cannon House
Office Building 20515; 225-5261.
Office Staff: Chief of Staff/Press
Secretary, H. West Richards.
Committees: Public Works &
Transportation; Science, Space &
Technology.

Ohio 17th — Northeast — Youngstown;
Warren. The district vote for George
Bush was 38% in 1988.

CQ Voting Studies

	1989	1990
Presidential	29%	19%
Party	83%	86%
Participation	100%	100%

Interest Groups

	1988	1989
ADA	95%	90%
ACU	8%	25%
AFL-CIO	100%	100%
CCUS	21%	40%

Elections

	1988	1990
General	77%	78%
Primary	86%	92%

Bob Traxler (D-Mich.)
Of Bay City • Elected 1974

Born: July 21, 1931, Kawkawlin, Mich.
Education: Michigan State U., B.A. 1952; Detroit College of Law, LL.B. 1959.
Military Career: Army, 1953-55.
Occupation: Lawyer.
Family: Divorced; three children.
Religion: Episcopalian.
Political Career: Mich. House, 1963-74.

Capitol Office: 2366 Rayburn House Office Building 20515; 225-2806.
Office Staff: Administrative Assistant, Roger Szemraj; Press Assistant, Bonnie Piper; Executive Assistant, Carmell Anderson.
Committees: Appropriations.

Michigan 8th — East — Bay City; Saginaw. The district vote for George Bush was 50% in 1988.

CQ Voting Studies

	1989	1990
Presidential	28%	25%
Party	83%	81%
Participation	93%	92%

Interest Groups

	1988	1989
ADA	80%	80%
ACU	14%	12%
AFL-CIO	100%	90%
CCUS	21%	33%

Elections

	1988	1990
General	72%	68%
Primary	u/o	u/o

CQ Voting Studies

	1989	1990
Presidential	29%	22%
Party	79%	76%
Participation	85%	85%

Interest Groups

	1988	1989
ADA	75%	95%
ACU	13%	16%
AFL-CIO	92%	92%
CCUS	29%	40%

Elections

	1988	1990
General	73%	66%
Primary	u/o	u/o

Morris K. Udall (D-Ariz.)
Of Tucson • Elected 1961

Born: June 15, 1922, St. Johns, Ariz.
Education: U. of Arizona, J.D. 1949.
Military Career: Army Air Corps, 1942-46.
Occupation: Lawyer.
Family: Wife, Norma Gilbert; six children.
Religion: Mormon.
Political Career: Pima County attorney, 1952-54; sought Democratic nomination for president, 1976.

Capitol Office: 235 Cannon House Office Building 20515; 225-4065.
Office Staff: Administrative Assistant, Matt James; Press Secretary, Erik Barnett; Executive Secretary, Joan Shycoff.
Committees: Foreign Affairs; Interior & Insular Affairs (Chairman); Post Office & Civil Service.

Arizona 2nd — Southwest — Western Tucson; Southern Phoenix; Yuma. The district vote for George Bush was 43% in 1988.

Jolene Unsoeld (D-Wash.)
Of Olympia • Elected 1988
Pronounced UN sold

Born: December 3, 1931, Corvallis, Ore.
Education: Oregon State U., 1950-51.
Occupation: Public official.
Family: Widowed; three children.
Religion: Theist.
Political Career: Democratic National Committee, 1983-88; Wash. House, 1985-89.

Capitol Office: 1508 Longworth House Office Building 20515; 225-3536.
Office Staff: Administrative Assistant, Dan Evans; Press Secretary, Doug Levy; Executive Assistant/Office Manager, Christine Cozadd.
Committees: Education & Labor; Merchant Marine & Fisheries.

Washington 3rd — Southwest — Olympia; Vancouver. The district vote for George Bush was 47% in 1988.

CQ Voting Studies

	1989	1990
Presidential	27%	15%
Party	95%	90%
Participation	99%	95%

Interest Groups

	1989
ADA	100%
ACU	4%
AFL-CIO	100%
CCUS	40%

Elections

	1988	1990
General	50%	54%
Primary	40%	52%

CQ Voting Studies

	1989	1990
Presidential	74%	61%
Party	85%	89%
Participation	99%	99%

Interest Groups

	1988	1989
ADA	30%	20%
ACU	64%	75%
AFL-CIO	50%	8%
CCUS	100%	100%

Elections

	1988	1990
General	71%	58%
Primary	u/o	63%

Fred Upton (R-Mich.)
Of St. Joseph • Elected 1986

Born: April 23, 1953, St. Joseph, Mich.
Education: U. of Michigan, B.A. 1975.
Occupation: Congressional aide; budget analyst.
Family: Wife, Amey Rulon-Miller; one child.
Religion: Protestant.
Political Career: No previous office.

Capitol Office: 1713 Longworth House Office Building 20515; 225-3761.
Office Staff: Administrative Assistant, Lynn S. Sachs; Press Secretary, Joan Hillebrands; Office Manager, Brynne Crowe.
Committees: Public Works & Transportation; Small Business.

Michigan 4th — Southwest — Holland; Benton Harbor-St. Joseph. The district vote for George Bush was 63% in 1988.

Tim Valentine (D-N.C.)
Of Nashville • Elected 1982

Born: March 15, 1926, Nash County, N.C.
Education: The Citadel, A.B. 1948; U. of North Carolina, LL.B. 1952.
Military Career: Army Air Force, 1944-46.
Occupation: Lawyer.
Family: Wife, Barbara Renyolds; four children; three stepchildren.
Religion: Baptist.
Political Career: N.C. House, 1955-61; N.C. Democratic Party chairman, 1966-68.

Capitol Office: 1510 Longworth House Office Building 20515; 225-4531.
Office Staff: Administrative Assistant, Ed Nagy; Press Assistant, Ben Finzel; Personal Secretary/Scheduler, Patricia A. Lawrence.
Committees: Public Works & Transportation; Science, Space & Technology.

North Carolina 2nd — North Central — Durham; Rocky Mount. The district vote for George Bush was 49% in 1988.

CQ Voting Studies

	1989	1990
Presidential	52%	42%
Party	69%	66%
Participation	98%	97%

Interest Groups

	1988	1989
ADA	45%	30%
ACU	48%	39%
AFL-CIO	71%	33%
CCUS	62%	70%

Elections

	1988	1990
General	u/o	75%
Primary	u/o	u/o

CQ Voting Studies

	1989	1990
Presidential	78%	66%
Party	57%	73%
Participation	86%	94%

Interest Groups

	1988	1989
ADA	15%	0%
ACU	91%	91%
AFL-CIO	21%	18%
CCUS	100%	90%

Elections

	1988	1990
General	70%	55%
Primary	u/o	u/o

Guy Vander Jagt (R-Mich.)
Of Luther • Elected 1966
Pronouced VAN der jack

Born: August 26, 1931, Cadillac, Mich.
Education: Hope College, A.B. 1953; Yale U., B.D. 1955; Bonn U., 1956; U. of Michigan, LL.B. 1960.
Occupation: Lawyer.
Family: Wife, Carol Doorn; one child.
Religion: Presbyterian.
Political Career: Mich. Senate, 1965-66.

Capitol Office: 2409 Rayburn House Office Building 20515; 225-3511.
Office Staff: Chief of Staff/Press Secretary, Jim Sparling; Appointments Secretary, Kathy Palmateer.
Committees: Ways & Means.

Michigan 9th — West — Muskegon; Traverse City. The district vote for George Bush was 62% in 1988.

Bruce F. Vento (D-Minn.)
Of St. Paul • Elected 1976

Born: October 7, 1940, St. Paul, Minn.
Education: U. of Minnesota, A.A. 1961; Wisconsin State U., B.S. 1965; U. of Minnesota, 1965-70.
Occupation: Science teacher.
Family: Wife, Mary Jean Moore; three children.
Religion: Roman Catholic.
Political Career: Minn. House, 1971-77.

Capitol Office: 2304 Rayburn House Office Building 20515; 225-6631.
Office Staff: Administrative Assistant, Larry Romans; Communications Director, Catherine Hope; Appointments Secretary, Mary Ann Daly.
Committees: Banking, Finance & Urban Affairs; Interior & Insular Affairs.

Minnesota 4th — St. Paul and Suburbs. The district vote for George Bush was 38% in 1988.

CQ Voting Studies

	1989	1990
Presidential	30%	13%
Party	92%	95%
Participation	99%	98%

Interest Groups

	1988	1989
ADA	90%	100%
ACU	4%	4%
AFL-CIO	100%	83%
CCUS	36%	30%

Elections

	1988	1990
General	72%	65%
Primary	93%	u/o

CQ Voting Studies

	1989	1990
Presidential	30%	22%
Party	89%	90%
Participation	98%	98%

Interest Groups

	1988	1989
ADA	100%	100%
ACU	0%	7%
AFL-CIO	100%	83%
CCUS	36%	40%

Elections

	1988	1990
General	77%	66%
Primary	84%	51%

Peter J. Visclosky (D-Ind.)

Of Merrillville • Elected 1984
Pronounced vis KLOSS key

Born: August 13, 1949, Gary, Ind.
Education: Indiana U., B.S. 1970; Notre Dame U., J.D. 1973; Georgetown U., LL.M. 1982.
Occupation: Lawyer.
Family: Wife, Ann Marie O'Keefe; one child.
Religion: Roman Catholic.
Political Career: No previous office.

Capitol Office: 330 Cannon House Office Building 20515; 225-2461.
Office Staff: Administrative Assistant, Chuck Brimmer; Press Assistant, Jeff O'Mara; Executive Assistant, Karen Hauck.
Committees: Interior & Insular Affairs; Public Works & Transportation.

Indiana 1st — Industrial Belt — Gary; Hammond. The district vote for George Bush was 41% in 1988.

Harold L. Volkmer (D-Mo.)
Of Hannibal • Elected 1976

Born: April 4, 1931, Jefferson City, Mo.
Education: U. of Missouri, LL.B. 1955.
Military Career: Army, 1955-57.
Occupation: Lawyer.
Family: Wife, Shirley Ruth Braskett; three children.
Religion: Roman Catholic.
Political Career: Marion County prosecuting attorney, 1960-66; Mo. House, 1967-77.

Capitol Office: 2411 Rayburn House Office Building 20515; 225-2956.
Office Staff: Administrative Assistant, Jim Spurling; Press Secretary, Mary Hicks; Appointments Secretary, Charlene Moore.
Committees: Agriculture; Science, Space & Technology.

Missouri 9th — Northeast — Columbia. The district vote for George Bush was 54% in 1988.

CQ Voting Studies

	1989	1990
Presidential	53%	35%
Party	72%	73%
Participation	100%	98%

Interest Groups

	1988	1989
ADA	60%	60%
ACU	35%	25%
AFL-CIO	93%	83%
CCUS	50%	40%

Elections

	1988	1990
General	68%	58%
Primary	u/o	u/o

CQ Voting Studies

	1989	1990
Presidential	79%	72%
Party	91%	84%
Participation	95%	94%

Interest Groups

	1988	1989
ADA	10%	5%
ACU	92%	89%
AFL-CIO	14%	8%
CCUS	77%	100%

Elections

	1988	1990
General	57%	59%
Primary	u/o	84%

Barbara F. Vucanovich (R-Nev.)
Of Reno • Elected 1982
Pronounced voo CAN oh vitch

Born: June 22, 1921, Camp Dix, N.J.
Education: Manhattanville College, 1938-39.
Occupation: Congressional aide; travel agent; franchise owner.
Family: Husband, George F. Vucanovich; five children.
Religion: Roman Catholic.
Political Career: No previous office.

Capitol Office: 206 Cannon House Office Building 20515; 225-6155.
Office Staff: Administrative Assistant, Michael Pieper; Press Secretary, Peggy Polk; Office Manager/ Personal Secretary, Sarah Willis.
Committees: Appropriations; Interior & Insular Affairs.

Nevada 2nd — North — Reno and the Cow Counties. The district vote for George Bush was 61% in 1988.

Robert S. Walker (R-Pa.)
Of East Petersburg • Elected 1976

Born: December 23, 1942, Bradford, Penn.
Education: Millersville U., B.S. 1964; U. of Delaware, M.A. 1968.
Military Career: Pa. National Guard, 1967-73.
Occupation: High school teacher; congressional aide.
Family: Wife, Sue Albertson.
Religion: Presbyterian.
Political Career: No previous office.

Capitol Office: 2445 Rayburn House Office Building 20515; 225-2411.
Office Staff: Administrative Assistant, Connie Thumma; Press Secretary, Melissa Sabatine; Executive Assistant, Lisa Zichar.
Committees: Science, Space & Technology (Ranking).

Pennsylvania 16th — Southeast — Lancaster. The district vote for George Bush was 70% in 1988.

CQ Voting Studies

	1989	1990
Presidential	79%	85%
Party	98%	95%
Participation	99%	99%

Interest Groups

	1988	1989
ADA	5%	10%
ACU	100%	93%
AFL-CIO	7%	0%
CCUS	93%	100%

Elections

	1988	1990
General	74%	66%
Primary	u/o	u/o

James T. Walsh (R-N.Y.)
Of Syracuse • Elected 1988

Born: June 19, 1947, Syracuse, N.Y.
Education: Saint Bonaventure U., B.A. 1970.
Occupation: Marketing executive; social worker.
Family: Wife, DeDe Ryan; three children.
Religion: Roman Catholic.
Political Career: Syracuse Common Council, 1978-88; president, 1986-88; sought nomination for Onondaga County executive, 1987.

Capitol Office: 1238 Longworth House Office Building 20515; 225-3701.
Office Staff: Administrative Assistant/Press Secretary, Art Jutton; Appointments Secretary, Mary Foti.
Committees: House Administration; Agriculture.

New York 27th — Central — Syracuse. The district vote for George Bush was 53% in 1988.

CQ Voting Studies

	1989	1990
Presidential	69%	44%
Party	57%	54%
Participation	98%	96%

Interest Groups

	1989
ADA	35%
ACU	64%
AFL-CIO	33%
CCUS	80%

Elections

	1988	1990
General	57%	63%
Primary	u/o	u/o

Craig Washington (D-Texas)
Of Houston • Elected 1989

Born: October 12, 1941, Longview, Texas.
Education: Prairie View A&M Univ., B.S. 1966; Texas Southern U., J.D. 1969.
Occupation: Lawyer.
Family: Separated; five children.
Religion: Baptist.
Political Career: Texas House, 1973-83; Texas Senate, 1983-90.

Capitol Office: 1711 Longworth House Office Building 20515; 225-3816.
Office Staff: Administrative Assistant/Press Secretary, Licia Green; Scheduling Secretary, Doyle Smart.
Committees: Education & Labor; Judiciary.

Texas 18th — Central Houston. The district vote for George Bush was 23% in 1988.

CQ Voting Studies

	1990
Presidential	12%
Party	73%
Participation	78%

Elections

	1989*	1990
General	57%	u/o
Primary		u/o

*Special election.

Elections

	1990
General	79%
Primary	88%

Maxine Waters (D-Calif.)
Of Los Angeles • Elected 1990

Born: August 31, 1938, St. Louis, Mo.
Education: California State U., B.A. 1970.
Occupation: Head Start official.
Family: Husband, Sidney Williams; two children.
Religion: Christian.
Political Career: Calif. Assembly, 1977-91.

Capitol Office: 1207 Longworth House Office Building 20515; 225-2201.
Office Staff: Administrative Assistant, Kay Hixson.
Committees: Banking, Finance & Urban Affairs; Veterans' Affairs.

California 29th — South-Central Los Angeles; Watts; Downey. The district vote for George Bush was 19% in 1988.

Henry A. Waxman (D-Calif.)
Of Los Angeles • Elected 1974

Born: September 12, 1939, Los Angeles, Calif.
Education: U.C.L.A., B.A. 1961; U.C.L.A., J.D. 1964.
Occupation: Lawyer.
Family: Wife, Janet Kessler; two children.
Religion: Jewish.
Political Career: Calif. Assembly, 1969-75.

Capitol Office: 2418 Rayburn House Office Building 20515; 225-3976.
Office Staff: Administrative Assistant/Press Secretary, Philip Schiliro; Office Manager, Norah Lucey-Mail.
Committees: Energy & Commerce; Government Operations.

California 24th — Hollywood; Part of San Fernando Valley. The district vote for George Bush was 34% in 1988.

CQ Voting Studies

	1989	1990
Presidential	28%	20%
Party	88%	90%
Participation	92%	94%

Interest Groups

	1988	1989
ADA	90%	100%
ACU	0%	4%
AFL-CIO	93%	100%
CCUS	21%	30%

Elections

	1988	1990
General	72%	69%
Primary	u/o	u/o

CQ Voting Studies

	1989	1990
Presidential	77%	63%
Party	84%	80%
Participation	97%	94%

Interest Groups

	1988	1989
ADA	15%	5%
ACU	96%	89%
AFL-CIO	14%	8%
CCUS	93%	100%

Elections

	1988	1990
General	58%	62%
Primary	u/o	u/o

Vin Weber (R-Minn.)
Of North Mankota • Elected 1980

Born: July 24, 1952, Slayton, Minn.
Education: U. of Minnesota, 1970-74.
Occupation: Congressional aide; publisher.
Family: Wife, Cheryl Foster; one child.
Religion: Roman Catholic.
Political Career: Republican nominee for Minn. Senate, 1976.

Capitol Office: 106 Cannon House Office Building 20515; 225-2331.
Office Staff: Administrative Assistant, Arne Christenson; Press Secretary, Sherri Burkholder; Scheduler, Amy Wolak.
Committees: Appropriations.

Minnesota 2nd — Southwest — Willmar. The district vote for George Bush was 51% in 1988.

Ted Weiss (D-N.Y.)
Of Manhattan • Elected 1976

Born: September 17, 1927, Hungary.
Education: Syracuse U., B.A. 1951;
Syracuse U., LL.B. 1952.
Military Career: Army, 1946-47.
Occupation: Lawyer.
Family: Wife, Sonya Hoover; two
children.
Religion: Jewish.
Political Career: N.Y. City Council, 1962-77; sought Democratic nomination for
U.S. House, 1966; sought Democratic
nomination for U.S. House, 1968.

Capitol Office: 2467 Rayburn House
Office Building 20515; 225-5635.
Office Staff: Administrative
Assistant/Press Secretary, Michael D.
Timmeny; Office Manager/Personal
Assistant, Joyce Power.
Committees: Banking, Finance & Urban
Affairs; Foreign Affairs; Government
Operations.

New York 17th — West Side Manhattan
— Part of the Bronx. The district vote for
George Bush was 21% in 1988.

CQ Voting Studies

	1989	1990
Presidential	28%	14%
Party	92%	92%
Participation	96%	99%

Interest Groups

	1988	1989
ADA	75%	95%
ACU	0%	0%
AFL-CIO	100%	91%
CCUS	21%	30%

Elections

	1988	1990
General	84%	80%
Primary	88%	u/o

Curt Weldon (R-Pa.)
Of Aston • Elected 1986

Born: July 22, 1947, Marcus Hook, Penn.
Education: West Chester State College,
B.A. 1969; Delaware County Community
College, A.A.S. 1972.
Occupation: Teacher.
Family: Wife, Mary Gallagher; five
children.
Religion: Protestant.
Political Career: Marcus Hook mayor,
1977-82; Delaware County Council, 1981-
86; Republican nominee for U.S. House,
1984.

Capitol Office: 316 Cannon House
Office Building 20515; 225-2011.
Office Staff: Administrative
Assistant/Press Secretary, Doug Ritter;
Executive Assistant, Kate Donahue Webb.
Committees: Armed Services; Merchant
Marine & Fisheries.

Pennsylvania 7th — Southwest
Philadelphia Suburbs. The district vote
for George Bush was 60% in 1988.

CQ Voting Studies

	1989	1990
Presidential	65%	50%
Party	56%	67%
Participation	96%	96%

Interest Groups

	1988	1989
ADA	30%	35%
ACU	59%	62%
AFL-CIO	77%	60%
CCUS	71%	89%

Elections

	1988	1990
General	68%	65%
Primary	u/o	u/o

Alan Wheat (D-Mo.)
Of Kansas City • Elected 1982

Born: October 16, 1951, San Antonio, Texas.
Education: Grinnell College, B.A. 1972.
Occupation: Legislative aide; federal economist.
Family: Wife, Yolanda Townsend; one child.
Religion: Church of Christ.
Political Career: Mo. House, 1977-83.

Capitol Office: 1210 Longworth House Office Building 20515; 225-4535.
Office Staff: Administrative Assistant, Margaret E. Broadaway; Press Secretary, Lynn Peebles; Appointments Secretary, Winsome Packer.
Committees: District of Columbia; Rules.

Missouri 5th — Kansas City and Eastern Suburbs. The district vote for George Bush was 39% in 1988.

CQ Voting Studies

	1989	1990
Presidential	27%	13%
Party	80%	95%
Participation	97%	98%

Interest Groups

	1988	1989
ADA	100%	95%
ACU	0%	0%
AFL-CIO	93%	100%
CCUS	21%	40%

Elections

	1988	1990
General	70%	62%
Primary	u/o	80%

Jamie L. Whitten (D-Miss.)
Of Charleston • Elected 1941

Born: April 18, 1910, Cascilla, Miss.
Education: U. of Mississippi, 1927-32.
Occupation: Grammar school teacher and principal; lawyer; author.
Family: Wife, Rebecca Thompson; two children.
Religion: Presbyterian.
Political Career: Miss. House, 1931-33; district attorney, 17th district, 1933-41.

Capitol Office: 2314 Rayburn House Office Building 20515; 225-4306.
Office Staff: Administrative Assistant, Hal DeCell; Press Secretary, Steve Burtt; Scheduler, Lisa Ulmer.
Committees: Appropriations (Chairman).

Mississippi 1st — North — Clarksdale. The district vote for George Bush was 59% in 1988.

CQ Voting Studies

	1989	1990
Presidential	52%	34%
Party	79%	79%
Participation	98%	94%

Interest Groups

	1988	1989
ADA	65%	50%
ACU	20%	42%
AFL-CIO	100%	67%
CCUS	15%	70%

Elections

	1988	1990
General	78%	65%
Primary	85%	u/o

Pat Williams (D-Mont.)
Of Missoula • Elected 1978

Born: October 30, 1937, Helena, Mont.
Education: U. of Montana, 1956-57; William Jewell College, 1958; U. of Denver, B.A. 1961; Western Montana College, 1962.
Military Career: Army, 1960-61; National Guard, 1962-69.
Occupation: Elementary and secondary school teacher.
Family: Wife, Carol Griffith; three children.
Religion: Roman Catholic.
Political Career: Mont. House, 1967-71; sought Democratic nomination for U.S. House, 1974.

Capitol Office: 2457 Rayburn House Office Building 20515; 225-3211.
Office Staff: Administrative Assistant, Jon Weintraub; Press Secretary, David Roach; Executive Assistant/Office Manager, Mary B. Flanagan.
Committees: Education & Labor; Interior & Insular Affairs.

Montana 1st — Western Mountains — Helena; Missoula. The district vote for George Bush was 50% in 1988.

CQ Voting Studies

	1989	1990
Presidential	31%	24%
Party	72%	77%
Participation	88%	90%

Interest Groups

	1988	1989
ADA	85%	80%
ACU	0%	7%
AFL-CIO	100%	91%
CCUS	15%	40%

Elections

	1988	1990
General	61%	61%
Primary	u/o	u/o

CQ Voting Studies

	1989	1990
Presidential	47%	35%
Party	61%	64%
Participation	84%	82%

Interest Groups

	1988	1989
ADA	35%	45%
ACU	55%	50%
AFL-CIO	82%	82%
CCUS	46%	40%

Elections

	1988	1990
General	88%	56%
Primary	u/o	u/o

Charles Wilson (D-Texas)
Of Lufkin • Elected 1972

Born: June 1, 1933, Trinity, Texas.
Education: Sam Houston State U., 1950-51; U. of Texas, 1951-52; U.S. Naval Academy, B.S. 1956.
Military Career: Navy, 1956-60.
Occupation: Lumberyard manager.
Family: Divorced.
Religion: Methodist.
Political Career: Texas House, 1961-67; Texas Senate, 1967-73.

Capitol Office: 2256 Rayburn House Office Building 20515; 225-2401.
Office Staff: Administrative Assistant, Payton Walters; Press Secretary, Elaine Lang; Personal Secretary, Lori White.
Committees: Appropriations; Select Intelligence.

Texas 2nd — East — Lufkin; Orange. The district vote for George Bush was 50% in 1988.

Bob Wise (D-W.Va.)
Of Clendenin • Elected 1982

Born: January 6, 1948, Washington, D.C.
Education: Duke U., A.B. 1970; Tulane U., J.D. 1975.
Occupation: Lawyer.
Family: Wife, Sandra Casber.
Religion: Episcopalian.
Political Career: W.Va. Senate, 1981-83.

Capitol Office: 1421 Longworth House Office Building 20515; 225-2711.
Office Staff: Administrative Assistant, Lowell Johnson; Press Assistant, Rod Blackstone; Staff Assistant/Scheduler, Carin Connell.
Committees: Budget; Government Operations.

West Virginia 3rd — Central — Charleston. The district vote for George Bush was 47% in 1988.

CQ Voting Studies

	1989	1990
Presidential	31%	19%
Party	85%	92%
Participation	93%	97%

Interest Groups

	1988	1989
ADA	75%	75%
ACU	12%	14%
AFL-CIO	100%	100%
CCUS	36%	30%

Elections

	1988	1990
General	74%	u/o
Primary	u/o	u/o

Frank R. Wolf (R-Va.)
Of Vienna • Elected 1980

Born: January 30, 1939, Philadelphia, Pa.
Education: Pennsylvania State U., B.A. 1961; Georgetown U., LL.B. 1965.
Military Career: Army, 1962-63; Army Reserve, 1963-67.
Occupation: Lawyer; federal official.
Family: Wife, Carolyn Stover; five children.
Religion: Presbyterian.
Political Career: Sought Republican nomination for U.S. House, 1976; Republican nominee for U.S. House, 1978.

Capitol Office: 104 Cannon House Office Building 20515; 225-5136.
Office Staff: Administrative Assistant, Charles E. White; Press Secretary, Ed Newberry; Personal Secretary, Susan Thompson.
Committees: Appropriations.

Virginia 10th — D.C. Suburbs; Arlington County. The district vote for George Bush was 57% in 1988.

CQ Voting Studies

	1989	1990
Presidential	81%	71%
Party	83%	78%
Participation	99%	99%

Interest Groups

	1988	1989
ADA	25%	10%
ACU	88%	89%
AFL-CIO	43%	17%
CCUS	86%	90%

Elections

	1988	1990
General	68%	62%
Primary	u/o	u/o

Howard Wolpe (D-Mich.)
Of Lansing • Elected 1978

Born: November 2, 1939, Los Angeles, Calif.
Education: Reed College, B.A. 1960; Massachusetts Institute of Technology, Ph.D. 1967.
Occupation: Professor of political science.
Family: Divorced; one child.
Religion: Jewish.
Political Career: Kalamazoo City Commission, 1969-72; Mich. House, 1973-77; Democratic nominee for U.S. House, 1976.

Capitol Office: 1535 Longworth House Office Building 20515; 225-5011.
Office Staff: Administrative Assistant, Marda Robillard; Press Secretary, Eileen Nicoll; Office Manager, Sarah Lisenby.
Committees: Foreign Affairs; Science, Space & Technology.

Michigan 3rd — South Central — Lansing; Kalamazoo. The district vote for George Bush was 54% in 1988.

CQ Voting Studies

	1989	1990
Presidential	28%	15%
Party	92%	90%
Participation	97%	95%

Interest Groups

	1988	1989
ADA	100%	100%
ACU	0%	4%
AFL-CIO	100%	100%
CCUS	36%	40%

Elections

	1988	1990
General	57%	58%
Primary	u/o	u/o

Ron Wyden (D-Ore.)
Of Portland • Elected 1980

Born: May 3, 1949, Wichita, Kan.
Education: Stanford U., B.A. 1971; U. of Oregon, J.D. 1974.
Occupation: Public interest lawyer; professor of gerontology; public interest organization executive; campaign aide.
Family: Wife, Laurie Oseran; two children.
Religion: Jewish.
Political Career: No previous office.

Capitol Office: 2452 Rayburn House Office Building 20515; 225-4811.
Office Staff: Administrative Assistant, Peter Newbould; Press Secretary, Wendy Horwitz; Scheduler, Annette Predeek.
Committees: Energy & Commerce; Small Business.

Oregon 3rd — Eastern Portland and Suburbs. The district vote for George Bush was 38% in 1988.

CQ Voting Studies

	1989	1990
Presidential	27%	24%
Party	91%	94%
Participation	98%	100%

Interest Groups

	1988	1989
ADA	90%	80%
ACU	16%	18%
AFL-CIO	86%	82%
CCUS	43%	50%

Elections

	1988	1990
General	u/o	81%
Primary	95%	93%

Chalmers P. Wylie   (R-Ohio)
Of Worthington • Elected 1966

Born: November 23, 1920, Norwich, Ohio.
Education: Otterbein College, 1939-40; Ohio State U., 1940-43; Harvard U., J.D. 1948.
Military Career: Army, 1943-45; Army Reserve, 1945-53; National Guard, 1958-78.
Occupation: Lawyer.
Family: Wife, Marjorie Siebold; two children.
Religion: Methodist.
Political Career: Columbus city attorney, 1954-57; Ohio House, 1961-67.

Capitol Office: 2310 Rayburn House Office Building 20515; 225-2015.
Office Staff: Administrative Assistant, Benson Hart; Personal Secretary, Angela Gambo.
Committees: Banking, Finance & Urban Affairs (Ranking); Veterans' Affairs.

Ohio 15th — Central — Western Columbus and Suburbs. The district vote for George Bush was 62% in 1988.

CQ Voting Studies

	1989	1990
Presidential	83%	69%
Party	68%	69%
Participation	95%	91%

Interest Groups

	1988	1989
ADA	30%	0%
ACU	80%	93%
AFL-CIO	36%	0%
CCUS	92%	90%

Elections

	1988	1990
General	75%	59%
Primary	u/o	78%

CQ Voting Studies

	1989	1990
Presidential	27%	17%
Party	93%	88%
Participation	98%	90%

Interest Groups

	1988	1989
ADA	80%	100%
ACU	5%	4%
AFL-CIO	100%	83%
CCUS	36%	20%

Elections

	1988	1990
General	66%	71%
Primary	u/o	70%

Sidney R. Yates (D-Ill.)
Of Chicago • Elected 1948

Born: August 27, 1909, Chicago, Ill.
Education: U. of Chicago, Ph.B. 1931; U. of Chicago, J.D. 1933.
Military Career: Navy, 1944-46.
Occupation: Lawyer.
Family: Wife, Adeline Holleb; one child.
Religion: Jewish.
Political Career: Democratic nominee for U.S. Senate, 1962; reelected to House, 1964.

Capitol Office: 2234 Rayburn House Office Building 20515; 225-2111.
Office Staff: Administrative Assistant/Press Secretary, Mary Bain; Scheduler, Kim Messineo.
Committees: Appropriations.

Illinois 9th — Chicago — North Side Lakefront; Northern Suburbs. The district vote for George Bush was 38% in 1988.

Gus Yatron (D-Pa.)
Of Reading • Elected 1968
Pronounced YAT ron

Born: October 16, 1927, Reading, Penn.
Education: Kutztown State U., 1950.
Occupation: Ice cream manufacturer; professional boxer.
Family: Wife, Millie Menzies; two children.
Religion: Greek Orthodox.
Political Career: Reading School Board, 1955-57; Pa. House, 1957-61; Pa. Senate, 1961-69.

Capitol Office: 2205 Rayburn House Office Building 20515; 225-5546.
Office Staff: Administrative Assistant, Joseph P. Gemmell; Press Secretary, Dale Morris; Staff Assistant/Scheduler, Ann Maruschak.
Committees: Foreign Affairs; Post Office & Civil Service.

Pennsylvania 6th — Southeast — Reading. The district vote for George Bush was 61% in 1988.

CQ Voting Studies

	1989	1990
Presidential	27%	34%
Party	56%	73%
Participation	72%	98%

Interest Groups

	1988	1989
ADA	65%	45%
ACU	24%	24%
AFL-CIO	100%	100%
CCUS	36%	25%

Elections

	1988	1990
General	63%	57%
Primary	u/o	u/o

C.W. Bill Young (R-Fla.)
Of St. Petersburg • Elected 1970

Born: December 16, 1930, Harmaville, Penn.
Education: Pennsylvania public schools.
Military Career: National Guard, 1948-57.
Occupation: Insurance executive.
Family: Wife, Beverly F. Angelo; three children.
Religion: Methodist.
Political Career: Fla. Senate, 1961-71; minority leader, 1967-71.

Capitol Office: 2407 Rayburn House Office Building 20515; 225-5961.
Office Staff: Administrative Assistant, Douglas Gregory; Press Secretary, Harry Glenn; Office Manager, Kevin Hardcastle.
Committees: Appropriations; Select Intelligence.

Florida 8th — West — St. Petersburg. The district vote for George Bush was 55% in 1988.

CQ Voting Studies

	1989	1990
Presidential	71%	68%
Party	83%	74%
Participation	97%	94%

Interest Groups

	1988	1989
ADA	10%	10%
ACU	88%	86%
AFL-CIO	36%	9%
CCUS	79%	89%

Elections

	1988	1990
General	73%	u/o
Primary	u/o	u/o

Don Young (R-Alaska)
Of Fort Yukon • Elected 1973

Born: June 9, 1933, Meridian, Calif.
Education: Yuba Junior College, A.A. 1952; Chico State College, B.A. 1958.
Military Career: Army, 1955-57.
Occupation: Elementary school teacher; riverboat captain.
Family: Wife, Lula Fredson; two children.
Religion: Episcopalian.
Political Career: Fort Yukon City Council, 1960-64; mayor of Fort Yukon, 1964-68; Alaska House, 1967-71; Alaska Senate, 1971-73; Republican nominee for U.S. House, 1972.

Capitol Office: 2331 Rayburn House Office Building 20515; 225-5765.
Office Staff: Administrative Assistant, C.J. Zane; Press Secretary, Steve Hansen; Executive Secretary/Scheduler, Nicholette Steube.
Committees: Interior & Insular Affairs (Ranking); Merchant Marine & Fisheries; Post Office & Civil Service.

Alaska — At Large. The district vote for George Bush was 60% in 1988.

CQ Voting Studies

	1989	1990
Presidential	70%	56%
Party	71%	60%
Participation	92%	91%

Interest Groups

	1988	1989
ADA	30%	15%
ACU	63%	77%
AFL-CIO	64%	50%
CCUS	69%	60%

Elections

	1988	1990
General	62%	52%
Primary	55%	57%

Bill Zeliff (R-N.H.)

Of Jackson • Elected 1990
Pronounced ZELL iff

Born: June 12, 1936, East Orange, N.J.
Education: U. of Connecticut, B.S. 1959.
Military Career: Army National Guard, 1959-64.
Occupation: Hotel owner.
Family: Wife, Sydna Taylor; three children.
Religion: Protestant.
Political Career: No previous office.

Capitol Office: 512 Cannon House Office Building 20515; 225-5456.
Office Staff: Chief of Staff, Brian Flood; Communications Director, Barbara Atkinson.
Committees: Government Operations; Public Works & Transportation.

New Hampshire 1st — East — Manchester. The district vote for George Bush was 64% in 1988.

Elections

	1990
General	55%
Primary	27%

Dick Zimmer (R-N.J.)
Of Flemington • Elected 1990

Born: August 16, 1944, Newark, N.J.
Education: Yale U., B.A. 1966; Yale U., LL.B. 1969.
Occupation: Lawyer.
Family: Wife, Marfy Goodspeed; two children.
Religion: Jewish.
Political Career: Republican nominee for N.J. Assembly, 1979; N.J. Assembly, 1982-87; N.J. Senate, 1987-91.

Capitol Office: 510 Cannon House Office Building 20515; 225-5801.
Office Staff: Administrative Assistant, David Karvelas; Press Secretary, Dave Barnes; Appointments Secretary, Gail Alexander.
Committees: Government Operations; Science, Space & Technology.

New Jersey 12th — North and Central — Morristown. The district vote for George Bush was 63% in 1988.

Elections

	1990
General	64%
Primary	38%

Ben Blaz (R-Guam)
Of Guam • Elected 1984
Pronounced BLAHS

Born: February 14, 1928, Agana, Guam.
Education: U. of Notre Dame, B.S. 1951;
George Washington U., M.A. 1963; Naval
War College, 1971.
Military Career: Marine Corps, 1951-80.
Occupation: Retired brigadier general.
Family: Wife, Ann Evers; two children.
Religion: Roman Catholic.
Political Career: No previous office.

Capitol Office: 1130 Longworth House
Office Building 20515; 225-1188.
Office Staff: Special Assistant, Eddie
Pangelinan; Press Secretary, Frank
Kalisiak; Personal Secretary, Vacant.
Committees: Armed Services; Foreign
Affairs; Interior & Insular Affairs.

Ron de Lugo (D-V.I.)
Of the Virgin Islands • Elected 1980

Born: August 2, 1930, Englewood, N.J.
Education: Colegio San Jose, attended.
Military Career: Army, 1948-50.
Occupation: Radio journalist.
Family: Wife, Sheila Paieworsky; four children.
Religion: Roman Catholic.
Political Career: V.I. Senate, 1956-66; administrator for St. Croix, 1961; Washington representative for the Virgin Islands, 1968; candidate for governor, 1978.

Capitol Office: 2238 Rayburn House Office Building 20515; 225-1790.
Office Staff: Administrative Assistant, Sheila Ross; Press Secretary, Page Stull; Executive Assistant/Office Manager, Yvonne Greene.
Committees: Interior & Insular Affairs; Public Works & Transportation.

Eni F.H. Faleomavaega
(D-Am. Samoa)
Of American Samoa • Elected 1988
Pronounced EN ee FALL eh oh mavah ENGA

Born: August 15, 1943, Vailoatai, American Samoa.
Education: Brigham Young U., B.A. 1966; U. of Houston, J.D. 1972; U. of California, Berkeley, LL.M. 1973.
Military Career: Army, 1966-69; Army Reserve, 1983-present.
Occupation: Lawyer.
Family: Wife, Hinanui Bambridge Cave; five children.
Religion: Mormon.
Political Career: Democratic candidate for U.S. House delegate, 1984; lieutenant governor, 1985-89.

Capitol Office: 413 Cannon House Office Building 20515; 225-8577.
Office Staff: Executive Assistant, Nancy M. Leong; Public Relations Coordinator, Ali'imau H. Sconlan.
Committees: Foreign Affairs; Interior & Insular Affairs; Merchant Marine & Fisheries.

Jaime B. Fuster (D-P.R.)
Of Puerto Rico • Elected 1984
Pronounced HI may foo STAIR

Born: January 12, 1941, Guayama, Puerto Rico.
Education: Notre Dame U., B.A. 1962; U. of Puerto Rico, J.D. 1965; Columbia U., LL.M. 1966; Harvard U., 1974.
Occupation: Law professor; university administrator; lawyer.
Family: Wife, Mary Jo Zalduondo; two children.
Religion: Roman Catholic.
Political Career: U.S. deputy assistant attorney general, 1980-81.

Capitol Office: 427 Cannon House Office Building 20515; 225-2615.
Office Staff: Administrative Assistant, Carmen Delgado Votaw; Special Assistant/Press Assistant, Ronald Walker; Scheduler, Alba Bernart.
Committees: Foreign Affairs; Interior & Insular Affairs.

Eleanor Holmes Norton
(D-D.C.)
Of Washington • *Elected 1990*

Born: June 13, 1937, Washington, D.C.
Education: Antioch College, B.A. 1960;
Yale U., M.A. 1963; Yale U., LL.B. 1964.
Occupation: Professor of law; lawyer.
Family: Husband, Edward Norton; two
children.
Religion: Episcopalian.
Political Career: No previous office.

Capitol Office: 1631 Longworth House
Office Building 20515; 225-8050.
Office Staff: Administrative Assistant,
Donna Brazile.
Committees: District of Columbia; Post
Office & Civil Service; Public Works &
Transportation.
District of Columbia — The District vote
for George Bush was 14% in 1988.

Appendixes

State Delegations to the 102nd Congress

The list below gives the names of senators and representatives of each state delegation for the 102nd Congress. The senators are listed by seniority and the representatives by district. As of January 18, 1991, there were 56 Democrats and 44 Republicans in the Senate and 267 Democrats, 167 Republicans, and 1 Independent in the House of Representatives.

Alabama
 Howell Heflin (D)
 Richard C. Shelby (D)
 1. Sonny Callahan (R)
 2. Bill Dickinson (R)
 3. Glen Browder (D)
 4. Tom Bevill (D)
 * 5. Bud Cramer (D)
 6. Ben Erdreich (D)
 7. Claude Harris (D)

Alaska
 Ted Stevens (R)
 Frank H. Murkowski (R)
 AL Don Young (R)

American Samoa
 AL Eni F.H. Faleomavaega (D)—
  Non-Voting Delegate.

Arizona
 Dennis DeConcini (D)
 John McCain (R)
 1. John J. Rhodes III (R)
 2. Morris K. Udall (D)
 3. Bob Stump (R)
 4. Jon Kyl (R)
 5. Jim Kolbe (R)

Arkansas
 Dale Bumpers (D)
 David Pryor (D)
 1. Bill Alexander (D)
 2. Ray Thornton (D)
 3. John Paul Hammerschmidt
  (R)
 4. Beryl Anthony Jr. (D)

California
 Alan Cranston (D)
 *John Seymour (R)
 * 1. Frank Riggs (R)
 2. Wally Herger (R)
 3. Robert T. Matsui (D)
 4. Vic Fazio (D)
 5. Nancy Pelosi (D)
 6. Barbara Boxer (D)
 7. George Miller (D)
 8. Ronald V. Dellums (D)
 9. Pete Stark (D)
 10. Don Edwards (D)
 11. Tom Lantos (D)
 12. Tom Campbell (R)
 13. Norman Y. Mineta (D)
 *14. John T. Doolittle (R)
 15. Gary Condit (D)
 16. Leon E. Panetta (D)

*17. Calvin Dooley (D)
18. Richard H. Lehman (D)
19. Robert J. Lagomarsino (R)
20. Bill Thomas (R)
21. Elton Gallegly (R)
22. Carlos J. Moorhead (R)
23. Anthony C. Beilenson (D)
24. Henry A. Waxman (D)
25. Edward R. Roybal (D)
26. Howard L. Berman (D)
27. Mel Levine (D)
28. Julian C. Dixon (D)
*29. Maxine Waters (D)
30. Matthew G. Martinez (D)
31. Mervyn M. Dymally (D)
32. Glenn M. Anderson (D)
33. David Dreier (R)
34. Esteban E. Torres (D)
35. Jerry Lewis (R)
36. George E. Brown Jr. (D)
37. Al McCandless (R)
38. Robert K. Dornan (R)
39. William E. Dannemeyer (R)
40. C. Christopher Cox (R)
41. Bill Lowery (R)
42. Dana Rohrabacher (R)
43. Ron Packard (R)
*44. Randy "Duke" Cunningham (R)
45. Duncan Hunter (R)

Colorado
Tim Wirth (D)
*Hank Brown (R)
1. Patricia Schroeder (D)
2. David E. Skaggs (D)
3. Ben Nighthorse Campbell (D)
* 4. Wayne Allard (R)
5. Joel Hefley (R)

6. Dan Schaefer (R)

Connecticut
Christopher J. Dodd (D)
Joseph I. Lieberman (D)
1. Barbara B. Kennelly (D)
2. Sam Gejdenson (D)
* 3. Rosa DeLauro (D)
4. Christopher Shays (R)
* 5. Gary Franks (R)
6. Nancy L. Johnson (R)

Delaware
William V. Roth Jr. (R)
Joseph R. Biden Jr. (D)
AL Thomas R. Carper (D)

District of Columbia
*AL Eleanor Holmes Norton (D)—
   Non-Voting Delegate.

Florida
Bob Graham (D)
Connie Mack (R)
1. Earl Hutto (D)
* 2. Pete Peterson (D)
3. Charles E. Bennett (D)
4. Craig T. James (R)
5. Bill McCollum (R)
6. Cliff Stearns (R)
7. Sam M. Gibbons (D)
8. C. W. Bill Young (R)
9. Michael Bilirakis (R)
10. Andy Ireland (R)
*11. Jim Bacchus (D)
12. Tom Lewis (R)
13. Porter J. Goss (R)
14. Harry A. Johnston (D)
15. E. Clay Shaw Jr. (R)
16. Lawrence J. Smith (D)

17. William Lehman (D)
18. Ileana Ros-Lehtinen (R)
19. Dante B. Fascell (D)

Georgia
Sam Nunn (D)
Wyche Fowler Jr. (D)
1. Lindsay Thomas (D)
2. Charles Hatcher (D)
3. Richard Ray (D)
4. Ben Jones (D)
5. John Lewis (D)
6. Newt Gingrich (R)
7. George "Buddy" Darden (D)
8. J. Roy Rowland (D)
9. Ed Jenkins (D)
10. Doug Barnard Jr. (D)

Guam
AL Ben Blaz (R)—Non-Voting
Delegate.

Hawaii
Daniel K. Inouye (D)
Daniel K. Akaka (D)
* 1. Neil Abercrombie (D)
2. Patsy T. Mink (D)

Idaho
Steve Symms (R)
*Larry E. Craig (R)
* 1. Larry LaRocco (D)
2. Richard Stallings (D)

Illinois
Alan J. Dixon (D)
Paul Simon (D)
1. Charles A. Hayes (D)
2. Gus Savage (D)
· 3. Marty Russo (D)

4. George E. Sangmeister (D)
5. William O. Lipinski (D)
6. Henry J. Hyde (R)
7. Cardiss Collins (D)
8. Dan Rostenkowski (D)
9. Sidney R. Yates (D)
10. John Porter (R)
11. Frank Annunzio (D)
12. Philip M. Crane (R)
13. Harris W. Fawell (R)
14. Dennis Hastert (R)
15. Edward Madigan (R)
*16. John W. Cox Jr. (D)
17. Lane Evans (D)
18. Robert H. Michel (R)
19. Terry L. Bruce (D)
20. Richard J. Durbin (D)
21. Jerry F. Costello (D)
22. Glenn Poshard (D)

Indiana
Richard G. Lugar (R)
Daniel R. Coats (R)
1. Peter J. Visclosky (D)
2. Philip R. Sharp (D)
* 3. Tim Roemer (D)
4. Jill Long (D)
5. Jim Jontz (D)
6. Dan Burton (R)
7. John T. Myers (R)
8. Frank McCloskey (D)
9. Lee H. Hamilton (D)
10. Andrew Jacobs Jr. (D)

Iowa
Charles E. Grassley (R)
Tom Harkin (D)
1. Jim Leach (R)
* 2. Jim Nussle (R)

* Freshman member

   3. Dave Nagle (D)
   4. Neal Smith (D)
   5. Jim Ross Lightfoot (R)
   6. Fred Grandy (R)

Kansas
  Bob Dole (R)
  Nancy Landon Kassebaum (R)
   1. Pat Roberts (R)
   2. Jim Slattery (D)
   3. Jan Meyers (R)
   4. Dan Glickman (D)
* 5. Dick Nichols (R)

Kentucky
  Wendell H. Ford (D)
  Mitch McConnell (R)
   1. Carroll Hubbard Jr. (D)
   2. William H. Natcher (D)
   3. Romano L. Mazzoli (D)
   4. Jim Bunning (R)
   5. Harold Rogers (R)
   6. Larry J. Hopkins (R)
   7. Carl C. Perkins (D)

Louisiana
  J. Bennett Johnston (D)
  John B. Breaux (D)
   1. Bob Livingston (R)
* 2. William J. Jefferson (D)
   3. W. J. "Billy" Tauzin (D)
   4. Jim McCrery (R)
   5. Jerry Huckaby (D)
   6. Richard H. Baker (R)
   7. Jimmy Hayes (D)
   8. Clyde C. Holloway (R)

Maine
  William S. Cohen (R)
  George J. Mitchell (D)

* 1. Thomas H. Andrews (D)
   2. Olympia J. Snowe (R)

Maryland
  Paul S. Sarbanes (D)
  Barbara A. Mikulski (D)
* 1. Wayne T. Gilchrest (R)
   2. Helen Delich Bentley (R)
   3. Benjamin L. Cardin (D)
   4. Tom McMillen (D)
   5. Steny H. Hoyer (D)
   6. Beverly B. Byron (D)
   7. Kweisi Mfume (D)
   8. Constance A. Morella (R)

Massachusetts
  Edward M. Kennedy (D)
  John Kerry (D)
   1. Silvio O. Conte (R)
   2. Richard E. Neal (D)
   3. Joseph D. Early (D)
   4. Barney Frank (D)
   5. Chester G. Atkins (D)
   6. Nicholas Mavroules (D)
   7. Edward J. Markey (D)
   8. Joseph P. Kennedy II (D)
   9. Joe Moakley (D)
  10. Gerry E. Studds (D)
  11. Brian Donnelly (D)

Michigan
  Donald W. Riegle Jr. (D)
  Carl Levin (D)
   1. John Conyers Jr. (D)
   2. Carl D. Pursell (R)
   3. Howard Wolpe (D)
   4. Fred Upton (R)
   5. Paul B. Henry (R)
   6. Bob Carr (D)

7. Dale E. Kildee (D)
8. Bob Traxler (D)
9. Guy Vander Jagt (R)
*10. Dave Camp (R)
11. Robert W. Davis (R)
12. David E. Bonior (D)
*13. Barbara-Rose Collins (D)
14. Dennis M. Hertel (D)
15. William D. Ford (D)
16. John D. Dingell (D)
17. Sander M. Levin (D)
18. William S. Broomfield (R)

Minnesota
Dave Durenberger (R)
*Paul Wellstone (D)
1. Timothy J. Penny (D)
2. Vin Weber (R)
* 3. Jim Ramstad (R)
4. Bruce F. Vento (D)
5. Martin Olav Sabo (D)
6. Gerry Sikorski (D)
* 7. Collin C. Peterson (D)
8. James L. Oberstar (D)

Mississippi
Thad Cochran (R)
Trent Lott (R)
1. Jamie L. Whitten (D)
2. Mike Espy (D)
3. G. V. "Sonny" Montgomery (D)
4. Mike Parker (D)
5. Gene Taylor (D)

Missouri
John C. Danforth (R)
Christopher S. Bond (R)
1. William L. Clay (D)

* 2. Joan Kelly Horn (D)
3. Richard A. Gephardt (D)
4. Ike Skelton (D)
5. Alan Wheat (D)
6. E. Thomas Coleman (R)
7. Mel Hancock (R)
8. Bill Emerson (R)
9. Harold L. Volkmer (D)

Montana
Max Baucus (D)
Conrad Burns (R)
1. Pat Williams (D)
2. Ron Marlenee (R)

Nebraska
Jim Exon (D)
Bob Kerrey (D)
1. Doug Bereuter (R)
2. Peter Hoagland (D)
* 3. Bill Barrett (R)

Nevada
Harry Reid (D)
Richard H. Bryan (D)
1. James Bilbray (D)
2. Barbara F. Vucanovich (R)

New Hampshire
Warren B. Rudman (R)
*Robert C. Smith (R)
* 1. Bill Zeliff (R)
* 2. Dick Swett (D)

New Jersey
Bill Bradley (D)
Frank R. Lautenberg (D)
* 1. Robert E. Andrews (D)
2. William J. Hughes (D)
3. Frank Pallone Jr. (D)

* Freshman member

4. Christopher H. Smith (R)
5. Marge Roukema (R)
6. Bernard J. Dwyer (D)
7. Matthew J. Rinaldo (R)
8. Robert A. Roe (D)
9. Robert G. Torricelli (D)
10. Donald M. Payne (D)
11. Dean A. Gallo (R)
*12. Dick Zimmer (R)
13. H. James Saxton (R)
14. Frank J. Guarini (D)

New Mexico
 Pete V. Domenici (R)
 Jeff Bingaman (D)
1. Steven H. Schiff (R)
2. Joe Skeen (R)
3. Bill Richardson (D)

New York
 Daniel Patrick Moynihan (D)
 Alfonse M. D'Amato (R)
1. George J. Hochbrueckner (D)
2. Thomas J. Downey (D)
3. Robert J. Mrazek (D)
4. Norman F. Lent (R)
5. Raymond J. McGrath (R)
6. Floyd H. Flake (D)
7. Gary L. Ackerman (D)
8. James H. Scheuer (D)
9. Thomas J. Manton (D)
10. Charles E. Schumer (D)
11. Ed Towns (D)
12. Major R. Owens (D)
13. Stephen J. Solarz (D)
14. Susan Molinari (R)
15. Bill Green (R)
16. Charles B. Rangel (D)
17. Ted Weiss (D)

18. Jose E. Serrano (D)
19. Eliot L. Engel (D)
20. Nita M. Lowey (D)
21. Hamilton Fish Jr. (R)
22. Benjamin A. Gilman (R)
23. Michael R. McNulty (D)
24. Gerald B. H. Solomon (R)
25. Sherwood Boehlert (R)
26. David O'B. Martin (R)
27. James T. Walsh (R)
28. Matthew F. McHugh (D)
29. Frank Horton (R)
30. Louise M. Slaughter (D)
31. Bill Paxon (R)
32. John J. LaFalce (D)
33. Henry J. Nowak (D)
34. Amo Houghton (R)

North Carolina
 Jesse Helms (R)
 Terry Sanford (D)
1. Walter B. Jones (D)
2. Tim Valentine (D)
3. H. Martin Lancaster (D)
4. David E. Price (D)
5. Stephen L. Neal (D)
6. Howard Coble (R)
7. Charlie Rose (D)
8. W. G. "Bill" Hefner (D)
9. Alex McMillan (R)
10. Cass Ballenger (R)
*11. Charles H. Taylor (R)

North Dakota
 Quentin N. Burdick (D)
 Kent Conrad (D)
 AL Byron L. Dorgan (D)

Ohio
 John Glenn (D)
 Howard M. Metzenbaum (D)
* 1. Charles Luken (D)
 2. Bill Gradison (R)
 3. Tony P. Hall (D)
 4. Michael G. Oxley (R)
 5. Paul E. Gillmor (R)
 6. Bob McEwen (R)
* 7. David L. Hobson (R)
* 8. John A. Boehner (R)
 9. Marcy Kaptur (D)
 10. Clarence E. Miller (R)
 11. Dennis E. Eckart (D)
 12. John R. Kasich (R)
 13. Don J. Pease (D)
 14. Thomas C. Sawyer (D)
 15. Chalmers P. Wylie (R)
 16. Ralph Regula (R)
 17. James A. Traficant Jr. (D)
 18. Doug Applegate (D)
 19. Edward F. Feighan (D)
 20. Mary Rose Oakar (D)
 21. Louis Stokes (D)

Oklahoma
 David L. Boren (D)
 Don Nickles (R)
 1. James M. Inhofe (R)
 2. Mike Synar (D)
* 3. Bill Brewster (D)
 4. Dave McCurdy (D)
 5. Mickey Edwards (R)
 6. Glenn English (D)

Oregon
 Mark O. Hatfield (R)
 Bob Packwood (R)
 1. Les AuCoin (D)

 2. Bob Smith (R)
 3. Ron Wyden (D)
 4. Peter A. DeFazio (D)
* 5. Mike Kopetski (D)

Pennsylvania
 John Heinz (R)
 Arlen Specter (R)
 1. Thomas M. Foglietta (D)
 2. William H. Gray III (D)
 3. Robert A. Borski (D)
 4. Joe Kolter (D)
 5. Richard T. Schulze (R)
 6. Gus Yatron (D)
 7. Curt Weldon (R)
 8. Peter H. Kostmayer (D)
 9. Bud Shuster (R)
 10. Joseph M. McDade (R)
 11. Paul E. Kanjorski (D)
 12. John P. Murtha (D)
 13. Lawrence Coughlin (R)
 14. William J. Coyne (D)
 15. Don Ritter (R)
 16. Robert S. Walker (R)
 17. George W. Gekas (R)
*18. Rick Santorum (R)
 19. Bill Goodling (R)
 20. Joseph M. Gaydos (D)
 21. Tom Ridge (R)
 22. Austin J. Murphy (D)
 23. William F. Clinger Jr. (R)

Puerto Rico
 AL Jaime B. Fuster (D)—Resident
  Commissioner.

Rhode Island
 Claiborne Pell (D)
 John H. Chafee (R)

* Freshman member

1. Ronald K. Machtley (R)
* 2. John R. Reed (D)

South Carolina
Strom Thurmond (R)
Ernest F. Hollings (D)
1. Arthur Ravenel Jr. (R)
2. Floyd D. Spence (R)
3. Butler Derrick (D)
4. Liz J. Patterson (D)
5. John M. Spratt Jr. (D)
6. Robin Tallon (D)

South Dakota
Larry Pressler (R)
Tom Daschle (D)
AL Tim Johnson (D)

Tennessee
Jim Sasser (D)
Al Gore (D)
1. James H. Quillen (R)
2. John J. "Jimmy" Duncan Jr. (R)
3. Marilyn Lloyd (D)
4. Jim Cooper (D)
5. Bob Clement (D)
6. Bart Gordon (D)
7. Don Sundquist (R)
8. John Tanner (D)
9. Harold E. Ford (D)

Texas
Lloyd Bentsen (D)
Phil Gramm (R)
1. Jim Chapman (D)
2. Charles Wilson (D)
3. Steve Bartlett (R)
4. Ralph M. Hall (D)
5. John Bryant (D)

6. Joe L. Barton (R)
7. Bill Archer (R)
8. Jack Fields (R)
9. Jack Brooks (D)
10. J. J. "Jake" Pickle (D)
*11. Chet Edwards (D)
12. Pete Geren (D)
13. Bill Sarpalius (D)
14. Greg Laughlin (D)
15. E. "Kika" de la Garza (D)
16. Ronald D. Coleman (D)
17. Charles W. Stenholm (D)
18. Craig Washington (D)
19. Larry Combest (R)
20. Henry B. Gonzalez (D)
21. Lamar Smith (R)
22. Tom DeLay (R)
23. Albert G. Bustamante (D)
24. Martin Frost (D)
25. Michael A. Andrews (D)
26. Dick Armey (R)
27. Solomon P. Ortiz (D)

Utah
Jake Garn (R)
Orrin G. Hatch (R)
1. James V. Hansen (R)
2. Wayne Owens (D)
* 3. Bill Orton (D)

Vermont
Patrick J. Leahy (D)
James M. Jeffords (R)
*AL Bernard Sanders (I)

Virgin Islands
AL Ron de Lugo (D)—Non-Voting Delegate.

Virginia
John W. Warner (R)
Charles S. Robb (D)
  1. Herbert H. Bateman (R)
  2. Owen B. Pickett (D)
  3. Thomas J. Bliley Jr. (R)
  4. Norman Sisisky (D)
  5. Lewis F. Payne Jr. (D)
  6. Jim Olin (D)
  7. D. French Slaughter Jr. (R)
* 8. James P. Moran Jr. (D)
  9. Rick Boucher (D)
 10. Frank R. Wolf (R)

Washington
Brock Adams (D)
Slade Gorton (R)
  1. John Miller (R)
  2. Al Swift (D)
  3. Jolene Unsoeld (D)
  4. Sid Morrison (R)
  5. Thomas S. Foley (D)
  6. Norm Dicks (D)
  7. Jim McDermott (D)
  8. Rod Chandler (R)

  * Freshman member

West Virginia
Robert C. Byrd (D)
John D. Rockefeller IV (D)
  1. Alan B. Mollohan (D)
  2. Harley O. Staggers Jr. (D)
  3. Bob Wise (D)
  4. Nick J. Rahall II (D)

Wisconsin
Bob Kasten (R)
Herb Kohl (D)
  1. Les Aspin (D)
* 2. Scott L. Klug (R)
  3. Steve Gunderson (R)
  4. Gerald D. Kleczka (D)
  5. Jim Moody (D)
  6. Thomas E. Petri (R)
  7. David R. Obey (D)
  8. Toby Roth (R)
  9. F. James Sensenbrenner Jr. (R)

Wyoming
Malcolm Wallop (R)
Alan K. Simpson (R)
AL Craig Thomas (R)

Congressional Leadership

Senate

Democrats

President Pro Tempore — Robert C. Byrd, W. Va.	224-2848
Majority Leader — George J. Mitchell, Maine	224-5556
Majority Whip — Wendell H. Ford, Ky.	224-2158
Conference Chairman — George J. Mitchell, Maine	224-5556
Conference Secretary — David Pryor, Ark.	224-3735
Policy Committee Chairman — George J. Mitchell, Maine	224-5556
Policy Committee Co-Chairman — Tom Daschle, S.D.	224-5551
Steering Committee Chairman — Daniel K. Inouye, Hawaii	224-3735
Democratic Senatorial Campaign Committee Chairmen —	
Charles S. Robb, Va.	224-2447
Phil Gramm, Texas	224-2943

Republicans

President — Dan Quayle	224-8391
Minority Leader — Bob Dole, Kan.	224-3135
Assistant Minority Leader — Alan K. Simpson, Wyo.	224-2708
Conference Chairman — Thad Cochran, Miss.	224-2764
Conference Secretary — Bob Kasten, Wis.	224-2764
Policy Committee Chairman — Don Nickles, Okla.	224-2946
Committee on Committees Chairman — Trent Lott, Miss.	224-5842
National Republican Senatorial Committee Chairman —	
Phil Gramm, Texas	224-6000

House

Democrats

Speaker of the House — Thomas S. Foley, Wash.	225-5604
Majority Leader — Richard A. Gephardt, Mo.	225-0100
Majority Whip — William H. Gray III, Pa.	225-3130

Caucus Chairman — Steny H. Hoyer, Md.   226-3210
Caucus Vice Chairman — Vic Fazio, Calif.   226-3210
Chief Deputy Whip — David E. Bonior, Mich.   225-0080
Steering and Policy Committee Chairman —
    Thomas S. Foley, Wash.   225-8550
Democratic Congressional Campaign Committee Chairman —
    Vic Fazio, Calif.   863-1500

Republicans
Committee on Committees Chairman —
    Robert H. Michel, Ill.   225-0600
Minority Leader — Robert H. Michel, Ill.   225-0600
Minority Whip — Newt Gingrich, Ga.   225-0197
Conference Chairman — Jerry Lewis, Calif.   225-5107
Conference Vice Chairman — Bill McCollum, Fla.   225-5107
Conference Secretary — Vin Weber, Minn.   225-5107
Chief Deputy Whips — Steve Gunderson, Wis.
    Robert S. Walker, Pa.   225-0197
Policy Committee Chairman — Mickey Edwards, Okla.   225-6168
Research Committee Chairman — Duncan Hunter, Calif.   225-0871
National Republican Congressional Committee Chairman —
    Guy Vander Jagt, Mich.   479-7000

Senate Committees

The standing committees of the U.S. Senate are listed below in alphabetical order; also listed is the Select Ethics Committee. The listing includes the room number, zip code, and telephone number for each full committee. Membership is given in order or seniority on the committee. Address abbreviations used are as follows: D (Dirksen Senate Office Bldg.), SH (Hart Senate Office Bldg.), SR (Russell Senate Office Bldg.), and CAP (Capitol). The telephone area code for Washington is 202.

Agriculture, Nutrition & Forestry

SR 328A 20510; 224-2035

Patrick J. Leahy, D-Vt., Chairman

Democrats	Republicans
David Pryor, Ark.	Richard G. Lugar, Ind.
David Boren, Okla.	Bob Dole, Kan.
Howell Heflin, Ala.	Jesse Helms, N.C.
Tom Harkin, Iowa	Thad Cochran, Miss.
Kent Conrad, N.D.	Mitch McConnell, Ky.
Wyche Fowler Jr., Ga.	Christopher S. Bond, Mo.
Tom Daschle, S.D.	Slade Gorton, Wash.
Max Baucus, Mont.	Larry E. Craig, Idaho
Bob Kerrey, Neb.	John Seymour, Calif.

Appropriations

CAP-S 128 20510; 224-3471

Robert C. Byrd, D-W.Va., Chairman

Democrats	Republicans
Daniel K. Inouye, Hawaii	Mark O. Hatfield, Ore.
Ernest F. Hollings, S.C.	Ted Stevens, Alaska
J. Bennett Johnston, La.	Jake Garn, Utah
Quentin N. Burdick, N.D.	Thad Cochran, Miss.
Patrick J. Leahy, Vt.	Bob Kasten, Wis.
Jim Sasser, Tenn.	Alfonse M. D'Amato, N.Y.
Dennis DeConcini, Ariz.	Warren B. Rudman, N.H.
Dale Bumpers, Ark.	Arlen Specter, Pa.

Appropriations (Continued)

Frank R. Lautenberg, N.J.	Pete V. Domenici, N.M.
Tom Harkin, Iowa	Charles E. Grassley, Iowa
Barbara A. Mikulski, Md.	Don Nickles, Okla.
Harry Reid, Nev.	Phil Gramm, Texas
Brock Adams, Wash.	Vacancy
Wyche Fowler Jr., Ga.	
Bob Kerrey, Neb.	

Armed Services   SR 228 20510; 224-3871

Sam Nunn, D-Ga., Chairman

Democrats	Republicans
Jim Exon, Neb.	John W. Warner, Va.
Carl Levin, Mich.	Strom Thurmond, S.C.
Edward M. Kennedy, Mass.	William S. Cohen, Maine
Jeff Bingaman, N.M.	John McCain, Ariz.
Alan J. Dixon, Ill.	Malcolm Wallop, Wyo.
John Glenn, Ohio	Slade Gorton, Wash.
Al Gore, Tenn.	Trent Lott, Miss.
Tim Wirth, Colo.	Daniel R. Coats, Ind.
Richard C. Shelby, Ala.	Robert C. Smith, N.H.
Robert C. Byrd, W.Va.	

Banking, Housing & Urban Affairs   SD 534 20510; 224-7391

Donald W. Riegle Jr., D-Mich., Chairman

Democrats	Republicans
Alan Cranston, Calif.	Jake Garn, Utah
Paul S. Sarbanes, Md.	John Heinz, Pa.
Christopher J. Dodd, Conn.	Alfonse M. D'Amato, N.Y.
Alan J. Dixon, Ill.	Phil Gramm, Texas
Jim Sasser, Tenn.	Christopher S. Bond, Mo.
Terry Sanford, N.C.	Connie Mack, Fla.
Richard C. Shelby, Ala.	William V. Roth Jr., Del.
Bob Graham, Fla.	Nancy Landon Kassebaum, Kan.
Tim Wirth, Colo.	Larry Pressler, S.D.
John Kerry, Mass.	
Richard H. Bryan, Nev.	

Budget

SD 621 20510; 224 0612

Jim Sasser, D-Tenn., Chairman

Democrats	Republicans
Ernest F. Hollings, S.C.	Pete V. Domenici, N.M.
J. Bennett Johnston, La.	Steve Symms, Idaho
Donald W. Riegle Jr., Mich.	Charles E. Grassley, Iowa
Jim Exon, Neb.	Bob Kasten, Wis.
Frank R. Lautenberg, N.J.	Don Nickles, Okla.
Paul Simon, Ill.	Warren B. Rudman, N.H.
Terry Sanford, N.C.	Phil Gramm, Texas
Tim Wirth, Colo.	Christopher S. Bond, Mo.
Wyche Fowler Jr., Ga.	
Kent Conrad, N.D.	
Christopher J. Dodd, Conn.	
Charles S. Robb, Va.	

Commerce, Science & Transportation

SD 508 20510; 224-5115

Ernest F. Hollings, D-S.C., Chairman

Democrats	Republicans
Daniel K. Inouye, Hawaii	John C. Danforth, Mo.
Wendell H. Ford, Ky.	Bob Packwood, Ore.
Jim Exon, Neb.	Larry Pressler, S.D.
Al Gore, Tenn.	Ted Stevens, Alaska
John D. Rockefeller IV, W.Va.	Bob Kasten, Wis.
Lloyd Bentsen, Texas	John McCain, Ariz.
John Kerry, Mass.	Conrad Burns, Mont.
John B. Breaux, La.	Slade Gorton, Wash.
Richard H. Bryan, Nev.	Trent Lott, Miss.
Charles S. Robb, Va.	

Energy & Natural Resources

SD 364 20510; 224-4971

J. Bennett Johnston, D-La., Chairman

Democrats	Republicans
Dale Bumpers, Ark.	Malcolm Wallop, Wyo.
Wendell H. Ford, Ky.	Mark O. Hatfield, Ore.
Bill Bradley, N.J.	Pete V. Domenici, N.M.

Energy and Natural Resources (Continued)

Jeff Bingaman, N.M.
Tim Wirth, Colo.
Kent Conrad, N.D.
Daniel K. Akaka, Hawaii
Wyche Fowler Jr., Ga.
Richard C. Shelby, Ala.
Paul Wellstone, Minn.

Frank H. Murkowski, Alaska
Don Nickles, Okla.
Conrad Burns, Mont.
Jake Garn, Utah
Larry E. Craig, Idaho
John Seymour, Calif.

Environment & Public Works   SD 458 20510; 224-6176

Quentin N. Burdick, D-N.D., Chairman

Democrats	Republicans
Daniel Patrick Moynihan, N.Y.	John H. Chafee, R.I.
George J. Mitchell, Maine	Alan K. Simpson, Wyo.
Max Baucus, Mont.	Steve Symms, Idaho
Frank R. Lautenberg, N.J.	Dave Durenberger, Minn.
Harry Reid, Nev.	John W. Warner, Va.
Bob Graham, Fla.	James M. Jeffords, Vt.
Joseph I. Lieberman, Conn.	Robert C. Smith, N.H.
Howard M. Metzenbaum, Ohio	

Ethics   SH 220 20510; 224-2981

Howell Heflin, D-Ala., Chairman

Democrats	Republicans
David Pryor, Ark.	Warren B. Rudman, N.H.
Terry Sanford, N.C.	Jesse Helms, N.C.
	Trent Lott, Miss.

Finance   SD 205 20510; 224-4515

Lloyd Bentsen, D-Texas, Chairman

Democrats	Republicans
Daniel Patrick Moynihan, N.Y.	Bob Packwood, Ore.
Max Baucus, Mont.	Bob Dole, Kan.
David Boren, Okla.	William V. Roth Jr., Del.
Bill Bradley, N.J.	John C. Danforth, Mo.
George J. Mitchell, Maine	John H. Chafee, R.I.

David Pryor, Ark
Donald W. Riegle Jr., Mich.
John D. Rockefeller IV, W.Va.
Tom Daschle, S.D.
John B. Breaux, La.

John Heinz, Pa.
Dave Durenberger, Minn.
Steve Symms, Idaho
Vacancy

Foreign Relations

SD 446 20510; 224-4651

Claiborne Pell, D-R.I., Chairman

Democrats	Republicans
Joseph R. Biden Jr., Del.	Jesse Helms, N.C.
Paul S. Sarbanes, Md.	Richard G. Lugar, Ind.
Alan Cranston, Calif.	Nancy Landon Kassebaum, Kan.
Christopher J. Dodd, Conn.	Larry Pressler, S.D.
John Kerry, Mass.	Frank H. Murkowski, Alaska
Paul Simon, Ill.	Mitch McConnell, Ky.
Terry Sanford, N.C.	Connie Mack, Fla.
Daniel Patrick Moynihan, N.Y.	Hank Brown, Colo.
Charles S. Robb, Va.	

Governmental Affairs

SD 340 20510; 224-4751

John Glenn, D-Ohio, Chairman

Democrats	Republicans
Sam Nunn, Ga.	William V. Roth Jr., Del.
Carl Levin, Mich.	Ted Stevens, Alaska
Jim Sasser, Tenn.	William S. Cohen, Maine
David Pryor, Ark.	Warren B. Rudman, N.H.
Herb Kohl, Wis.	John Heinz, Pa.
Joseph I. Lieberman, Conn.	Vacancy
Daniel K. Akaka, Hawaii	

Judiciary

SD 224 20510; 224-5225

Joseph R. Biden Jr., D-Del., Chairman

Democrats	Republicans
Edward M. Kennedy, Mass.	Strom Thurmond, S.C.
Howard M. Metzenbaum, Ohio	Orrin G. Hatch, Utah
Dennis DeConcini, Ariz.	Alan K. Simpson, Wyo.

Judiciary (Continued)

Patrick J. Leahy, Vt.	Charles E. Grassley, Iowa
Howell Heflin, Ala.	Arlen Specter, Pa.
Paul Simon, Ill.	Hank Brown, Colo.
Herb Kohl, Wis.	

Labor & Human Resources   SD 428 20510; 224-5375

Edward M. Kennedy, D-Mass., Chairman

Democrats	Republicans
Claiborne Pell, R.I.	Strom Thurmond, S.C.
Howard M. Metzenbaum, Ohio	Nancy Landon Kassebaum, Kan.
Christopher J. Dodd, Conn.	James M. Jeffords, Vt.
Paul Simon, Ill.	Daniel R. Coats, Ind.
Tom Harkin, Iowa	Strom Thurmond, S.C.
Brock Adams, Wash.	Dave Durenberger, Minn.
Barbara A. Mikulski, Md.	Thad Cochran, Miss.
Jeff Bingaman, N.M.	
Paul Wellstone, Minn.	

Rules & Administration   SR 305 20510; 224-6352

Wendell H. Ford, D-Ky., Chairman

Democrats	Republicans
Claiborne Pell, R.I.	Ted Stevens, Alaska
Robert C. Byrd, W.Va.	Mark O. Hatfield, Ore.
Daniel K. Inouye, Hawaii	Jesse Helms, N.C.
Dennis DeConcini, Ariz.	Bob Dole, Kan.
Al Gore, Tenn.	Jake Garn, Utah
Daniel Patrick Moynihan, N.Y.	Mitch McConnell, Ky.
Christopher J. Dodd, Conn.	
Brock Adams, Wash.	

Small Business   SR 428A 20510; 224-9126

Dale Bumpers, D-Ark., Chairman

Democrats	Republicans
Sam Nunn, Ga.	Bob Kasten, Wis.
Max Baucus, Mont.	Larry Pressler, S.D.

Carl Levin, Mich.
Alan J. Dixon, Ill.
David Boren, Okla.
Tom Harkin, Iowa
John Kerry, Mass.
Barbara A. Mikulski, Md.
Joseph I. Lieberman, Conn.

Malcolm Wallop, Wyo.
Christopher S. Bond, Mo.
Charles E. Grassley, Iowa
Trent Lott, Miss.
Conrad Burns, Mont.
Ted Stevens, Alaska

Veterans' Affairs

SR 414 20510; 224-9126

Alan Cranston, D-Calif., Chairman

Democrats	Republicans
Dennis DeConcini, Ariz.	Frank H. Murkowski, Alaska
George J. Mitchell, Maine	Alan K. Simpson, Wyo.
John D. Rockefeller IV, W.Va.	Strom Thurmond, S.C.
Bob Graham, Fla.	Arlen Specter, Pa.
Daniel K. Akaka, Hawaii	James M. Jeffords, Vt.

House Committees

The standing committees of the U.S. House of Representatives are listed below in alphabetical order; also listed is the Select Intelligence Committee. The listing includes the room number, zip code, and telephone number for each full committee. Address abbreviations used are as follows: CHOB (Cannon House Office Bldg.), LHOB (Longworth House Office Bldg.), RHOB (Rayburn House Office Bldg.), HOB Annex #1 (House Office Bldg. at 300 New Jersey Ave. S.E), HOB Annex #2 (House Office Bldg. at 2nd and D Sts. S.W.), and CAP (Capitol). The telephone area code for Washington is 202.

Agriculture   1301 LHOB 20515; 225-2171
E. de la Garza, D-Texas, Chairman

Democrats	Republicans
Walter B. Jones, N.C.	Edward Madigan, Ill.
George E. Brown Jr., Calif.	Tom Coleman, Mo.
Charlie Rose, N.C.	Ron Marlenee, Mont.
Glenn English, Okla.	Larry J. Hopkins, Ky.
Leon E. Panetta, Calif.	Pat Roberts, Kan.
Jerry Huckaby, La.	Bill Emerson, Mo.
Dan Glickman, Kan.	Sid Morrison, Wash.
Charles W. Stenholm, Texas	Steve Gunderson, Wis.
Harold L. Volkmer, Mo.	Tom Lewis, Fla.
Charles Hatcher, Ga.	Bob Smith, Ore.
Robin Tallon, S.C.	Larry Combest, Texas
Harley O. Staggers Jr., W.Va.	Wally Herger, Calif.
Jim Olin, Va.	James T. Walsh, N.Y.
Timothy J. Penny, Minn.	Dave Camp, Mich.
Richard Stallings, Idaho	Wayne Allard, Colo.
Dave Nagle, Iowa	Bill Barrett, Neb.
Jim Jontz, Ind.	Jim Nussle, Iowa
Tim Johnson, S.D.	John A. Boehner, Ohio
Ben Nighthorse Campbell, Colo.	
Mike Espy, Miss.	

Agriculture (Continued)

Bill Sarpalius, Texas
Jill Long, Ind.
Gary Condit, Calif.
Calvin Dooley, Calif.
Mike Kopetski, Ore.
Collin C. Peterson, Minn.

Appropriations

CAP-H 218; 225-2771

Jamie L. Whitten, D-Miss., Chairman

Democrats	Republicans
William H. Natcher, Ky.	Silvio O. Conte, Mass.
Neal Smith, Iowa	Joseph M. McDade, Pa.
Sidney R. Yates, Ill.	John T. Myers, Ind.
David R. Obey, Wis.	Clarence E. Miller, Ohio
Edward R. Roybal, Calif.	Lawrence Coughlin, Pa.
Louis Stokes, Ohio	C.W. Bill Young, Fla.
Tom Bevill, Ala.	Ralph Regula, Ohio
Bill Alexander, Ark.	Carl D. Pursell, Mich.
John P. Murtha, Pa.	Mickey Edwards, Okla.
Bob Traxler, Mich.	Robert L. Livingston, La.
Joseph D. Early, Mass.	Bill Green, N.Y.
Charles Wilson, Texas	Jerry Lewis, Calif.
Norm Dicks, Wash.	John Porter, Ill.
Matthew F. McHugh, N.Y.	Harold Rogers, Ky.
William Lehman, Fla.	Joe Skeen, N.M.
Martin Olav Sabo, Minn.	Frank R. Wolf, Va.
Julian C. Dixon, Calif.	Bill Lowery, Calif.
Vic Fazio, Calif.	Vin Weber, Minn.
W.G. Hefner, N.C.	Tom DeLay, Texas
Les AuCoin, Ore.	Jim Kolbe, Ariz.
William H. Gray III, Pa.	Dean A. Gallo, N.J.
Bernard J. Dwyer, N.J.	Barbara F. Vucanovich, Nev.
Steny H. Hoyer, Md.	
Bob Carr, Mich.	
Robert J. Mrazek, N.Y.	
Richard J. Durbin, Ill.	
Ronald D. Coleman, Texas	

Alan B. Mollohan, W.Va.
Lindsay Thomas, Ga.
Chester G. Atkins, Mass.
Jim Chapman, Texas
Marcy Kaptur, Ohio
Lawrence J. Smith, Fla.
David E. Skaggs, Colo.
David Price, N.C.
Nancy Pelosi, Calif.

Armed Services

2120 RHOB 20515; 225-4151

Les Aspin, D-Wis., Chairman

Democrats	Republicans
Charles E. Bennett, Fla.	Bill Dickinson, Ala.
G.V. Montgomery, Miss.	Floyd D. Spence, S.C.
Ronald V. Dellums, Calif.	Bob Stump, Ariz.
Patricia Schroeder, Colo.	Larry J. Hopkins, Ky.
Beverly B. Byron, Md.	Robert W. Davis, Mich.
Nicholas Mavroules, Mass.	Duncan Hunter, Calif.
Earl Hutto, Fla.	David O'B. Martin, N.Y.
Ike Skelton, Mo.	John R. Kasich, Ohio
Dave McCurdy, Okla.	Herbert H. Bateman, Va.
Thomas M. Foglietta, Pa.	Ben Blaz, Guam
Dennis M. Hertel, Mich.	Andy Ireland, Fla.
Marilyn Lloyd, Tenn.	James V. Hansen, Utah
Norman Sisisky, Va.	Curt Weldon, Pa.
Richard Ray, Ga.	Jon Kyl, Ariz.
John M. Spratt Jr., S.C.	Arthur Ravenel Jr., S.C.
Frank McCloskey, Ind.	Robert K. Dornan, Calif.
Solomon P. Ortiz, Texas	Joel Hefley, Colo.
George Darden, Ga.	Jim McCrery, La.
Albert G. Bustamante, Texas	Ronald K. Machtley, R.I.
Barbara Boxer, Calif.	H. James Saxton, N.J.
George J. Hochbrueckner, N.Y.	Randy Cunningham, Calif.
Owen B. Pickett, Va.	Gary Franks, Conn.
H. Martin Lancaster, N.C.	
Lane Evans, Ill.	
James Bilbray, Nev.	

Armed Services (Continued)

John Tanner, Tenn.
Michael R. McNulty, N.Y.
Glen Browder, Ala.
Gene Taylor, Miss.
Neil Abercrombie, Hawaii
Thomas H. Andrews, Maine
Chet Edwards, Texas

Banking, Finance & Urban Affairs   2129 RHOB 20515; 225-4247

Henry B. Gonzalez, D-Texas, Chairman

Democrats	Republicans
Frank Annunzio, Ill.	Chalmers P. Wylie, Ohio
Stephen L. Neal, N.C.	Jim Leach, Iowa
Carroll Hubbard Jr., Ky.	Bill McCollum, Fla.
John J. LaFalce, N.Y.	Marge Roukema, N.J.
Mary Rose Oakar, Ohio	Doug Bereuter, Neb.
Bruce F. Vento, Minn.	Tom Ridge, Pa.
Doug Barnard Jr., Ga.	Steve Bartlett, Texas
Charles E. Schumer, N.Y.	Toby Roth, Wis.
Barney Frank, Mass.	Al McCandless, Calif.
Ben Erdreich, Ala.	Richard H. Baker, La.
Thomas R. Carper, Del.	Cliff Stearns, Fla.
Esteban E. Torres, Calif.	Paul E. Gillmor, Ohio
Gerald D. Kleczka, Wis.	Bill Paxon, N.Y.
Paul E. Kanjorski, Pa.	John J. Duncan Jr., Tenn.
Liz J. Patterson, S.C.	Tom Campbell, Calif.
Joseph P. Kennedy II, Mass.	Mel Hancock, Mo.
Floyd H. Flake, N.Y.	Frank Riggs, Calif.
Kweisi Mfume, Md.	Jim Nussle, Iowa
Peter Hoagland, Neb.	Vacancy
Richard E. Neal, Mass.	Vacancy
Charles Luken, Ohio	
Maxine Waters, Calif.	**Independent**
Larry LaRocco, Idaho	Bernard Sanders, Vt.
Bill Orton, Utah	
Jim Bacchus, Fla.	

James P. Moran Jr., Va.
John W. Cox Jr., Ill.
Ted Weiss, N.Y.
Jim Slattery, Kan.
Gary L. Ackerman, N.Y.

Budget   214 HOB1 20515; 225-7290

Leon E. Panetta, D-Calif., Chairman

Democrats	Republicans
Richard A. Gephardt, Mo.	Bill Gradison, Ohio
James L. Oberstar, Minn.	Alex McMillan, N.C.
Frank J. Guarini, N.J.	Bill Thomas, Calif.
Richard J. Durbin, Ill.	Harold Rogers, Ky.
Mike Espy, Miss.	Dick Armey, Texas
Dale E. Kildee, Mich.	Amo Houghton, N.Y.
Anthony C. Beilenson, Calif.	Jim McCrery, La.
Jerry Huckaby, La.	John R. Kasich, Ohio
Martin Olav Sabo, Minn.	Dean A. Gallo, N.J.
Bernard J. Dwyer, N.J.	Helen Delich Bentley, Md.
Howard L. Berman, Calif.	William E. Dannemeyer, Calif.
Bob Wise, W.Va.	John Miller, Wash.
John Bryant, Texas	Christopher Shays, Conn.
John M. Spratt Jr., S.C.	Rick Santorum, Pa.
Don J. Pease, Ohio	
Charles W. Stenholm, Texas	
Robert T. Matsui, Calif.	
Barney Frank, Mass.	
Jim Cooper, Tenn.	
Louise M. Slaughter, N.Y.	
Lewis F. Payne Jr., Va.	
Mike Parker, Miss.	

District of Columbia   1310 LHOB 20515; 225-4457

Ronald V. Dellums, D-Calif., Chairman

Democrats	Republicans
Pete Stark, Calif.	Thomas J. Bliley Jr., Va.
William H. Gray III, Pa.	Larry Combest, Texas

District of Columbia (Continued)

Mervyn M. Dymally, Calif.
Alan Wheat, Mo.
Jim McDermott, Wash.
Eleanor Holmes Norton, D.C.
Vacancy

Dana Rohrabacher, Calif.
Vacancy

Education & Labor   2181 RHOB 20515; 225-4527

William D. Ford, D-Mich., Chairman

Democrats	Republicans
Joseph M. Gaydos, Pa.	Bill Goodling, Pa.
William L. Clay, Mo.	Tom Coleman, Mo.
George Miller, Calif.	Tom Petri, Wis.
Austin J. Murphy, Pa.	Marge Roukema, N.J.
Dale E. Kildee, Mich.	Steve Gunderson, Wis.
Pat Williams, Mont.	Steve Bartlett, Texas
Matthew G. Martinez, Calif.	Dick Armey, Texas
Major R. Owens, N.Y.	Harris W. Fawell, Ill.
Charles A. Hayes, Ill.	Paul B. Henry, Mich.
Carl C. Perkins, Ky.	Cass Ballenger, N.C.
Tom Sawyer, Ohio	Susan Molinari, N.Y.
Donald M. Payne, N.J.	Bill Barrett, Neb.
Nita M. Lowey, N.Y.	John A. Boehner, Ohio
Jolene Unsoeld, Wash.	Scott L. Klug, Wis.
Craig Washington, Texas	
Jose E. Serrano, N.Y.	
Patsy T. Mink, Hawaii	
Robert E. Andrews, N.J.	
William J. Jefferson, La.	
John F. Reed, R.I.	
Tim Roemer, Ind.	
Peter J. Visclosky, Ind.	
Ron de Lugo, V.I.	
Jaime B. Fuster, P.R.	

Energy & Commerce

2125 RHOB 20515; 225-2927

John D. Dingell, D-Mich., Chairman

Democrats	Republicans
James H. Scheuer, N.Y.	Norman F. Lent, N.Y.
Henry A. Waxman, Calif.	Edward Madigan, Ill.
Philip R. Sharp, Ind.	Carlos J. Moorhead, Calif.
Edward J. Markey, Mass.	Matthew J. Rinaldo, N.J.
Al Swift, Wash.	William E. Dannemeyer, Calif.
Cardiss Collins, Ill.	Don Ritter, Pa.
Mike Synar, Okla.	Thomas J. Bliley Jr., Va.
W.J. Tauzin, La.	Jack Fields, Texas
Ron Wyden, Ore.	Michael G. Oxley, Ohio
Ralph M. Hall, Texas	Michael Bilirakis, Fla.
Dennis E. Eckart, Ohio	Dan Schaefer, Colo.
Bill Richardson, N.M.	Joe L. Barton, Texas
Jim Slattery, Kan.	Sonny Callahan, Ala.
Gerry Sikorski, Minn.	Alex McMillan, N.C.
John Bryant, Texas	Dennis Hastert, Ill.
Rick Boucher, Va.	Clyde C. Holloway, La.
Jim Cooper, Tenn.	
Terry L. Bruce, Ill.	
J. Roy Rowland, Ga.	
Thomas J. Manton, N.Y.	
Edolphus Towns, N.Y.	
Tom McMillen, Md.	
Gerry E. Studds, Mass.	
Peter H. Kostmayer, Pa.	
Richard H. Lehman, Calif.	
Claude Harris, Ala.	

Foreign Affairs

2170 RHOB 20515; 225-5021

Dante B. Fascell, D-Fla., Chairman

Democrats	Republicans
Lee H. Hamilton, Ind.	William S. Broomfield, Mich.
Gus Yatron, Pa.	Benjamin A. Gilman, N.Y.
Stephen J. Solarz, N.Y.	Robert J. Lagomarsino, Calif.
Gerry E. Studds, Mass.	Bill Goodling, Pa.

Foreign Affairs (Continued)

Howard Wolpe, Mich.
Sam Gejdenson, Conn.
Mervyn M. Dymally, Calif.
Tom Lantos, Calif.
Peter H. Kostmayer, Pa.
Robert G. Torricelli, N.J.
Howard L. Berman, Calif.
Mel Levine, Calif.
Edward F. Feighan, Ohio
Ted Weiss, N.Y.
Gary L. Ackerman, N.Y.
Morris K. Udall, Ariz.
Jaime B. Fuster, P.R.
Wayne Owens, Utah
Harry A. Johnston, Fla.
Eliot L. Engel, N.Y.
Eni F.H. Faleomavaega, Am.Samoa
Austin J. Murphy, Pa.
Thomas M. Foglietta, Pa.
Frank McCloskey, Ind.
Tom Sawyer, Ohio
Donald M. Payne, N.J.
Bill Orton, Utah

Jim Leach, Iowa
Toby Roth, Wis.
Olympia J. Snowe, Maine
Henry J. Hyde, Ill.
Doug Bereuter, Neb.
Christopher H. Smith, N.J.
Dan Burton, Ind.
Jan Meyers, Kan.
John Miller, Wash.
Ben Blaz, Guam
Elton Gallegly, Calif.
Amo Houghton, N.Y.
Porter J. Goss, Fla.
Ileana Ros-Lehtinen, Fla.

Government Operations

2157 RHOB 20515; 225-5051

John Conyers Jr., D-Mich., Chairman

Democrats	Republicans
Cardiss Collins, Ill.	Frank Horton, N.Y.
Glenn English, Okla.	William F. Clinger, Pa.
Henry A. Waxman, Calif.	Al McCandless, Calif.
Ted Weiss, N.Y.	Dennis Hastert, Ill.
Mike Synar, Okla.	Jon Kyl, Ariz.
Stephen L. Neal, N.C.	Christopher Shays, Conn.
Doug Barnard Jr., Ga.	Steven H. Schiff, N.M.
Tom Lantos, Calif.	C. Christopher Cox, Calif.

Bob Wise, W.Va.
Barbara Boxer, Calif.
Major R. Owens, N.Y.
Edolphus Towns, N.Y.
Ben Erdreich, Ala.
Gerald D. Kleczka, Wis.
Albert G. Bustamante, Texas
Matthew G. Martinez, Calif.
Donald M. Payne, N.J.
Gary Condit, Calif.
Patsy T. Mink, Hawaii
Ray Thornton, Ark.
Collin C. Peterson, Minn.
Rosa DeLauro, Conn.
Charles Luken, Ohio
John W. Cox Jr., Ill.

Craig Thomas, Wyo.
Ileana Ros-Lehtinen, Fla.
Ronald K. Machtley, R.I.
Dick Zimmer, N.J.
Bill Zeliff, N.H.
David L. Hobson, Ohio
Scott L. Klug, Wis.

House Administration

CAP-H 326 20515; 225-2061

Charlie Rose, D-N.C., Chairman

Democrats	Republicans
Frank Annunzio, Ill.	Bill Thomas, Calif.
Joseph M. Gaydos, Pa.	Bill Dickinson, Ala.
Leon E. Panetta, Calif.	Newt Gingrich, Ga.
Al Swift, Wash.	Pat Roberts, Kan.
Mary Rose Oakar, Ohio	Paul E. Gillmor, Ohio
William L. Clay, Mo.	James T. Walsh, N.Y.
Sam Gejdenson, Conn.	Vacancy
Joe Kolter, Pa.	Vacancy
Martin Frost, Texas	Vacancy
Thomas J. Manton, N.Y.	
Marty Russo, Ill.	
William H. Gray III, Pa.	
Steny H. Hoyer, Md.	
Gerald D. Kleczka, Wis.	

Intelligence

CAP-H 405; 225-4121

Dave McCurdy, D-Okla., Chairman

Democrats	Republicans
Charles Wilson, Texas	Bud Shuster, Pa.
Barbara B. Kennelly, Conn.	Larry Combest, Texas
Dan Glickman, Kan.	Doug Bereuter, Neb.
Nicholas Mavroules, Mass.	Robert K. Dornan, Calif.
Bill Richardson, N.M.	C. W. Bill Young, Fla.
Stephen J. Solarz, N.Y.	David O'B. Martin, N.Y.
Norm Dicks, Wash.	George W. Gekas, Pa.
Ronald V. Dellums, Calif.	
David E. Bonior, Mich.	
Martin Olav Sabo, Minn.	
Wayne Owens, Utah	

Interior & Insular Affairs

1324 LHOB 20515; 225-2761

Morris K. Udall, D-Ariz., Chairman

Democrats	Republicans
George Miller, Calif.	Don Young, Alaska
Philip R. Sharp, Ind.	Robert J. Lagomarsino, Calif.
Edward J. Markey, Mass.	Ron Marlenee, Mont.
Austin J. Murphy, Pa.	James V. Hansen, Utah
Nick J. Rahall II, W.Va.	Ben Blaz, Guam
Bruce F. Vento, Minn.	John J. Rhodes III, Ariz.
Pat Williams, Mont.	Elton Gallegly, Calif.
Beverly B. Byron, Md.	Bob Smith, Ore.
Ron de Lugo, V.I.	Jim Ross Lightfoot, Iowa
Sam Gejdenson, Conn.	Craig Thomas, Wyo.
Peter H. Kostmayer, Pa.	John J. Duncan Jr., Tenn.
Richard H. Lehman, Calif.	Dick Schulze, Pa.
Bill Richardson, N.M.	Joel Hefley, Colo.
George Darden, Ga.	Charles H. Taylor, N.C.
Peter J. Visclosky, Ind.	John T. Doolittle, Calif.
Jaime B. Fuster, P.R.	Wayne Allard, Colo.
Mel Levine, Calif.	
Wayne Owens, Utah	

John Lewis, Ga.
Ben Nighthorse Campbell, Colo.
Peter A. DeFazio, Ore.
Eni F.H. Faleomavaega, Am.Samoa
Tim Johnson, S.D.
Charles E. Schumer, N.Y.
Jim Jontz, Ind.
Peter Hoagland, Neb.
Harry A. Johnston, Fla.
Larry LaRocco, Idaho

Judiciary   2138 RHOB 20515; 225-3951
Jack Brooks, D-Texas, Chairman

Democrats	Republicans
Don Edwards, Calif.	Hamilton Fish Jr., N.Y.
John Conyers Jr., Mich.	Carlos J. Moorhead, Calif.
Romano L. Mazzoli, Ky.	Henry J. Hyde, Ill.
William J. Hughes, N.J.	F. James Sensenbrenner Jr., Wis.
Mike Synar, Okla.	Bill McCollum, Fla.
Patricia Schroeder, Colo.	George W. Gekas, Pa.
Dan Glickman, Kan.	Howard Coble, N.C.
Barney Frank, Mass.	D. French Slaughter Jr., Va.
Charles E. Schumer, N.Y.	Lamar Smith, Texas
Edward F. Feighan, Ohio	Craig T. James, Fla.
Howard L. Berman, Calif.	Tom Campbell, Calif.
Rick Boucher, Va.	Steven H. Schiff, N.M.
Harley O. Staggers Jr., W.Va.	Jim Ramstad, Minn.
John Bryant, Texas	
Mel Levine, Calif.	
George E. Sangmeister, Ill.	
Craig Washington, Texas	
Peter Hoagland, Neb.	
Mike Kopetski, Ore.	
John F. Reed, R.I.	

Merchant Marine & Fisheries
1334 LHOB 20515; 225-4047

Walter B. Jones, D-N.C., Chairman

Democrats	Republicans
Gerry E. Studds, Mass.	Robert W. Davis, Mich.
Carroll Hubbard Jr., Ky.	Don Young, Alaska
William J. Hughes, N.J.	Norman F. Lent, N.Y.
Earl Hutto, Fla.	Jack Fields, Texas
W.J. Tauzin, La.	Herbert H. Bateman, Va.
Thomas M. Foglietta, Pa.	H. James Saxton, N.J.
Dennis M. Hertel, Mich.	Howard Coble, N.C.
William O. Lipinski, Ill.	Curt Weldon, Pa.
Robert A. Borski, Pa.	Wally Herger, Calif.
Thomas R. Carper, Del.	James M. Inhofe, Okla.
Robin Tallon, S.C.	Porter J. Goss, Fla.
Solomon P. Ortiz, Texas	Arthur Ravenel Jr., S.C.
Charles E. Bennett, Fla.	Sonny Callahan, Ala.
Thomas J. Manton, N.Y.	Wayne T. Gilchrest, Md.
Owen B. Pickett, Va.	John T. Doolittle, Calif.
George J. Hochbrueckner, N.Y.	Randy Cunningham, Calif.
Bob Clement, Tenn.	Vacancy
Stephen J. Solarz, N.Y.	
Frank Pallone Jr., N.J.	
Greg Laughlin, Texas	
Nita M. Lowey, N.Y.	
Jolene Unsoeld, Wash.	
Gene Taylor, Miss.	
Glenn M. Anderson, Calif.	
John F. Reed, R.I.	
William J. Jefferson, La.	
Neil Abercrombie, Hawaii	
Eni F. H. Faleomavaega, Am. Samoa	

Post Office & Civil Service
309 CHOB 20515; 225-4054

William L. Clay, D-Mo., Chairman

Democrats	Republicans
Patricia Schroeder, Colo.	Benjamin A. Gilman, N.Y.
Gus Yatron, Pa.	Frank Horton, N.Y.

Mary Rose Oakar, Ohio
Gerry Sikorski, Minn.
Frank McCloskey, Ind.
Gary L. Ackerman, N.Y.
Mervyn M. Dymally, Calif.
Tom Sawyer, Ohio
Paul E. Kanjorski, Pa.
Charles A. Hayes, Ill.
Michael R. McNulty, N.Y.
James P. Moran Jr., Va.
Eleanor Holmes Norton, D.C.
Morris K. Udall, Ariz.

John T. Myers, Ind.
Don Young, Alaska
Dan Burton, Ind.
Constance A. Morella, Md.
Tom Ridge, Pa.
Rod D. Chandler, Wash.

Public Works & Transportation

2165 RHOB 20515; 225-4472

Robert A. Roe, D-N.J., Chairman

Democrats	Republicans
Glenn M. Anderson, Calif.	John Paul Hammerschmidt, Ark.
Norman Y. Mineta, Calif.	Bud Shuster, Pa.
James L. Oberstar, Minn.	William F. Clinger, Pa.
Henry J. Nowak, N.Y.	Tom Petri, Wis.
Nick J. Rahall II, W.Va.	Ron Packard, Calif.
Douglas Applegate, Ohio	Sherwood Boehlert, N.Y.
Ron de Lugo, V.I.	Helen Delich Bentley, Md.
Gus Savage, Ill.	Jim Ross Lightfoot, Iowa
Robert A. Borski, Pa.	James M. Inhofe, Okla.
Joe Kolter, Pa.	Cass Ballenger, N.C.
Tim Valentine, N.C.	Fred Upton, Mich.
William O. Lipinski, Ill.	Bill Emerson, Mo.
Peter J. Visclosky, Ind.	John J. Duncan Jr., Tenn.
James A. Traficant Jr., Ohio	Mel Hancock, Mo.
John Lewis, Ga.	C. Christopher Cox, Calif.
Peter A. DeFazio, Ore.	Susan Molinari, N.Y.
Jimmy Hayes, La.	David L. Hobson, Ohio
Bob Clement, Tenn.	Frank Riggs, Calif.
Lewis F. Payne Jr., Va.	Charles H. Taylor, N.C.
Jerry F. Costello, Ill.	Dick Nichols, Kan.
Frank Pallone Jr., N.J.	Bill Zeliff, N.H.
Ben Jones, Ga.	

Public Works & Transportation (Continued)

Mike Parker, Miss.
Greg Laughlin, Texas
Pete Geren, Texas
George E. Sangmeister, Ill.
Glenn Poshard, Ill.
Dick Swett, N.H.
Bill Brewster, Okla.
Bud Cramer, Ala.
Rosa DeLauro, Conn.
Joan Kelly Horn, Mo.
Barbara-Rose Collins, Mich.
Pete Peterson, Fla.
Eleanor Holmes Norton, D.C.

Rules   CAP-H 312 20515; 225-9486

Joe Moakley, D-Mass., Chairman

Democrats	Republicans
Butler Derrick, S.C.	Gerald B.H. Solomon, N.Y.
Anthony C. Beilenson, Calif.	James H. Quillen, Tenn.
Martin Frost, Texas	David Dreier, Calif.
David E. Bonior, Mich.	Bob McEwen, Ohio
Tony P. Hall, Ohio	
Alan Wheat, Mo.	
Bart Gordon, Tenn.	
Louise M. Slaughter, N.Y.	

Science, Space & Technology   2321 RHOB 20515; 225-6371

George E. Brown Jr., D-Calif., Chairman

Democrats	Republicans
James H. Scheuer, N.Y.	Robert S. Walker, Pa.
Marilyn Lloyd, Tenn.	F. James Sensenbrenner Jr., Wis.
Dan Glickman, Kan.	Sherwood Boehlert, N.Y.
Harold L. Volkmer, Mo.	Tom Lewis, Fla.
Howard Wolpe, Mich.	Don Ritter, Pa.
Ralph M. Hall, Texas	Sid Morrison, Wash.
Dave McCurdy, Okla.	Ron Packard, Calif.

Norman Y. Mineta, Calif.
Tim Valentine, N.C.
Robert G. Torricelli, N.J.
Rick Boucher, Va.
Terry L. Bruce, Ill.
Richard Stallings, Idaho
James A. Traficant Jr., Ohio
Henry J. Nowak, N.Y.
Carl C. Perkins, Ky.
Tom McMillen, Md.
Dave Nagle, Iowa
Jimmy Hayes, La.
Jerry F. Costello, Ill.
John Tanner, Tenn.
Glen Browder, Ala.
Pete Geren, Texas
Ray Thornton, Ark.
Jim Bacchus, Fla.
Tim Roemer, Ind.
Bud Cramer, Ala.
Dick Swett, N.H.
Mike Kopetski, Ore.
Joan Kelly Horn, Mo.
Barbara-Rose Collins, Mich.

Paul B. Henry, Mich.
Harris W. Fawell, Ill.
D. French Slaughter Jr., Va.
Lamar Smith, Texas
Constance A. Morella, Md.
Dana Rohrabacher, Calif.
Steven H. Schiff, N.M.
Tom Campbell, Calif.
John J. Rhodes III, Ariz.
Joe L. Barton, Texas
Dick Zimmer, N.J.
Wayne T. Gilchrest, Md.

Small Business

2361 RHOB 20515; 225-5821

John J. LaFalce, D-N.Y., Chairman

Democrats	Republicans
Neal Smith, Iowa	Joseph M. McDade, Pa.
Ike Skelton, Mo.	Silvio O. Conte, Mass.
Romano L. Mazzoli, Ky.	William S. Broomfield, Mich.
Nicholas Mavroules, Mass.	Andy Ireland, Fla.
Charles Hatcher, Ga.	D. French Slaughter Jr., Va.
Ron Wyden, Ore.	Jan Meyers, Kan.
Dennis E. Eckart, Ohio	Larry Combest, Texas
Gus Savage, Ill.	Richard H. Baker, La.
Norman Sisisky, Va.	Joel Hefley, Colo.
Esteban E. Torres, Calif.	Fred Upton, Mich.

Small Business (Continued)

Jim Olin, Va.
Richard Ray, Ga.
John Conyers Jr., Mich.
James Bilbray, Nev.
Kweisi Mfume, Md.
Floyd H. Flake, N.Y.
H. Martin Lancaster, N.C.
Bill Sarpalius, Texas
Richard E. Neal, Mass.
Glenn Poshard, Ill.
Eliot L. Engel, N.Y.
Jose E. Serrano, N.Y.
Robert E. Andrews, N.J.
Thomas H. Andrews, Maine
Calvin Dooley, Calif.
Robert E. Andrews, N.J.
Bill Orton, Utah

Mel Hancock, Mo.
Ronald K. Machtley, R.I.
Jim Ramstad, Minn.
Dave Camp, Mich.
Gary Franks, Conn.
Wayne Allard, Colo.
John A. Boehner, Ohio

Veterans' Affairs   335 CHOB 20515; 225-3527

G. V. "Sonny" Montgomery, D-Miss., Chairman

Democrats	Republicans
Don Edwards, Calif.	Bob Stump, Ariz.
Douglas Applegate, Ohio	John Paul Hammerschmidt, Ark.
Lane Evans, Ill.	Chalmers P. Wylie, Ohio
Timothy J. Penny, Minn.	Christopher H. Smith, N.J.
Harley O. Staggers Jr., W.Va.	Dan Burton, Ind.
J. Roy Rowland, Ga.	Michael Bilirakis, Fla.
Jim Slattery, Kan.	Tom Ridge, Pa.
Claude Harris, Ala.	Craig T. James, Fla.
Joseph P. Kennedy II, Mass.	Cliff Stearns, Fla.
Liz J. Patterson, S.C.	Bill Paxon, N.Y.
George E. Sangmeister, Ill.	Floyd D. Spence, S.C.
Ben Jones, Ga.	Dick Nichols, Kan.
Jill Long, Ind.	Rick Santorum, Pa.
Pete Peterson, Fla.	
Maxine Waters, Calif.	

Chet Edwards, Texas
Bill Brewster, Okla.
Owen B. Pickett, Va.
Pete Geren, Texas
Vacancy

Ways & Means   1102 LHOB 20515; 225-3625

Dan Rostenkowski, D-Ill., Chairman

Democrats	Republicans
Sam M. Gibbons, Fla.	Bill Archer, Texas
J.J. Pickle, Texas	Guy Vander Jagt, Mich.
Charles B. Rangel, N.Y.	Philip M. Crane, Ill.
Pete Stark, Calif.	Dick Schulze, Pa.
Andy Jacobs Jr., Ind.	Bill Gradison, Ohio
Harold E. Ford, Tenn.	Bill Thomas, Calif.
Ed Jenkins, Ga.	Raymond J. McGrath, N.Y.
Thomas J. Downey, N.Y.	Rod D. Chandler, Wash.
Frank J. Guarini, N.J.	E. Clay Shaw Jr., Fla.
Marty Russo, Ill.	Don Sundquist, Tenn.
Don J. Pease, Ohio	Nancy L. Johnson, Conn.
Robert T. Matsui, Calif.	Fred Grandy, Iowa
Beryl Anthony Jr., Ark.	Jim Bunning, Ky.
Byron L. Dorgan, N.D.	
Barbara B. Kennelly, Conn.	
Brian Donnelly, Mass.	
William J. Coyne, Pa.	
Michael A. Andrews, Texas	
Sander M. Levin, Mich.	
Jim Moody, Wis.	
Benjamin L. Cardin, Md.	
Jim McDermott, Wash.	

Key Votes for 1990

Since 1945, Congressional Quarterly has selected a series of key votes on major issues of the year.

An issue is judged by the extent that it represents:

- A matter of major controversy.
- A matter of presidential or political power.
- A decision of potentially great impact on the nation and lives of Americans.

For each group of related votes on an issue, one key vote usually is chosen—the one that, in the opinion of CQ editors, was important in determining the outcome.

Charts showing how each member of Congress voted on these issues can be found after the vote descriptions.

Key Senate Votes

1. HR 2712. Chinese Students/Veto Override. Passage, over President Bush's Nov. 30 veto, of the bill to defer indefinitely the deportation of Chinese students whose visas expire and to waive for students on "J" visas a requirement that they return to their home country for two years before applying for permanent residence in the United States. Rejected 62-37: R 8-37; D 54-0 (ND 38-0, SD 16-0), Jan. 25, 1990. A two-thirds majority of those present and voting (66 in this case) of both houses is required to override a veto. A "nay" was a vote supporting the president's position.

2. S 695. Education Programs/National Standards. Helms, R-N.C., amendment to delete $25 million in federal matching funds for the National Board for Professional Teaching Standards, which is developing guidelines for voluntary certification of teachers. Rejected 35-64: R 35-10; D 0-54 (ND 0-37, SD 0-17), Feb. 6, 1990. A "yea" was a vote supporting the president's position.

3. S 1630. Clean Air Act Reauthorization/Motor Vehicles. Mitchell, D-Maine, motion to table (kill) the Wirth, D-Colo., amendment to provide for a second round of tailpipe emissions reductions in the year 2003; to require cleaner-burning reformulated gasoline in all ozone non-attainment areas; to require light-duty vehicles to meet new-car emission standards for 100,000 miles; and to provide for use of clean fuels and clean-fuel vehicles in the nation's smoggiest cities. Motion agreed to

52-46: R 25-19; D 27-27 (ND 14-23, SD 13-4), March 20, 1990. A "yea" was a vote supporting the president's position.

4. S 1630. Clean Air Act Reauthorization/Coal Miner Benefits. Byrd, D-W.Va., amendment to provide severance pay and retraining benefits to coal miners who lose their jobs as a result of provisions to control acid rain. Rejected 49-50: R 11-34; D 38-16 (ND 29-9, SD 9-7), March 29, 1990. A "nay" was a vote supporting the president's position.

5. S 1970. Omnibus Crime Package/Assault-Style Weapons. Hatch, R-Utah, amendment to strike provisions that would prohibit for three years making, selling and possessing nine types of semiautomatic assault-style weapons. Rejected 48-52: R 36-9; D 12-43 (ND 5-33, SD 7-10), May 23, 1990. A "yea" was a vote supporting the president's position.

6. S J Res 332. Constitutional Amendment on the Flag/ Passage. Passage of the joint resolution to propose an amendment to the Constitution to prohibit the physical desecration of the U.S. flag. Rejected 58-42: R 38-7; D 20-35 (ND 10-28, SD 10-7), June 26, 1990. A two-thirds majority of those present and voting (67 in this case) of both houses is required for passage of a joint resolution proposing an amendment to the Constitution. A "yea" was a vote supporting the president's position.

7. S 933. Americans with Disabilities Act/Conference Report. Adoption of the conference report (thus clearing the measure for the president) on the bill to prohibit discrimination against the disabled in public facilities and employment and to guarantee them access to mass transit and telecommunications services. Adopted 91-6: R 37-6; D 54-0 (ND 37-0, SD 17-0), July 13, 1990. A "yea" was a vote supporting the president's position.

8. S 2830. Farm Programs Reauthorization/Sugar Price Supports. Akaka, D-Hawaii, motion to table (kill) the Bradley, D-N.J., amendment to extend the current sugar program for five years and lower the sugar price-support program loan rate from 18 cents per pound to 16 cents per pound. Motion agreed to 54-44: R 17-26; D 37-18 (ND 22-16, SD 15-2), July 24, 1990.

9. S 137. Campaign Finance Overhaul/Taxpayer Funding. McConnell, R-Ky., amendment to the Boren, D-Okla., substitute amendment to eliminate all taxpayer funding of Senate campaigns. Rejected 46-49: R 44-0; D 2-49 (ND 1-34, SD 1-15), July 30, 1990.

10. HR 5257. Fiscal 1991 Labor, HHS and Education Appropriations/Abortion. Harkin, D-Iowa, motion to table (kill) the Armstrong, R-Colo., amendment to the committee amendment to permit federal funding of abortion in cases of rape or incest. The Armstrong amendment would require organizations receiving funds to notify a parent or legal

Southern states - Ala., Ark., Fla., Ga., Ky., La., Miss., N.C., Okla., S.C., Tenn., Texas, Va.

guardian 48 hours before performing an abortion for a minor, unless there is a medical emergency. Motion rejected 48-48: R 8-34; D 40-14 (ND 31-6, SD 9-8), Oct. 12, 1990. (Subsequently, the Armstrong amendment was adopted by voice vote.)

11. S 3189. Fiscal 1991 Defense Appropriations/Troop Cuts. Conrad, D-N.D., amendment to reduce U.S. forces in NATO by 30,000 troops below the Senate-passed authorization level and reduce the Department of Defense military personnel level by a corresponding 30,000 below the authorized level. Rejected 46-50: R 8-34; D 38-16 (ND 31-6, SD 7-10), Oct. 15, 1990. A "nay" was a vote supporting the president's position.

12. S 3189. Fiscal 1991 Defense Appropriations/B-2 Bomber. Leahy, D-Vt., amendment to cut funds for the two additional B-2 bombers in the bill, thereby terminating the expansion of the program with the 15 bombers being produced and tested. Rejected 44-50: R 9-32; D 35-18 (ND 30-7, SD 5-11), Oct. 15, 1990. A "nay" was a vote supporting the president's position.

13. S 3209. Fiscal 1991 Budget Reconciliation Act/Passage. Passage of the bill to cut spending and raise revenues as required by the reconciliation instructions in the budget resolution and make changes in the budget process. Passed 54-46: R 23-22; D 31-24 (ND 20-18, SD 11-6), in the session that began, and the Congressional Record dated, Oct. 18, 1990. (The Senate subsequently passed HR 5835 by voice vote after striking everything after the enacting clause and inserting in lieu thereof the text of S 3209.)

14. HR 5114. Fiscal 1991 Foreign Operations Appropriations/El Salvador. Leahy, D-Vt., amendment to the committee amendment, to reduce military aid to the government of El Salvador by 50 percent and link future military aid to improvements in human rights and progress toward a negotiated peace settlement. Adopted 74-25: R 19-25; D 55-0 (ND 38-0, SD 17-0), Oct. 19, 1990. A "nay" was a vote supporting the president's position.

15. HR 5114. Fiscal 1991 Foreign Operations Appropriations/Egyptian Debt. Harkin, D-Iowa, amendment to the committee amendment, to strike provisions canceling Egypt's debt to the United States and to require the president to develop in cooperation with Congress a proposal to restructure that debt and convene an international conference to develop a comprehensive and multilateral solution to Egypt's international debt problem. Rejected 42-55: R 10-34; D 32-21 (ND 20-16, SD 12-5), Oct. 19, 1990. A "nay" was a vote supporting the president's position.

16. S 2104. Civil Rights Act of 1990/Veto Override. Passage, over

ND Northern Democrats   SD Southern Democrats

President Bush's Oct. 22 veto, of the bill to reverse or modify six recent Supreme Court decisions that narrowed the reach and remedies of job discrimination law and to authorize monetary damages under Title VII of the 1964 Civil Rights Act. Rejected 66-34: R 11-34; D 55-0 (ND 38-0, SD 17-0), Oct. 24, 1990. A two-thirds majority of those present and voting (67 in this case) of both houses is required to override a veto. A "nay" was a vote supporting the president's position.

Southern states - Ala., Ark., Fla., Ga., Ky., La., Miss., N.C., Okla., S.C., Tenn., Texas, Va.

Senate Key Votes	1	2	3	4	5	6	7	8	9	10	11	12	13	14	15	16
ALABAMA																
Heflin	Y	N	Y	Y	Y	Y	Y	Y	?	N	N	N	N	Y	Y	Y
Shelby	Y	N	Y	Y	Y	Y	Y	Y	N	N	Y	N	N	Y	Y	Y
ALASKA																
Murkowski	N	Y	Y	N	Y	Y	Y	N	Y	N	N	N	Y	Y	N	N
Stevens	N	Y	?	Y	Y	Y	Y	Y	Y	Y	N	N	Y	Y	N	N
ARIZONA																
DeConcini	Y	N	N	Y	N	Y	Y	Y	-	N	Y	Y	N	Y	N	Y
McCain	N	Y	N	N	Y	Y	Y	N	Y	N	N	Y	N	N	N	N
ARKANSAS																
Bumpers	Y	N	Y	Y	N	N	Y	Y	N	Y	Y	Y	Y	Y	Y	Y
Pryor	Y	N	Y	N	N	N	Y	Y	N	Y	Y	Y	Y	Y	Y	Y
CALIFORNIA																
Cranston	Y	N	N	Y	N	N	Y	Y	N	Y	Y	Y	Y	Y	N	Y
Wilson	Y	Y	N	N	N	Y	Y	Y	Y	?	?	?	N	N	N	N
COLORADO																
Wirth	Y	N	N	Y	N	N	Y	Y	N	Y	Y	Y	Y	Y	N	Y
Armstrong	Y	Y	N	N	Y	Y	Y	N	?	N	N	N	N	N	N	N
CONNECTICUT																
Dodd	Y	N	Y	N	N	N	Y	Y	N	Y	Y	N	Y	Y	Y	Y
Lieberman	Y	N	N	N	N	N	Y	N	N	Y	Y	N	Y	Y	Y	Y
DELAWARE																
Biden	Y	N	N	N	N	N	Y	Y	N	Y	Y	Y	N	Y	Y	Y
Roth	N	N	N	N	Y	Y	Y	N	Y	N	N	Y	N	Y	N	N
FLORIDA																
Graham	Y	N	N	N	N	Y	Y	Y	N	Y	N	N	N	Y	Y	Y
Mack	N	Y	Y	N	Y	Y	Y	Y	N	N	N	N	N	N	N	N
GEORGIA																
Fowler	Y	N	N	N	N	Y	Y	Y	N	Y	Y	N	Y	Y	N	Y
Nunn	Y	N	N	N	N	Y	Y	N	N	N	N	N	Y	Y	Y	Y
HAWAII																
Inouye	Y	N	Y	Y	N	N	Y	Y	N	N	N	N	Y	Y	N	Y
Akaka †					N	N	Y	Y	N	Y	N	Y	N	Y	Y	Y
IDAHO																
McClure	N	Y	N	Y	Y	Y	?	Y	Y	N	N	Y	Y	N	N	N
Symms	N	Y	N	N	Y	Y	N	Y	Y	N	N	N	N	N	N	N

	Democrats	**Republicans**	

Y Voted for "yea"	# Paired for	C Voted "present" to avoid
N Voted against "nay"	X Paired against	possible conflict of interest
	- Announced against	? Did not vote or otherwise
+ Announced for	P Voted "present"	make a position known

† Daniel K. Akaka was appointed April 28, 1990.

Senate Key Votes	1	2	3	4	5	6	7	8	9	10	11	12	13	14	15	16
ILLINOIS																
Dixon	Y	N	Y	Y	N	Y	Y	Y	N	N	Y	N	Y	Y	Y	Y
Simon	Y	N	N	Y	N	N	Y	Y	N	Y	Y	Y	N	Y	Y	Y
INDIANA																
Coats	N	Y	Y	Y	Y	Y	Y	N	Y	N	N	N	N	N	Y	N
Lugar	N	Y	Y	N	Y	Y	Y	N	Y	N	N	N	Y	N	N	N
IOWA																
Harkin	Y	N	N	Y	N	N	Y	Y	N	Y	Y	Y	N	Y	Y	Y
Grassley	N	Y	Y	Y	Y	Y	Y	N	Y	N	N	Y	N	Y	Y	N
KANSAS																
Dole	N	Y	Y	N	N	Y	Y	N	Y	N	N	N	Y	N	N	Y
Kassebaum	N	Y	N	N	N	Y	Y	N	Y	N	?	?	Y	Y	Y	N
KENTUCKY																
Ford	Y	N	Y	Y	Y	Y	Y	Y	N	N	N	N	Y	Y	Y	Y
McConnell	N	Y	Y	Y	Y	Y	Y	N	Y	N	N	N	N	N	N	N
LOUISIANA																
Breaux	?	N	Y	N	Y	Y	Y	Y	N	N	N	N	Y	Y	Y	Y
Johnston	Y	N	Y	+	Y	Y	Y	Y	N	N	N	N	N	Y	Y	Y
MAINE																
Mitchell	Y	N	Y	N	N	N	Y	N	N	Y	Y	Y	Y	Y	N	Y
Cohen	Y	N	N	N	Y	Y	Y	N	Y	Y	Y	Y	N	Y	Y	Y
MARYLAND																
Mikulski	Y	N	N	Y	N	N	Y	Y	?	Y	Y	Y	Y	Y	Y	Y
Sarbanes	Y	N	Y	N	N	N	Y	N	N	Y	Y	Y	Y	Y	N	Y
MASSACHUSETTS																
Kennedy	Y	N	N	Y	N	N	Y	N	N	Y	Y	Y	Y	Y	N	Y
Kerry	Y	N	N	Y	N	N	Y	N	N	Y	+	#	N	Y	Y	Y
MICHIGAN																
Levin	Y	N	Y	N	N	N	Y	Y	N	Y	Y	Y	N	Y	Y	Y
Riegle	Y	N	Y	N	N	N	Y	Y	N	Y	Y	Y	N	Y	?	Y
MINNESOTA																
Boschwitz	Y	Y	N	N	Y	Y	Y	Y	Y	N	N	N	Y	Y	Y	Y
Durenberger	N	N	Y	N	Y	N	Y	Y	Y	N	N	N	Y	Y	N	Y
MISSISSIPPI																
Cochran	N	N	Y	Y	Y	Y	Y	Y	Y	N	N	N	Y	N	N	N
Lott	N	Y	Y	N	Y	Y	Y	Y	Y	N	N	N	N	N	Y	N
MISSOURI																
Bond	N	Y	Y	Y	Y	Y	N	N	Y	N	N	N	Y	N	N	N
Danforth	N	Y	Y	Y	Y	N	Y	N	Y	N	N	N	Y	Y	N	Y
MONTANA																
Baucus	Y	N	Y	N	Y	Y	Y	Y	N	Y	Y	Y	N	Y	Y	Y
Burns	N	Y	N	N	Y	Y	Y	Y	Y	N	N	N	N	N	N	N

Senate Key Votes	1	2	3	4	5	6	7	8	9	10	11	12	13	14	15	16
NEBRASKA																
Exon	Y	N	Y	Y	Y	Y	Y	Y	Y	N	Y	N	N	Y	Y	Y
Kerrey	Y	N	Y	Y	N	N	Y	Y	N	Y	Y	Y	N	Y	Y	Y
NEVADA																
Bryan	Y	N	N	Y	Y	Y	Y	N	Y	Y	Y	N	Y	Y	Y	Y
Reid	Y	-	N	Y	Y	Y	Y	N	N	N	Y	Y	Y	Y	Y	Y
NEW HAMPSHIRE																
Humphrey	N	Y	Y	N	Y	N	N	N	Y	N	Y	Y	N	N	Y	N
Rudman	N	Y	Y	N	Y	N	Y	N	Y	Y	N	N	Y	N	N	N
NEW JERSEY																
Bradley	Y	N	N	Y	N	N	Y	N	N	N	Y	Y	N	Y	N	Y
Lautenberg	Y	N	N	Y	N	N	Y	N	N	N	Y	Y	N	Y	N	Y
NEW MEXICO																
Bingaman	Y	N	N	Y	Y	N	Y	N	N	Y	N	Y	Y	Y	N	Y
Domenici	N	Y	Y	N	Y	Y	Y	N	Y	?	N	N	Y	Y	N	Y
NEW YORK																
Moynihan	Y	N	N	Y	N	N	Y	N	N	Y	Y	Y	Y	Y	N	Y
D'Amato	N	Y	N	N	N	Y	Y	Y	Y	Y	N	Y	N	Y	N	N
NORTH CAROLINA																
Sanford	Y	N	Y	Y	Y	N	Y	N	N	Y	Y	X	N	Y	Y	Y
Helms	Y	Y	Y	Y	Y	Y	N	Y	N	N	N	N	Y	N	N	N
NORTH DAKOTA																
Burdick	Y	N	Y	Y	N	Y	Y	Y	N	Y	Y	Y	Y	Y	Y	Y
Conrad	Y	N	N	Y	N	Y	Y	Y	N	N	Y	Y	N	Y	Y	Y
OHIO																
Glenn	Y	N	Y	Y	N	N	Y	N	N	Y	N	Y	Y	Y	N	Y
Metzenbaum	Y	N	Y	Y	N	N	Y	N	N	?	Y	Y	Y	Y	N	Y
OKLAHOMA																
Boren	Y	N	Y	N	N	N	Y	Y	N	Y	Y	N	Y	Y	N	Y
Nickles	N	Y	Y	N	Y	Y	Y	N	Y	N	Y	N	N	N	N	N
OREGON																
Hatfield	N	N	N	Y	N	Y	Y	N	Y	?	+	#	N	Y	Y	Y
Packwood	N	Y	N	N	N	Y	Y	N	Y	Y	Y	Y	Y	Y	N	Y
PENNSYLVANIA																
Heinz	N	N	Y	Y	Y	Y	Y	N	Y	Y	N	Y	Y	Y	N	Y
Specter	N	N	Y	Y	Y	Y	Y	N	Y	Y	N	N	Y	Y	N	Y

	Democrats	*Republicans*

Y Voted for "yea"	# Paired for	C Voted "present" to avoid
N Voted against	X Paired against	possible conflict of interest
"nay"	- Announced against	? Did not vote or otherwise
+ Announced for	P Voted "present"	make a position known

Senate Key Votes	1	2	3	4	5	6	7	8	9	10	11	12	13	14	15	16
RHODE ISLAND																
Pell	Y	N	N	Y	N	N	Y	N	-	Y	Y	Y	N	Y	Y	Y
Chafee	N	N	Y	N	N	N	Y	N	Y	Y	N	N	Y	Y	N	Y
SOUTH CAROLINA																
Hollings	Y	N	Y	Y	Y	Y	Y	Y	Y	Y	N	Y	N	Y	Y	Y
Thurmond	N	Y	Y	N	Y	Y	Y	Y	Y	N	N	N	Y	N	N	N
SOUTH DAKOTA																
Daschle	Y	N	N	N	N	N	Y	Y	N	Y	Y	Y	Y	Y	+	Y
Pressler	Y	Y	N	N	Y	Y	Y	?	Y	N	Y	Y	N	Y	Y	N
TENNESSEE																
Gore	Y	N	N	Y	N	N	Y	Y	N	Y	N	N	Y	Y	N	Y
Sasser	Y	N	Y	Y	N	N	Y	Y	N	Y	Y	Y	Y	Y	Y	Y
TEXAS																
Bentsen	Y	N	Y	Y	N	Y	Y	Y	N	N	N	N	Y	Y	N	Y
Gramm	N	Y	Y	N	Y	Y	Y	Y	Y	N	N	N	N	?	?	N
UTAH																
Garn	N	Y	N	N	Y	Y	N	?	Y	N	N	N	Y	N	N	N
Hatch	N	N	N	N	Y	Y	Y	Y	Y	N	N	N	Y	N	N	N
VERMONT																
Leahy	Y	N	N	N	N	N	Y	Y	N	Y	N	Y	Y	Y	N	Y
Jeffords	N	N	Y	N	N	N	Y	N	Y	Y	N	X	Y	Y	N	Y
VIRGINIA																
Robb	Y	N	Y	N	N	N	Y	N	N	Y	N	N	Y	Y	N	Y
Warner	N	Y	Y	N	N	Y	Y	N	Y	N	N	N	Y	Y	N	N
WASHINGTON																
Adams	Y	N	N	Y	N	N	Y	Y	N	Y	Y	Y	N	Y	N	Y
Gorton	Y	Y	N	N	Y	Y	Y	N	Y	N	N	N	N	N	N	N
WEST VIRGINIA																
Byrd	Y	N	N	Y	N	Y	Y	Y	N	N	N	Y	Y	Y	Y	Y
Rockefeller	Y	N	N	Y	N	Y	?	Y	N	Y	Y	Y	Y	Y	Y	Y
WISCONSIN																
Kohl	Y	N	N	Y	N	N	Y	N	N	Y	Y	Y	Y	Y	Y	Y
Kasten	Y	Y	Y	N	Y	Y	Y	N	Y	N	Y	N	N	N	N	N
WYOMING																
Simpson	N	Y	Y	N	Y	Y	+	Y	Y	N	N	N	Y	N	N	N
Wallop	N	Y	N	N	Y	Y	N	Y	Y	N	N	N	N	N	N	N

Key House Votes

1. HR 4636. Fiscal 1990 Foreign Aid Supplemental Authorizations/Military Aid. Moakley, D-Mass., amendment to suspend 50 percent of El Salvador's military aid planned for fiscal years 1990 and 1991, depending on actions by the Salvadoran government or by the leftist guerrillas. Adopted 250-163: R 31-135; D 219-28 (ND 166-4, SD 53-24), May 22, 1990. A "nay" was a vote supporting the president's position.

2. HR 3030. Clean Air Act Reauthorization/Transition Aid. Wise, D-W.Va., amendment to authorize $250 million over a five-year period for a Clean Air Employment Transition Assistance program to provide workers who lose their jobs or have their wages reduced as a result of the bill with retraining assistance and up to six months of additional unemployment benefits. Adopted 274-146: R 43-126; D 231-20 (ND 169-2, SD 62-18), May 23, 1990. A "nay" was a vote supporting the president's position.

3. HR 3030. Clean Air Act Reauthorization/Passage. Passage of the bill (thus clearing for the president) to amend the Clean Air Act to attain and maintain national ambient air quality standards, require reductions of emissions in motor vehicles, control toxic air pollutants, reduce acid rain, establish a system of federal permits and enforcement, and otherwise improve the quality of the nation's air. Passed 401-21: R 154-16; D 247-5 (ND 169-4, SD 78-1), May 23, 1990.

4. H J Res 350. Constitutional Amendment on the Flag/Passage. Brooks, D-Texas, motion to suspend the rules and pass the joint resolution to propose an amendment to the Constitution to prohibit the physical desecration of the U.S. flag. Rejected 254-177: R 159-17; D 95-160 (ND 43-130, SD 52-30), June 21, 1990. A two-thirds majority of those present and voting (288 in this case) of both houses is required for passage of a joint resolution proposing an amendment to the Constitution. A "yea" was a vote supporting the president's position.

5. HR 770. Family and Medical Leave Act/Veto Override. Passage, over President Bush's June 29 veto, of the bill to require public and private employers to give unpaid leave to care for a newborn child or a seriously ill child, parent or spouse, or to use as medical leave due to a serious health condition. Rejected 232-195: R 38-138; D 194-57 (ND 156-14, SD 38-43), July 25, 1990. A two-thirds majority or those present and voting (285 in this case) of both houses is required to override a veto. A "nay" was a vote supporting the president's position.

6. HR 3950. Farm Programs Reauthorization/High-Income Farmers. Schumer, D-N.Y., amendment to prohibit all payments, purchases and loans under the wheat, feed grains, cotton, honey, rice, oil seeds, and wool and mohair programs for any person with an adjusted gross income of $100,000 or more. Rejected 159-263: R 66-109; D 93-154 (ND 85-82, SD 8-72), July 25, 1990.

7. H Res 440. Frank Reprimand/Censure. Gingrich, R-Ga., motion to recommit the resolution reprimanding Frank to the Committee on Standards of Official Conduct with instructions to report back a recommendation of censure instead of reprimand. Motion rejected 141-287: R 129-46; D 12-241 (ND 1-171, SD 11-70), July 26, 1990.

8. HR 4739. Fiscal 1991 Defense Authorization/SDI Funding. Bennett, D-Fla., amendment to reduce spending for the strategic defense initiative by $600 million to a new level of $2.3 billion. Adopted 225-189: R 20-150; D 205-39 (ND 157-7, SD 48-32), Sept. 18, 1990. A "nay" was a vote supporting the president's position.

9. HR 4739. Fiscal 1991 Defense Authorization/Abortion Services. Fazio, D-Calif., amendment to provide military personnel and their dependents stationed overseas with reproductive health services, including privately paid abortions, at military hospitals. Rejected 200-216: R 35-139; D 165-77 (ND 113-50, SD 52-27), Sept. 18, 1990. A "nay" was a vote supporting the president's position.

10. HR 4300. Legal Immigration Revision/Passage. Passage of the bill to increase the number of visas for relatives and people coming to the United States to work; suspend deportation for the spouses and children of newly legalized aliens; establish diversity visas for immigrants from countries that currently account for a low number of immigrants to the United States; and reform and revise other immigration procedures. Passed 231-192: R 45-127; D 186-65 (ND 159-13, SD 27-52), Oct. 3, 1990. A "nay" was a vote supporting the president's position.

11. H Con Res 310. Fiscal 1991 Budget Resolution/Conference Report. Adoption of the conference report to set binding budget levels for fiscal 1991: budget authority, $1.49 trillion; outlays, $1.24 trillion; revenues, $1.173 trillion; deficit, $64 billion, by incorporating the spending and revenue targets announced Sept. 30 at the budget summit. The agreement contains reconciliation instructions providing cost-saving changes in entitlement programs, increases in various user fees and taxes, and caps on annual appropriations for defense, international affairs and domestic programs to reduce the deficit by $40.1 billion in fiscal 1991 and $500 billion in fiscal 1991 through 1995. Rejected 179-254: R 71-105; D 108-149 (ND 63-111, SD 45-38), Oct. 5, 1990 (in the session that began, and the Congressional Record dated, Oct. 4, 1990). A "yea" was a vote supporting the president's position.

12. HR 4328. Textile Trade Act/Veto Override. Passage, over President Bush's Oct. 5 veto, of the bill to limit the growth of imports of textiles and apparel to 1 percent annually, establish permanent quotas for

Southern states - Ala., Ark., Fla., Ga., Ky., La., Miss., N.C., Okla., S.C., Tenn., Texas, Va.

most non-rubber footwear imports at 1989 levels, authorize the special allocation of textile quotas for countries increasing their purchases of U.S. agricultural goods, and for other purposes. Rejected 275-152: R 70-103; D 205-49 (ND 131-41, SD 74-8), Oct. 10, 1990. A two-thirds majority of those present and voting (285 in this case) of both chambers is required to override a veto. A "nay" was a vote supporting the president's position.

13. HR 4825. Fiscal 1991-95 NEA Authorization/NEA Funding Standards. Williams, D-Mont., substitute amendment to require the chairman of the National Endowment for the Arts (NEA) in funding projects to take into account not only artistic excellence and merit but general standards of decency and respect for the diverse beliefs and values of Americans. The amendment also gives states a larger share of NEA funds and leaves the courts to decide what constitutes obscenity; requires artists convicted of obscenity to repay their grants; and makes changes in the grant application process. Adopted 382-42: R 142-31; D 240-11 (ND 160-11, SD 80-0), Oct. 11, 1990.

14. HR 5835. Fiscal 1991 Omnibus Reconciliation Act/Democratic Alternative. Rostenkowski, D-Ill., en bloc amendment to provide smaller increases in the Medicare premium and deductible; delete revenue provisions, including the gas tax, the petroleum fuels tax, the extension of the Medicare tax to additional state and local employees, and the limit on itemized deductions; eliminate the "bubble" and lift the top marginal tax rate to 33 percent; create a 10 percent surtax on income above $1 million; increase the minimum tax rate; delay indexing for one year; provide a limited tax break for capital gains; and for other purposes. Adopted 238-192: R 10-164; D 228-28 (ND 157-16, SD 71-12), Oct. 16, 1990. A "nay" was a vote supporting the president's position.

15. S 2104. Civil Rights Act of 1990/Conference Report. Adoption of the conference report on the bill to reverse or modify six recent Supreme Court decisions that narrowed the reach and remedies of job discrimination laws and to authorize monetary damages under Title VII of the 1964 Civil Rights Act. Adopted 273-154: R 34-139; D 239-15 (ND 169-3, SD 70-12), Oct. 17, 1990. A "nay" was a vote supporting the president's position.

16. HR 5422. Fiscal 1991 Intelligence Appropriations/Aid to UNITA. Separate vote at the request of Hyde, R-Ill., on the Solarz, D-N.Y., amendment to suspend military aid to the National Union for the Total Independence of Angola (UNITA) — a rebel group fighting the Angolan government — if the government of Angola agrees to accept a cease-fire and a political settlement for the conflict in Angola; receives no military aid from the Soviet Union; and offers free and fair multiparty elections in which UNITA is free to participate. Adopted 207-206: R 12-156; D 195-50 (ND 158-10, SD 37-40), Oct. 17, 1990. A "nay" was a vote supporting the president's position.

ND Northern Democrats   **SD** Southern Democrats

House Key Votes	1	2	3	4	5	6	7	8	9	10	11	12	13	14	15	16
ALABAMA																
1 *Callahan*	Y	N	Y	Y	N	N	N	N	N	N	N	Y	Y	N	N	N
2 *Dickinson*	N	N	Y	Y	N	Y	Y	N	N	N	Y	Y	Y	N	N	N
3 Browder	Y	Y	Y	Y	N	N	N	N	N	N	N	Y	Y	Y	Y	N
4 Bevill	Y	Y	Y	Y	N	N	N	N	N	N	Y	Y	Y	Y	Y	N
5 Flippo	?	?	?	Y	Y	N	N	N	N	?	Y	Y	Y	Y	Y	Y
6 Erdreich	Y	Y	Y	Y	N	N	N	N	Y	N	Y	Y	Y	Y	Y	N
7 Harris	Y	Y	Y	Y	N	N	N	N	N	N	N	Y	Y	Y	Y	N
ALASKA																
AL *Young*	N	N	Y	Y	Y	N	N	N	N	Y	Y	Y	Y	N	N	N
ARIZONA																
1 *Rhodes*	N	N	Y	Y	N	N	Y	N	N	N	Y	N	Y	N	N	N
2 Udall	Y	Y	Y	N	Y	N	N	Y	Y	Y	Y	N	Y	Y	Y	Y
3 *Stump*	N	N	N	N	Y	C	Y	N	N	N	N	N	N	N	N	N
4 *Kyl*	N	N	N	Y	N	N	Y	N	N	N	N	N	N	N	N	N
5 *Kolbe*	X	N	N	N	N	N	Y	N	Y	N	Y	N	N	N	N	N
ARKANSAS																
1 Alexander	?	?	?	Y	N	N	N	Y	Y	N	Y	Y	Y	Y	Y	Y
2 *Robinson*	?	?	?	Y	N	N	Y	N	N	N	Y	N	N	N	N	N
3 *Hammerschmidt*	?	N	Y	Y	N	N	Y	N	N	N	Y	Y	Y	Y	N	N
4 Anthony	Y	Y	Y	N	Y	N	N	Y	Y	Y	N	Y	Y	Y	Y	Y
CALIFORNIA																
1 Bosco	Y	Y	Y	N	N	N	Y	Y	Y	N	Y	Y	Y	N	Y	Y
2 *Herger*	N	Y	Y	Y	N	N	Y	?	N	N	N	N	N	N	N	N
3 Matsui	Y	Y	Y	N	Y	N	N	Y	Y	Y	N	Y	Y	Y	Y	Y
4 Fazio	Y	Y	Y	N	Y	N	N	Y	Y	Y	Y	Y	Y	Y	Y	Y
5 Pelosi	Y	Y	Y	N	Y	Y	N	Y	Y	Y	N	Y	N	Y	Y	Y
6 Boxer	Y	Y	Y	N	Y	Y	N	Y	Y	Y	N	Y	N	Y	Y	Y
7 Miller	Y	Y	Y	N	Y	Y	N	Y	Y	Y	N	Y	N	Y	Y	Y
8 Dellums	Y	Y	Y	N	Y	Y	N	Y	Y	Y	N	Y	N	Y	Y	Y
9 Stark	Y	Y	Y	N	Y	Y	N	Y	Y	Y	N	Y	N	Y	Y	Y
10 Edwards	Y	Y	Y	N	Y	N	N	Y	Y	Y	N	Y	N	Y	Y	Y
11 Lantos	Y	Y	Y	N	Y	Y	N	Y	Y	Y	Y	Y	Y	Y	Y	N
12 *Campbell*	Y	N	Y	Y	Y	Y	N	Y	Y	?	N	N	N	N	Y	N
13 Mineta	Y	Y	Y	N	Y	N	N	N	Y	Y	Y	Y	Y	Y	Y	Y
14 *Shumway*	N	N	Y	Y	N	N	Y	N	Y	N	Y	N	N	N	N	N
15 Condit	Y	Y	Y	N	N	N	Y	N	Y	Y	N	Y	N	Y	Y	Y

	Democrats	*Republicans*

Y Voted for "yea"	# Paired for	C Voted "present" to avoid
N Voted against	X Paired against	possible conflict of interest
"nay"	- Announced against	? Did not vote or otherwise
+ Announced for	P Voted "present"	make a position known

House Key Votes	1	2	3	4	5	6	7	8	9	10	11	12	13	14	15	16
16 Panetta	Y	Y	Y	N	Y	Y	N	Y	Y	Y	Y	N	Y	Y	Y	Y
17 *Pashayan*	Y	Y	Y	Y	N	N	N	N	N	Y	N	Y	Y	N	N	N
18 Lehman	Y	Y	Y	N	Y	N	N	Y	Y	N	Y	N	Y	Y	Y	Y
19 *Lagomarsino*	N	N	Y	Y	N	Y	Y	N	N	N	N	N	N	N	N	N
20 *Thomas*	X	X	?	Y	N	Y	N	Y	Y	N	Y	Y	Y	?	N	N
21 *Gallegly*	N	N	Y	Y	N	N	N	N	N	N	N	N	Y	N	N	N
22 *Moorhead*	N	N	Y	Y	N	N	N	N	N	N	N	N	N	N	N	N
23 Beilenson	Y	N	Y	N	Y	Y	N	Y	Y	N	Y	N	Y	Y	Y	Y
24 Waxman	Y	Y	Y	N	Y	Y	N	Y	Y	N	N	N	N	Y	Y	Y
25 Roybal	Y	Y	Y	N	Y	N	N	Y	Y	Y	N	Y	Y	Y	Y	Y
26 Berman	Y	Y	Y	N	Y	Y	N	Y	Y	Y	N	N	Y	Y	Y	?
27 Levine	Y	Y	Y	N	Y	Y	N	Y	Y	N	N	N	Y	Y	Y	Y
28 Dixon	Y	Y	Y	N	Y	N	N	Y	Y	Y	N	Y	Y	Y	Y	Y
29 Hawkins	#	Y	Y	N	Y	N	N	?	?	Y	N	Y	Y	Y	Y	?
30 Martinez	Y	Y	Y	Y	Y	?	N	Y	Y	Y	N	Y	Y	Y	Y	Y
31 Dymally	Y	Y	Y	N	Y	N	N	Y	Y	Y	N	Y	Y	Y	Y	Y
32 Anderson	Y	Y	Y	N	Y	N	N	Y	Y	Y	Y	N	Y	Y	Y	Y
33 *Dreier*	N	N	Y	Y	N	Y	Y	N	N	N	N	N	N	N	N	N
34 Torres	Y	Y	Y	N	Y	N	N	Y	Y	N	Y	Y	Y	Y	Y	Y
35 *Lewis*	N	N	Y	Y	N	N	N	N	N	N	N	N	N	N	N	N
36 Brown	?	Y	Y	N	Y	N	N	Y	Y	N	Y	N	Y	Y	Y	Y
37 *McCandless*	N	N	Y	Y	N	N	N	Y	N	N	N	N	N	N	N	N
38 *Dornan*	N	N	Y	Y	N	Y	N	N	N	N	N	N	N	N	N	N
39 *Dannemeyer*	N	N	N	N	Y	Y	Y	N	N	N	N	N	N	N	N	N
40 *Cox*	N	N	Y	Y	N	Y	N	Y	N	N	N	N	N	N	N	N
41 *Lowery*	N	N	Y	Y	N	N	N	N	N	N	N	N	N	N	N	N
42 *Rohrabacher*	N	N	Y	Y	N	Y	Y	N	N	N	N	N	N	N	N	N
43 *Packard*	N	N	Y	Y	N	Y	N	Y	N	N	N	N	N	N	N	N
44 Bates	Y	Y	Y	N	Y	Y	N	Y	Y	N	Y	N	Y	Y	Y	Y
45 *Hunter*	N	N	Y	Y	N	N	Y	N	N	Y	N	Y	N	N	N	N
COLORADO																
1 Schroeder	Y	Y	Y	N	Y	Y	N	Y	Y	N	N	Y	Y	Y	Y	Y
2 Skaggs	Y	Y	Y	N	Y	N	N	Y	Y	Y	Y	N	Y	Y	Y	Y
3 Campbell	Y	Y	Y	Y	N	N	N	Y	Y	N	N	Y	Y	Y	N	N
4 *Brown*	N	N	Y	Y	N	Y	Y	N	Y	N	N	N	Y	Y	N	N
5 *Hefley*	N	N	Y	Y	N	N	Y	N	N	N	N	N	N	Y	N	N
6 *Schaefer*	N	Y	Y	Y	N	N	N	N	N	N	N	Y	Y	N	N	N
CONNECTICUT																
1 Kennelly	Y	Y	Y	N	Y	Y	N	Y	Y	Y	Y	N	Y	Y	Y	Y
2 Gejdenson	Y	Y	Y	N	Y	Y	N	Y	Y	Y	Y	Y	Y	Y	Y	Y
3 Morrison	Y	Y	Y	N	Y	Y	N	Y	Y	Y	N	Y	+	Y	+	+
4 *Shays*	Y	N	Y	N	Y	Y	Y	Y	Y	Y	Y	N	Y	Y	N	Y
5 *Rowland*	N	N	Y	Y	Y	Y	Y	N	Y	?	N	X	?	?	?	?
6 *Johnson*	N	Y	Y	N	Y	Y	Y	N	Y	Y	Y	N	Y	N	Y	N

House Key Votes	1	2	3	4	5	6	7	8	9	10	11	12	13	14	15	16
DELAWARE																
AL Carper	Y	Y	Y	N	Y	Y	Y	N	Y	Y	Y	Y	Y	Y	Y	Y
FLORIDA																
1 Hutto	N	N	Y	Y	N	N	Y	N	N	N	N	Y	Y	Y	N	N
2 *Grant*	N	N	Y	Y	N	N	Y	Y	N	N	N	Y	Y	N	Y	N
3 Bennett	Y	Y	Y	Y	Y	Y	N	Y	Y	Y	Y	Y	Y	Y	Y	Y
4 *James*	N	N	N	Y	N	N	Y	N	N	N	N	N	N	Y	N	N
5 *McCollum*	N	N	Y	Y	N	Y	N	N	N	N	N	N	N	N	N	N
6 *Stearns*	N	N	Y	Y	N	Y	Y	N	N	N	N	N	N	Y	N	N
7 Gibbons	Y	Y	Y	N	Y	Y	N	Y	Y	Y	N	Y	N	Y	Y	Y
8 *Young*	N	N	Y	Y	N	Y	Y	N	N	N	N	N	Y	N	N	N
9 *Bilirakis*	N	N	Y	Y	N	N	?	?	N	N	N	N	N	Y	N	N
10 *Ireland*	N	N	Y	Y	N	N	Y	N	N	N	N	N	N	Y	N	N
11 Nelson	#	#	+	Y	+	-	-	N	Y	N	Y	N	N	Y	N	Y
12 *Lewis*	N	N	Y	Y	N	N	Y	N	N	N	N	N	N	N	N	N
13 *Goss*	N	N	Y	Y	N	Y	Y	N	N	N	N	N	N	Y	N	N
14 Johnston	Y	Y	Y	N	Y	Y	N	Y	Y	N	N	Y	Y	Y	Y	Y
15 *Shaw*	N	N	Y	Y	N	N	Y	N	N	N	N	N	N	Y	N	N
16 Smith	Y	Y	Y	N	Y	Y	N	Y	Y	N	Y	Y	Y	Y	Y	Y
17 Lehman	Y	Y	Y	N	Y	Y	N	Y	Y	Y	N	Y	Y	Y	Y	Y
18 *Ros-Lehtinen*	N	N	Y	Y	N	Y	Y	N	N	N	N	N	Y	N	N	N
19 Fascell	Y	Y	Y	N	Y	N	Y	Y	Y	Y	Y	Y	Y	Y	Y	N
GEORGIA																
1 Thomas	N	Y	Y	Y	N	N	Y	Y	Y	N	Y	Y	Y	Y	Y	N
2 Hatcher	N	Y	Y	Y	N	N	Y	Y	Y	N	Y	Y	Y	Y	Y	N
3 Ray	N	N	Y	Y	N	N	Y	N	N	Y	Y	Y	Y	Y	Y	N
4 Jones	Y	Y	Y	N	N	N	N	Y	Y	?	N	Y	N	Y	N	N
5 Lewis	Y	Y	Y	N	Y	N	N	Y	Y	Y	N	Y	Y	Y	Y	Y
6 *Gingrich*	N	N	Y	Y	N	N	Y	N	N	N	Y	Y	Y	N	N	N
7 Darden	N	Y	Y	Y	N	N	Y	Y	N	Y	Y	Y	Y	Y	N	N
8 Rowland	Y	Y	Y	Y	N	N	Y	Y	Y	N	Y	Y	Y	Y	Y	Y
9 Jenkins	N	N	Y	Y	Y	N	N	Y	N	N	N	Y	Y	Y	N	N
10 Barnard	#	Y	Y	Y	N	N	Y	?	N	N	N	Y	Y	N	N	N
HAWAII																
1 *Saiki*	N	N	Y	Y	Y	N	Y	N	Y	Y	N	N	Y	N	Y	N
2 Mink †										Y	N	Y	Y	Y	Y	Y

	Democrats	***Republicans***

Y	Voted for "yea"	#	Paired for	C	Voted "present" to avoid
N	Voted against	X	Paired against		possible conflict of interest
	"nay"	-	Announced against	?	Did not vote or otherwise
+	Announced for	P	Voted "present"		make a position known

† *Patsy T. Mink was sworn in September 27, 1990.*

House Key Votes	1	2	3	4	5	6	7	8	9	10	11	12	13	14	15	16
IDAHO																
1 *Craig*	X	X	Y	Y	N	N	Y	N	N	N	N	N	N	N	N	N
2 Stallings	Y	?	Y	Y	N	N	N	Y	N	N	N	N	Y	N	Y	N
ILLINOIS																
1 Hayes	Y	Y	Y	N	Y	N	N	Y	Y	Y	N	Y	?	Y	Y	Y
2 Savage	Y	Y	Y	N	Y	Y	P	Y	Y	N	N	Y	Y	N	Y	Y
3 Russo	Y	Y	Y	N	Y	Y	N	Y	N	Y	N	Y	Y	Y	N	Y
4 Sangmeister	Y	Y	Y	Y	Y	N	N	Y	N	Y	N	N	Y	N	Y	Y
5 Lipinski	N	Y	Y	Y	Y	Y	N	N	N	Y	N	Y	Y	Y	N	Y
6 *Hyde*	N	N	Y	Y	Y	N	Y	N	N	Y	N	N	Y	N	N	N
7 Collins	Y	Y	Y	N	Y	N	N	Y	Y	Y	N	Y	Y	Y	Y	Y
8 Rostenkowski	Y	Y	Y	N	Y	Y	N	Y	N	Y	Y	N	Y	Y	Y	Y
9 Yates	Y	Y	Y	N	Y	Y	N	Y	Y	N	Y	N	Y	Y	Y	Y
10 *Porter*	N	N	Y	N	N	Y	Y	N	Y	Y	Y	N	Y	N	N	N
11 Annunzio	Y	Y	Y	Y	Y	Y	N	Y	N	Y	N	Y	Y	N	N	Y
12 *Crane*	N	N	N	Y	N	Y	Y	N	N	N	N	N	N	N	N	N
13 *Fawell*	N	N	Y	Y	N	Y	Y	N	Y	N	N	N	Y	N	N	N
14 *Hastert*	N	N	N	Y	N	Y	Y	N	N	N	Y	N	Y	N	N	N
15 *Madigan*	N	N	Y	Y	N	N	Y	N	N	Y	Y	N	Y	N	?	?
16 *Martin*	N	Y	Y	Y	Y	N	N	N	Y	N	N	N	Y	N	?	?
17 Evans	Y	Y	Y	N	Y	N	N	Y	Y	Y	N	Y	Y	Y	Y	Y
18 *Michel*	N	N	Y	Y	N	N	Y	N	N	Y	N	N	Y	N	N	N
19 Bruce	Y	Y	Y	N	Y	N	N	Y	N	Y	N	Y	Y	Y	Y	Y
20 Durbin	Y	Y	Y	N	Y	N	N	Y	N	Y	N	Y	Y	Y	Y	Y
21 Costello	Y	Y	N	Y	Y	N	N	Y	N	Y	N	Y	Y	Y	Y	Y
22 Poshard	Y	Y	N	N	Y	N	Y	Y	N	Y	N	Y	Y	Y	Y	Y
INDIANA																
1 Visclosky	Y	Y	Y	N	Y	Y	N	Y	Y	Y	N	Y	Y	Y	Y	Y
2 Sharp	Y	Y	Y	Y	Y	N	N	?	Y	Y	N	Y	Y	Y	Y	Y
3 *Hiler*	N	N	Y	Y	N	N	Y	N	N	N	N	N	Y	N	N	N
4 Long	Y	Y	Y	Y	Y	N	N	Y	Y	N	N	Y	Y	N	Y	Y
5 Jontz	Y	Y	Y	N	Y	N	N	Y	Y	Y	N	Y	Y	N	N	N
6 *Burton*	N	N	N	Y	N	N	Y	N	N	N	N	N	Y	N	N	N
7 *Myers*	N	N	N	Y	N	N	N	N	N	N	N	N	Y	N	N	N
8 McCloskey	Y	Y	Y	N	Y	N	N	Y	Y	Y	N	Y	Y	Y	Y	Y
9 Hamilton	Y	Y	Y	N	N	N	N	Y	Y	Y	N	Y	Y	Y	Y	Y
10 Jacobs	Y	Y	Y	N	Y	Y	N	Y	Y	N	N	Y	Y	Y	Y	Y
IOWA																
1 *Leach*	Y	N	Y	N	N	N	N	Y	Y	Y	Y	N	Y	Y	Y	Y
2 *Tauke*	Y	N	Y	Y	N	N	N	N	N	Y	N	N	Y	N	N	Y
3 Nagle	Y	Y	Y	N	N	N	N	Y	Y	Y	Y	Y	Y	Y	Y	Y
4 Smith	Y	Y	Y	N	Y	N	N	Y	Y	Y	Y	N	Y	Y	Y	Y
5 *Lightfoot*	N	N	N	Y	N	N	Y	N	N	N	N	Y	N	N	N	N
6 *Grandy*	Y	N	Y	N	N	N	N	Y	N	N	Y	N	Y	N	N	Y

House Key Votes	1	2	3	4	5	6	7	8	9	10	11	12	13	14	15	16
KANSAS																
1 *Roberts*	N	N	Y	Y	N	N	Y	N	N	N	Y	N	Y	N	N	N
2 Slattery	Y	Y	Y	N	N	N	N	Y	Y	Y	Y	N	Y	Y	Y	Y
3 *Meyers*	N	N	Y	Y	N	N	N	Y	N	N	Y	N	Y	N	Y	N
4 Glickman	Y	Y	Y	N	N	N	N	Y	Y	Y	Y	N	Y	Y	Y	Y
5 *Whittaker*	N	N	Y	Y	N	N	N	N	N	N	N	N	N	N	N	N
KENTUCKY																
1 Hubbard	Y	Y	N	Y	N	N	N	Y	Y	N	N	Y	Y	N	Y	N
2 Natcher	Y	Y	Y	Y	Y	N	N	Y	N	N	N	Y	Y	Y	Y	Y
3 Mazzoli	Y	Y	Y	Y	Y	Y	N	Y	N	N	N	Y	Y	Y	Y	Y
4 *Bunning*	N	Y	Y	Y	N	N	Y	N	N	N	N	N	N	N	N	N
5 *Rogers*	N	Y	Y	Y	N	N	Y	N	N	N	Y	N	N	N	N	N
6 *Hopkins*	N	Y	Y	Y	N	N	Y	N	N	N	Y	N	N	N	N	N
7 Perkins	Y	Y	Y	Y	Y	N	N	Y	Y	Y	Y	Y	Y	Y	Y	Y
LOUISIANA																
1 *Livingston*	N	N	Y	Y	N	Y	Y	N	N	N	Y	N	N	N	N	N
2 Boggs	Y	Y	Y	N	Y	N	N	N	?	?	Y	?	?	Y	Y	Y
3 Tauzin	N	N	Y	Y	N	N	N	N	N	N	Y	N	Y	N	N	N
4 *McCrery*	N	N	Y	Y	N	N	N	N	N	N	N	N	Y	N	N	N
5 Huckaby	N	N	Y	Y	N	N	N	N	N	N	Y	Y	Y	N	Y	N
6 *Baker*	N	N	Y	Y	N	N	Y	N	N	N	Y	N	N	N	N	N
7 Hayes	Y	Y	Y	Y	N	Y	Y	N	N	N	N	N	Y	N	Y	?
8 *Holloway*	N	?	?	?	N	N	Y	N	N	N	N	N	N	N	N	N
MAINE																
1 Brennan	Y	Y	Y	N	Y	Y	N	Y	Y	Y	N	N	Y	?	?	?
2 *Snowe*	N	N	Y	Y	Y	Y	N	Y	Y	Y	N	Y	Y	N	Y	N
MARYLAND																
1 Dyson	Y	Y	Y	Y	Y	N	N	N	N	N	N	Y	Y	N	Y	Y
2 *Bentley*	N	Y	Y	Y	N	N	Y	N	N	N	N	N	Y	N	N	N
3 Cardin	Y	Y	Y	N	Y	N	Y	Y	Y	Y	Y	Y	Y	Y	Y	Y
4 McMillen	Y	Y	Y	N	Y	N	Y	N	Y	Y	Y	Y	Y	Y	Y	Y
5 Hoyer	Y	Y	Y	N	Y	N	N	Y	Y	Y	Y	Y	Y	Y	Y	Y
6 Byron	N	Y	Y	Y	N	N	N	N	N	N	Y	Y	Y	Y	Y	Y
7 Mfume	Y	Y	Y	N	Y	N	N	Y	Y	Y	N	Y	Y	Y	Y	N
8 *Morella*	Y	N	Y	Y	Y	N	N	Y	Y	Y	Y	N	Y	Y	Y	Y
MASSACHUSETTS																
1 *Conte*	Y	N	Y	N	Y	Y	N	Y	N	Y	Y	Y	Y	Y	Y	N

Democrats **Republicans**

Y	Voted for "yea"	#	Paired for	C Voted "present" to avoid possible conflict of interest
N	Voted against "nay"	X	Paired against	? Did not vote or otherwise make a position known
+	Announced for	-	Announced against	
		P	Voted "present"	

House Key Votes	1	2	3	4	5	6	7	8	9	10	11	12	13	14	15	16
2 Neal	Y	Y	Y	Y	Y	Y	N	+	+	Y	N	#	Y	Y	Y	Y
3 Early	Y	N	Y	N	Y	?	N	Y	N	N	N	Y	Y	Y	Y	Y
4 Frank	Y	Y	Y	N	Y	Y	C	Y	Y	Y	N	Y	Y	Y	Y	Y
5 Atkins	Y	Y	Y	N	Y	Y	N	Y	Y	Y	N	Y	Y	Y	Y	Y
6 Mavroules	Y	Y	Y	N	Y	Y	N	Y	N	Y	N	Y	Y	Y	Y	Y
7 Markey	Y	Y	Y	N	Y	Y	N	Y	Y	Y	N	Y	Y	Y	Y	Y
8 Kennedy	Y	Y	Y	N	Y	Y	N	Y	Y	Y	N	Y	Y	Y	Y	Y
9 Moakley	Y	Y	Y	Y	Y	N	N	Y	N	Y	Y	Y	Y	Y	Y	Y
10 Studds	Y	Y	Y	N	Y	Y	N	Y	Y	Y	N	Y	Y	Y	Y	Y
11 Donnelly	Y	Y	Y	Y	N	Y	N	Y	N	Y	N	Y	Y	Y	Y	N
MICHIGAN																
1 Conyers	Y	Y	Y	N	Y	N	N	Y	Y	Y	Y	Y	Y	Y	Y	Y
2 *Pursell*	Y	Y	Y	Y	N	N	Y	Y	N	N	N	N	Y	N	Y	N
3 Wolpe	Y	Y	Y	N	Y	N	N	Y	Y	Y	N	Y	Y	Y	Y	Y
4 *Upton*	Y	Y	Y	Y	N	N	N	N	N	N	N	N	Y	N	N	N
5 *Henry*	Y	Y	Y	N	N	N	Y	N	N	N	N	?	Y	N	Y	N
6 Carr	Y	Y	Y	N	N	N	N	Y	Y	Y	N	Y	Y	Y	Y	Y
7 Kildee	Y	Y	Y	N	N	N	N	Y	N	Y	N	Y	Y	Y	Y	Y
8 Traxler	Y	Y	Y	Y	N	N	N	N	N	Y	Y	Y	Y	Y	Y	Y
9 *Vander Jagt*	N	N	Y	Y	N	N	Y	N	N	N	Y	N	N	N	N	N
10 *Schuette*	N	Y	Y	Y	N	N	Y	N	N	N	N	?	?	N	?	?
11 *Davis*	N	Y	Y	Y	Y	N	N	?	N	N	N	Y	Y	Y	Y	N
12 Bonior	Y	Y	Y	N	N	N	Y	N	Y	N	Y	Y	Y	Y	Y	Y
13 Crockett	Y	Y	Y	N	Y	?	N	?	?	?	?	N	Y	Y	Y	?
14 Hertel	Y	Y	Y	N	Y	Y	N	Y	N	Y	N	Y	Y	Y	Y	?
15 Ford	Y	Y	Y	N	Y	N	N	Y	?	Y	N	Y	Y	Y	Y	?
16 Dingell	Y	Y	Y	N	Y	N	N	Y	Y	Y	Y	Y	Y	Y	Y	Y
17 Levin	Y	Y	Y	N	Y	Y	N	Y	Y	Y	Y	Y	Y	Y	Y	Y
18 *Broomfield*	N	Y	Y	Y	N	Y	Y	N	N	N	N	N	Y	Y	N	N
MINNESOTA																
1 Penny	Y	Y	Y	N	N	N	N	N	N	N	Y	N	Y	Y	Y	Y
2 *Weber*	N	N	Y	Y	N	N	Y	N	N	Y	N	N	N	N	N	N
3 *Frenzel*	N	N	?	Y	Y	N	N	Y	N	Y	N	N	Y	N	N	?
4 Vento	Y	Y	Y	N	Y	Y	N	Y	Y	Y	N	Y	Y	Y	Y	Y
5 Sabo	Y	Y	Y	N	Y	Y	N	Y	Y	Y	N	Y	Y	Y	Y	Y
6 Sikorski	Y	Y	Y	N	Y	N	N	Y	Y	Y	Y	Y	Y	Y	Y	Y
7 *Stangeland*	N	Y	Y	N	N	N	N	N	N	Y	N	N	N	N	N	N
8 Oberstar	Y	Y	Y	N	Y	N	N	Y	N	Y	N	Y	Y	Y	Y	Y
MISSISSIPPI																
1 Whitten	Y	Y	Y	Y	Y	N	N	N	N	?	N	Y	Y	Y	Y	N
2 Espy	Y	Y	Y	N	Y	N	N	Y	Y	Y	N	Y	Y	Y	Y	Y
3 Montgomery	N	N	Y	Y	N	N	N	N	N	N	Y	Y	Y	Y	N	N
4 Parker	N	N	Y	Y	N	N	N	N	N	N	N	Y	Y	Y	N	N
5 Taylor	Y	Y	Y	Y	N	N	Y	N	N	N	N	N	Y	Y	N	N

House Key Votes	1	2	3	4	5	6	7	8	9	10	11	12	13	14	15	16
MISSOURI																
1 Clay	Y	Y	Y	N	Y	N	N	Y	Y	Y	N	Y	Y	Y	Y	Y
2 *Buechner*	N	N	Y	Y	N	Y	Y	Y	N	N	N	Y	N	Y	N	N
3 Gephardt	Y	Y	Y	N	Y	N	N	Y	?	Y	Y	Y	Y	Y	Y	Y
4 Skelton	N	Y	Y	Y	N	N	N	N	N	N	N	Y	Y	Y	Y	Y
5 Wheat	Y	Y	Y	Y	N	N	N	N	Y	Y	N	Y	Y	Y	Y	Y
6 *Coleman*	N	N	Y	N	N	N	N	N	N	N	Y	Y	Y	N	N	?
7 *Hancock*	N	N	N	Y	N	Y	Y	N	N	N	N	N	N	N	N	N
8 *Emerson*	N	Y	Y	Y	N	Y	Y	N	N	N	N	N	Y	N	N	N
9 Volkmer	Y	Y	Y	Y	Y	N	N	Y	N	N	N	Y	Y	Y	Y	Y
MONTANA																
1 Williams	Y	#	Y	N	Y	N	N	Y	Y	Y	N	Y	Y	Y	Y	?
2 *Marlenee*	X	N	N	Y	N	N	N	N	N	N	N	N	Y	N	N	N
NEBRASKA																
1 *Bereuter*	Y	N	Y	Y	N	N	N	N	N	N	N	N	Y	N	N	N
2 Hoagland	N	Y	Y	N	N	N	N	Y	Y	N	N	Y	Y	Y	Y	Y
3 *Smith*	N	N	Y	Y	N	N	Y	N	N	N	N	Y	N	N	N	N
NEVADA																
1 Bilbray	Y	Y	Y	Y	Y	Y	N	N	Y	Y	Y	Y	N	N	N	N
2 *Vucanovich*	N	N	Y	Y	N	N	Y	N	N	?	Y	Y	Y	N	N	N
NEW HAMPSHIRE																
1 *Smith*	N	N	Y	Y	N	Y	Y	N	N	N	N	Y	N	N	N	N
2 *Douglas*	N	N	Y	Y	N	Y	Y	Y	N	N	N	Y	Y	N	N	N
NEW JERSEY																
1 Vacancy																
2 Hughes	Y	Y	Y	N	?	Y	N	Y	Y	N	N	N	Y	Y	Y	N
3 Pallone	Y	Y	Y	Y	Y	Y	N	Y	Y	Y	N	Y	Y	N	Y	Y
4 *Smith*	N	Y	Y	Y	Y	Y	Y	N	N	Y	N	Y	Y	N	N	N
5 *Roukema*	Y	N	Y	Y	Y	Y	Y	Y	Y	N	N	Y	Y	N	Y	N
6 Dwyer	Y	Y	Y	N	Y	Y	N	Y	Y	Y	N	Y	Y	Y	Y	Y
7 *Rinaldo*	Y	Y	Y	Y	Y	Y	Y	N	N	Y	N	Y	Y	Y	Y	Y
8 Roe	Y	Y	Y	Y	Y	?	N	Y	N	Y	N	Y	Y	Y	Y	Y
9 Torricelli	Y	Y	Y	N	Y	N	N	?	?	Y	N	Y	Y	Y	Y	Y
10 Payne	Y	Y	Y	N	Y	Y	N	Y	Y	Y	N	Y	Y	Y	Y	Y
11 *Gallo*	N	N	Y	Y	N	Y	Y	N	N	Y	N	Y	N	N	N	N
12 *Courter*	N	N	Y	Y	N	Y	Y	N	Y	Y	Y	N	Y	N	N	?
13 *Saxton*	N	N	Y	Y	N	Y	Y	Y	N	N	N	N	Y	N	N	N
14 Guarini	Y	Y	Y	Y	Y	Y	N	Y	Y	Y	N	Y	Y	Y	Y	Y

Democrats **Republicans**

Y Voted for "yea"
N Voted against "nay"
+ Announced for
\# Paired for
X Paired against
- Announced against
P Voted "present"
C Voted "present" to avoid possible conflict of interest
? Did not vote or otherwise make a position known

House Key Votes	1	2	3	4	5	6	7	8	9	10	11	12	13	14	15	16
NEW MEXICO																
1 *Schiff*	N	Y	Y	Y	N	N	N	N	Y	Y	Y	Y	Y	N	Y	N
2 *Skeen*	N	N	Y	Y	N	N	Y	N	N	Y	Y	Y	Y	N	N	N
3 Richardson	Y	Y	Y	Y	Y	N	N	N	?	Y	Y	Y	Y	Y	Y	Y
NEW YORK																
1 Hochbrueckner	Y	Y	Y	Y	Y	Y	N	Y	N	N	N	Y	Y	Y	Y	Y
2 Downey	Y	Y	Y	N	Y	Y	N	Y	Y	Y	N	N	Y	Y	Y	Y
3 Mrazek	Y	Y	Y	N	Y	Y	N	Y	Y	Y	Y	N	Y	Y	Y	Y
4 *Lent*	N	N	Y	Y	N	Y	N	N	N	Y	Y	N	Y	N	N	N
5 *McGrath*	Y	Y	Y	Y	Y	Y	N	N	N	Y	N	Y	Y	Y	Y	N
6 Flake	Y	Y	Y	N	?	?	N	Y	Y	Y	Y	Y	Y	Y	Y	Y
7 Ackerman	Y	Y	Y	N	Y	N	N	Y	Y	Y	Y	Y	N	Y	Y	?
8 Scheuer	Y	Y	Y	N	Y	Y	N	Y	Y	Y	Y	Y	Y	Y	Y	Y
9 Manton	Y	Y	Y	Y	Y	Y	N	Y	N	Y	Y	Y	Y	Y	Y	Y
10 Schumer	Y	Y	Y	N	Y	Y	N	Y	Y	Y	N	N	Y	Y	Y	Y
11 Towns	Y	Y	Y	N	Y	N	N	Y	Y	Y	N	Y	Y	Y	Y	Y
12 Owens	Y	Y	Y	N	Y	Y	N	Y	Y	Y	N	#	Y	Y	Y	Y
13 Solarz	Y	Y	Y	N	Y	Y	N	Y	Y	Y	N	Y	Y	Y	Y	Y
14 *Molinari*	N	N	Y	Y	Y	Y	N	N	Y	Y	Y	N	Y	Y	N	N
15 *Green*	Y	N	Y	N	Y	Y	N	Y	Y	Y	Y	Y	Y	N	Y	Y
16 Rangel	Y	Y	Y	?	Y	Y	N	Y	Y	Y	N	Y	Y	Y	Y	Y
17 Weiss	Y	Y	Y	N	Y	Y	N	Y	Y	Y	N	Y	N	Y	Y	Y
18 Serrano	Y	Y	Y	N	Y	Y	N	Y	Y	Y	Y	Y	Y	Y	Y	Y
19 Engel	Y	Y	Y	N	Y	Y	N	Y	Y	?	N	Y	Y	Y	Y	Y
20 Lowey	Y	Y	Y	N	Y	Y	N	Y	Y	Y	N	Y	Y	Y	Y	?
21 *Fish*	?	Y	Y	Y	Y	Y	N	N	N	Y	Y	Y	Y	Y	Y	Y
22 *Gilman*	Y	Y	Y	Y	Y	Y	N	N	N	Y	Y	N	Y	N	Y	Y
23 McNulty	Y	Y	Y	Y	Y	Y	N	N	N	Y	Y	Y	Y	Y	Y	Y
24 *Solomon*	N	Y	Y	Y	Y	N	Y	N	N	N	N	Y	Y	N	N	N
25 *Boehlert*	Y	N	Y	Y	Y	N	N	N	Y	Y	Y	Y	Y	Y	Y	N
26 *Martin*	N	Y	Y	Y	Y	N	N	N	N	N	N	Y	Y	N	N	N
27 *Walsh*	Y	Y	Y	Y	N	Y	N	N	Y	Y	N	N	Y	Y	Y	N
28 McHugh	Y	Y	Y	N	Y	N	N	Y	Y	Y	Y	Y	Y	Y	Y	Y
29 *Horton*	Y	Y	Y	Y	Y	Y	N	Y	Y	Y	Y	Y	Y	Y	Y	Y
30 Slaughter	Y	Y	Y	N	Y	Y	N	Y	Y	Y	N	Y	Y	Y	Y	Y
31 *Paxon*	N	N	Y	Y	N	N	Y	N	N	N	N	N	Y	N	N	N
32 LaFalce	Y	Y	Y	N	Y	N	Y	N	Y	Y	N	Y	Y	Y	Y	Y
33 Nowak	Y	Y	Y	N	Y	Y	N	Y	Y	Y	N	Y	Y	Y	Y	Y
34 *Houghton*	N	Y	Y	N	N	N	N	N	Y	N	Y	Y	Y	N	Y	Y
NORTH CAROLINA																
1 Jones	Y	Y	Y	Y	N	N	N	Y	Y	Y	N	Y	Y	Y	Y	N
2 Valentine	Y	N	Y	N	N	N	N	Y	Y	N	Y	Y	Y	Y	Y	Y
3 Lancaster	N	Y	Y	Y	N	N	N	N	Y	Y	Y	Y	Y	Y	Y	N
4 Price	Y	Y	Y	N	Y	Y	N	Y	Y	Y	N	Y	Y	Y	Y	Y
5 Neal	Y	N	Y	N	N	N	N	N	Y	Y	N	N	Y	Y	Y	?

House Key Votes	1	2	3	4	5	6	7	8	9	10	11	12	13	14	15	16
6 *Coble*	N	Y	N	Y	N	Y	Y	Y	N	N	N	Y	Y	N	N	N
7 Rose	Y	Y	Y	N	Y	N	N	Y	Y	Y	Y	Y	?	Y	?	Y
8 Hefner	Y	Y	Y	Y	N	N	N	Y	Y	N	N	Y	Y	Y	Y	Y
9 *McMillan*	N	N	Y	Y	N	Y	N	N	N	N	Y	Y	Y	N	N	N
10 *Ballenger*	N	N	Y	Y	N	Y	Y	Y	N	N	N	Y	Y	N	N	N
11 Clarke	Y	N	Y	Y	N	Y	N	Y	N	N	N	Y	Y	Y	Y	Y

NORTH DAKOTA

	1	2	3	4	5	6	7	8	9	10	11	12	13	14	15	16
AL Dorgan	Y	Y	Y	N	Y	N	N	Y	N	Y	N	N	Y	Y	Y	Y

OHIO

	1	2	3	4	5	6	7	8	9	10	11	12	13	14	15	16
1 Luken	Y	Y	Y	Y	Y	N	N	Y	N	Y	Y	Y	Y	Y	Y	Y
2 *Gradison*	N	N	Y	Y	N	Y	Y	N	N	Y	Y	N	Y	N	N	N
3 Hall	Y	Y	Y	Y	Y	N	N	Y	N	Y	Y	Y	?	Y	Y	Y
4 *Oxley*	N	Y	Y	Y	N	Y	N	N	N	N	Y	N	Y	N	N	N
5 *Gillmor*	N	N	Y	Y	Y	N	Y	N	N	N	Y	N	Y	N	N	N
6 *McEwen*	N	Y	N	Y	Y	N	Y	N	N	N	N	Y	Y	Y	Y	Y
7 *DeWine*	N	Y	N	Y	Y	N	Y	N	N	Y	Y	N	Y	N	N	N
8 *Lukens*	?	?	?	Y	N	N	P	N	N	N	Y	Y	Y	N	N	N
9 Kaptur	Y	Y	Y	N	?	N	N	Y	N	Y	Y	Y	Y	Y	Y	Y
10 *Miller*	N	Y	N	Y	N	Y	Y	?	N	N	Y	N	Y	N	N	N
11 Eckart	Y	Y	Y	Y	Y	Y	N	Y	Y	Y	N	Y	Y	Y	Y	Y
12 *Kasich*	N	Y	N	N	Y	N	Y	N	N	N	N	N	Y	N	N	N
13 Pease	Y	Y	Y	N	Y	N	Y	Y	Y	Y	Y	N	Y	Y	Y	Y
14 Sawyer	Y	Y	Y	N	Y	N	N	Y	Y	Y	Y	N	Y	Y	Y	Y
15 *Wylie*	N	N	Y	Y	N	Y	Y	Y	N	N	Y	N	?	N	N	N
16 *Regula*	Y	Y	Y	Y	Y	Y	Y	N	N	N	Y	Y	Y	N	N	N
17 Traficant	Y	Y	Y	Y	Y	N	N	Y	N	N	Y	Y	Y	N	Y	Y
18 Applegate	Y	Y	N	Y	Y	Y	N	Y	N	N	Y	Y	Y	N	Y	Y
19 Feighan	Y	Y	Y	N	Y	N	?	?	Y	N	Y	N	Y	Y	Y	Y
20 Oakar	Y	Y	Y	N	Y	N	N	Y	N	N	Y	Y	Y	Y	Y	Y
21 Stokes	#	Y	Y	N	Y	N	N	N	N	N	Y	Y	Y	Y	Y	Y

OKLAHOMA

	1	2	3	4	5	6	7	8	9	10	11	12	13	14	15	16
1 *Inhofe*	N	N	Y	Y	N	N	Y	N	N	N	N	N	Y	N	N	N
2 Synar	Y	Y	Y	N	Y	N	N	N	Y	Y	N	N	Y	Y	Y	Y
3 Watkins	?	Y	Y	Y	N	N	Y	?	?	N	Y	Y	Y	Y	Y	N
4 McCurdy	N	N	Y	N	Y	N	N	Y	Y	N	Y	N	Y	Y	Y	Y
5 *Edwards*	N	N	Y	Y	N	N	Y	N	N	N	N	N	Y	N	N	N
6 English	N	Y	Y	Y	Y	N	N	N	N	N	N	Y	N	Y	N	N

House Key Votes	1	2	3	4	5	6	7	8	9	10	11	12	13	14	15	16
OREGON																
1 AuCoin	Y	Y	Y	N	Y	N	N	?	?	Y	Y	N	Y	Y	Y	Y
2 *Smith, B.*	N	Y	Y	Y	N	N	Y	N	N	N	N	N	N	N	N	N
3 Wyden	Y	Y	Y	N	Y	Y	N	Y	Y	Y	N	N	Y	Y	Y	Y
4 DeFazio	Y	Y	Y	N	Y	N	N	Y	Y	Y	N	N	Y	Y	Y	Y
5 *Smith, D.*	-	N	Y	Y	N	N	Y	N	N	N	N	Y	Y	N	N	N
PENNSYLVANIA																
1 Foglietta	Y	Y	Y	N	Y	Y	N	Y	N	Y	Y	Y	Y	Y	Y	Y
2 Gray	Y	Y	Y	N	Y	Y	N	Y	Y	Y	Y	Y	Y	Y	Y	Y
3 Borski	Y	Y	Y	N	Y	Y	N	Y	N	Y	N	Y	Y	Y	Y	Y
4 Kolter	Y	Y	Y	Y	Y	?	N	Y	Y	Y	N	Y	Y	N	Y	Y
5 *Schulze*	N	Y	Y	Y	N	Y	Y	N	N	N	N	N	Y	Y	Y	N
6 Yatron	Y	Y	Y	Y	Y	Y	N	Y	N	Y	N	Y	Y	Y	Y	Y
7 *Weldon*	Y	Y	Y	Y	Y	Y	N	N	N	+	Y	Y	Y	N	N	N
8 Kostmayer	Y	Y	Y	N	Y	Y	N	Y	Y	Y	Y	Y	N	Y	Y	Y
9 *Shuster*	N	N	N	Y	N	Y	Y	N	N	N	N	Y	N	N	N	N
10 *McDade*	N	Y	Y	Y	Y	N	N	?	?	Y	Y	Y	Y	N	N	N
11 Kanjorski	Y	Y	Y	Y	Y	Y	N	Y	N	Y	N	Y	Y	Y	Y	Y
12 Murtha	Y	Y	Y	Y	Y	N	N	?	N	Y	N	Y	Y	Y	Y	Y
13 *Coughlin*	Y	N	Y	Y	Y	Y	N	Y	N	Y	N	Y	N	Y	Y	N
14 Coyne	Y	Y	Y	N	Y	Y	N	Y	Y	Y	Y	Y	Y	Y	Y	Y
15 *Ritter*	N	Y	Y	Y	N	N	N	N	N	N	N	N	Y	N	N	N
16 *Walker*	N	N	Y	Y	N	Y	Y	N	N	N	N	N	N	N	N	N
17 *Gekas*	N	N	Y	Y	N	N	Y	?	N	N	Y	Y	Y	N	N	N
18 Walgren	Y	Y	Y	N	Y	Y	N	Y	Y	Y	Y	Y	Y	Y	Y	Y
19 *Goodling*	N	Y	Y	Y	N	Y	Y	N	N	N	N	Y	Y	Y	N	N
20 Gaydos	Y	Y	Y	Y	Y	Y	N	Y	N	Y	N	Y	Y	Y	Y	Y
21 *Ridge*	Y	Y	Y	Y	N	N	N	Y	Y	Y	Y	Y	Y	N	N	N
22 Murphy	Y	Y	Y	Y	Y	Y	N	Y	N	Y	N	Y	Y	Y	Y	Y
23 *Clinger*	N	+	+	N	N	N	N	N	N	N	Y	Y	Y	Y	N	N
RHODE ISLAND																
1 *Machtley*	Y	N	Y	Y	Y	Y	N	Y	Y	Y	N	Y	Y	N	Y	Y
2 *Schneider*	Y	N	Y	N	Y	Y	N	Y	Y	Y	N	Y	Y	N	Y	Y
SOUTH CAROLINA																
1 *Ravenel*	N	N	Y	Y	Y	N	N	N	N	N	N	Y	Y	N	N	N
2 *Spence*	N	N	Y	Y	N	N	N	N	N	N	N	Y	Y	N	N	N
3 Derrick	Y	Y	Y	Y	N	N	N	Y	Y	Y	N	Y	Y	Y	Y	Y
4 Patterson	Y	Y	Y	Y	N	N	Y	N	Y	N	N	Y	Y	Y	Y	Y
5 Spratt	Y	Y	Y	N	N	N	N	N	Y	N	Y	Y	Y	Y	Y	Y
6 Tallon	N	Y	Y	N	N	N	N	N	N	N	Y	Y	Y	Y	Y	N
SOUTH DAKOTA																
AL Johnson	Y	Y	Y	Y	N	N	N	Y	Y	Y	N	Y	Y	Y	Y	Y
TENNESSEE																
1 *Quillen*	N	Y	Y	Y	N	N	Y	N	N	N	Y	Y	Y	N	N	N

House Key Votes	1	2	3	4	5	6	7	8	9	10	11	12	13	14	15	16
2 *Duncan*	N	Y	Y	Y	N	Y	Y	N	N	N	N	Y	Y	N	N	N
3 Lloyd	N	Y	Y	Y	Y	N	N	N	N	N	Y	Y	Y	Y	Y	N
4 Cooper	N	N	Y	N	N	C	N	Y	Y	N	Y	Y	Y	Y	Y	N
5 Clement	Y	Y	Y	Y	Y	N	N	Y	Y	N	Y	Y	Y	Y	Y	Y
6 Gordon	Y	Y	Y	N	Y	N	N	Y	Y	N	Y	Y	Y	Y	Y	N
7 *Sundquist*	N	N	Y	Y	N	N	N	N	N	N	N	N	Y	N	N	N
8 Tanner	Y	Y	Y	N	N	N	N	Y	Y	N	Y	Y	Y	Y	Y	N
9 Ford	Y	Y	Y	N	Y	?	N	Y	Y	Y	N	Y	Y	Y	Y	?
TEXAS																
1 Chapman	Y	Y	Y	Y	Y	N	?	Y	Y	N	Y	Y	Y	Y	Y	Y
2 Wilson	N	Y	Y	Y	Y	Y	N	N	N	Y	Y	Y	?	Y	Y	?
3 *Bartlett*	N	N	Y	Y	N	N	Y	N	N	N	N	N	N	N	N	N
4 Hall	N	N	Y	?	N	N	Y	N	N	N	Y	Y	Y	N	N	Y
5 Bryant	Y	Y	Y	N	Y	N	N	Y	Y	N	Y	Y	Y	Y	Y	Y
6 *Barton*	?	?	Y	Y	N	N	Y	N	N	N	N	N	N	N	N	N
7 *Archer*	N	N	Y	N	N	Y	Y	N	N	N	N	N	N	N	N	N
8 *Fields*	N	N	Y	Y	N	N	Y	N	N	N	N	N	N	N	N	N
9 Brooks	Y	Y	Y	Y	N	N	Y	Y	Y	Y	N	Y	Y	Y	Y	?
10 Pickle	Y	N	Y	N	N	N	N	N	Y	Y	Y	Y	Y	Y	Y	Y
11 Leath	?	Y	?	Y	N	N	N	?	?	N	Y	Y	N	N	N	Y
12 Geren	N	Y	Y	Y	N	N	N	Y	Y	N	N	N	N	Y	N	N
13 Sarpalius	N	N	Y	N	N	N	Y	N	N	N	N	N	Y	N	N	N
14 Laughlin	N	Y	Y	Y	N	N	Y	Y	N	N	N	Y	N	Y	N	N
15 de la Garza	Y	Y	Y	Y	Y	N	N	N	Y	N	Y	Y	Y	Y	Y	?
16 Coleman	Y	Y	Y	N	Y	N	N	Y	Y	Y	Y	Y	Y	Y	Y	Y
17 Stenholm	N	N	Y	N	N	N	N	N	N	N	Y	Y	Y	N	N	N
18 Washington	Y	Y	Y	N	?	N	N	Y	Y	Y	Y	Y	Y	Y	Y	Y
19 *Combest*	N	N	N	Y	N	N	Y	N	N	N	Y	Y	N	N	N	N
20 Gonzalez	Y	Y	Y	N	Y	N	N	Y	Y	Y	N	Y	Y	Y	Y	Y
21 *Smith*	N	N	Y	Y	Y	N	Y	Y	N	N	N	N	N	N	N	N
22 *DeLay*	N	N	N	Y	N	N	Y	N	N	N	N	Y	N	N	N	N
23 Bustamante	Y	Y	Y	Y	Y	N	N	Y	?	Y	Y	Y	Y	Y	Y	Y
24 Frost	Y	Y	Y	N	Y	N	N	Y	Y	Y	Y	Y	Y	Y	Y	Y
25 Andrews	Y	N	Y	Y	Y	N	N	Y	Y	Y	N	Y	Y	Y	Y	Y
26 *Armey*	N	N	N	Y	N	Y	Y	N	N	N	N	N	N	N	N	N
27 Ortiz	Y	Y	Y	Y	Y	N	N	Y	N	Y	Y	Y	Y	Y	Y	Y
UTAH																
1 *Hansen*	N	N	Y	Y	N	Y	Y	N	N	N	N	N	N	N	N	N

House Key Votes	1	2	3	4	5	6	7	8	9	10	11	12	13	14	15	16
2 Owens	Y	Y	Y	N	Y	Y	N	Y	Y	Y	Y	N	Y	Y	Y	Y
3 *Nielson*	N	N	Y	Y	N	Y	Y	N	N	N	N	N	Y	N	N	N
VERMONT																
AL *Smith*	Y	N	Y	N	Y	N	Y	Y	Y	Y	Y	Y	Y	Y	Y	?
VIRGINIA																
1 *Bateman*	N	N	Y	Y	N	N	Y	N	N	N	Y	N	Y	N	N	N
2 Pickett	N	N	Y	Y	N	N	N	N	Y	Y	N	Y	Y	Y	Y	Y
3 *Bliley*	N	N	Y	Y	N	Y	Y	N	N	N	N	Y	Y	N	Y	N
4 Sisisky	N	N	Y	Y	N	N	N	N	Y	N	Y	Y	Y	Y	Y	Y
5 Payne	Y	Y	Y	Y	N	N	N	N	Y	N	Y	Y	Y	Y	Y	Y
6 Olin	Y	Y	Y	Y	N	N	N	Y	Y	N	Y	Y	Y	Y	Y	Y
7 *Slaughter*	N	N	Y	Y	N	N	Y	N	N	N	N	Y	Y	N	N	N
8 *Parris*	N	N	Y	Y	N	N	Y	N	N	N	N	Y	Y	N	N	N
9 Boucher	Y	Y	Y	N	Y	Y	N	Y	Y	Y	Y	Y	Y	Y	Y	Y
10 *Wolf*	N	N	Y	Y	N	Y	Y	N	N	N	Y	N	Y	N	N	N
WASHINGTON																
1 *Miller*	Y	N	Y	Y	Y	Y	N	N	Y	Y	Y	N	Y	N	N	Y
2 Swift	Y	Y	Y	N	Y	N	N	Y	Y	Y	Y	N	Y	Y	Y	Y
3 Unsoeld	Y	Y	Y	N	Y	N	N	+	+	Y	N	N	Y	Y	Y	Y
4 *Morrison*	Y	N	Y	Y	Y	N	N	N	Y	Y	Y	N	Y	N	N	Y
5 Foley				N			N				Y					Y
6 Dicks	Y	Y	Y	N	Y	N	N	Y	Y	Y	Y	N	Y	Y	Y	Y
7 McDermott	Y	Y	Y	N	Y	N	N	Y	Y	Y	Y	N	N	Y	Y	Y
8 *Chandler*	Y	N	Y	N	N	N	N	Y	Y	N	Y	N	Y	N	N	Y
WEST VIRGINIA																
1 Mollohan	Y	Y	N	Y	Y	N	N	Y	N	Y	Y	Y	Y	Y	Y	N
2 Staggers	Y	Y	Y	Y	Y	N	N	Y	N	Y	N	Y	Y	Y	Y	Y
3 Wise	Y	Y	Y	Y	Y	Y	N	Y	Y	Y	Y	N	Y	Y	Y	Y
4 Rahall	Y	Y	Y	Y	Y	N	N	Y	N	Y	N	Y	Y	Y	Y	Y
WISCONSIN																
1 Aspin	Y	Y	Y	N	N	Y	N	Y	Y	Y	Y	Y	Y	Y	Y	Y
2 Kastenmeier	Y	Y	Y	N	Y	N	N	Y	Y	Y	N	Y	Y	Y	Y	Y
3 *Gunderson*	N	N	Y	Y	N	N	N	N	N	Y	N	Y	N	N	N	N
4 Kleczka	Y	Y	Y	N	Y	Y	N	Y	N	Y	N	N	Y	Y	Y	Y
5 Moody	Y	Y	Y	N	Y	N	N	Y	Y	Y	N	Y	Y	Y	Y	Y
6 *Petri*	N	N	Y	N	N	Y	Y	N	N	N	N	N	N	N	N	N
7 Obey	Y	Y	Y	N	Y	Y	N	Y	Y	Y	N	Y	Y	Y	Y	Y
8 *Roth*	N	N	Y	Y	N	Y	Y	N	N	N	N	Y	Y	N	N	N
9 *Sensenbrenner*	N	N	Y	Y	N	Y	Y	N	N	N	N	N	N	N	N	N
WYOMING																
AL *Thomas*	N	N	Y	Y	N	N	N	N	N	N	N	N	Y	N	N	N

Senate Terms of Office

Term Expires 1992

Adams, Brock, D-Wash.
Bond, Christopher S., R-Mo.
Breaux, John B., D-La.
Bumpers, Dale, D-Ark.
Coats, Daniel R., R-Ind.
Conrad, Kent, D-N.D.
Cranston, Alan, D-Calif.
D'Amato, Alfonse M., R-N.Y.
Daschle, Tom, D-S.D.
Dixon, Alan J., D-Ill.
Dodd, Christopher J., D-Conn.
Dole, Bob, R-Kan.
Ford, Wendell H., D-Ky.
Fowler, Wyche Jr., D-Ga.
Garn, Jake, R-Utah
Glenn, John, D-Ohio
Graham, Bob, D-Fla.
Grassley, Charles E., R-Iowa

Hollings, Ernest F., D-S.C.
Inouye, Daniel K., D-Hawaii
Kasten, Bob, R-Wis.
Leahy, Patrick J., D-Vt.
McCain, John, R-Ariz.
Mikulski, Barbara A., D-Md.
Murkowski, Frank H., R-Alaska
Nickles, Don, R-Okla.
Packwood, Bob, R-Ore.
Reid, Harry, D-Nev.
Rudman, Warren B., R-N.H.
Sanford, Terry, D-N.C.
Seymour, John, R-Calif.*
Shelby, Richard C., D-Ala.
Specter, Arlen, R-Pa.
Symms, Steve, R-Idaho
Wirth, Tim, D-Colo.

Term Expires 1994

Akaka, Daniel K., D-Hawaii
Bentsen, Lloyd, D-Texas
Bingaman, Jeff, D-N.M.
Bryan, Richard H., D-Nev.
Burdick, Quentin N., D-N.D.
Burns, Conrad, R-Mont.
Byrd, Robert C., D-W.Va.
Chafee, John H., R-R.I.
Danforth, John C., R-Mo.
DeConcini, Dennis, D-Ariz.

Durenberger, Dave, R-Minn.
Gorton, Slade, R-Wash.
Hatch, Orrin G., R-Utah
Heinz, John, R-Pa.
Jeffords, James M., R-Vt.
Kennedy, Edward M., D-Mass.
Kerrey, Bob, D-Neb.
Kohl, Herbert, D-Wis.
Lautenberg, Frank R., D-N.J.
Lieberman, Joseph I., D-Conn.

* Appointed by Gov. Pete Wilson. Seymour will face a special election in 1992 to secure the right to the final two years of the term originally won by Wilson in 1988. If Seymour wins in 1992, his seat will be up again in 1994.

Lott, Trent, R-Miss.
Lugar, Richard G., R-Ind.
Mack, Connie, R-Fla.
Metzenbaum, Howard M., D-Ohio
Mitchell, George J., D-Maine
Moynihan, Daniel Patrick, D-N.Y.

Riegle, Donald W. Jr., D-Mich.
Robb, Charles S., D-Va.
Roth, William V. Jr., R-Del.
Sarbanes, Paul S., D-Md.
Sasser, Jim, D-Tenn.
Wallop, Malcolm, R-Wyo.

Term Expires 1996

Baucus, Max, D-Mont.
Biden, Joseph R. Jr., D-Del.
Boren, David L., D-Okla.
Bradley, Bill, D-N.J.
Brown, Hank, R-Colo.
Cochran, Thad, R-Miss.
Cohen, William S., R-Maine
Craig, Larry E., R-Idaho
Domenici, Pete V., R-N.M.
Exon, Jim, D-Neb.
Gore, Al, D-Tenn.
Gramm, Phil, R-Texas
Harkin, Tom, D-Iowa
Hatfield, Mark O., R-Ore.
Heflin, Howell, D-Ala.
Helms, Jesse, R-N.C.
Johnston, J. Bennett, D-La.

Kassebaum, Nancy Landon, R-Kan.
Kerry, John, D-Mass.
Levin, Carl, D-Mich.
McConnell, Mitch, R-Ky.
Nunn, Sam, D-Ga.
Pell, Claiborne, D-R.I.
Pressler, Larry, R-S.D.
Pryor, David, D-Ark.
Rockefeller, John D. IV, D-W.Va.
Simon, Paul, D-Ill.
Simpson, Alan K., R-Wyo.
Smith, Robert C., R-N.H.
Stevens, Ted, R-Alaska
Thurmond, Strom, R-S.C.
Warner, John W., R-Va.
Wellstone, Paul, D-Minn.

TV Guide to Senate Floor Action

Cable television viewers accustomed to watching the normally fastpaced, well orchestrated action of the House of Representatives have found that the Senate operates quite differently.

In contrast to the 435-member House, where the leadership sets the agenda for the week and usually makes it stick, the Senate often operates at the mercy of its 100 members.

Many of the Senate rules are designed to assure that members who hold minority views have a chance to make their point.

One determined senator can take advantage of the rules to delay action for days or weeks on legislation he opposes.

The Senate often meanders through hours of cursory debate and quorum calls, during which a clerk slowly calls the roll. No one answers, not even members who are present.

Proceedings are broadcast by the Cable Satellite Public Affairs Network (C-SPAN).

Typical Day

A typical day in the Senate might go like this:

- The Senate is **called to order** by the presiding officer. The constitutional presiding officer, the vice president, seldom is in attendance. Usually the president pro tempore presides over the opening minutes of the Senate session.

During the course of the day, other members of the majority party take turns presiding over the Senate for an hour at a time. Whoever is in the chair is addressed as Mr. (or Madame) President.

- The Senate chaplain delivers the **opening prayer.**
- The majority leader and the minority leader are recognized for opening remarks. The majority leader usually announces his plan for the day's business, which is developed in consultation with the minority leadership.

• Several senators, usually fewer than half a dozen, who have requested time in advance are recognized for **special orders,** during which they may speak about any topic for five minutes. (Before TV came to the Senate, special orders were fifteen minutes.) Some senators ask for special order time every day.

• After special orders, the Senate usually conducts **morning business.** During morning business—which need not be in the morning—members conduct routine administrative chores. They introduce bills and receive reports from committees and messages from the president.

• After morning business, the Senate begins work on **legislative or executive** matters. If the majority leader wants the Senate to begin work on a piece of legislation, he normally asks for unanimous consent to call up the measure.

If any member objects, the leader may make a debatable **motion** that the Senate begin work on the bill.

The debatable motion gives opponents the opportunity to launch a **filibuster,** or extended debate, even before the Senate officially begins work on the bill.

Sponsors of the bill may file a **cloture petition** seeking to shut off debate.

Under normal circumstances, the Senate votes on the petition two days after it is filed. To terminate debate, sixty votes are needed, regardless of how many members are voting.

Even after cloture is invoked, debate on the motion can continue for thirty hours. In addition, opponents can keep a filibuster going by demanding votes on all amendments filed before cloture.

A few measures, such as the budget resolution and conference reports, are privileged and a motion to consider them is not debatable.

After the Senate begins work on a bill, floor debate is generally handled by **managers,** usually the chairman and the ranking minority member of the committee with jurisdiction over the measure.

Some measures are considered under a **time agreement** in which the Senate unanimously agrees to limit debate and to divide the time in some prearranged fashion. Usually, however, legislation is considered with no limit on debate.

In the absence of a time agreement, any senator may seek recognition from the chair, and once recognized, may speak for as long as he or she wishes.

Unless the Senate has unanimously agreed to limit **amendments,** senators may offer as many as they wish. Generally, amendments need not be **germane,** or directly related, to the bill.

Most bills are passed by a voice vote with only a handful of senators present.

Any member can request a **roll call,** or recorded vote, on an amendment or on final passage of a measure. Although Senate rules require a **sufficient second** by at least eleven members, the presiding officer often orders a roll call vote when fewer members second the request.

The Senate leadership tries to schedule roll call votes at a time convenient to members; thus few votes are held on Mondays or Fridays, when members are often in their home states.

Senate roll calls are casual affairs. Few members answer the clerk as their names are called. Instead, senators stroll in from the cloakrooms or their offices and congregate in the well (the area between the front row of desks and the desk occupied by the presiding officer and the other officials of the Senate). When they are ready to vote, senators catch the eye of the clerk and vote, often by indicating thumbs-up or thumbs-down.

Roll call votes are supposed to last fifteen minutes, but some have lasted for more than an hour, as members waited for late-comers to arrive from other appointments.

- Often, near the end of the day, the majority leader and the minority leader quickly move through a **wrap-up** period, during which minor bills that previously had been cleared by all members are passed by unanimous consent.

It is not uncommon for the Senate to pass as many as a dozen bills on the Senate **calendar** in just a few minutes during the wrap-up.

- Just before the Senate finishes its work for the day, the majority leader will seek unanimous consent for his agenda for the next session—when the Senate will convene, which senators will be given special orders and, sometimes, specific time agreements for consideration of legislation.

TV Guide to House Floor Action

The House of Representatives has supplanted soap operas as preferred daytime viewing for millions of Americans.

Since the House opened its chambers to television in 1979, C-SPAN has brought the often rambunctious antics of the 435 congressmen and the representatives of the District of Columbia, Puerto Rico, Guam, American Samoa, and the Virgin Islands to life with far more impact than history books.

Because its membership is so large, the House has developed rigid rules to expedite its business. As a result, the House is actually more manageable and efficient than the Senate, with just 100 members.

There is little "dead" air—no quorum calls or desultory speeches as in the Senate. Members, who usually have less than five minutes to make their points, must get right to the heart of the issue.

In just one or two days, the House can pass major legislation that would take weeks in the Senate.

Typical Day

A typical day in the House might go like this:
- The chaplain delivers the **opening prayer.**
- The speaker approves the *Journal,* the record of the previous day's proceedings. Often a member will demand a roll call vote on the approval of the *Journal.* The vote gives party leaders an opportunity to find out which members are absent. On days when hotly contested legislation is to be considered, the absence of just a few members might alter the outcome of a vote.
  - After some procedural activities—receiving messages from the Senate or the president, granting committees permission to file reports or to meet during the session, etc.—members are recognized for **one minute speeches.**

On a typical day, ten or twenty members come to the well to deliver their brief statements, which can be on any topic—current events, a bill due on the floor that day, a tribute to a prominent constituent, or a Republican harangue against some action of the Democratic leadership.

• The House then turns to its legislative business.

Virtually every major bill is considered under a **rule** that sets forth guidelines for floor action. The rule, which is a resolution reported by the Rules Committee, sets a time limit for general debate on the bill and specifies which, if any, amendments are permitted.

The Rules panel works closely with the Democratic leadership: Democrats hold nine of the thirteen seats on the committee and all Democratic members are appointed by the Speaker (with the approval of the Democratic Caucus).

The rule is generally approved with little opposition. However, rules are occasionally defeated by members opposed to the bill, or by members who want a more favorable rule that will allow them to offer their amendments.

Sometimes members approve an **open rule,** which permits unlimited amendments, or a **closed rule,** which permits no amendments. However, most major bills are considered under a **modified open/closed rule,** which permits only specific amendments identified in the rule.

Privileged matters such as conference reports, the budget resolution, and appropriations bills can come to the floor without a rule.

After the rule is adopted, the House resolves into the Committee of the Whole House on the State of the Union (known simply as the **Committee of the Whole)** to consider the bill. The Speaker relinquishes the gavel to a chairman, who presides over the Committee.

The debate time is controlled by the **managers** of the bill, usually the chairman and ranking minority member of the standing committee with jurisdiction over the measure. After time for general debate has expired, amendments that are permitted under the rule can be offered.

Debate on the amendments is conducted under a **five-minute rule:** Supporters and opponents are limited to five minutes. However, members may obtain additional time for debate by offering pro-forma amendments to **strike out the last word.**

Voting is by voice (the usual procedure); division (members stand to be counted); teller (a seldom-used procedure in which members walk past designated tellers); or by electronic device. When members vote electronically, they insert a plastic card into one of the many voting stations on the House floor and press a button to record a "yea," a "nay," or a "present." Their vote is immediately recorded on a big screen on the wall above the Speaker's desk and tabulated, giving a running vote total.

Most electronic votes last fifteen minutes.

Votes cannot technically be taken without a **quorum** (although they often are because no one objects). A point of order that a quorum is not present mandates an electronic vote. A quorum in the Committee of the Whole is 100; a House quorum is 218.

After the amending process is complete, the Committee **rises,** and the chairman reports to the Speaker on the actions taken.

Acting once again as the House, the members vote on final passage of the bill, sometimes after voting on a motion to recommit the bill to its committee of origin.

• On many noncontroversial bills, the House leadership wants to speed up action, bypassing the Rules Committee and the Committee of the Whole.

It can do that by waiving, or **suspending** the rules. Bills under **suspension,** sometimes as many as a dozen at a time, are usually brought up early in the week.

Suspensions cannot be amended. Debate is limited to forty minutes. Then members are asked to vote on whether they want to suspend the rules and pass the bill. A single vote accomplishes both steps. A two-thirds vote is needed to suspend the House rules, making it a gamble sometimes to bring up legislation under suspension.

If a bill is defeated under the two-thirds requirement, it often is brought back to the floor later under regular procedures, where only a simple majority is sufficient.

To accommodate many members who have not returned from their districts on Mondays, recorded votes on suspensions are usually delayed until Tuesday. Roughly half the measures under suspension are passed by voice vote.

• Measures that are even less controversial are placed on the **consent**

calendar or are passed by **unanimous consent.** These measures, such as resolutions expressing congratulations to a winning sports team, expressing support for a Soviet dissident, or approving a minor transfer of government land, are cleared through the leadership of both parties. A single objection on the floor can block passage.

• After the House completes its legislative business, members are allowed to speak for up to sixty minutes under **special orders.** They must reserve the time in advance but can speak on any topic. The television cameras record the speeches, which often are made to an almost deserted chamber.

Congressional Bell System

On days Congress is in session, a system of electric lights and buzzers is used to inform members of proceedings on the floor. The clocks in the House and Senate office buildings light up with the respective number of buzzer rings, signaling members of impending votes or other legislative action. In the House, the signals include:

1 ring — teller vote (not a recorded vote).

1 long ring, pause, followed by 3 rings — the start or continuation of a notice quorum call.

1 long ring — termination of a notice quorum call.

2 rings — electronically recorded vote.

2 rings, pause, followed by 2 rings — a manual roll-call vote.

2 rings, pause, followed by 5 rings — first 15-minute vote in a series, where subsequent votes are to be five minutes in length.

3 rings — quorum call.

3 rings, pause, followed by 5 rings — quorum call in the Committee of the Whole, which may be immediately followed by a five-minute recorded vote.

4 rings — adjournment of the House.

5 rings — five-minute electronically recorded vote.

6 rings — recess of the House.

In the Senate, one long ring signifies that a session is convening; one red light on the right-hand side of the clock remains lighted at all times while the Senate is in actual session. In the Senate, the signals include:

1 ring — yeas and nays.

2 rings — quorum call.

3 rings — call of absentees.

4 rings — adjournment or recess.

5 rings — five minutes remaining on yea-and-nay vote.

6 rings — morning business concluded or temporary recess.

Glossary of Legislative Terms

Act. The term for legislation once it has passed both houses of Congress and has been signed by the president or passed over his veto, thus becoming law.

Amendment. A proposal to alter the language or provisions in a bill or in another amendment.

Amendment in the Nature of a Substitute. An amendment that seeks to replace the entire text of a bill or replaces a large portion of it.

Appropriations Bill. A bill that gives legal authority to spend or obligate money from the Treasury. An appropriations bill generally cannot provide more money than has been authorized for a particular program under separate legislation.

Authorization. Basic, substantive legislation that establishes or continues the legal operation of a federal program or agency, either indefinitely or for a specific period of time. An authorization normally is a prerequisite for an appropriation and sets a ceiling for it.

Bills. Most legislative proposals before Congress are in the form of bills and are designated by HR in the House of Representatives or S in the Senate, according to the house in which they originate, and by a number assigned in the order in which they are introduced during the two-year period of a Congress. "Public bills" deal with general questions and become public laws if approved by Congress and signed by the president. "Private bills" deal with such matters as an individual's claim against the government or special immigration request, and become private laws if approved and signed.

Bills Introduced. Any number of members may join in introducing a bill or resolution. The first member listed is the sponsor of the bill; the others are cosponsors.

Bills Referred. When introduced, a bill is referred to the committee or committees that have jurisdiction over the subject of the bill.

Budget. The document sent to Congress by the president early each year estimating government revenue and expenditures for the ensuing fiscal year.

Budget Resolution. A concurrent resolution passed by both houses of Congress, but not requiring the president's signature, setting forth or revising the congressional budget for the following three fiscal years.

By Request. A phrase used when a member introduces a bill at the request of an executive agency or private organization but does not necessarily endorse it.

Calendar. An agenda of business awaiting possible action by the chamber. The House uses five legislative calendars—the Consent, Discharge, House, Private, and Union calendars, according to the type of bill involved. The Senate uses only an executive calendar.

Clean Bill. Frequently after a committee has finished a major revision of a bill, one of the committee members will assemble the changes and what is left of the original bill into a new measure and introduce it as a "clean bill." The revised measure, which is given a new number, then is referred back to the committee, which reports it to the floor for consideration.

Clerk of the House. Chief administrative officer of the House of Representatives.

Cloture. The process in the Senate for ending a filibuster other than by unanimous consent. A petition to limit debate must be signed by sixteen senators, and the motion to invoke cloture then must be agreed to by three-fifths of the Senate's membership.

Committee. A division of the House or Senate that prepares legislation for action by the parent chamber or makes investigations as directed by the parent chamber. Most committees are divided into subcommittees, which study legislation, hold hearings, and report bills to the full committee.

Committee of the Whole. The working title of what is formally "The Committee of the Whole House on the State of the Union." To expedite business, the House resolves itself into the Committee of the Whole to consider amendments to most major bills. The Speaker is supplanted with a "chairman" who presides over debate and voting on amendments. When work on a measure is complete, the Committee "rises," the Speaker returns to the chair, and the full House then votes on passage of the legislation.

Concurrent Resolution. A statement expressing the sense of Congress on some issue. Designated H Con Res or S Con Res, depending on the chamber of origin, it must be adopted by both houses, but it does not go to the president or have the force of law.

Conference. A meeting between selected members of the House and Senate to reconcile differences between the two chambers' versions of the same legislation.

Congressional Record. The daily, printed account of proceedings in the House and Senate, with a substantially verbatim account of debate. Members are allowed to revise their spoken remarks.

Continuing Resolution. A joint resolution to continue appropriations for a department or agency when a fiscal year is beginning and Congress has not enacted the department's regular appropriations bill. Also called "CR" or continuing appropriations.

Division Vote. A vote in which all members present who favor a bill are asked to stand, followed by all those opposed. No record is kept of how members voted (also called "standing vote").

Entitlement Program. A federal program such as Social Security or unemployment compensation that guarantees a certain level of benefits to persons who meet requirements set by law.

Filibuster. A time-delaying strategy of debate, quorum calls, amendments, and other procedures used by a minority to defeat or achieve compromise on a proposition favored by the majority.

Fiscal Year. Financial operations of the government are carried out in a twelve-month period beginning October 1 each year. Fiscal 1990, for example, began October 1, 1989, and will end September 30, 1990.

Five-Minute Rule. A debate-limiting rule of the House that, while the Committee of the Whole sits, allows a member offering an amendment to speak for five minutes in its favor, followed by an opponent who also speaks for five minutes.

Floor Manager. A member who has the task of steering legislation through floor debate and the amending process to a final vote in the chamber. The floor manager is usually the chairman or ranking minority member of the committee that reported the legislation.

Frank. A member's facsimile signature, which is used on envelopes in lieu of stamps, for the member's official outgoing mail. The "franking privilege" is the right to send mail postage-free.

Germane. Pertaining to the subject matter of the measure at hand.

Gramm-Rudman-Hollings Deficit Reduction Act. Legislation to balance the federal budget by fiscal year 1993. The law established annual maximum deficit targets and mandated across-the-board automatic cuts ("sequestration") in most federal programs if the deficit goals were not achieved through regular budget actions.

Hearings. Committee sessions for taking testimony from witnesses. The public and press may attend open hearings; the vast majority of hearings are open to the public.

Hopper. Box on House clerk's desk where members deposit bills and resolutions to be introduced.

Joint Resolution. A resolution requiring approval of both the House and Senate. It becomes law if signed by the president or passed over his veto. Differing in no substantive way from a bill, a joint resolution often is used to address a limited matter. A joint resolution also is used for a constitutional amendment, which requires passage by two-thirds of each chamber but does not go to the president.

Law. An act of Congress that has been signed by the president or passed over his veto by Congress. Public bills, when signed, become public laws and are cited by the letters PL and a hyphenated number.

Majority Leader. In the Senate, the majority leader, in consultation with the minority leader, directs the legislative schedule for the chamber. He also is his party's spokesperson and chief strategist. In the House, the majority leader is second to the Speaker and serves as his party's legislative strategist. There also is a minority leader, who is the floor leader for the minority party in each chamber.

Majority Whip. In effect, the assistant majority leader, in either the House or Senate. His job is to help marshal majority forces in support of party strategy and legislation. There also is a minority whip, who performs duties of whip for the minority party.

Marking Up a Bill. Working on legislation in committee or subcommittee; approving, amending, or rejecting each provision and the bill as a whole.

Morning Hour. Time set aside for the conduct of routine business. The House rarely has a morning hour.

Motion. A request by a member to institute any one of a wide array of parliamentary actions. He "moves" for a certain procedure, such as the consideration of a measure.

Nominations. Presidential appointments to government and diplomatic posts that are subject to Senate confirmation.

One-Minute Speeches. Delivered at the beginning of a legislative day in the House, these may cover any topic but are limited to one minute in duration.

Override a Veto. If the president disapproves a bill and sends it back to Congress with his objections, Congress may try to override his veto and enact the bill into law. The override requires a recorded vote with a two-thirds majority in each chamber.

Pair. A "gentleman's agreement" between two lawmakers who are on opposite sides of an issue, made in advance of a vote to cancel out the effects of absences. Notices of pairs are printed in the *Congressional Record*.

Parliamentarian. Each chamber employs several parliamentarians to assist the presiding officer in making rulings and conducting business of the chamber.

Pocket Veto. The act of the president in withholding his approval of a bill after Congress has adjourned.

Point of Order. An objection raised by a member that the chamber is departing from rules governing its conduct of business. The chair then must rule on whether the objection is justified.

President of the Senate. The vice president of the United States presides over the Senate. In his absence, a president pro tempore presides.

President Pro Tempore. The presiding officer of the Senate in the absence of the vice president of the United States.

Previous Question. A motion that, if approved, has the effect of cutting off all debate, preventing further amendments, and forcing a vote on the pending matter.

Quorum. The number of members whose presence is necessary for transaction of business. In the Senate, a majority of the membership comprises a quorum. In the House, a quorum also is a majority of the members, except in the Committee of the Whole House, where it is one hundred members.

Readings of Bills. Traditionally, a bill has to be read three times before passage. In modern practice, a bill is considered to have been read first upon introduction, second upon floor consideration, and third after all floor debate. Seldom are bills actually read aloud in their entirety.

Recommit to Committee. A motion made after a bill has been debated to return it to the committee that reported it. Recommittal usually is a death blow to a bill, unless done with instructions to adopt a particular amendment and report the bill back to the chamber.

Reconciliation. The 1974 budget act provides for a "reconciliation" procedure for bringing tax and appropriations bills into conformity with congressional budget resolutions. Congress instructs its legislative committees to approve measures adjusting revenues and expenditures by a certain amount by a given deadline. The recommendations of these committees are consolidated without change by the Budget committees into an omnibus reconciliation bill, which then must be approved by both houses of Congress.

Reconsider a Vote. A motion to reconsider the vote by which an action was taken has the effect, until disposed of, of putting the action in abeyance. Such a motion can be made only by a member who voted on the prevailing side.

Recorded Vote. A vote on which a public record is kept of each member's stand. In the Senate, this is accomplished through a roll call of the senators. The House uses an electronic voting system, and a recorded vote can be obtained on demand of one-fifth of a quorum (forty-four members) of the full house, or one-fourth (twenty-five) during Committee of the Whole.

Report. Both a verb and a noun as a congressional term. After completing a markup of a bill, a committee reports its recommendations to the chamber along with the measure. It usually publishes a written report containing an explanation of the bill as approved and the committee's reasons for its action.

Resolution. Designated H Res or S Res, a "simple" resolution deals with matters entirely within the prerogatives of one house. It does not require passage by the other chamber or approval by the president, and it does not have the force of law.

Rider. An amendment, usually not germane, that a sponsor offers to a bill to enhance the amendment's chances of enactment.

Rules. The term has two congressional meanings. Both houses of Congress have standing rules governing procedure. In the House, the term also refers to resolutions reported by the Rules Committee, which, upon approval by the full House, govern the length and terms of debate for most bills considered on the floor.

Secretary of the Senate. Chief administrative officer of the Senate.

Speaker. The presiding officer of the House of Representatives.

Strike Out the Last Word. In the House's Committee of the Whole, when debate is limited by the five-minute rule, a member may gain recognition from the chair by moving to "strike out the last word" of the amendment or section of a bill under consideration. The motion is pro forma, requires no vote, and does not alter the measure being debated. Members also use "strike out the requisite number of words."

Supplemental Appropriations Bill. Legislation appropriating added funds for a department during the current fiscal year after its regular appropriations bill has been enacted.

Suspend the Rules. A time-saving procedure used for considering bills in the House under which no amendments may be offered and debate is limited to twenty minutes per side. A two-thirds vote is required for passage under suspension of the rules, a procedure reserved mostly for noncontroversial bills.

Table a Bill. A motion to "lay on the table" effectively kills a bill if approved.

Treaties. Executive proposals, such as arms control proposals, that must be submitted to the Senate for approval by two-thirds of the senators present.

Unanimous Consent. The Senate or House can do almost anything it wishes, regardless of its rules, upon unanimous consent of the chamber. But objection from a single member can block action.

Unanimous Consent Agreement. Also called a time limitation agreement, it is an agreement negotiated by the Senate leadership to govern one or more aspects of action on a measure. In effect, it is similar to a rule in the House.

Veto. Disapproval by the president of a bill or joint resolution. When Congress is in session, the president must veto a bill within ten days, excluding Sundays, after he has received it; otherwise, it becomes law without his signature.

Voice Vote. Members answer "aye" or "no" in chorus, and the presiding officer decides the result. No record is made of how individual members voted.

Yeas and Nays. A recorded vote (see above).

Yield. When a member has been recognized to speak, no other member may speak unless he obtains permission from the member recognized. Requests are made in the form, "Will the gentleman yield?"